THE WANING OF THE MIDDLE AGES

PORTRAIT OF PHILIP THE GOOD, DUKE OF BURGUNDY. BY ROGIER VAN DER WEYDEN.

THE WANING OF
THE MIDDLE AGES

A STUDY OF THE FORMS OF LIFE,
THOUGHT AND ART IN FRANCE AND
THE NETHERLANDS IN THE XIVᵀᴴ
AND XVᵀᴴ CENTURIES

BY

J. HUIZINGA

ST. MARTIN'S PRESS
New York

ISBN O-312-85540-0

Library of Congress Cataloging in Publication Data

Huizinga, Johan, 1872-1945.
  The Waning of the Middle Ages.

  Translation of: Herfsttijd der Middeleeuwen.
  Bibliography: p. 309
  Includes index.
  1. France—Civilization—1328-1600. 2. Netherlands—
Civilization. 3. Civilization, Medieval. I. Title.
DC33.2.H83 1984   944   84-9980
ISBN 0-312-85540-0

PREFACE

History has always been far more engrossed by problems of origins than by those of decline and fall. When studying any period, we are always looking for the promise of what the next is to bring. Ever since Herodotus, and earlier still, the questions imposing themselves upon the mind have been concerned with the rise of families, nations, kingdoms, social forms or ideas. So, in medieval history, we have been searching so diligently for the origins of modern culture, that at times it would seem as though what we call the Middle Ages had been little more than the prelude to the Renaissance.

But in history, as in nature, birth and death are equally balanced. The decay of overripe forms of civilization is as suggestive a spectacle as the growth of new ones. And it occasionally happens that a period in which one had, hitherto, been mainly looking for the coming to birth of new things, suddenly reveals itself as an epoch of fading and decay.

The present work deals with the history of the fourteenth and fifteenth centuries regarded as a period of termination, as the close of the Middle Ages. Such a view of them presented itself to the author of this volume, whilst endeavouring to arrive at a genuine understanding of the art of the brothers Van Eyck and their contemporaries, that is to say, to grasp its meaning by seeing it in connection with the entire life of their times. Now the common feature of the various manifestations of civilization of that epoch proved to be inherent rather in that which links them to the past than in the germs which they contain of the future. The significance, not of the artists alone, but also of theologians, poets, chroniclers, princes and statesmen, could be best appreciated by considering them, not as the harbingers of a coming culture, but as perfecting and concluding the old.

This English edition is not a simple translation of the original

Dutch (second edition 1921, first 1919), but the result of a work of adaptation, reduction and consolidation under the author's directions. The references, here left out, may be found in full in the original.

Verse quotations are given in the original French throughout the work. In order to avoid an undue increase in length, quotations in prose are, as a rule, given in translations only, except in the concluding chapters where the literary expression as such is discussed, and the actual language becomes important. Here the old French prose also is set out in full.

The author wishes to express his sincere thanks to Sir J. Rennell Rodd, whose kind interest in the book gave rise to this edition, and to the translator, Mr. F. Hopman, of Leiden, whose clear insight into the exigencies of translation rendered the recasting possible, and whose endless patience with the wishes of an exacting author made the difficult task a work of friendly co-operation.

LEIDEN,   J. H.
 April, 1924.

CONTENTS

LIST OF ILLUSTRATIONS

THE
WANING OF THE MIDDLE AGES

CHAPTER I

THE VIOLENT TENOR OF LIFE

To the world when it was half a thousand years younger, the outlines of all things seemed more clearly marked than to us. The contrast between suffering and joy, between adversity and happiness, appeared more striking. All experience had yet to the minds of men the directness and absoluteness of the pleasure and pain of child-life. Every event, every action, was still embodied in expressive and solemn forms, which raised them to the dignity of a ritual. For it was not merely the great facts of birth, marriage and death which, by the sacredness of the sacrament, were raised to the rank of mysteries ; incidents of less importance, like a journey, a task, a visit, were equally attended by a thousand formalities : benedictions, ceremonies, formulæ.

Calamities and indigence were more afflicting than at present ; it was more difficult to guard against them, and to find solace. Illness and health presented a more striking contrast ; the cold and darkness of winter were more real evils. Honours and riches were relished with greater avidity and contrasted more vividly with surrounding misery. We, at the present day, can hardly understand the keenness with which a fur coat, a good fire on the hearth, a soft bed, a glass of wine, were formerly enjoyed.

Then, again, all things in life were of a proud or cruel publicity. Lepers sounded their rattles and went about in processions, beggars exhibited their deformity and their misery in churches. Every order and estate, every rank and profession, was distinguished by its costume. The great lords

1

never moved about without a glorious display of arms and liveries, exciting fear and envy. Executions and other public acts of justice, hawking, marriages and funerals, were all announced by cries and processions, songs and music. The lover wore the colours of his lady ; companions the emblem of their confraternity ; parties and servants the badges or blazon of their lords. Between town and country, too, the contrast was very marked. A medieval town did not lose itself in extensive suburbs of factories and villas ; girded by its walls, it stood forth as a compact whole, bristling with innumerable turrets. However tall and threatening the houses of noblemen or merchants might be, in the aspect of the town the lofty mass of the churches always remained dominant.

The contrast between silence and sound, darkness and light, like that between summer and winter, was more strongly marked than it is in our lives. The modern town hardly knows silence or darkness in their purity, nor the effect of a solitary light or a single distant cry.

All things presenting themselves to the mind in violent contrasts and impressive forms, lent a tone of excitement and of passion to everyday life and tended to produce that per- petual oscillation between despair and distracted joy, between cruelty and pious tenderness which characterize life in the Middle Ages.

One sound rose ceaselessly above the noises of busy life and lifted all things unto a sphere of order and serenity : the sound of bells. The bells were in daily life like good spirits, which by their familiar voices, now called upon the citizens to mourn and now to rejoice, now warned them of danger, now exhorted them to piety. They were known by their names : big Jacqueline, or the bell Roland. Every one knew the difference in meaning of the various ways of ringing. However continuous the ringing of the bells, people would seem not to have become blunted to the effect of their sound.

Throughout the famous judicial duel between two citizens of Valenciennes, in 1455, the big bell, " which is hideous to hear," says Chastellain, never stopped ringing. What in- toxication the pealing of the bells of all the churches, and of all the monasteries of Paris, must have produced, sounding from morning till evening, and even during the night, when a peace was concluded or a pope elected.

The frequent processions, too, were a continual source of pious agitation. When the times were evil, as they often were, processions were seen winding along, day after day, for weeks on end. In 1412 daily processions were ordered in Paris, to implore victory for the king, who had taken up the oriflamme against the Armagnacs. They lasted from May to July, and were formed by ever-varying orders and corporations, going always by new roads, and always carrying different relics. The Burgher of Paris calls them " the most touching processions in the memory of men." People looked on or followed, " weeping piteously, with many tears, in great devotion." All went barefooted and fasting, councillors of the Parlement as well as the poorer citizens. Those who could afford it, carried a torch or a taper. A great many small children were always among them. Poor country-people of the environs of Paris came barefooted from afar to join the procession. And nearly every day the rain came down in torrents.

Then there were the entries of princes, arranged with all the resources of art and luxury belonging to the age. And, lastly, most frequent of all, one might almost say, uninterrupted, the executions. The cruel excitement and coarse compassion raised by an execution formed an important item in the spiritual food of the common people. They were spectacular plays with a moral. For horrible crimes the law invented atrocious punishments. At Brussels a young incendiary and murderer is placed in the centre of a circle of burning fagots and straw, and made fast to a stake by means of a chain running round an iron ring. He addresses touching words to the spectators, " and he so softened their hearts that every one burst into tears and his death was commended as the finest that was ever seen." During the Burgundian terror in Paris in 1411, one of the victims, Messire Mansart du Bois, being requested by the hangman, according to custom, to forgive him, is not only ready to do so with all his heart, but begs the executioner to embrace him. " There was a great multitude of people, who nearly all wept hot tears."

When the criminals were great lords, the common people

had the satisfaction of seeing rigid justice done, and at the
same time finding the inconstancy of fortune exemplified
more strikingly than in any sermon or picture. The magistrate took care that nothing should be wanting to the effect
of the spectacle : the condemned were conducted to the scaffold, dressed in the garb of their high estate. Jean de Mon-
taigu, grand maître d'hôtel to the king, the victim of Jean
sans Peur, is placed high on a cart, preceded by two trumpeters.
He wears his robe of state, hood, cloak, and hose half red
and half white, and his gold spurs, which are left on the feet
of the beheaded and suspended corpse. By special order of
Louis XI, the head of maître Oudart de Bussy, who had
refused a seat in the Parlement, was dug up and exhibited
in the market-place of Hesdin, covered with a scarlet hood
lined with fur " selon la mode des conseillers de Parlement,"
with explanatory verses.

Rarer than processions and executions were the sermons
of itinerant preachers, coming to shake people by their eloquence. The modern reader of newspapers can no longer
conceive the violence of impression caused by the spoken
word on an ignorant mind lacking mental food. The Franciscan friar Richard preached in Paris in 1429 during ten
consecutive days. He began at five in the morning and spoke
without a break till ten or eleven, for the most part in the
cemetery of the Innocents. When, at the close of his tenth
sermon, he announced that it was to be his last, because he
had no permission to preach more, " great and small wept as
touchingly and as bitterly as if they were watching their
best friends being buried ; and so did he." Thinking that he
would preach once more at Saint Denis on the Sunday, the
people flocked thither on Saturday evening, and passed the
night in the open, to secure good seats.

Another Minorite friar, Antoine Fradin, whom the magistrate of Paris had forbidden to preach, because he inveighed
against the bad government, is guarded night and day in the
Cordeliers monastery, by women posted around the building,
armed with ashes and stones. In all the towns where the
famous Dominican preacher Vincent Ferrer is expected, the
people, the magistrates, the lower clergy, and even prelates
and bishops, set out to greet him with joyous songs. He

journeys with a numerous and ever-increasing following of adherents, who every night make a circuit of the town in procession, with chants and flagellations. Officials are appointed to take charge of lodging and feeding these multitudes. A large number of priests of various religious orders accompany him everywhere, to assist him in celebrating mass and in confessing the faithful. Also several notaries, to draw up, on the spot, deeds embodying the reconciliations which this holy preacher everywhere brings about. His pulpit has to be protected by a fence against the pressure of the congregation which wants to kiss his hand or habit. Work is at a stand-still all the time he preaches. He rarely fails to move his auditors to tears. When he spoke of the Last Judgment, of Hell, or of the Passion, both he and his hearers wept so copiously that he had to suspend his sermon till the sobbing had ceased. Malefactors threw themselves at his feet, before every one, confessing their great sins. One day, while he was preaching, he saw two persons, who had been condemned to death—a man and a woman—being led to execution. He begged to have the execution delayed, had them both placed under the pulpit, and went on with his sermon, preaching about their sins. After the sermon, only some bones were found in the place they had occupied, and the people were convinced that the word of the saint had consumed and saved them at the same time.

After Olivier Maillard had been preaching Lenten sermons at Orleans, the roofs of the houses surrounding the place whence he had addressed the people had been so damaged by the spectators who had climbed on to them, that the roofer sent in a bill for repairs extending over sixty-four days.

The diatribes of the preachers against dissoluteness and luxury produced violent excitement which was translated into action. Long before Savonarola started bonfires of " vanities " at Florence, to the irreparable loss of art, the custom of these holocausts of articles of luxury and amusement was prevalent both in France and in Italy. At the summons of a famous preacher, men and women would hasten to bring cards, dice, finery, ornaments, and burn them with great pomp. Renunciation of the sin of vanity in this way had taken a fixed and solemn form of public manifestation, in accordance with the tendency of the age to invent a style for everything.

All this general facility of emotions, of tears and spiritual upheavals, must be borne in mind in order to conceive fully how violent and high-strung was life at that period.

Public mourning still presented the outward appearance of a general calamity. At the funeral of Charles VII, the people are quite appalled on seeing the cortège of all the court dignitaries, "dressed in the deepest mourning, which was most pitiful to see ; and because of the great sorrow and grief they exhibited for the death of their master, many tears were shed and lamentations uttered throughout the town." People were especially touched at the sight of six pages of the king mounted on horses quite covered with black velvet. One of the pages, according to a rumour, had neither eaten nor drunk for four days. "And God knows what doleful and piteous plaints they made, mourning for their master."

Solemnities of a political character also led to abundant weeping. An ambassador of the king of France repeatedly bursts into tears while addressing a courteous harangue to Philip the Good. At the meeting of the kings of France and of England at Ardres, at the reception of the dauphin at Brussels, at the departure of John of Coïmbre from the court of Burgundy, all the spectators weep hot tears. Chastellain describes the dauphin, the future Louis XI, during his voluntary exile in Brabant, as subject to frequent fits of weeping.

Unquestionably there is some exaggeration in these descriptions of the chroniclers. In describing the emotion caused by the addresses of the ambassadors at the peace congress at Arras, in 1435, Jean Germain, bishop of Chalons, makes the auditors throw themselves on the ground, sobbing and groaning. Things, of course, did not happen thus, but thus the bishop thought fit to represent them, and the palpable exaggeration reveals a foundation of truth. As with the sentimentalists of the eighteenth century, tears were considered fine and honourable. Even nowadays an indifferent spectator of a public procession sometimes feels himself suddenly moved to inexplicable tears. In an age filled with religious reverence for all pomp and grandeur, this propensity will appear altogether natural.

A simple instance will suffice to show the high degree of irritability which distinguishes the Middle Ages from our own time. One can hardly imagine a more peaceful game than that of chess. Still like the *chansons de gestes* of some centuries back, Olivier de la Marche mentions frequent quarrels arising over it : " le plus saige y pert patience."

A scientific historian of the Middle Ages, relying first and foremost on official documents, which rarely refer to the passions, except violence and cupidity, occasionally runs the risk of neglecting the difference of tone between the life of the expiring Middle Ages and that of our own days. Such documents would sometimes make us forget the vehement pathos of medieval life, of which the chroniclers, however defective as to material facts, always keep us in mind.

In more than one respect life had still the colours of a fairy-story ; that is to say, it assumed those colours in the eyes of contemporaries. The court chroniclers were men of culture, and they observed the princes, whose deeds they recorded, at close quarters, yet even they give these records a somewhat archaic, hieratic air. The following story, told by Chastellain, serves to prove this. The young count of Charolais, the later Charles the Bold, on arriving at Gorcum, in Holland, on his way from Sluys, learns that his father, the duke, has taken all his pensions and benefices from him. Thereupon he calls his whole court into his presence, down to the scullions, and in a touching speech imparts his misfortune to them, dwelling on his respect for his ill-informed father, and on his anxiety about the welfare of all his retinue. Let those who have the means to live, remain with him awaiting the return of good fortune ; let the poor go away freely, and let them come back when they hear that the count's fortune has been re-established : they will all return to their old places, and the count will reward them for their patience. " Then were heard cries and sobs, and with one accord they shouted : ' We all, we all, my lord, will live and die with thee.' " Profoundly touched, Charles accepts their devotion : " Well, then, stay and suffer, and I will suffer for you, rather than that you should be in want." The nobles then come and offer him what they possess, " one saying, I have a thousand, another, ten thousand ; I have this,

I have that to place at thy service, and I am ready to share all that may befall thee." And in this way everything went on as usual, and there was never a hen the less in the kitchen.

Clearly this story has been more or less touched up. What interests us is that Chastellain sees the prince and his court in the epic guise of a popular ballad. If this is a literary man's conception, how brilliant must royal life have appeared, when displayed in almost magic splendour, to the naïve imagination of the uneducated !

Although in reality the mechanism of government had already assumed rather complicated forms, the popular mind pictures it in simple and fixed figures. The current political ideas are those of the Old Testament, of the romaunt and the ballad. The kings of the time are reduced to a certain number of types, every one of which corresponds, more or less, to a literary motif. There is the wise and just prince, the prince deceived by evil counsellors, the prince who avenges the honour of his family, the unfortunate prince to whom his servants remain faithful. In the mind of the people political questions are reduced to stories of adventure. Philip the Good knew the political language which the people understands. To convince the Hollanders and Frisians that he was perfectly able to conquer the bishopric of Utrecht, he exhibits, during the festivities of the Hague, in 1456, precious plate to the value of thirty thousand silver marks. Everybody may come and look at it. Amongst other things, two hundred thousand gold lions have been brought from Lille contained in two chests which every one may try to lift up. The demonstration of the solvency of the state took the form of an entertainment at a fair.

Often we find a fantastic element in the life of princes which reminds us of the caliph of the *Arabian Nights*. Charles VI, disguised and mounted with a friend on a single horse, witnesses the entrance of his betrothed and is knocked about in the crowd by petty constables. Philip the Good, whom the physicians ordered to have his head shaved, issues a command to all the nobles to do likewise, and charges Pierre de Hagenbach with the cropping of any whom he finds recalcitrant. In the midst of coolly calculated enterprises princes sometimes act with an impetuous temerity, which endangers their lives

and their policy. Edward III does not hesitate to expose his
life and that of the prince of Wales in order to capture some
Spanish merchantmen, in revenge for deeds of piracy. Philip
the Good interrupts the most serious political business to
make the dangerous crossing from Rotterdam to Sluys for the
sake of a mere whim. On another occasion, mad with rage
in consequence of a quarrel with his son, he leaves Brussels
in the night alone, and loses his way in the woods. The knight
Philippe Pot, to whom fell the delicate task of pacifying him
on his return, lights upon the happy phrase : " Good day, my
liege, good day, what is this ? Art thou playing King Arthur,
now, or Sir Lancelot ? "

The custom of princes, in the fifteenth century, frequently
to seek counsel in political matters from ecstatic preachers
and great visionaries, maintained a kind of religious tension
in state affairs which at any moment might manifest itself in
decisions of a totally unexpected character.

At the end of the fourteenth century and at the beginning
of the fifteenth, the political stage of the kingdoms of Europe
was so crowded with fierce and tragic conflicts that the peoples
could not help seeing all that regards royalty as a succession
of sanguinary and romantic events : in England, King Richard
II dethroned and next secretly murdered, while nearly at the
same time the highest monarch in Christendom, his brother-
in-law Wenzel, king of the Romans, is deposed by the electors ;
in France, a mad king and soon afterwards fierce party strife,
openly breaking out with the appalling murder of Louis of
Orleans in 1407, and indefinitely prolonged by the retaliation
of 1419 when Jean sans Peur is murdered at Montereau. With
their endless train of hostility and vengeance, these two
murders have given to the history of France, during a whole
century, a sombre tone of hatred. For the contemporary
mind cannot help seeing all the national misfortunes which
the struggle of the houses of Orleans and of Burgundy was to
unchain, in the light of that sole dramatic motive of princely
vengeance. It finds no explanation for historic events save
in personal quarrels and motives of passion.

In addition to all these evils came the increasing obsession
of the Turkish peril, and the still vivid recollection of the
catastrophe of Nicopolis in 1396, where a reckless attempt

to save Christendom had ended in the wholesale slaughter of French chivalry. Lastly, the great schism of the West had lasted already for a quarter of a century, unsettling all notions about the stability of the Church, dividing every land and community. Two, soon three, claimants contending for the papacy! One of them, the obstinate Aragonese Peter of Luna, or Benedict XIII, was commonly called in France " le Pappe de la Lune." What can an ignorant populace have imagined when hearing such a name ?

The familiar image of Fortune's wheel from which kings are falling with their crowns and their sceptres took a living shape in the person of many an expelled prince, roaming from court to court, without means, but full of projects and still decked with the splendour of the marvellous East whence he had fled—the king of Armenia, the king of Cyprus, before long the emperor of Constantinople. It is not surprising that the people of Paris should have believed in the tale of the Gipsies, who presented themselves in 1427, " a duke and a count and ten men, all on horseback," while others, to the number of 120, had to stay outside the town. They came from Egypt, they said ; the pope had ordered them, by way of penance for their apostasy, to wander about for seven years, without sleeping in a bed ; there had been 1,200 of them, but their king, their queen and all the others had died on the way ; as a mitigation the pope had ordered that every bishop and abbot was to give them ten pounds tournois. The people of Paris came in great numbers to see them, and have their fortunes told by women who eased them of their money " by magic art or in other ways."

The inconstancy of the fortune of princes was strikingly embodied in the person of King René. Having aspired to the crowns of Hungary, of Sicily, and of Jerusalem, he had lost all his opportunities, and reaped nothing but a series of defeats, and imprisonments, chequered by perilous escapes. The royal poet, a lover of the arts, consoled himself for all his disappointments on his estates in Anjou and in Provence ; his cruel fate had not cured him of his predilection for pastoral enjoyment. He had seen all his children die but one, a daughter for whom was reserved a fate even harder than his own. Married at sixteen to an imbecile bigot, Henry VI of

England, Margaret of Anjou, full of wit, ambition and passion, after living for many years in that hell of hatred and of persecution, the English court, lost her crown when the quarrel between York and Lancaster at last broke out into civil war. Having found refuge, after many dangers and suffering, at the court of Burgundy, she told Chastellain the story of her adventures : how she had been forced to commit herself and her young son to the mercy of a robber, how at mass she had had to ask a Scotch archer a penny for her offering, " who reluctantly and with regret took a groat scots for her out of his purse and lent it her." The good historiographer, moved by so much misfortune, dedicated to her " a certain little treatise on fortune, based on its inconstancy and deceptive nature," which he entitled *Le Temple de Bocace*. He could not guess that still graver calamities were in store for the unfortunate queen. At the battle of Tewkesbury, in 1471, the fortunes of Lancaster went down for ever. Her only son perished there, probably slaughtered after the battle. Her husband was secretly murdered ; she herself was imprisoned in the Tower of London, where she remained for five years, to be at last given up by Edward IV to Louis XI, who made her renounce her father's inheritance as the price of her liberty.

An atmosphere of passion and adventure enveloped the lives of princes. It was not popular fancy alone which lent it that colour.

A present-day reader, studying the history of the Middle Ages based on official documents, will never sufficiently realize the extreme excitability of the medieval soul. The picture drawn mainly from official records, though they may be the most reliable sources, will lack one element : that of the vehement passion possessing princes and peoples alike. To be sure, the passionate element is not absent from modern politics, but it is now restrained and diverted for the most part by the complicated mechanism of social life. Five centuries ago it still made frequent and violent irruptions into practical politics, upsetting rational schemes. In princes this violence of sentiment is doubled by pride and the consciousness of power, and therefore operates with a twofold impetus. It is not surprising, says Chastellain, that princes often live in hostility, "for princes are men, and their affairs are high and perilous, and their natures are subject to many passions, such as hatred and envy ; their hearts are veritable dwelling-places of these, because of their pride in reigning."

In writing the history of the house of Burgundy, the *leit-motiv* should constantly keep before our minds the spirit of revenge. Nobody, of course, will now seek the explanation of the whole conflict of power and interests, whence proceeded the secular struggle between France and the house of Austria, in the family feud between Orleans and Burgundy. All sorts of causes of a general nature—political, economic, ethnographic—have contributed to the genesis of that great conflict. But we should never forget that the apparent origin of it, and the central motive dominating it, was, to the men of the fifteenth century and even later, the thirst for revenge. To them Philip the Good is always, in the first place, the avenger, "he who, to avenge the outrage done to the person of Duke John, sustained the war for sixteen years." He had undertaken it as a sacred duty : "with the most violent and deadly hatred he would give himself up to revenge the dead, as far as ever God would permit him, and he would devote to it body and soul, substance and lands, submitting everything to Fortune, considering it more a salutary task and agreeable to God to undertake it, than to leave it."

Read the long list of expiatory deeds which the treaty of Arras demanded in 1435—chapels, monasteries, churches, chapters to be founded, crosses to be erected, masses to be chanted—then one realizes the immensely high rate at which men valued the need of vengeance and of reparations to out-raged honour. The Burgundians were not alone in thinking after this fashion ; the most enlightened man of his century, Aeneas Sylvius, in one of his letters praises Philip above all the other princes of his time, for his anxiety to avenge his father.

According to La Marche, this duty of honour and revenge was to the duke's subjects also the cardinal point of policy. All the dominions of the duke, he says, were clamouring for vengeance along with him. We shall find it difficult to believe this, when we remember, for instance, the commercial relations between Flanders and England, a more important political factor, it would seem, than the honour of the ducal family. But to understand the sentiment of the age itself, one should look for the avowed and conscious political ideas. There can be no doubt that no other political motive could be better understood by the people than the primitive motives of hatred and of vengeance. Attachment to princes had still an emotional character; it was based on the innate and immediate sentiments of fidelity and fellowship, it was still feudal sentiment at bottom. It was rather party feeling than political. The last three centuries of the Middle Ages are the time of the great party struggles. From the thirteenth century onward inveterate party quarrels arise in nearly all countries : first in Italy, then in France, the Netherlands, Germany and England. Though economic interests may sometimes have been at the bottom of these quarrels, the attempts which have been made to disengage them often smack somewhat of arbitrary construction. The desire to discover economic causes is to some degree a craze with us, and sometimes leads us to forget a much simpler psychological explanation of the facts.

In the feudal age the private wars between two families have no other discernible reason than rivalry of rank and covetousness of possessions. Racial pride, thirst of vengeance, fidelity, are their primary and direct motives. There are no grounds to ascribe another economic basis to them than mere greed of one's neighbour's riches. Accordingly as the central power consolidates and extends, these isolated quarrels unite, agglomerate to groups ; large parties are formed, are polarized, so to say ; while their members know of no other grounds for their concord or enmity than those of honour, tradition and fidelity. Their economic differences are often only a consequence of their relation towards their rulers.

Every page of medieval history proves the spontaneous and passionate character of the sentiments of loyalty and devotion to the prince. At Abbeville, in 1462, a messenger comes at night, bringing the news of a dangerous illness of the duke of Burgundy. His son requests the good towns to pray for him. At once the aldermen order the bells of the church of Saint Vulfran to be rung ; the whole population wakes up and goes to church, where it remains all night in prayer, kneeling or

prostrate on the ground, with "grandes allumeries merveil-
leuses," while the bells keep tolling.

It might be thought that the schism, which had no dogmatic
cause, could hardly awaken religious passions in countries
distant from Avignon and of Rome, in which the two popes
were only known by name. Yet in fact it immediately
engendered a fanatical hatred, such as exists between the
faithful and infidels. When the town of Bruges went over to
the " obedience " of Avignon, a great number of people left
their house, trade or prebend, to go and live according to their
party views in some diocese of the Urbanist obedience : Liège,
Utrecht, or elsewhere. In 1382 the oriflamme, which might
only be unfurled in a holy cause, was taken up against the
Flemings, because they were Urbanists, that is, infidels.
Pierre Salmon, a French political agent, arriving at Utrecht
about Easter, could not find a priest there willing to admit
him to the communion service, " because they said I was a
schismatic and believed in Benedict the anti-pope."

The emotional character of party sentiments and of fidelity
was further heightened by the powerfully suggestive effect of
all the outward signs of these divergences : liveries, colours,
badges, party cries. During the first years of the war between
the Armagnacs and the Burgundians, these signs succeeded
each other in Paris with a dangerous alternation : a purple
hood with the cross of Saint Andrew, white hoods, then violet
ones. Even priests, women and children wore distinctive
signs. The images of saints were decorated with them ; it
was asserted that certain priests, during mass and in baptizing,
refused to make the sign of the cross in the orthodox way, but
made it in the form of a Saint Andrew cross.

In the blind passion with which people followed their lord
or their party, the unshakable sentiment of right, characteristic of the Middle Ages, is trying to find expression. Man at
that time is convinced that right is absolutely fixed and
certain. Justice should prosecute the unjust everywhere and
to the end. Reparation and retribution have to be extreme,
and assume the character of revenge. In this exaggerated
need of justice, primitive barbarism, pagan at bottom, blends
with the Christian conception of society. The Church, on
the one hand, had inculcated gentleness and clemency, and

tried, in that way, to soften judicial morals. On the other hand, in adding to the primitive need of retribution the horror of sin, it had, to a certain extent, stimulated the sentiment of justice. And sin, to violent and impulsive spirits, was only too frequently another name for what their enemies did. The barbarous idea of retaliation was reinforced by fanaticism. The chronic insecurity made the greatest possible severity on the part of the public authorities desirable ; crime came to be regarded as a menace to order and society, as well as an insult to divine majesty. Thus it was natural that the late Middle Ages should become the special period of judicial cruelty. That the criminal deserved his punishment was not doubted for a moment. The popular sense of justice always sanctioned the most rigorous penalties. At intervals the magistrate undertook regular campaigns of severe justice, now against brigandage, now against sorcery or sodomy.

What strikes us in this judicial cruelty and in the joy the people felt at it, is rather brutality than perversity. Torture and executions are enjoyed by the spectators like an entertainment at a fair. The citizens of Mons bought a brigand, at far too high a price, for the pleasure of seeing him quartered, " at which the people rejoiced more than if a new holy body had risen from the dead." The people of Bruges, in 1488, during the captivity of Maximilian, king of the Romans, cannot get their fill of seeing the tortures inflicted, on a high platform in the middle of the market-place, on the magistrates suspected of treason. The unfortunates are refused the death-blow which they implore, that the people may feast again upon their torments.

Both in France and in England, the custom existed of refusing confession and the extreme unction to a criminal condemned to death. Sufferings and fear of death were to be aggravated by the certainty of eternal damnation. In vain had the council of Vienne in 1311 ordered to grant them at least the sacrament of penitence. Towards the end of the fourteenth century the same custom still existed. Charles V himself, moderate though he was, had declared that no change would be made in his lifetime. The chancellor Pierre d'Orgemont, whose " forte cervelle," says Philippe de Mézières, was more difficult to turn than a mill-stone, remained deaf to the humane remonstrances of the latter. It was only after Gerson had joined his voice to that of Mézières that a royal decree of the 12th of February, 1397, ordered that confession should be accorded to the condemned. A stone cross erected by the care of Pierre de Craon, who had interested himself in the decree, marked the place where the Minorite friars might assist penitents going to execution. And even then the barbarous custom did not disappear. Etienne Ponchier, bishop of Paris, had to renew the decree of 1311 in 1500.

In 1427 a noble brigand is hanged in Paris. At the moment when he is going to be executed, the great treasurer of the regent appears on the scene and vents his hatred against him ; he prevents his confession, in spite of his prayers ; he climbs the ladder behind him, shouting insults, beats him with a stick, and gives the hangman a thrashing for exhorting the victim to think of his salvation. The hangman grows nervous and bungles his work ; the cord snaps, the wretched criminal falls on the ground, breaks a leg and some ribs, and in this condition has to climb the ladder again.

The Middle Ages knew nothing of all those ideas which have rendered our sentiment of justice timid and hesitating : doubts as to the criminal's responsibility ; the conviction that society is, to a certain extent, the accomplice of the individual; the desire to reform instead of inflicting pain ; and, we may even add, the fear of judicial errors. Or rather these ideas were implied, unconsciously, in the very strong and direct feeling of pity and of forgiveness which alternated with extreme severity. Instead of lenient penalties, inflicted with hesitation, the Middle Ages knew but the two extremes : the fulness of cruel punishment, and mercy. When the condemned criminal is pardoned, the question whether he deserves it for any special reasons is hardly asked ; for mercy has to be gratuitous, like the mercy of God. In practice, it was not always pure pity which determined the question of pardon. The princes of the fifteenth century were very liberal of " lettres de rémission " for misdeeds of all sorts, and contemporaries thought it quite natural, that they were obtained by the intercession of noble relatives. The majority of these documents, however, concern poor common people.

The contrast of cruelty and of pity recurs at every turn in

the manners and customs of the Middle Ages. On the one hand, the sick, the poor, the insane, are objects of that deeply moved pity, born of a feeling of fraternity akin to that which is so strikingly expressed in modern Russian literature ; on the other hand, they are treated with incredible hardness or cruelly mocked. The chronicler Pierre de Fenin, having described the death of a gang of brigands, winds up naïvely : " and people laughed a good deal, because they were all poor men." In 1425, an " esbatement " takes place in Paris, of four blind beggars, armed with sticks, with which they hit each other in trying to kill a pig, which is the prize of the combat. On the evening before they are led through the town, " all armed, with a great banner in front, on which was pictured a pig, and preceded by a man beating a drum."

In the fifteenth century, female dwarfs were objects of amusement, as they still were at the court of Spain when Velazquez painted their infinitely sad faces. Madame d'Or, the blond dwarf of Philip the Good, was famous. She was made to wrestle, at a court festival, with the acrobat Hans. At the wedding-feasts of Charles the Bold, in 1468, Madame de Beaugrant, the female dwarf of Mademoiselle of Burgundy, enters dressed like a shepherdess, mounted on a golden lion, larger than a horse ; she is presented to the young duchess and placed on the table. As to the fate of these small creatures, the account-books are more eloquent for us than any sentimental complaint could be. They tell us of a dwarf-girl whom a duchess caused to be fetched from her home, and how her parents came to visit her from time to time and receive a gratuity. " Au père de Belon la folle, qui estoit venu veoir sa fille. . . . 27*s*. 6*d*." The poor fellow perhaps went home well pleased and much elated about the court function of his daughter. That same year a locksmith of Blois furnished two iron collars, the one " to make fast Belon, the fool, and the other to put round the neck of the monkey of her grace the Duchess."

In the harshness of those times there is something ingenuous which almost forbids us to condemn it. When the massacre of the Armagnacs was in full swing in 1418, the Parisians founded a brotherhood of Saint Andrew in the church of Saint Eustache : every one, priest or layman, wore a wreath of red roses, so that the church was perfumed by them, " as if it had been washed with rose-water." The people of Arras celebrate the annulment of the sentences for witchcraft, which during the whole year 1461 had infested the town like an epidemic, by joyous festivals and a competition in acting " folies moralisées," of which the prizes were a gold fleur-de-lis, a brace of capons, etc.; nobody, it seems, thought any more of the tortured and executed victims.

So violent and motley was life, that it bore the mixed smell of blood and of roses. The men of that time always oscillate between the fear of hell and the most naïve joy, between cruelty and tenderness, between harsh asceticism and insane attachment to the delights of this world, between hatred and goodness, always running to extremes.

After the close of the Middle Ages the mortal sins of pride, anger and covetousness have never again shown the unabashed insolence with which they manifested themselves in the life of preceding centuries. The whole history of the house of Burgundy is like an epic of overweening and heroic pride, which takes the form of bravura and ambition with Philippe le Hardi, of hatred and envy with Jean sans Peur, of the lust of vengeance and fondness for display with Philip the Good, of foolhardy temerity and obstinacy with Charles the Bold.

Medieval doctrine found the root of all evil either in the sin of pride or in cupidity. Both opinions were based on Scripture texts : *A superbia initium sumpsit omnis perditio.— Radix omnium malorum est cupiditas.* It seems, nevertheless, that from the twelfth century downward people begin to find the principle of evil rather in cupidity than in pride. The voices which condemn blind cupidity, " la cieca cupidigia " of Dante, become louder and louder. Pride might perhaps be called the sin of the feudal and hierarchic age. Very little property is, in the modern sense, liquid, while power is not yet associated, predominantly, with money ; it is still rather inherent in the person and depends on a sort of religious awe which he inspires ; it makes itself felt by pomp and magnificence, or a numerous train of faithful followers. Feudal or hierarchic thought expresses the idea of grandeur by visible signs, lending to it a symbolic shape, of homage paid kneeling, of ceremonial reverence. Pride, therefore, is a symbolic sin, and from the fact that, in the last resort, it derives from the pride of Lucifer, the author of all evil, it assumes a metaphysical character.

Cupidity, on the other hand, has neither this symbolic character nor these relations with theology. It is a purely worldly sin, the impulse of nature and of the flesh. In the later Middle Ages the conditions of power had been changed by the increased circulation of money, and an illimitable field opened to whosoever was desirous of satisfying his ambitions by heaping up wealth. To this epoch cupidity becomes the predominant sin. Riches have not acquired the spectral impalpability which capitalism, founded on credit, will give them later ; what haunts the imagination is still the tangible yellow gold. The enjoyment of riches is direct and primitive ; it is not yet weakened by the mechanism of an automatic and invisible accumulation by investment ; the satisfaction of being rich is found either in luxury and dissipation, or in gross avarice.

Towards the end of the Middle Ages feudal and hierarchic pride had lost nothing, as yet, of its vigour ; the relish for pomp and display is as strong as ever. This primitive pride has now united itself with the growing sin of cupidity, and it is this mixture of the two which gives the expiring Middle Ages a tone of extravagant passion that never appears again.

A furious chorus of invectives against cupidity and avarice rises up everywhere from the literature of that period. Preachers, moralists, satirical writers, chroniclers and poets speak with one voice. Hatred of rich people, especially of the new rich, who were then very numerous, is general. Official records confirm the most incredible cases of unbridled avidity told by the chronicles. In 1436 a quarrel between two beggars, in which a few drops of blood had been shed, had soiled the church of the Innocents at Paris. The bishop, Jacques du Châtelier, "a very ostentatious, grasping man, of a more worldly disposition than his station required," refused to consecrate the church anew, unless he received a certain sum of money from the two poor men, which they did not possess, so that the service was interrupted for twenty-two days. Even worse happened under his successor, Denys de Moulins. During four months of the year 1441, he prohibited both burials and processions in the cemetery of the Innocents, the

most favoured of all, because the church could not pay the
tax he demanded. This Denys de Moulins was reputed " a
man who showed very little pity to people, if he did not receive
money or some equivalent ; and it was told for truth that he
had more than fifty lawsuits before the Parlement, for nothing
could be got out of him without going to law."

A general feeling of impending calamity hangs over all.
Perpetual danger prevails everywhere. To realize the continuous insecurity in which the lives of great and small alike were
passed, it suffices to read the details which Monsieur Pierre
Champion has collected regarding the persons mentioned by
Villon in his *Testament*, or the notes of Monsieur A. Tuetey
to the diary of a Burgher of Paris. They present to us an
interminable string of lawsuits, crimes, assaults and persecutions. A chronicle like that of Jacques du Clercq, or a diary
such as that of the citizen of Metz, Philippe de Vigneulles,
perhaps lay too much stress on the darker side of contemporary
life, but every investigation of the careers of individual persons
seems to confirm them, by revealing to us strangely troubled
lives.

In reading the chronicle of Mathieu d'Escouchy, simple,
exact, impartial, moralizing, one would think that the author
was a studious, quiet and honest man. His character was
unknown before Monsieur du Fresne de Beaucourt had elicited
the history of his life from the archives. But what a life
it was, that of this representative of " colérique Picardie."
Alderman, then, towards 1445 provost, of Péronne, we find
him from the outset engaged in a family quarrel with Jean
Froment, the city syndic. They harass each other recipro-
cally with lawsuits, for forgery and murder, for " excès et
attemptaz." The attempt of the provost to get the widow
of his enemy condemned for witchcraft costs him dear.
Summoned before the Parlement of Paris himself, d'Escouchy
is imprisoned. We find him again in prison as an accused
on five more occasions, always in grave criminal causes, and
more than once in heavy chains. A son of Froment wounds
him in an encounter. Each of the parties hires brigands to
assail the other. After this long feud ceases to be mentioned
in the records, others arise of similar violence. All this does
not check the career of d'Escouchy : he becomes bailiff, provost

of Ribemont, "procureur du roi" at Saint Quentin; he is ennobled. He is taken prisoner at Montlhéry, then comes back maimed from a later campaign. Next he marries, but not to settle down to a quiet life. Once more, he appears accused of counterfeiting seals, conducted to Paris "comme larron et murdrier," forced into confessions by torture, prevented from appealing, condemned; then rehabilitated and again condemned, till the traces of this career of hatred and persecutions disappear from the records.

Is it surprising that the people could see their fate and that of the world only as an endless succession of evils? Bad government, exactions, the cupidity and violence of the great, wars and brigandage, scarcity, misery and pestilence—to this is contemporary history nearly reduced in the eyes of the people. The feeling of general insecurity which was caused by the chronic form wars were apt to take, by the constant menace of the dangerous classes, by the mistrust of justice, was further aggravated by the obsession of the coming end of the world, and by the fear of hell, of sorcerers and of devils. The background of all life in the world seems black. Everywhere the flames of hatred arise and injustice reigns. Satan covers a gloomy earth with his sombre wings. In vain the militant Church battles, preachers deliver their sermons; the world remains unconverted. According to a popular belief, current towards the end of the fourteenth century, no one, since the beginning of the great Western schism, had entered Paradise.

CHAPTER II

PESSIMISM AND THE IDEAL OF THE SUBLIME LIFE

At the close of the Middle Ages, a sombre melancholy weighs on people's souls. Whether we read a chronicle, a poem, a sermon, a legal document even, the same impression of immense sadness is produced by them all. It would sometimes seem as if this period had been particularly unhappy, as if it had left behind only the memory of violence, of covetousness and mortal hatred, as if it had known no other enjoyment but that of intemperance, of pride and of cruelty.

Now in the records of all periods misfortune has left more traces than happiness. Great evils form the groundwork of history. We are perhaps inclined to assume without much evidence that, roughly speaking, and notwithstanding all calamities, the sum of happiness can have hardly changed from one period to another. But in the fifteenth century, as in the epoch of romanticism, it was, so to say, bad form to praise the world and life openly. It was fashionable to see only its suffering and misery, to discover everywhere signs of decadence and of the near end—in short, to condemn the times or to despise them.

We look in vain in the French literature of the beginning of the fifteenth century for the vigorous optimism which will spring up at the Renaissance—though, by the way, the optimist tendency of the Renaissance is sometimes exaggerated. The exulting exclamation of Ulrich von Hutten, which has become trite from much quoting, "O saeculum, O literae! juvat vivere!"[1] expresses the enthusiasm of the scholar rather than that of the man. With the humanists optimism is still tempered by the ancient contempt, both Christian and

[1] "O world, O letters, it is a delight to live!"

Stoic, for the world. A passage extracted from a letter written by Erasmus in 1518, may serve better than Hutten's exclamation to show the average valuation put upon life by a humanist. " I am not so greatly attached to life ; having entered upon my fifty-first year, I judge I have lived long enough ; and on the other hand, I see in this life nothing so excellent or agreeable that a man might wish for it, on whom the Christian creed has conferred the hope of a much happier life, in store for those who have attached themselves closely to piety. Nevertheless, at present, I could almost wish to be rejuvenated for a few years, for this only reason that I believe I see a golden age dawning in the near future." He then describes the concord reigning among the princes of Christendom and their inclination to peace—which was so dear to him personally— then he continues : " Everything confirms my hope that not only good morals and Christian piety will be reborn and flourish, but also pure and true literature and good learning." Thanks to the protection of princes, be it understood. " It is to their pious feelings that we are indebted for seeing everywhere, as at a given signal, illustrious spirits awakening and conspiring to restore good learning."

In short, the appreciation of the joys of life, which Erasmus manifests, is fairly cool ; moreover, he soon changed his mood of hopeful expectation, never to find it again. However, compared with current feeling in the preceding century, except in Italy, Erasmus's appreciation might rather be called warm. The men of letters at the court of Charles VII, or at that of Philip the Good, never tire of inveighing against life and the age. The note of despair and profound dejection is predominantly sounded not by ascetic monks, but by the court poets and the chroniclers—laymen, living in aristocratic circles and amid aristocratic ideas. Possessing only a slight intellectual and moral culture, being for the most part strangers to study and learning, and of only a feebly religious temper, they were incapable of finding consolation or hope in the spectacle of universal misery and decay, and could only bewail the decline of the world and despair of justice and of peace.

No one has been so lavish of complaints of this nature as Eustache Deschamps :

" Temps de doleur et de temptacion,
Aages de plour, d'envie et de tourment,
Temps de langour et de dampnacion,
Aages meneur près du definement,
Temps plains d'orreur qui tout fait faussement,
Aage menteur, plain d'orgueil et d'envie,
Temps sanz honeur et sanz vray jugement,
Aage en tristesse qui abrege la vie." [1]

The ballads he has composed in this spirit may be counted
by the dozen : monotonous and gloomy variations of the same
dismal theme. There must have prevailed among the nobility
a general disposition to melancholy ; otherwise we could not
account for the manifest popularity of these poems.

" Toute léesse deffaut,
Tous cueurs ont prins par assaut
Tristesse et merencolie." [2]

Towards the end of the fifteenth century, the tone is still
unchanged ; Jean Meschinot sighs as did Deschamps.

" O miserable et très dolente vie ! . . .
La guerre avons, mortalité, famine ;
Le froid, le chaud, le jour, la nuit nous mine ;
Puces, cirons et tant d'autre vermine
Nous guerroyent. Bref, miserere domine
Noz meschans corps, dont le vivre est très court." [3]

He too is convinced that all goes wrong in the world ; there
is no justice any more ; the great exploit the small, and the
small exploit each other. He pretends to have been led by
his hypochondria within an ace of suicide. He depicts himself in the following terms :

[1] Time of mourning and of temptation, Age of tears, of envy and of torment, Time of languor and of damnation, Age of decline nigh to the end,
Time full of horror which does all things falsely, Lying age, full of pride and
of envy, Time without honour and without true judgment, Age of sadness
which shortens life.

[2] All mirth is lost, All hearts have been taken by storm By sadness and
melancholy.

[3] O miserable and very sad life ! . . . We suffer from warfare, death
and famine ; Cold and heat, day and night, sap our strength ; Fleas, scab-
mites and so much other vermin Make war upon us. In short, have mercy,
Lord, upon our wicked persons, whose life is very short.

" Et je, le pouvre escrivain,
Au cueur triste, faible et vain,
Voyant de chascun le deuil,
Soucy me tient en sa main ;
Toujours les larmes à l'œil,
Rien fors mourir je ne vueil." [1]

All that we get to know of the moral state of the nobles points to a sentimental need of enrobing their souls with the garb of woe. There is hardly one who does not come forward to affirm that he has seen nothing but misery during his life and expects only worse things from the future. Georges Chastellain, the historiographer of the dukes of Burgundy and chief of the Burgundian rhetorical school, speaks thus of himself in the prologue to his chronicle : " I, man of sadness, born in an eclipse of darkness, and thick fogs of lamentation." His successor, Olivier de la Marche, chooses for his device the lament, " tant a souffert La Marche." [2] It would be interesting to study from the point of view of physiognomy the portraits of that time, which for the most part strike us by their sad expression.

It is curious to notice the variation of meaning which the word melancholy shows in the fourteenth century. The ideas of sadness, of reflection, and of fancy, are blended in the term. For example, in speaking of Philip of Artevelde, lost in thought, in consequence of a message he had just received, Froissart expresses himself thus : " Quant il eut merancoliet une espasse, il s'avisa que il rescriproit aus commissaires dou roi de France." [3] Deschamps says of something that is uglier than could be imagined : no artist is " merencolieux " enough to be able to paint it. The change of meaning evidently shows a tendency to identify all serious occupation of the mind with sadness.

The poetry of Eustache Deschamps is full of petty reviling of life and its inevitable troubles. Happy is he who has no children, for babies mean nothing but crying and stench ;

[1] And I, poor writer, With the sad, feeble and vain heart, When I see every one mourning, Then Affliction holds me in her hand ; I have always tears in my eye, I wish for nothing but to die.

[2] So much has La Marche suffered.

[3] When he had reflected for a space, he resolved to answer the emissaries of the king of France.

they give only trouble and anxiety ; they have to be clothed
shod, fed ; they are always in danger of falling and hurting
themselves ; they contract some illness and die.   When they
grow up, they may go to the bad and be put in prison.   Nothing
but cares and sorrows ; no happiness compensates us for our
anxiety, for the trouble and expenses of their education.   Is
there a greater evil than to have deformed children ?   The
poet has no word of pity for their misfortune ; he holds

> " Que homs de membre contrefais
> Est en sa pensée meffais,—
> Plains de pechiez et plains de vices." [1]

Happy are bachelors, for a man who has an evil wife has a
bad time of it, and he who has a good one always fears to lose
her.   In other words, happiness is feared together with misfortune.   In old age the poet sees only evil and disgust, a
lamentable decline of the body and the mind, ridicule and
insipidity.   It comes soon, at thirty for a woman, at fifty for
a man, and neither lives beyond sixty, for the most part.   It
is a far cry to the serene ideality of Dante's conception of noble
old age in the *Convivio* !

The world, says Deschamps, is like an old man fallen into
dotage.   He has begun by being innocent, then he has been
wise for a long time, just, virtuous and strong :

> " Or est laches, chetis et molz,
> Vieulx, convoiteux et mal parlant :
> Je ne voy que foles et folz. . . .
> La fin s'approche, en vérité. . . .
> Tout va mal." [2]

In another place he laments :

> " Pour quoy est si obscurs le temps,
> Que li uns l'autre ne cognoist,
> Mais muent les gouvernements
> De mal en pis, si comme on voit ?

---

[1] That a man with deformed limbs is misshapen of mind,—Full of sins
and full of vices.

[2] Now the world is cowardly, decayed and weak, Old, covetous, confused
of speech : I see only female and male fools. . . . The end approaches, in
sooth. . . . All goes badly.

Le temps passé trop mieulx valoit.
Qui règne ? Tristesse et Ennuy ;
Il ne court justice ne droit ;
Je ne scé mais desquelz je suy." [1]

And again :

" Se ce temps tient, je deviendray hermite,
Car je n'i voys fors que dueil et tourment." [2]

Pessimism of this kind has hardly anything to do with
religion. Deschamps only gives an off-hand pious purport
to his reflections. Despondency and spleen are at the bottom
of them, not piety. A contempt of the world, which is dominated by fear of weariness and of sorrow, of disease and of old
age, is but an asceticism of the blasé, born of disillusion and
of satiety. It has nothing in common with religion but its
terminology.

Even in ascetic utterances of a purer and loftier kind such
fear of life, such recoiling before its inevitable sorrows, is not
seldom mingled. The series of arguments which Jean Gerson
propounds in his *Discours de l'excellence de Virginité*, written
for his sisters, with a view to keep them from marrying,
does not essentially differ from Deschamps' gloomy lamentations. All the evils attaching to wedlock are found there.
The husband may be a drunkard, a spendthrift, a miser. If
he be honest and good, bad harvests, death of cattle, a ship-
wreck may occur, robbing him of all he possesses. What
misery it is to be pregnant ! How many women die in childbed. The woman who suckles her baby knows neither rest
nor pleasure. Children may be deformed or disobedient ; the
husband may die, and leave his widow behind in care and
poverty.

Thus, always and everywhere in the literature of the age,
we find a confessed pessimism. As soon as the soul of these
men has passed from childlike mirth and unreasoning enjoy-

---

[1] Why are the times so dark That men do not know each other, But governments move From bad to worse, as we see ? The past was much better.
Who reigns ? Affliction and annoyance ; Justice nor law are current ; I
know no more where I belong.

[2] If the times remain so, I shall become a hermit, For I see nothing but
grief and torment.

ment to reflection, deep dejection about all earthly misery takes their place and they see only the woe of life. Still this very pessimism is the ground whence their soul will soar up to the aspiration of a life of beauty and serenity. For at all times the vision of a sublime life has haunted the souls of men, and the gloomier the present is, the more strongly this aspiration will make itself felt.

Three different paths, at all times, have seemed to lead to the ideal life. Firstly, that of forsaking the world. The perfection of life here seems only to be reached beyond the domain of earthly labour and delight, by a loosening of all ties. The second path conducts to amelioration of the world itself, by consciously improving political, social and moral institutions and conditions. Now, in the Middle Ages, Christian faith had so strongly implanted in all minds the ideal of renunciation as the base of all personal and social perfection, that there was scarcely any room left for entering upon this path of material and political progress. The idea of a purposed and continual reform and improvement of society did not exist. Institutions in general are considered as good or as bad as they can be ; having been ordained by God, they are intrinsically good, only the sins of men pervert them. What therefore is in need of remedy is the individual soul. Legislation in the Middle Ages never aims consciously and avowedly at creating a new organism ; professedly it is always opportunistic, it only restores good old law (or at least thinks it does no more) or mends special abuses. It looks more towards an ideal past than towards an earthly future. For the true future is the Last Judgment, and that is near at hand.

It goes without saying that this mental disposition must have greatly contributed to the general pessimism. If in all that regards the things of this world there is no hope of improvement and of progress, however slow, those who love the world too much to give up its delights, and who nevertheless cannot help aspiring to a better order of things, see nothing before them but a gulf. We will have to wait till the eighteenth century—for even the Renaissance does not truly bring the idea of progress—before men resolutely enter the path of social optimism ;—only then the perfectibility of man and society is raised to the rank of a central dogma, and the next century will only lose the naïveté of this belief, but not the courage and optimism which it inspired.

It would be a mistake to think that the medieval mind, lacking the ideas of progress and conscious reform, had only known the religious form of the aspiration to ideal life. For there is a third path to a world more beautiful, trodden in all ages and civilizations, the easiest and also the most fallacious of all, that of the dream. A promise of escape from the gloomy actual is held out to all; we have only to colour life with fancy, to enter upon the quest of oblivion, sought in the delusion of ideal harmony. After the religious and the social solution we here have the poetical.

A simple tune suffices for the enrapturing fugue to develop itself; an outlook on the heroism, the virtue or the happiness of an ideal past is all that is wanted. The themes are few in number, and have hardly changed since antiquity; we may call them the heroic and the bucolic theme. Nearly all the literary culture of later ages has been built upon them.

But *was* it only a question of literature, this third path to the sublime life, this flight from harsh reality into illusion? Surely it has been more. History pays too little attention to the influence of these dreams of a sublime life on civilization itself and on the forms of social life. The content of the ideal is a desire to return to the perfection of an imaginary past. All aspiration to raise life to that level, be it in poetry only or in fact, is an imitation. The essence of chivalry is the imitation of the ideal hero, just as the imitation of the ancient sage is the essence of humanism. Strongest and most lasting of all is the illusion of a return to nature and its innocent charms by an imitation of the shepherd's life. Since Theocritus it has never lost its hold upon civilized society.

Now, the more primitive a society is, the more the need of conforming real life to an ideal standard overflows beyond literature into the sphere of the actual. Modern man is a worker. To work is his ideal. The modern male costume since the end of the eighteenth century is essentially a workman's dress. Since political progress and social perfection have stood foremost in general appreciation, and the ideal itself is sought in the highest production and most equitable distribution of goods, there is no longer any need for playing the hero or the sage. The ideal itself has become democratic. In aristocratic periods, on the other hand, to be representative of true culture means to produce by conduct, by customs, by manners, by costume, by deportment, the illusion of a heroic being, full of dignity and honour, of wisdom and, at all events, of courtesy. This seems possible by the aforesaid imitation of an ideal past. The dream of past perfection ennobles life and its forms, fills them with beauty and fashions them anew as forms of art. Life is regulated like a noble game. Only a small aristocratic group can come up to the standard of this artistic game. To imitate the hero and the sage is not everybody's business. Without leisure or wealth one does not succeed in giving life an epic or idyllic colour. The aspiration to realize a dream of beauty in the forms of social life bears as a *vitium originis* the stamp of aristocratic exclusiveness.

Here, then, we have attained a point of view from which we can consider the lay culture of the waning Middle Ages : aristocratic life decorated by ideal forms, gilded by chivalrous romanticism, a world disguised in the fantastic gear of the Round Table.

The quest of the life beautiful is much older than the Italian *quattrocento*. Here, as elsewhere, the line of demarcation between the Middle Ages and the Renaissance has been too much insisted upon. Florence had but to adopt and develop ancient motifs which the Middle Ages had known. In spite of the æsthetic distance separating the *Giostre* of the Medici from the barbarous pageantry of the dukes of Burgundy, the inspiration is the same. Italy, indeed, discovered new worlds of beauty, and tuned life to a new tone ; but the impulse itself to force it up to a thing of art, generally taken as typical of the Renaissance, was not its invention.

In the Middle Ages the choice lay, in principle, only between God and the world, between contempt or eager acceptance, at the peril of one's soul, of all that makes up the beauty and the charm of earthly life. All terrestrial beauty bore the stain of sin. Even where art and piety succeeded in hallowing it by placing it in the service of religion, the artist or the lover of art had to take care not to surrender to the charms of colour and line. Now, all noble life was in its essential manifestations full of such beauty tainted by sin. Knightly exercises and courteous fashions with their worship of bodily strength ; honours and dignities with their vanity and their pomp, and especially love ;—what were they but pride, envy, avarice and lust, all condemned by religion ! To be admitted as elements of higher culture all these things had to be ennobled and raised to the rank of virtue.

It was here that the path of fancy proved its civilizing value. All aristocratic life in the later Middle Ages is a wholesale attempt to act the vision of a dream. In cloaking itself in the fanciful brilliance of the heroism and probity of a past age, the life of the nobles elevated itself towards the sublime. By this trait the Renaissance is linked to the times of feudalism.

The need of high culture found its most direct expression in all that constitutes ceremonial and etiquette. The actions of princes, even daily and common actions, all assume a quasi-symbolic form and tend to raise themselves to the rank of mysteries. Births, marriages, deaths, are framed in an apparatus of solemn and sublime formalities. The emotions which accompany them are dramatized and amplified. Byzantinism is nothing but the expression of the same tendency, and to realize that it survived the Middle Ages, it is sufficient to remember the Roi-Soleil.

The court was pre-eminently the field where this æstheticism flourished. Nowhere did it attain to greater development than at the court of the dukes of Burgundy, which was more pompous and better arranged than that of the kings of France. It is well known how much importance the dukes attached to the magnificence of their household. A splendid court could, better than anything else, convince rivals of the high rank the dukes claimed to occupy among the princes of Europe. "After the deeds and exploits of war, which are claims to glory," says Chastellain, "the household is the first thing that strikes the eye, and which it is, therefore, most necessary to conduct and arrange well." It was boasted that the Burgundian court was the richest and best regulated of all. Charles the Bold, especially, had the passion of magnificence. The archaic and idyllic function of justice administered by the prince in person, even to the humblest of his subjects, was practised by the duke, who was in the habit of sitting in audience with great solemnity two or three times a week, when every one might tender his petition. He would deliver judgment in the presence of all the noblemen of his household, seated on a " hautdos " covered with gold-cloth, and assisted by two " maîtres des requêtes," the warrant-officer and the clerk kneeling before him. The noblemen were a good deal bored, but there was no help for it, says Chastellain, who expresses some doubt as to the use of these audiences. " It seemed to be a magnificent and very praiseworthy thing, whatever fruit it might bear. But I have neither heard nor seen such a thing done in my time by a prince or a king."

For amusements, too, Charles felt the need of solemn and showy forms. " He was in the habit of devoting part of his day to serious occupations, and, with games and laughter mixed, pleased himself with fine speeches and with exhorting his nobles, like an orator, to practise virtue. And in this regard he was often seen sitting in a chair of state, with his nobles before him, remonstrating with them according to time and circumstances. And always, as the prince and chief of all, he was richly and magnificently dressed, more so than all the others."

This " haute magnificence de cœur pour estre vu et regardé en singulières choses,"[1] is it not altogether according to the spirit of the Renaissance, in spite of its naïve and somewhat stiff outward appearance ?

The meals of the duke were ceremonies of a dignity that was almost liturgic. The descriptions by the master of ceremonies, Olivier de la Marche, are well worth reading. His treatise, *L'Etat de la Maison du duc Charles de Bourgogne*, composed at the request of the king of England, Edward IV, to serve him for a model, expounds the complicated service of breadmasters, carvers, cup-bearers, cooks, and the ordered course of the banquet, which was crowned by all the noblemen filing past the duke, who was still seated at table, " pour lui donner gloire."

The kitchen regulations are truly Pantagruelistic. We may picture them in operation in the kitchen of heroic dimensions, with its seven gigantic chimneys, which can still be seen in the ducal palace of Dijon. The chief cook is seated on a

---

[1] High magnificence of heart to be seen and regarded in extraordinary things.

CHARLES THE BOLD AND HIS COURT.
From a MS. in the British Museum.

[See page 32.

MINIATURE FROM "LE JOUVENCEL." BY ALEXANDER BENING.

From a MS. at Munich, Library of the University.

[See page 63.

raised chair, overlooking the whole apartment ; " and he must hold in his hand a big wooden ladle which serves him for a double purpose : on the one hand to taste soup and broth, on the other to chase the scullions from the kitchen to their work, and to strike them, if need be."

La Marche speaks of the ceremonies which he describes, in as respectful and quasi-scholastic a tone as if he were treating of sacred mysteries. He submits to his readers grave questions of precedence and of service, and answers them most knowingly. —Why is the chief-cook present at the meals of his lord and not the " écuyer de la cuisine " ? How does one proceed to nominate the chief-cook ? To which he replies in his wisdom : When the office of chief-cook falls vacant at the court of the prince, the " maîtres d'hôtel " call the " écuyers " and all the kitchen servants to them one by one. Each one solemnly gives his vote, attested by an oath, and in this way the chief-cook is elected.—Who is to take the chief-cook's place in case he is absent : the " spit-master," or the " soup-master " ?— Answer : Neither ; the substitute will be designated by election.—Why do the " panetiers " and cup-bearers form the first and second ranks, above the carvers and cooks ?—Because they are in charge of bread and wine, to which the sanctity of the sacrament gives a holy character.

The extreme importance which attaches to questions of precedence and etiquette can only be explained by the almost religious significance ascribed to them wherever tradition is strong, and where a primitive spirit still prevails. They contain, so to say, a ritualistic element. All forms of etiquette are elaborated so as to constitute a noble game, which, although artificial, has not yet degenerated altogether into a vain parade. Sometimes the polite form takes such an importance that the gravity of the matter in hand is lost sight of.

Before the battle of Crécy, four French knights returned from reconnoitring the English lines. The incident is told by Froissart. Impatient to hear the news they bring, the king rides forward to meet them and stops as soon as he sees them. They force their way through the ranks of the men-at-arms and reach the king. " What news, my lords ? " asks the king. Then they look at each other without speaking a word, for not one is willing to speak before his companions. And one said

to the other : " Lord, do you say it, speak to the king. I shall
not speak before you." So, for a time they were debating,
as none would begin to speak " par honneur." Till at last the
king ordered Sir Monne de Basele to tell what he knew.

Messire Gaultier Rallart, " chevalier du guet " at Paris,
in 1418, was in the habit of never going his rounds without
being preceded " by three or four musicians playing brass
instruments, which appeared a strange thing to the people, for
they said that it seemed that he said to malefactors : ' Get
away, for I am coming.' " This case, reported by the Burgher
of Paris, of a chief of police warning malefactors of his approach,
is not an isolated one. Jean de Roye tells the same thing of
Jean Balue, bishop of Evreux in 1465. At night he went his
rounds, " with clarions, trumpets and other instruments of
music, through the streets and on the walls, which was not a
customary thing to do for men of the watch."

Even on the scaffold the honours due to rank are strictly
observed. Thus the scaffold mounted by the Constable of
Saint Pol is richly shrouded with black velvet strewn with
fleurs-de-lis ; the cloth with which his eyes are bandaged, the
cushion on which he kneels, are of crimson velvet, and the
hangman is a fellow who has never yet executed a single
criminal—rather a doubtful privilege for the noble victim.

The struggles of politeness, which some forty years ago
were still characteristic of lower-middle-class etiquette, were
extraordinarily developed in the court life of the fifteenth
century. A person of fashion would have considered himself
dishonoured by not according to a superior the place which
belonged to him. The dukes of Burgundy give precedence
scrupulously to their royal relations of France. Jean sans
Peur never fails to show exaggerated respect to his daughter-
in-law, the young princess Michelle of France ; he calls her
Madame ; he bends his knee to the earth before her and at
table always tries to help her, which she will not suffer him
to do. When Philip the Good learns that his cousin, the
dauphin, in consequence of a quarrel with his father, has
removed to Brabant, he at once raises the siege of Deventer,
which formed the first step to his very important scheme of
conquering Friesland. He travels in hot haste to Brussels,
there to receive his royal guest. As the moment of the

meeting approaches, there follows a veritable race to be the first in doing homage to the other. At the news that the dauphin is coming to meet him, the old duke is extremely vexed ; he sends him " three, four messages, one after the other, to tell him, that if he should ride forward to meet him, he had taken an oath, he would quickly return to where he came from, and would retire before him so quickly and so far, that the other would not find him for a whole year, nor would see him, whatever he did ; for, he said, it would mean to him, the duke, ridicule and shame, which would never cease, but be imputed to him throughout the world, to all eternity as a great outrage and a foolish thing ; which he was very anxious to avoid." Out of reverence for the blood of France, the duke, although in the territory of the Empire, prohibits his sword to be carried before him, on entering Brussels ; before reaching the palace, he hastily alights from his horse, enters the court and passes on quickly on perceiving the king's son, "who has come down from his apartment, holding the duchess by the hand, and rapidly goes to him in the inner court with wide-open arms." At once the old duke bares his head, kneels down for a moment and passes on quickly. The duchess holds the dauphin to prevent his advancing a step, the dauphin vainly seizes the duke to prevent him from kneeling, and makes a fruitless attempt to make him rise. Both cried with emotion, says Chastellain, and so did all the spectators.

In the royal receptions of modern times we undoubtedly find ceremonies bordering on the ludicrous, but we shall look in vain for this passionate anxiety about formalities, which attests that towards the close of the Middle Ages a moral significance still attached to them.

After the young count of Charolais, out of modesty, has obstinately refused to use the wash-basin before a meal at the same time with the queen of England, the court talks the whole day of the incident ; the duke, to whom the case is submitted, charges two noblemen to argue the case on both sides. Humble refusals to take precedence of another last upwards of a quarter of an hour ; the longer one resists, the more one is praised. People hide their hands to avoid the honour of a hand-kiss ; the queen of Spain does so on meeting the young archduke Philippe le Beau ; the latter waits patiently, for a moment of inattentiveness on the part of the queen, to seize her hand and kiss it.   For once Spanish gravity was at fault ; the court laughed.

All the trifling amenities of social intercourse are minutely regulated.   Etiquette not only prescribes which ladies of the court may hold each other by the hand, but also which lady is entitled to encourage others to this mark of intimacy, by beckoning them.   This right of beckoning, " hucher," is a technical question for the old court lady Aliénor de Poitiers, who has described the ceremonial of the court of Burgundy. The departure of a guest is opposed with troublesome insistence.   Philip the Good refuses to let the queen of France go on the day fixed by the king, in spite of the fear which the poor queen and her train felt for the anger of Louis XI.

Goethe has said that there is not an outward sign of politeness which has not a profound moral foundation, and Emerson expresses almost the same thought when calling politeness " virtue gone to seed."   It would, perhaps, be an exaggeration to say that at the end of the Middle Ages people were still fully conscious of the ethical value of politeness ; but surely people still felt its æsthetic value, which marks the transition of these forms from sincere professions of affection to arid formalities of civility.

It is obvious that this rich adornment of life flourished nowhere so much as at the court of princes, where people could devote time to it and had room for it.   This same cult of forms, however, spread downwards from the nobility to the middle classes, where they lingered on, after having become obsolete in higher circles.   Customs such as that of urging a guest to have another helping of a dish, or to prolong his visit, of refusing to take precedence, now hardly fashionable, were in full bloom in the fifteenth century, scrupulously observed, though at the same time an object of satire.

Above all, public worship offered ample occasion for lengthy displays of civility.   In the first place, there is the " offrande " ; no one is willing to be the first to place his alms on the altar :

> " Passez.—Non feray.—Or avant !
> Certes si ferez, ma cousine.
> —Non feray.—Huchez no voisine,
> Qu'elle doit mieux devant offrir.

> —Vous ne le devriez souffrir."
> Dist la voisine ; "n'appartient
> A moy ; offrez, qu'a vous ne tient
> Que li prestres ne se delivre." [1]

When at last the person of highest rank has led the way, the same debate will be repeated in connection with the " pax," a disc of wood, silver or ivory, that was kissed after the *Agnus Dei*. Amid polite refusals to kiss first, the " pax " went from hand to hand among the notabilities, with the result of a prolonged interruption of the service.

> " Respondre doit la juene fame :
> —Prenez, je ne prendray pas, dame.
> — Si ferez, prenez, douce amie.
> —Certes, je ne le prandray mie ;
> L'en me tendroit pour une sote.
> —Baillez, damoiselle Marote.
> —Non feray, Jhesucrist m'en gart !
> Portez a ma dame Ermagart.
> —Dame, prenez.—Saincte Marie,
> Portez la paix a la baillie
> —Non, mais a la gouverneresse." [2]

Even a holy man like François de Paule thought it his duty to take part in these childish observances ; the witnesses in the process for his canonization considered this behaviour a mark of great humility and merit, which shows that satire can have hardly exaggerated and that the ethical idea of these forms had not completely disappeared.

With all this business of compliments, attending public worship became almost like dancing a minuet. For on leaving the church similar scenes are enacted, in getting a superior to walk on the right hand, or to be the first to cross a plank-bridge or enter a narrow lane. Arrived at home, the whole company has to be invited to enter and drink some wine

---

[1] " Go on—I shall not—Come forward ! Certainly, you will do so, cousin —I shall not—Call to our neighbour, That she should offer before you—You should not suffer it," the neighbour says : " it does not belong To me ; offer, only for you The priest has to wait."

[2] The young woman should answer, Take it, I shall not, lady—Yes, do, take it, dear friend—I shall certainly not take it, dear ; People would take me for a fool—Pass it, miss Marote—I shall not, Jesus Christ forbid ! Take it to the lady Ermagart—Lady, take it—Holy Mary, Take the pax to the bailiff's wife—No, but to the governor's wife.

(as Spanish courtesy demands to this day). The company excuse themselves politely, upon which it becomes requisite to accompany them part of the way, in spite of their repeated protestations.

These futile forms become touching, and their moral and civilizing value is better understood, on remembering they emanated from the passionate soul of a savage race, struggling to tame its pride and its anger. Quarrels and acts of violence go hand in hand with the ceremonious abdication of all pride, of which they are the reverse. Noble families disputed fiercely for that same precedence in church by which they courteously pretended to set little store.

Often enough native rudeness pierces through the thin veneer of politeness. Duke John of Bavaria, the elect of Liège, is a guest at Paris. At the festivities given in his honour by the great nobles, he wins all their money from them in gaming. One of the princes cannot restrain himself any longer, and exclaims : " What devil of a priest have we got here ? " (It is the chronicler of Liège, Jean de Stavelot, who reports the fact.) "What, is he to win all our money ? Whereupon my lord of Liège rose from the table and said angrily : I am not a priest and I do not want your money. And he took it and threw it all about the room ; and many marvelled greatly at his liberality."

The magnificent order maintained at the court of Burgundy, praised by Christine de Pisan, by Chastellain, and by the Bohemian nobleman Leon of Rozmital, acquires its full significance only when compared with the disorder which reigned at the court of France, Burgundy's older and more illustrious model. In a number of his ballads Eustache Deschamps complains of the misery at court, and these complaints are not merely variations on the familiar theme of disparagement of court life. Bad fare and poor lodgings ; continual noise and disorder ; swearing and quarrels ; jealousies and injuries ; in short, the court is an abyss of sins, the gate of hell.

Neither the sacred respect for royalty, nor the almost sacramental value attaching to ceremonies, could prevent decorum from being occasionally ignominiously thrust aside on the most solemn occasions. At the coronation banquet of Charles VI, in 1380, the duke of Burgundy seeks, by force, to take the place to which he is entitled, as doyen of the peers, between the king and the duke of Anjou. Already the train of the duke begins to thrust aside their opponents ; threatening cries arise, a scuffle is breaking out when the king prevents it, by doing justice to the claims of the duke of Burgundy.

Even the infractions of solemn forms tended to become forms themselves. It seems that it was more or less a custom for the funeral of a king of France to be interrupted by a quarrel, of which the object was the possession of the utensils of the ceremony. In 1422 the corporation of the " henouars," or salt-weighers, of Paris, whose privilege it was to carry the king's corpse to Saint-Denis, came to blows with the monks of the abbey, as both parties claimed the pall covering the bier of Charles VI.

An analogous case occurred in 1461, at the funeral of Charles VII. In consequence of an altercation with the monks, the " henouars " put down the coffin when they have come half-way and refuse to carry it any further, unless they are paid ten pounds Paris. The Lord Grand Master of the Horse quiets them by promising to pay them out of his own pocket, but the delay had been so long that the cortège arrives at Saint-Denis only towards eight at night. After the interment, a new conflict arises with regard to the pall of gold-cloth, between the monks and the Grand Master of the Horse himself.

The great publicity which it was customary to give to all important events in the life of a king, and which survived to the times of Louis XIV, sometimes led to a pitiable breakdown of discipline on the most solemn occasions. At the coronation banquet of 1380, the throng of spectators, guests and servants was such that the constable and the marshal of Sancerre had to serve up the dishes on horseback. At the coronation of Henry VI of England at Paris, in 1431, the people force their way at daybreak into the great hall where the feast was to take place, " some to look on, others to regale themselves, others to pilfer or to steal victuals or other things." The members of the Parlement and of the University, the provost of the merchants and the aldermen, after having succeeded with great difficulty in entering the hall, find the tables assigned to them occupied by all sorts of artisans. An attempt is made to remove them, " but when they had

succeeded in driving away one or two, six or eight sat down on
the other side." At the inauguration of Louis XI, in 1461,
the precaution had been taken of closing the doors of the
cathedral of Reims early and placing a guard there, so that
not more persons should enter the church than the choir could
hold. Nevertheless, the spectators so pressed round the altar
where the king was anointed, that the prelates assisting the
archbishop could scarcely move, and the princes of the blood
were nearly squeezed to death in their seats of honour.

The passionate and violent soul of the age, always vacillating between tearful piety and frigid cruelty, between
respect and insolence, between despondency and wantonness,
could not dispense with the severest rules and the strictest
formalism. All emotions required a rigid system of conventional forms, for without them passion and ferocity would
have made havoc of life. By this sublimating faculty each
event became a spectacle for others ; mirth and sorrow were
artificially and theatrically made up. For want of the faculty
to express emotions in a simple and natural way, recourse
must needs be had to æsthetic representations of sorrow and
of joy.

The ceremonies accompanying birth, marriage and death
fully assumed this character of spectacles. Æsthetic values
have here taken the place of their old religious (pagan for the
most part) or magic signification.

Nowhere does the formalizing of the emotions assume a
more suggestive appearance than in the sphere of mourning
rites. There is a tendency in primitive times to exaggerate
the expression of grief, like that of joy. Pompous mourning
is the counterpart of immoderate rejoicings and of insane
luxury. At the death of Jean sans Peur the mourning is
organized with incomparable magnificence, in which there
was, no doubt, also a political by-purpose. The retinue
escorting Philip of Burgundy, who went out to meet the kings
of France and of England, carry two thousand black vanes,
to say nothing of the standards and banners seven yards long,
of the same colour. The carriage of the duke and also the
state seats have been painted black for the occasion. At
the meeting of Troyes, Philip wears a mantle of black velvet

which is so long as to hang down from his horse to the ground. For a long time afterwards he and his court only show themselves dressed in black.

Amidst the general black of court mourning the red worn only by the king of France (not even by the queen) must have made a most startling contrast. In 1393 the Parisians had the surprise of a pompous funeral all in white : that of the king of Armenia, Léon de Lusignan, who died in exile.

The manifestations of sorrow at the death of a prince, if at times purposely exaggerated, undoubtedly often enfolded a deep and unfeigned grief. The general instability of the soul, the extreme horror of death, the fervour of family attachment and loyalty, all contributed to make the decease of a king or a prince an afflicting event. A savage exuberance of grief breaks out when the news is brought to Ghent of the murder of Jean sans Peur. All chronicles confirm it ; Chastellain is diffuse on the subject. His heavy and trailing style is wonderfully well adapted for reporting the long harangue of the bishop of Tournay to prepare the young duke for the awful tidings, as well as for the majestic lamentations of Philip and of Michelle of France, his consort. Half a century later we see Charles the Bold, at the death-bed of his father, weeping, crying out, wringing his hands, falling on the ground, " so as to make every one wonder at his unmeasured grief."

Whatever may be the share of the court style in these narratives, what they tell us fits in too well with the overstrung sensibility of the epoch, and at the same time with the craving for clamorous mourning as an edifying thing, not to be substantially true. Primitive custom demanding that the dead should be publicly and loudly lamented still survived in considerable strength in the fifteenth century. Noisy manifestations of sorrow were thought fine and becoming, and all things connected with a deceased person had to bear witness to unmeasured grief.

The extreme fear of announcing a death likewise bears testimony to the same intermingling of primitive ritual and passionate emotionalism. The death of her father is kept a secret from the countess of Charolais, who is pregnant. During an illness of Philip the Good, the court does not dare to announce to him a single death touching him at all nearly ;

Adolphus of Cleves is forbidden to go into mourning for his wife, out of consideration for the duke, who is ill. The chancellor Nicolas Rolin dies : the duke is left in ignorance of his decease. Yet he begins to suspect it and asks the bishop of Tournay, who has come to visit him, to tell him the truth. " My liege, says the bishop—in sooth, he is dead, indeed, for he is old and broken, and cannot live long.—Déa ! says the duke, I do not ask that. I ask if he is truly dead and gone.— Hà ! my liege—the bishop retorts, he is not dead, but paralysed on one side, and therefore practically dead.—The duke grows angry.—Vechy merveilles ! Tell me clearly, now, whether he is dead. Only then says the bishop : Yes, truly, my liege, he is really dead."

Does not this curious way of announcing a death suggest some trace of ancient superstition, more even than the wish to spare a sick man ? The anxiety to exclude systematically the thought of death denotes a state of mind analogous to that of Louis XI, who would never again wear the dress he had on, nor use the horse he was riding at the moment when evil tidings were announced to him, and who even had a part of the forest of Loches cut down where the tidings of the death of a new-born son were brought to him. " Monsieur the Chancellor," the king writes on May 25, 1483, " I thank you for the letters etc., but I beg you to send me no more by him who brought them, for I found his face terribly changed since I last saw him, and I tell you on my word that he made me much afraid, and farewell."

The cultural value of mourning is that it gives grief its form and rhythm. It transfers actual life to the sphere of the drama. It shoes it with the cothurnus. Mourning at the court of France or of Burgundy, at the time with which we are concerned, has to be regarded as a sort of acted elegy. Funeral ceremonial and funeral poetry, which in primitive civilizations are still undistinguished (in Ireland, for instance), had not yet been completely separated. Mourning still continued a remnant of its poetical functions. It dramatized the effects of grief.

The nobler the deceased and the survivors are, the more heroic the mourning. For a whole year the queen of France may not leave the room in which the death of her consort was announced to her. For the princesses the seclusion lasts six weeks. During all the time that Madame de Charolais is in mourning for her father, she remains in bed, propped up by cushions and dressed in bands, coif and mantle. The rooms are upholstered in black ; the floor is covered with a large black cloth. Aliénor de Poitiers has described for us all the gradations of the ceremonial, varying according to rank.

Under this fine outward show the feelings which are thus exhibited and formalized often tend to disappear. The pathetic posture belies itself behind the scenes. " State " and real life are clearly and naïvely distinguished. Aliénor, having described the sumptuous mourning of the countess of Charolais, adds : " When Madame was ' en son particulier ' she by no means always lay in bed, nor confined herself to one room."

Next to mourning, the lying-in chamber affords ample opportunity for fine ceremonial and differentiation according to rank. The colours and materials of coverings and clothes all have a meaning. Green is the privilege of queens and of princesses, whereas it was white in preceding ages. " La chambre verde " was forbidden even to countesses. During the lying-in of Isabelle de Bourbon, mother of Mary of Burgundy, five large state beds, all draped with an artful fabric of green curtain, remain empty, like state coaches at funerals, only to serve for ceremonious use at the baptism, while the mother reposes on a low couch near the fire. The blinds are kept closed all the time, and the room is lighted by candles.

Through all the ranks of society a severe hierarchy of material and colour kept classes apart, and gave to each estate or rank an outward distinction, which preserved and exalted the feeling of dignity.

Moreover, outside the sphere of birth, marriage and death, a strongly felt æsthetic need tends to create a solemn and decorous form for every event and every notable deed. A sinner who humbles himself, a condemned prisoner who repents, a holy person sacrificing himself, all afford a kind of public spectacle. Public life in this way almost presents the appearance of a perpetual " morale en action."

Even intimate relations in medieval society are rather paraded than kept secret. Not only love, but friendship too, has its finely made up forms. Two friends dress in the same way, share the same room, or the same bed, and call one another by the name of " mignon." It is good form for the prince to have his minion. We must not let the well-known case of Henry III of France affect for us the ordinary accept-ance of the word " mignon " in the fifteenth century. There have been princes and favourites in the Middle Ages too who were accused of culpable relations—Richard II of England and Robert de Vere, for instance—but minions would not have been spoken of so freely, if we had to regard this institution as connoting anything but sentimental friendship. It was a distinction of which the friends boasted in public. On the occasion of solemn receptions the prince leans on the shoulder of the minion, as Charles V at his abdication leaned on William of Orange. To understand the duke's sentiment towards Cesario in *Twelfth Night*, we must recall this form of sentimental friendship, which maintained itself as a formal institution till the days of James I and George Villiers.

The complex of all these fine forms, veiling cruel reality under apparent harmony, made life an art. This art leaves no traces, and it is for this reason that its cultural importance has been noticed too little. The tenderness of compliments, the charming fiction of modesty and altruism, the hieratic pomp of ceremonies, the pageant of marriage, all this is ephe-meral and may seem culturally sterile. That which gives them their style and expression is fashion, not art, and fashion leaves no monuments behind.

And yet, at the close of the Middle Ages, the connections between art and fashion were closer than at present. Art had not yet fled to transcendental heights ; it formed an integral part of social life. In the domain of costume art and fashion were still inextricably blended, style in dress stood nearer to artistic style than later, and the function of costume in social life, that of accentuating the strict order of society itself, almost partook of the liturgic. The amazing extravagance of dress during the last centuries of the Middle Ages was, as it were, the expression of an overflowing æsthetic craving, which art alone did not suffice to satisfy.

All relations, all dignities, all actions, all sentiments, had found their style. The higher the moral value of a social function, the nearer its form of expression approached to pure art. Whereas ceremony and courtesy have no other expression than conversation and luxury, and pass away without visible residue, the rites of mourning do not exhaust themselves in funeral pomp and fictions of etiquette, but leave a durable and artistic expression in the sepulchral monument. As in the case of marriage and baptism, the link of mourning with religion heightens its cultural value.

Still, the richest flower of beautiful forms was reserved for three other elements of life—courage, honour and love.

CHAPTER III

THE HIERARCHIC CONCEPTION OF SOCIETY

When, somewhat more than a hundred years ago, medieval history began to assert itself as an object of interest and admiration, the first element of it to draw general attention and to become a source of enthusiasm and inspiration was chivalry. To the epoch of romanticism the Middle Ages and Chivalry were almost synonymous terms. Historical imagination dwelt by preference on crusades, tournaments, knights-errant. Since then history has become democratic. Chivalry is now only seen as a very special efflorescence of civilization, which, far from having controlled the course of medieval history, has been rather a secondary factor in the political and social evolution of the epoch. For us the problems of the Middle Ages lie first of all in the development of communal organization, of economic conditions, of monarchic power, of administrative and judicial institutions; and, in the second place, in the domain of religion, scholasticism and art. Towards the end of the period our attention is almost entirely occupied by the genesis of new forms of political and economic life (absolutism, capitalism), and new modes of expression (Renaissance). From this point of view feudalism and chivalry appear as little more than a remnant of a superannuated order already crumbling into insignificance, and, for the understanding of the epoch, almost negligible.

Nevertheless, an assiduous reader of the chronicles and literature of the fifteenth century will hardly resist the impression that nobility and chivalry occupy a much more considerable place there than our general conception of the epoch would imply. The reason of this disproportion lies in the fact, that long after nobility and feudalism had ceased to be really essential factors in the state and in society, they continued to impress the mind as dominant forms of life. The

men of the fifteenth century could not understand that the
real moving powers of political and social evolution might be
looked for anywhere else than in the doings of a warlike or
courtly nobility. They persisted in regarding the nobility
as the foremost of social forces and attributed a very exaggerated importance to it, undervaluing altogether the social
significance of the lower classes.

So the mistake, it may be argued, is theirs, and our conception of the Middle Ages is right. This would be so if, to
understand the spirit of an age, it sufficed to know its real and
hidden forces and not its illusions, its fancies and its errors.
But for the history of civilization every delusion or opinion of
an epoch has the value of an important fact. In the fifteenth
century chivalry was still, after religion, the strongest of all
the ethical conceptions which dominated the mind and the
heart. It was thought of as the crown of the whole social
system. Medieval political speculation is imbued to the
marrow with the idea of a structure of society based upon
distinct orders. This notion of " orders " is itself by no means
fixed. The words " estate " and " order," almost synonymous, designate a great variety of social realities. The idea
of an " estate " is not at all limited to that of a class ; it extends
to every social function, to every profession, to every group.
Side by side with the French system of the three estates of
the realm, which in England, according to Professor Pollard,
was only secondarily and theoretically adopted after the
French model, we find traces of a system of twelve social
estates. The functions or groupings, which the Middle Ages
designated by the words " estate " and " order," are of very
diverse natures. There are, first of all, the estates of the
realm, but there are also the trades, the state of matrimony
and that of virginity, the state of sin. At court there are the
" four estates of body and mouth " : bread-masters, cup-bearers,
carvers, and cooks. In the Church there are sacerdotal orders
and monastic orders. Finally, there are the different orders
of chivalry. That which, in medieval thought, establishes
unity in the very dissimilar meanings of the word, is the
conviction that every one of these groupings represents a
divine institution, an element of the organism of Creation
emanating from the will of God, constituting an actual entity,

and being, at bottom, as venerable as the angelic hierarchy.

Now, if the degrees of the social edifice are conceived as the lower steps of the throne of the Eternal, the value assigned to each order will not depend on its utility, but on its sanctity— that is to say, its proximity to the highest place. Even if the Middle Ages had recognized the diminishing importance of the nobility as a limb of the social body, that would not have changed the conception they had of its high value, no more than the spectacle of a violent and dissipated nobility ever hindered the veneration of the order in itself. To the catholic soul the unworthiness of the persons never compromises the sacred character of the institution. The morals of the clergy, or the decadence of chivalrous virtues, might be stigmatized, without deviating for a moment from the respect due to the Church or the nobility as such. The estates of society cannot but be venerable and lasting, because they all have been ordained by God. The conception of society in the Middle Ages is statical, not dynamical.

The aspect which society and politics assume under the influence of these general ideas is bound to be a strange one. The chroniclers of the fifteenth century have, nearly all, been the dupes of an absolute misappreciation of their times, of which the real moving forces escaped their attention. Chastellain, the historiographer of the dukes of Burgundy, may serve as an instance. A Fleming by birth, he had been face to face, in the Netherlands, with the power and the wealth of the commoners, nowhere stronger and more self-conscious than there. The extraordinary fortune of the Burgundian branch of Valois transplanted to Flanders was in reality based on the wealth of the Flemish and Brabant towns. Nevertheless, dazzled by the splendour and magnificence of an extravagant court, Chastellain imagined that the power of the house of Burgundy was especially due to the heroism and the devotion of knighthood.

God, he says, created the common people to till the earth and to procure by trade the commodities necessary for life ; he created the clergy for the works of religion ; the nobles that they should cultivate virtue and maintain justice, so that the deeds and the morals of these fine personages might be a pattern to others. All the highest tasks in the state are assigned by Chastellain to the nobility; notably those of protecting the Church, augmenting the faith, defending the people from oppression, maintaining public prosperity, combating violence and tyranny, confirming peace. Veracity, courage, integrity, liberality, appertain properly to the noble class, and French nobility, according to this pompous panegyrist, comes up to this ideal image. In spite of his general pessimism, Chastellain does his best to see his times through the tinted glasses of this aristocratic conception.

This failing to see the social importance of the common people, which is proper to nearly all authors of the fifteenth century, may be regarded as a kind of mental inertia, which is a phenomenon of frequent occurrence and vital importance in history. The idea which people had of the third estate had not yet been corrected and remodelled in accordance with altered realities. This idea was simple and summary, like those miniatures of breviaries, or those bas-reliefs of cathedrals, representing the tasks of the year in the shape of the toiling labourer, the industrious artisan, or the busy merchant. Among archaic types like these there is neither place for the figure of the wealthy patrician encroaching upon the power of the nobleman, nor for that of the militant representative of a revolutionary craft-guild. Nobody perceived that the nobility only maintained itself, thanks to the blood and the riches of the commoners. No distinction in principle was made, in the third estate, between rich and poor citizens, nor between townsmen and country-people. The figure of the poor peasant alternates indiscriminately with that of the wealthy burgher, but a sound definition of the economic and political functions of these different classes does not take shape. In 1412 the reform programme of an Augustinian friar demanded in all earnest that every non-noble person in France should either devote himself to some handicraft or to labour, or be banished from the kingdom, evidently considering commerce and law as useless occupations.

Chastellain, who is very naïve in political matters and very susceptible to ethical delusions, attributes sublime virtues only to the nobility, and only inferior ones to the common people. " Coming to the third estate, making up the kingdom as a whole, it is the estate of the good towns, of merchants and

of labouring men, of whom it is not becoming to give such a
long exposition as of the others, because it is hardly possible
to attribute great qualities to them, as they are of a servile
degree." Humility, diligence, obedience to the king, and
docility in bowing " voluntarily to the pleasure of the lords,"
those are the qualities which bring credit to " cestuy bas estat
de François."[1]

May not this strange infatuation, by preventing them from
foreseeing future times of economic expansion have contributed to engender pessimism in minds such as that of Chastellain, who could only expect the good of mankind from the
virtues of the nobility ?

Chastellain still calls the rich burghers simply villeins. He
has not the slightest notion of middle-class honour. Duke
Philip the Good was wont to abuse his power by marrying his
archers or other servants of lesser gentility to rich burgher
widows or heiresses. To avoid those alliances, the parents on
their side married their daughters as soon as they reached
marriageable age. Jacques du Clercq mentions the case of a
widow, who for this reason remarried two days after the
burial of her husband. Once the duke, while engaged in such
marriage-broking, met with an obstinate refusal from a rich
brewer of Lille, who felt affronted at such an alliance for his
daughter. The duke secured the person of the young girl ;
the father removed with all his possessions to Tournay, outside
the ducal jurisdiction, in order to be able to bring the matter
before the Parlement of Paris. This brought him nothing
but vexation, and he fell ill with grief. At last he sent his
wife to Lille " in order to beg mercy of the duke and give up
his daughter to him." The latter, in honour of Good Friday,
gave her back to the mother, but with scornful and humilia-
ting words.—Chastellain's sympathies are all on the side of his
master, though, on other occasions, he did not at all fear
to record his disapproval of the duke's conduct. For the
injured father he has no other terms than " this rebellious
rustic brewer," " and such a naughty villein too."

There are in the sentiments of the aristocratic class towards
the people two parallel currents. Side by side with this
haughty disdain of the small man, already a little out of date,

[1] This low estate of Frenchmen.

we notice a sympathetic attitude in the nobility, which seems in absolute contrast with it. Whereas feudal satire goes on expressing hatred mixed with contempt and sometimes with fear, as in the *Proverbes del Vilain* and in the *Kerelslied,* the song of the Flemish villagers, the code of aristocratic ethics teaches, on the other hand, a sentimental compassion for the miseries of the oppressed and defenceless people. Despoiled by war, exploited by the officials, the people live in the greatest distress.

> " Si fault de faim perir les innocens
> Dont les grans loups font chacun jour ventrée,
> Qui amassent à milliers et à cens
> Les faulx trésors ; c'est le grain, c'est le blée,
> Le sang, les os qui ont la terre arée
> Des povres gens, dont leur esperit crie
> Vengence à Dieu, vé à la seignourie." [1]

They suffer in patience. " The prince knows nothing of this." If, at times, they murmur, " poor sheep, poor foolish people," a word from the prince will suffice to appease them. The devastation and insecurity which in consequence of the Hundred Years' War had finally spread over almost all France, gave these laments a sad actuality. From the year 1400 downwards there is no end to the complaints about the fate of the peasants, plundered, squeezed, maltreated by gangs of enemies or friends, robbed of their cattle, driven from their homes. They are expressed by the great Churchmen who favoured reform, such as Nicolas de Clemanges, in his *Liber de lapsu et reparatione justitiæ,* or Gerson in his political sermon *Vivat rex,* preached on November 7, 1405, in the queen's palace at Paris, before the regents and the court. " The poor man "—said the brave chancellor—" will not have bread to eat, except perhaps a handful of rye or barley ; his poor wife will lie in and they will have four or six little ones about the hearth or the oven, which perchance will be warm ; they will ask for bread, they will scream, mad with hunger. The poor mother will but have a very little salted bread to put into their mouths.

[1] The innocents must starve With which the big wolves fill their belly every day, Who by thousands and hundreds hoard Ill-gotten treasures ; it is the grain, it is the corn, The blood, the bones of poor people, which have ploughed the earth And therefore their souls call Upon God for vengeance and woe to lordship.

Now such misery ought to suffice ; but no :—the plunderers
will come, who will seek everything. . . . Everything will be
taken and snapped up ; and we need not ask who pays."
Statesmen, too, make themselves the spokesmen of the
miserable people, and utter their complaints. Jean Jouvenel
laid them before the States of Blois in 1433, and those of Orléans
in 1439. In a petition presented to the king at the meeting
of the States of Tours in 1484, these complaints take the direct
form of a political " remonstrance."

The chroniclers could not help reverting to the subject again
and again : it was bound up with their subject-matter.

The poets in their turn took hold of the motif. Alain
Chartier treats it in his *Quadriloge Invectif*, and Robert Gaguin
in his *Debat du Laboureur, du Prestre et du Gendarme*, inspired
by Chartier. A hundred years after *La Complainte du povre
Commun et des povres Laboureurs de France* of about 1400,
Jean Molinet was to compose a *Resource du petit Peuple*. Jean
Meschinot never tires of reminding the ruling classes of the
fact that the common people are being neglected.

> " O Dieu, voyez du commun l'indigence,
> Pourvoyez-y à toute diligence :
> Las ! par faim, froid, paour et misere tremble.
> S'il a peché ou commis negligence
> Encontre vous, il demande indulgence.
> N'est-ce pitié des biens que l'on lui emble ?
> Il n'a plus bled pour porter au molin,
> On lui oste draps de laine et de lin,
> L'eaue, sans plus, lui demeure pour boire." [1]

This pity, however, remains sterile. It does not result in
acts, not even in programmes, of reform. The felt need of
serious reform is wanting to it and will be wanting for a long
time. In La Bruyère, in Fénelon, perhaps in the elder Mira-
beau, the theme is still the same ; even they have not yet got
beyond theoretical and stereotyped commiseration.

It is natural that the belated chivalrous spirits of the fifteenth

---

[1] O God, see the indigence of the common people, Provide for it with all
speed : Alas ! with hunger, cold, fear and misery they tremble, If they
have sinned or are guilty of negligence Toward Thee, they beg indulgence.
Is it not a pity that they are bereft of their goods ? They have no more
corn to take to the mill, Woollen and linen goods are taken from them, Only
water is left to them to drink.

century join in this chorus of pity for the people. Was it not the knight's duty to protect the weak ? The ideal of chivalry implied, after all, two ideas which might seem to concur in forbidding a haughty contempt for the small man ; the ideas, namely, that true nobility is based on virtue, and that all men are equal.

We should be careful not to overrate the importance of these two ideas. They were equally stereotyped and theoretical. To acknowledge true chivalry a matter of the heart should not be considered a victory over the spirit of feudalism or an achievement of the Renaissance. This medieval notion of equality is by no means a manifestation of the spirit of revolt. It does not owe its origin to radical reformers. In quoting the text of John Ball, who preached the revolt of 1381, " When Adam delved and Eve span, who was then the gentleman ? " one is inclined to fancy that the nobles must have trembled on hearing it. But, in fact, it was the nobility themselves who for a long time had been repeating this ancient theme.

The two ideas of the equality of men and of the nature of true nobility were commonplaces of courteous literature, just as they were in the salons of the " ancien régime." Both derived from antiquity. The poetry of the troubadours had sung and popularized them. Every one applauded them.

> "Dont vient a tous souveraine noblesse ?
> Du gentil cuer, paré de nobles mours.
> . . . Nulz n'est villains se du cuer ne lui muet." [1]

The notion of equality had been borrowed by the Fathers of the Church from Cicero and Seneca. Gregory the Great, the great initiator of the Middle Ages, had given a text for coming ages in his *Omnes namque homines natura aequales sumus.* It had been repeated in all keys, but an actual social purport was not attached to it. It was a moral sentence, nothing more ; to the men of the Middle Ages it meant the approaching equality of death, and was far from holding out, as a consolation for the iniquities of this world, a deceptive prospect of equality on earth. The thought of equality in

---

[1] Whence comes to all sovereign nobility ? From a gentle heart, adorned by noble morals. . . . No one is a villein unless it comes from his heart.

the Middle Ages is closely akin to a *memento mori*. Thus we find it in a ballad by Eustache Deschamps, where Adam addresses his posterity:

> "Enfans, enfans, de moy, Adam, venuz,
> Qui après Dieu suis peres premerain
> Créé de lui, tous estes descenduz
> Naturelment de ma coste et d'Evain ;
> Vo mere fut. Comment est l'un villain
> Et l'autre prant le nom de gentillesce
> De vous, freres ? dont vient tele noblesce ?
> Je ne le sçay, se ce n'est des vertus,
> Et les villains de tout vice qui blesce :
> Vous estes tous d'une pel revestuz.

> "Quant Dieu me fist de la boe ou je fus,
> Homme mortel, faible, pesant et vain,
> Eve de moy, il nous crea tous nuz,
> Mais l'esperit nous inspira a plain
> Perpetuel puis eusmes soif et faim,
> Labour, dolour, et enfans en tristesce ;
> Pour noz pechiez enfantent a destresce
> Toutes femmes ; vilment estes conçuz.
> Vous estes tous d'une pel revestuz.

> "Les roys puissans, les contes et les dus,
> Le gouverneur du peuple et souverain,
> Quant ilz naissent, de quoy sont ilz vestuz ?
> D'une orde pel.
>   . . . Prince, pensez, sans avoir en desdain
> Les povres gens, que la mort tient le frain." [1]

---

[1] Children, descended from me, Adam, Who am the first father, after God, Created by him, you are all born Naturally of my rib and of Eve ; She was your mother. How is it that one is a villein And the other assumes the name of gentility, Of you, brothers ? Whence comes such nobility ? I do not know, unless it springs from virtues And the villeins from all vice, which wounds : You are all covered by the same skin.

When God made me out of the mud where I lay, A mortal man, feeble, heavy and vain, Eve out of me, he created us quite nude, But the spirit fully inspired us, Afterwards we were perpetually thirsty and hungry, We laboured, suffered, children were born in sorrow ; For our sins, all women bear children In pain ; vilely you are conceived. Whence then comes this name : villein that wounds the hearts ? You are all covered by the same skin.

The mighty kings, the counts and the dukes, The governor of the people and sovereign, When they are born, with what are they clothed ? By a dirty skin. . . . Prince, remember, without disdaining The poor people, that death holds the reins.

Jean le Maire de Belges, in *Les Chansons de Namur*, purposely mentions the exploits of rustic heroes, to acquaint the nobles with the fact that those whom they treat as villeins are sometimes animated by the greatest gallantry. For the reason of these poetical admonitions on the subject of true nobility and human equality generally lies in the stimulus they impart to the nobles to adapt themselves to the true ideal of knighthood, and thereby to support and to purify the world. In the virtues of the nobles, says Chastellain, lies the remedy for the evils of the time ; the weal of the kingdom, the peace of the Church, the rule of justice, depend on them.—" Two things," it is said in *Le Livre des Faicts du Mareschal Boucicaut*, " have, by the will of God, been established in the world, like two pillars to sustain the order of divine and human laws . . . and without which the world would be like a confused thing and without any order . . . these two flawless pillars are Chivalry and Learning, which go very well together." "Learning, Faith and Chivalry " are the three flowers of the *Chapel des Fleurs-de-lis* of Philippe de Vitri ; it is the duty of knighthood to preserve and protect the two others.

Long after the Middle Ages a certain equivalence of knighthood and a doctor's degree was generally acknowledged. This parallelism indicates the high ethical value attaching to the idea of chivalry. The two dignities of a knight and of a doctor are conceived as the sacred forms of two superior functions, that of courage and of knowledge. By being knighted the man of action is raised to an ideal level ; by taking his doctor's degree the man of knowledge receives a badge of superiority. They are stamped, the one as a hero, the other as a sage. The devotion to a higher life-work is expressed by a ceremonial consecration. If as an element of social life the idea of chivalry has been of much greater importance, it was because it contained, besides its ethical value, an abundance of æsthetic value of the most suggestive kind.

CHAPTER IV

THE IDEA OF CHIVALRY

Medieval thought in general was saturated in every part with the conceptions of the Christian faith. In a similar way and in a more limited sphere the thought of all those who lived in the circles of court or castle was impregnated with the idea of chivalry. Their whole system of ideas was permeated by the fiction that chivalry ruled the world. This conception even tends to invade the transcendental domain. The primordial feat of arms of the archangel Michael is glorified by Jean Molinet as "the first deed of knighthood and chivalrous prowess that was ever achieved." From the archangel "terrestrial knighthood and human chivalry" take their origin, and in so far are but an imitation of the host of the angels around God's throne.

This illusion of society based on chivalry curiously clashed with the reality of things. The chroniclers themselves, in describing the history of their time, tell us far more of covetousness, of cruelty, of cool calculation, of well-understood self-interest, and of diplomatic subtlety, than of chivalry. None the less, all, as a rule, profess to write in honour of chivalry, which is the stay of the world. Froissart, Monstrelet, d'Escouchy, Chastellain, La Marche, Molinet, all, with the exception only of Philippe de Commines and Thomas Basin, open their works by high-sounding declarations of their purpose of glorifying knightly bravery and virtues, of recording "noble enterprises, conquests, feats of heroism and of arms," "the great marvels and the fine feats of arms that have come to pass because of the great wars." History, to them, is illumined throughout by this their ideal. Later, when writing, they forget it more or less. Froissart, himself the author of a super-romantic epic of chivalry, *Méliador*, narrates endless treasons and cruelties, without being aware of the contra-

56

diction between his general conceptions and the contents of his narrative. Molinet, in his chronicle, from time to time remembers his chivalrous intention, and interrupts his matter-of-fact account of events, to unbosom himself in a flood of high-flown terms.

The conception of chivalry constituted for these authors a sort of magic key, by the aid of which they explained to themselves the motives of politics and of history. The confused image of contemporaneous history being much too complicated for their comprehension, they simplified it, as it were, by the fiction of chivalry as a moving force (not consciously, of course). A very fantastic and rather shallow point of view, no doubt. How much vaster is ours, embracing all sorts of economic and social forces and causes. Still, this vision of a world ruled by chivalry, however superficial and mistaken it might be, was the best they had in the matter of general political ideas. It served them as a formula to understand, in their poor way, the appalling complexity of the world's way. What they saw about them looked primarily mere violence and confusion. War in the fifteenth century tended to be a chronic process of isolated raids and incursions ; diplomacy was mostly a very solemn and very verbose procedure, in which a multitude of questions about juridical details clashed with some very general traditions and some points of honour. All notions which might have enabled them to discern in history a social development were lacking to them. Yet they required a form for their political conceptions, and here the idea of chivalry came in. By this traditional fiction they succeeded in explaining to themselves, as well as they could, the motives and the course of history, which thus was reduced to a spectacle of the honour of princes and the virtue of knights, to a noble game with edifying and heroic rules.

As a principle of historiography, this point of view is a very inferior one. History thus conceived becomes a summary of feats of arms and of ceremonies. The historians *par excellence* will be heralds and kings-at-arms—Froissart thinks so—for they are the witnesses of these sublime deeds ; they are experts in matters of honour and of glory, and it is to record honour and glory that history is written. The statutes of the Golden Fleece enjoined that the feats of arms of the knights be noted down. Types of this combination of herald and historiographer are the king-at-arms of the Golden Fleece, Lefèvre de Saint Remy, and Gilles le Bouvier, dit le héraut Berry.

The conception of chivalry as a sublime form of secular life might be defined as an æsthetic ideal assuming the appearance of an ethical ideal. Heroic fancy and romantic sentiment form its basis. But medieval thought did not permit ideal forms of noble life, independent of religion. For this reason piety and virtue have to be the essence of a knight's life. Chivalry, however, will always fall short of this ethical function. Its earthly origin draws it down. For the source of the chivalrous idea is pride aspiring to beauty, and formalized pride gives rise to a conception of honour, which is the pole of noble life. The sentiment of honour, says Burckhardt, this strange mixture of conscience and of egotism, " is compatible with many vices and susceptible to extravagant delusions ; nevertheless, all that has remained pure and noble in man may find support in it and draw new strength from it." Is not this almost what Chastellain tried to say, when he expressed himself thus :

> "Honneur semont toute noble nature
> D'aimer tout ce qui noble est en son estre.
> Noblesse aussi y adjoint sa droiture." [1]

And again :

"La gloire des princes pend en orgueil et en haut peril emprendre ; toutes principales puissances conviengnent en un point estroit qui se dit orgueil." [2]

According to the celebrated Swiss historian, the quest of personal glory was the characteristic attribute of the men of the Renaissance. The Middle Ages proper, according to him, knew honour and glory only in collective forms, as the honour due to groups and orders of society, the honour of rank, of

---

[1] Honour urges every noble nature To love all that is noble in being. Nobility also adds its uprightness to it.

[2] The glory of princes is in their pride and in undertaking great peril ; all principal forces meet in a small point, which is called pride.

class, or of profession. It was in Italy, he thinks, under the influence of antique models, that the craving for individual glory originated. Here, as elsewhere, Burckhardt has exaggerated the distance separating Italy from the Western countries and the Renaissance from the Middle Ages.

The thirst for honour and glory proper to the men of the Renaissance is essentially the same as the chivalrous ambition of earlier times, and of French origin. Only it has shaken off the feudal form and assumed an antique garb. The passionate desire to find himself praised by contemporaries or by posterity was the source of virtue with the courtly knight of the twelfth century and the rude captain of the fourteenth, no less than with the beaux-esprits of the *quattrocento*. When Beaumanoir and Bamborough fix the conditions of the famous combat of the Thirty, the English captain, according to Froissart, expresses himself in these terms : " And let us right there try ourselves and do so much that people will speak of it in future times in halls, in palaces, in public places and elsewhere throughout the world." The saying may not be authentic, but it teaches us what Froissart thought.

The quest of glory and of honour goes hand in hand with a hero-worship which also might seem to announce the Renaissance. The somewhat factitious revival of the splendour of chivalry that we find everywhere in European courts after 1300 is already connected with the Renaissance by a real link. It is a naïve prelude to it. In reviving chivalry the poets and princes imagined that they were returning to antiquity. In the minds of the fourteenth century, a vision of antiquity had hardly yet disengaged itself from the fairy-land sphere of the Round Table. Classical heroes were still tinged with the general colour of romance. On the one hand, the figure of Alexander had long ago entered the sphere of chivalry ; on the other, chivalry was supposed to be of Roman origin. " And he maintained the discipline of chivalry well, as did the Romans formerly," thus a Burgundian chronicler praised Henry V of England. The blazons of Cæsar, of Hercules, and of Troilus, are placed in a fantasy of King René, side by side with those of Arthur and of Lancelot. Certain coincidences of terminology played a part in tracing back the origin of chivalry to Roman antiquity. How could people have known that the word *miles* with Roman authors did not mean a *miles* in the sense of medieval Latin, that is to say, a knight, or that a Roman *eques* differed from a feudal knight ? Consequently, Romulus, because he raised a band of a thousand mounted warriors, was taken to be the founder of chivalry.

The life of a knight is an imitation ; that of princes is so too, sometimes. No one was so consciously inspired by models of the past, or manifested such desire to rival them, as Charles the Bold. In his youth he made his attendants read out to him the exploits of Gauvain and of Lancelot. Later he preferred the ancients. Before retiring to rest, he listens for an hour or two to the " lofty histories of Rome." He especially admires Cæsar, Hannibal and Alexander, " whom he wished to follow and imitate." All his contemporaries attach great importance to this eagerness to imitate the heroes of antiquity, and agree in regarding it as the mainspring of his conduct. " He desired great glory "—says Commines—" which more than anything else led him to undertake his wars ; and longed to resemble those ancient princes who have been so much talked of after their death." The anecdote is well known of the jester who, after the defeat of Granson, called out to him : " My lord, we are well Hannibaled this time ! " His love of the " beau geste " in antique style was observed by Chastellain at Mechlin in 1467, when he made his first entry there as duke. He had to punish a rising. He sat down facing the scaffold erected for the leader of the insurgents. Already the hangman has drawn the sword and is preparing to strike the blow. " Stop," said the duke then, " take the bandage from his eyes and help him up." " And then I perceived"—says Chastellain—" that he had set his heart on high and singular purposes for the future, and on acquiring glory and renown by extraordinary works."

Thus the aspiration to the splendour of antique life, which is the characteristic of the Renaissance, has its roots in the chivalrous ideal. Between the ponderous spirit of the Burgundian and the classical instinct of an Italian of the same period there is only a difference of nuance. The forms which Charles the Bold affected are still flamboyant Gothic, and he still read his classics in translations.

The chivalrous element and the Renaissance element are

also confounded in the cult of the Nine Worthies ("les neuf preux"). The grouping of three pagans, three Jews, and three Christians in a sort of gallery of heroism is found for the first time in a work of the beginning of the fourteenth century, *Les Vœux du Paon*, by Jacques de Longuyon. The choice of the heroes betrays a close connection with the romances of chivalry. They are Hector, Cæsar, Alexander, Josuah, David, Judas Maccabæus, Arthur, Charlemagne, Godfrey of Bouillon. Eustache Deschamps adopted the idea of the "neuf preux" from his master, Guillaume de Machaut, and devoted many of his ballads to the subject. The craving for symmetry, so strong in the Middle Ages, demanded that the series should be completed by counterparts of the female sex. Deschamps satisfied the demand by choosing from fiction and history a group of rather bizarre heroines. Among them we find Penthesilea, Tomyris, Semiramis. His idea was successful. Literature and tapestry popularized the female as well as the male worthies. Blazons were invented for them. On the occasion of his entry into Paris, in 1431, the English king, Henry VI, is preceded by all the eighteen worthies of both sexes. How popular the idea was, is attested by the parody which Molinet composed of the "nine worthies of gluttony." Francis I still occasionally dressed himself "in the antique style," in order to represent one of the worthies.

Deschamps went further. He completed the series of the nine worthies by adding a tenth, Bertrand du Guesclin, the brave and prudent Breton warrior to whom France owed her recovery from Crécy and Poitiers. In this way he linked the cult of ancient heroes to the budding sentiment of national military glory. His idea was generally adopted. Louis of Orleans had the statue of Du Guesclin, as tenth of the "preux," erected in the great hall of the castle of Coucy. His special reason for honouring the constable's memory was the fact that the latter had held him at the baptismal font and put a sword into his little hand.

The inventories of the Burgundian dukes enumerate curious relics of ancient and modern heroes, such as "the sword of Saint George," with his coat of arms; "another war-sword which belonged to Messire Bertran de Claiquin"; "a big boar's fang, said to be the fang of the boar of Garin le Loherain";

" the psalter of Saint Louis, out of which he learned in his child-hood." How curiously the spheres of imagination of chival-rous romance, and of religious veneration, blend here with the coming spirit of the Renaissance !

About 1300 the sword of Sir Tristram, with an inscription in French verse, was said to have been discovered in Lom-bardy, in an ancient tomb.¹ Here we are only a step from Pope Leo X, who accepted solemnly, as though it were a relic, a humerus of Livy, offered him by the Venetians.

This hero-worship of the declining Middle Ages finds its literary expression in the biography of the perfect knight. In this genre the figures of recent history gradually superseded the legendary ones like that of Gillon de Trazegnies.   Three of these lives of contemporary and illustrious knights are cha-racteristic, although very different from each other : those of Marshal Boucicaut, of Jean de Bueil, and of Jacques de Lalaing.

The military career of Jean le Meingre, surnamed the Marshal Boucicaut, had led him from the defeat of Nicopolis to that of Agincourt, where he was taken prisoner, to die in captivity, six years later.   As early as 1409 one of his admirers wrote his biography from reliable information, but with the intention of producing, not a book of contemporary history, but a mirror of chivalrous life.   The real facts of this hard life of a captain and statesman disappear beneath the appear-ances of ideal heroism.   The marshal is depicted as the type of a frugal and pious knight, at once courtly and well read. He is not rich.   His father would neither augment nor diminish his possessions, saying : " If my children are honest and brave, they will have enough ; if they are worthless, it would be a pity to leave them much."   Boucicaut's piety has a Puritan flavour.   He rises early and remains in prayer for three hours. However occupied or hurried he may be, he hears, on his knees, two masses a day.   On Fridays he dresses in black. On Sundays and festal days he makes pilgrimages on foot, discourses of holy matters, or has some life of a saint read out to him or some story of " the valiant dead—Roman or other." He lives soberly, he speaks little, and when he speaks it is of

¹ A sword of Tristram figures also among King John's jewels lost in the Wash in 1216.

God and the saints, or of chivalry and virtue. He has accustomed his servants to practise piety and observe decency; they have given up the habit of swearing. We shall find him again as one of the propagandists of faithful and chaste love, and as the founder of the order of "l'escu vert à la dame blanche," for the defence of women, for which Christine de Pisan praised him. At Genoa, as a regent of the king of France, one day he courteously returned the curtsy of two ladies whom he met. "My lord"—said his squire—"who are those two women to whom you bowed so deeply ? "—"Huguenin," said he, "I do not know." Then he said to him : "My lord, they are harlots." "Harlots," said he, "Huguenin, I would rather have paid my salutations to ten harlots than have omitted them to one respectable woman." His device, resigned and enigmatical, is "What you will."

Such are the colours of piety, austerity and fidelity in which the ideal image of a knight is painted. The real Boucicaut did not altogether resemble this portrait ; no one would have expected it. He was neither free from violence nor from avarice, common faults in his class.

There are, however, patterns of chivalry of another type. The biographical romance about Jean de Bueil, entitled *Le Jouvencel*, was written half a century after *Le Livre des Faicts* of Boucicaut, which partly explains the differences. Jean de Bueil had fought under the banner of Joan of Arc. He had taken part in the rising called the Praguerie and in the war "du bien public" ; he died in 1477. Fallen in disgrace with the king, he dictated, or rather suggested, about 1465, an account of his life to three of his servants. In contrast with the *Life* of Boucicaut, of which the historical form hardly conceals the romantic purpose, *Le Jouvencel* contains in fictitious garb a great deal of simple realism ; this is so, at least, in the first part, for further on the authors have lost themselves in very insipid romanticism.

Jean de Bueil must have given his scribes a very lively narrative of his exploits. It would hardly be possible to quote in the literature of the fifteenth century another work giving as sober a picture as *Le Jouvencel* of the wars of those times. We find the small miseries of military life, its privations and boredom, gay endurance of hardships and courage in danger.

A castellan musters his garrison ; there are but fifteen horses, lean and old beasts, most of them unshod. He puts two men on each horse, but of the men also most are blind of one eye or lame. They set out to seize the enemy's laundry in order to patch the captain's clothes. A captured cow is courteously returned to a hostile captain at his request. Reading the description of a nocturnal march, one feels as though surrounded by the silence and the freshness of the night. It is not saying too much that here military France is announcing herself in literature, which will give birth to the types of the " mousquetaire," the " grognard," and the " poilu." The feudal knight is merging into the soldier of modern times ; the universal and religious ideal is becoming national and military. The hero of the book releases his prisoners without a ransom, on condition that they shall become good Frenchmen. Having risen to great dignities, he yearns for the old life of adventure and liberty.

Le Jouvencel is an expression of true French sentiment. Literature in the Burgundian sphere, being more old-fashioned, more feudal and more solemn, would not have been able as yet to create so realistic a type of a knight. By the side of the Jouvencel, the figure of the Hainault pattern knight of the fifteenth century, Jacques de Lalaing, is an antique curiosity, more or less modelled on the knights-errant of a preceding age. *Le Livre des Faits du bon Chevalier Messire Jacques de Lalaing* is far more concerned with tournaments and jousts than with real war.

In the *Jouvencel* we find a remarkable portrayal, hardly to be surpassed, of the psychology of warlike courage of a simple and touching kind. " It is a joyous thing, is war. . . . You love your comrade so in war. When you see that your quarrel is just and your blood is fighting well, tears rise to your eye. A great sweet feeling of loyalty and of pity fills your heart on seeing your friend so valiantly exposing his body to execute and accomplish the command of our Creator. And then you prepare to go and die or live with him, and for love not to abandon him. And out of that there arises such a delectation, that he who has not tasted it is not fit to say what a delight it is. Do you think that a man who does that fears death ? Not at all ; for he feels so strengthened, he is so elated, that he does not know where he is. Truly he is afraid of nothing."

These sentiments have nothing specifically chivalrous or medieval. The words might have been spoken by a modern soldier. They show us the very core of courage : man, in the excitement of danger, stepping out of his narrow egotism, the ineffable feeling caused by a comrade's bravery, the rapture of fidelity and of sacrifice,—in short, the primitive and spontaneous asceticism, which is at the bottom of the chivalrous ideal.

CHAPTER V

THE DREAM OF HEROISM AND OF LOVE

A conception of military life resembling that of medieval chivalry is found nearly everywhere, notably with the Hindus of the *Mahâbhârata* and in Japan. Warlike aristocracies need an ideal form of manly perfection. The aspiration to a pure and beautiful life, expressed in the *Kalokagathia* of the Hellenes, in the Middle Ages gives birth to chivalry. And during several centuries that ideal remains a source of energy, and at the same time a cloak for a whole world of violence and self-interest.

The ascetic element is never absent from it. It is most accentuated in the times when the function of knighthood is most vital, as in the times of the early crusades. The noble warrior has to be poor and exempt from worldly ties. "This ideal of the well-born man without possessions"—says William James—"was embodied in knight-errantry and templardom, and, hideously corrupted as it has always been, it still dominates sentimentally, if not practically, the military and aristocratic view of life. We glorify the soldier as the man absolutely unincumbered. Owning nothing but his bare life, and willing to toss that up at any moment when the cause commands him, he is the representative of unhampered freedom in ideal directions." Medieval chivalry, in its first bloom, was bound to blend with monachism. From this union were born the military orders of the Templars, of Saint John, of the Teutonic knights, and also those of Spain. Soon, however, or rather from the very beginning, reality gives the lie to the ideal, and accordingly the ideal will soar more and more towards the regions of fantasy, there to preserve the traits of asceticism and sacrifice too rarely visible in real life. The knight-errant, fantastic and useless, will always be poor and without ties, as the first Templars had been.

66

It would thus be unjust to regard as factitious or superficial the religious elements of chivalry, such as compassion, fidelity, justice. They are essential to it. Yet the complex of aspirations and imaginings, forming the idea of chivalry, in spite of its strong ethical foundation and the combative instinct of man, would never have made so solid a frame for the life beautiful if love had not been the source of its constantly revived ardour.

These very traits, moreover, of compassion, of sacrifice, and of fidelity, which characterize chivalry, are not purely religious ; they are erotic at the same time. Here, again, it must be remembered that the desire of bestowing a form, a style, on sentiment, is not expressed exclusively in art and literature ; it also unfolds in life itself : in courtly conversation, in games, in sports. There, too, love incessantly seeks a sublime and romantic expression. If, therefore, life borrows motifs and forms from literature, literature, after all, is only copying life. The chivalrous aspect of love had somehow to make its appearance in life before it expressed itself in literature.

The knight and his lady, that is to say, the hero who serves for love, this is the primary and invariable motif from which erotic fantasy will always start. It is sensuality transformed into the craving for self-sacrifice, into the desire of the male to show his courage, to incur danger, to be strong, to suffer and to bleed before his lady-love.

From the moment when the dream of heroism through love has intoxicated the yearning heart, fantasy grows and overflows. The first simple theme is soon left behind, the soul thirsts for new fancies, and passion colours the dream of suffering and of renunciation. The man will not be content merely to suffer, he will want to save from danger, or from suffering, the object of his desire. A more vehement stimulus is added to the primary motif : its chief feature will be that of defending imperilled virginity—in other words, that of ousting the rival. This, then, is the essential theme of chivalrous love poetry : the young hero, delivering the virgin. The sexual motif is always behind it, even when the aggressor is only an artless dragon ; a glance at Burne-Jones's famous picture suffices to prove it.

One is surprised that comparative mythology should have

looked so indefatigably to meteorological phenomena for the explanation of such an immediate and perpetual motif as the deliverance of the virgin, which is the oldest of literary motifs, and one which can never grow antiquated. It may from time to time become stale from overmuch repetition, and yet it will reappear, adapting itself to all times and surroundings. New romantic types will arise, just as the cowboy has succeeded the corsair.

The Middle Ages cultivated these motifs of a primitive romanticism with a youthful insatiability. Whereas in some higher genres of literature, such as lyrical poetry, the expression of desire and fulfilment became more refined, the romance of adventure always preserved it in its crude and naïve form, without ever losing its charm to its contemporaries. We might have expected that the last centuries of the Middle Ages would have lost their relish for these childish fancies. We are inclined to suppose that *Méliador*, the super-romantic novel by Froissart, or *Perceforest*, those belated fruits of chivalrous romance, were anachronisms even in their own day. They were no more so than the sensational novel is at present. Erotic imagination always requires similar models, and it finds them here. In the hey-day of the Renaissance we see them revive in the cycle of Amadis of Gaul. When, a good while after the middle of the sixteenth century, François de la Noue affirms that the novels of Amadis had caused " un esprit de vertige " among his generation—the generation of the Huguenots, which had passed through humanism with its vein of rationalism—we can imagine what must have been the romantic susceptibility of the ill-balanced and ignorant generation of 1400.

Literature did not suffice for the almost insatiable needs of the romantic imagination of the age. Some more active form of expression was required. Dramatic art might have supplied it, but the medieval drama in the real sense of the word treated love matters only exceptionally ; sacred subjects were its substance. There was, however, another form of representation, namely, noble sports, tourneys and jousts. Sportive struggles always and everywhere contain a strong dramatic element and an erotic element. In the medieval tournament these two elements. had so much got the upper hand, that its character of a contest of force and courage had been almost obliterated by its romantic purport. With its bizarre accoutrements and pompous staging, its poetical illusion and pathos, it filled the place of the drama of a later age.

The life of aristocracies when they are still strong, though of small utility, tends to become an all-round game. In order to forget the painful imperfection of reality, the nobles turn to the continual illusion of a high and heroic life. They wear the mask of Lancelot and of Tristram. It is an amazing self-deception. The crying falsehood of it can only be borne by treating it with some amount of raillery. The whole chivalrous culture of the last centuries of the Middle Ages is marked by an unstable equilibrium between sentimentality and mockery. Honour, fidelity and love are treated with unimpeachable seriousness ; only from time to time the solemn rigidity relaxes into a smile, but downright parody never prevails. Even after the *Morgante* of Pulci and the *Orlando Innamorato* of Boiardo had made the heroic pose ridiculous, Ariosto recaptured the absolute serenity of chivalrous sentiment.

In French circles, of about 1400, the cult of chivalry was treated with perfect gravity. It is not easy for us to understand this seriousness, and not to be startled by the contrast between the literary note of a Boucicaut and the facts of his career. He is represented as the indefatigable defender of courtesy and of chivalry, serving his lady according to the old rules of courteous love. " He served all, he honoured all, for the love of one. His speech was graceful, courteous and diffident before his lady." During his travels in the Near East in 1388, he and his companions in arms amuse themselves by composing a poetical defence of the faithful and chaste love of a knight—the *Livre des Cent Ballades*. One might have supposed him cured of all chivalrous delusions after the catastrophe of Nicopolis. There he had seen the lamentable consequences of statecraft recklessly embarking on an enterprise of vital import in the spirit of a chivalrous adventure. His companions of the *Cent Ballades* had perished. That would suffice, one would think, to make him turn his back on old-fashioned forms of courtesy. Yet he remains devoted

to them and resumes his moral task in founding the order
" de la dame blanche à l'escu vert."

Like all romantic forms that are worn out as an instrument
of passion, this apparatus of chivalry and of courtesy affects
us at first sight as a silly and ridiculous thing. The accents
of passion are heard in it no more save in some rare products
of literary genius. Still, all these costly elaborated forms of
social conduct have played their part as a decoration of life,
as a framework for a living passion. In reading this antiquated love poetry, or the clumsy descriptions of tournaments,
no exact knowledge of historical details avails without the
vision of the smiling eyes, long turned to dust, which at one
time were infinitely more important than the written word
that remains.

Only a stray glimmer now reminds us of the passionate
significance of these cultural forms. In the *Vœu du Héron*
the unknown author makes Jean de Beaumont speak :

> " Quant sommes ès tavernes, de ces fors vins buvant,
> Et ces dames delès qui nous vont regardant,
> A ces gorges polies, ces coliés tirant,
> Chil œil vair resplendissent de biauté souriant,
> Nature nous semont d'avoir cœur désirant,
> . . . Adonc conquerons-nous Yaumont et Agoulant
> Et li autre conquierrent Olivier et Rollant.
> Mais, quant sommes as camps sus nos destriers courans,
> Nos escus à no col et nos lansses bais(s)ans,
> Et le froidure grande nous va tout engelant,
> Li membres nous effondrent, et derrière et devant,
> Et nos ennemies sont envers nous approchant,
> Adonc vorrièmes estre en un chélier si grant
> Que jamais ne fussions veu tant ne quant." [1]

Nowhere does the erotic element of the tournament appear
more clearly than in the custom of the knight's wearing the

[1] When we are in the tavern, drinking strong wines, And the ladies pass
and look at us, With those white throats, and tight bodices, Those sparkling
eyes resplendent with smiling beauty, Then nature urges us to have a desiring
heart, . . . Then we could overcome Yaumont and Agoulant And the others
would conquer Oliver and Roland. But when we are in camp on our trotting
chargers, Our bucklers round our necks and our lances lowered, And the
great cold is congealing us altogether, And our limbs are crushed before and
behind, And our enemies are approaching us, Then we should wish to be in
a cellar so large That we might never be seen by any means.

veil or the dress of his lady. In *Perceforest* we read how the
lady spectators of the combat take off their finery, one article
after another, to throw them to the knights in the lists. At
the end of the fight they are bareheaded and without sleeves.
A poem of the thirteenth century, the work of a Picard or a
Hainault minstrel, entitled *Des trois Chevaliers et del Chainse*,[1]
has worked out this motif in all its force. The wife of a nobleman of great liberality, but not very fond of fighting, sends her
shirt to three knights who serve her for love, that one of them
at the tournament which her husband is going to give may
wear it as a coat-armour, without any mail underneath. The
first and the second knights excuse themselves. The third,
who is poor, takes the shirt in his arms at night, and kisses it
passionately. He appears at the tournament, dressed in the
shirt and without a coat of mail ; he is grievously wounded,
the shirt, stained with his blood, is torn. Then his extraordinary bravery is perceived and he is awarded the prize.
The lady gives him her heart. The lover asks something in
his turn. He sends back the garment, all blood-stained, to
the lady, that she may wear it over her gown at the meal
which is to conclude the feast. She embraces it tenderly and
shows herself dressed in the shirt as the knight had demanded.
The majority of those present blame her, the husband is confounded, and the minstrel winds up by asking the question :
Which of the two lovers sacrificed most for the sake of the
other ?

The Church was openly hostile to tournaments ; it repeatedly
prohibited them, and there is no doubt that the fear of the
passionate character of this noble game, and of the abuses
resulting from it, had a great share in this hostility. Moralists
were not favourably disposed towards tournaments, neither
were the humanists. Where do we read, Petrarch asks, that
Cicero or Scipio jousted ? The burghers thought them useless
and ridiculous. Only the world of the nobility continued to
cultivate all that regarded tournaments and jousts, as things
of the highest importance. Monuments were erected on the
sites of famous combats, as the Pélerine Cross near Saint
Omer, in remembrance of the Passage of Arms of la Pélerine,
and of the exploits of the bastard of Saint Pol and a Spanish

[1] Of the three knights and the shirt.

knight. Bayard piously went to visit this cross, as if on a pilgrimage. In the church of Notre Dame of Boulogne were preserved the decorations of the Passage of Arms of the Fontaine des Pleurs, solemnly dedicated to the Holy Virgin.

The warlike sports of the Middle Ages differ from Greek and modern athletics by being far less simple and natural. Pride, honour, love and art give additional stimulus to the competition itself. Overloaded with pomp and decoration, full of heroic fancy, they serve to express romantic needs too strong for mere literature to satisfy. The realities of court life or a military career offered too little opportunity for the fine make-belief of heroism and love, which filled the soul. So they had to be acted. The staging of the tournament, therefore, had to be that of romance; that is to say, the imaginary world of Arthur, where the fancy of a fairy-tale was enhanced by the sentimentality of courtly love.

A Passage of Arms of the fifteenth century is based on a fictitious case of chivalrous adventure, connected with an artificial scene called by a romantic name, as, for instance, *La fontained es pleurs, L'arbre Charlemagne*. A fountain is expressly constructed, and beside it a pavilion, where during a whole year a lady is to reside (in effigy, be it understood), holding a unicorn which bears three shields. The first day of each month knights come to touch the shields, and in this way to pledge themselves for a combat of which the " Chapters " of the Passage of Arms lay down the rules. They will find horses in readiness, for the shields have to be touched on horseback. Or, in the case of the *Emprise du dragon*, four knights will be stationed at a cross-road where, unless she gives a gage, no lady may pass without a knight breaking two lances for her. There is an unmistakable connection between these primitive forms of warlike and erotic sport and the children's play of forfeits. One of the rules of the " Chapters " of the *Fontaine des pleurs* runs thus : he who, in a combat, is unhorsed, will during a year wear a gold bracelet, until he finds the lady who holds the key to it and who can free him, on condition that he shall serve her.

The nobles liked to throw a veil of mystery and melancholy over the procedure. The knight should be unknown. He is called " le blanc chevalier," " le chevalier mesconnu," or he wears the crest of Lancelot or Palamedes. The shields of the Fount of Tears are white, violet and black, and overspread with white tears; those of the Tree of Charlemagne are sable and violet, with gold and sable tears. At the *Emprise du dragon*, celebrated on the occasion of the departure of his daughter Margaret for England, King René was present, dressed all in black, and his whole outfit, caparison, horse and all, down to the wood of his lance, was of the same colour.

CHAPTER VI

ORDERS OF CHIVALRY AND VOWS

The ideal of courage, of honour, and of fidelity found other forms of expression, besides those of the tournament. Apart from martial sport, the orders of chivalry opened an ample field where the taste for high aristocratic culture might expand. Like the tournaments and the accolade, the orders of chivalry have their roots in the sacred rites of a very remote past. Their religious origins are pagan, only the feudal system of thought had Christianized them. Strictly speaking, the several orders of chivalry are only ramifications of the order of knighthood itself. For knighthood was a sacred brotherhood, into which admittance was effected by means of solemn rites of initiation. The more elaborate form of these rites shows a most curious blending of Christian and heathen elements : the shaving, the bath, and the vigil of arms undoubtedly go back to pre-Christian times. Those who had gone through these ceremonies were called Knights of the Bath, in distinction from those who were knighted by the simple accolade. The term afterwards gave rise to the legend of a special Order of the Bath instituted by Henry IV, and thus to the establishment of the real one by George I.

The first great orders, those of the Temple, of Saint John, and of the Teutonic Knights, born of the mutual penetration of monastic and feudal ideas, early assumed the character of great political and economic institutions. Their aim was no longer in the first place the practice of chivalry ; that element, as well as their spiritual aspirations, had been more or less effaced by their political and financial importance. It was in the orders of more recent origin that the primitive conception of a club, of a game, of an aristocratic federation, reappeared. In the fourteenth and fifteenth centuries the real importance of chivalrous orders, which were founded in great numbers, was very slight, but the aspirations professed in founding them were always those of the very highest ethical and political idealism. Philippe de Mézières, an unrivalled political dreamer, wishes to remedy all the evils of the century by a new order of chivalry, that of the Passion, which is to unite Christendom in a common effort to expel the Turks. Burgesses and labourers are to find a place in it, side by side with the nobles. The three monastic vows are to be modified for practical reasons : instead of celibacy he only requires conjugal fidelity. Mézières adds a fourth vow, unknown to preceding orders, that of individual, moral perfection, *summa perfectio*. He confided the task of propagating the *Militia Passionis Jhesu Christi* to four " messaiges de Dieu et de la chevalerie " (among whom was the celebrated Othe de Granson), who were to go to " divers lands and kingdoms to preach and to announce the aforesaid holy chivalry, like four evangelists."

The word " order " thus still preserved much of its spiritual meaning ; it alternates with " religion," which usually designated a monastic order. We hear of the " religion " of the Golden Fleece, of a " knight of the religion of Avys." The rules of the Golden Fleece are conceived in a truly ecclesiastical spirit ; mass and obsequies occupy a large place in them ; the knights are seated in choir-stalls like canons. The membership of an order of chivalry constituted a sacred and exclusive tie. The knights of the Star of John the Good are required to withdraw from every other order. Philip the Good declines the honour of the Garter, in spite of the urgency of the duke of Bedford, in order not to tie himself too closely to England. Charles the Bold, on accepting it, was accused by Louis XI of having broken the peace of Péronne, which forbade alliance with England without the king's consent.

In spite of these serious airs, the founders of new orders had to defend themselves from the reproach of pursuing merely a vain amusement. The Golden Fleece, says the poet Michault, was instituted,

> "Non point pour jeu ne pour esbatement,
> Mais à la fin que soit attribuée
> Loenge à Dieu trestout premièrement,
> Et aux bons gloire et haulte renommée." [1]

---

[1] Not for amusement, nor for recreation, But for the purpose that praise shall be given To God, in the first place, And glory and high renown to the good.

Similarly, Guillaume Fillastre writes his book of the Golden Fleece to demonstrate the high interest and the sacred importance of the order, that it might not be regarded as a work of vanity. It was not superfluous to draw attention to the high objects of the duke, so that his creation might be distinguished from the numerous orders of recent foundation. There was not a prince or great noble who did not desire to have his own order. Orléans, Bourbon, Savoie, Hainaut-Bavière, Lusignan, Coucy, all eagerly exerted themselves in inventing bizarre emblems and striking devices. The chain of Pierre de Lusignan's Sword-order was made of gold S's, which meant " silence." The Porcupine of Louis of Orléans threatens Burgundy with its spines, which it shoots, according to popular belief, *cominus et eminus*.

If the Golden Fleece eclipsed all the other orders, it is because the dukes of Burgundy placed at its disposal the resources of their enormous wealth. In their view, the order was to serve as the symbol of their power. The fleece was primarily that of Colchis ; the fable of Jason was familiar to all. Jason, however, was, as an eponymous hero, not absolutely irreproachable. Had he not broken his word ? There was an opening here for nasty allusions to the policy of the dukes towards France. *La Ballade de Fougères* of Alain Chartier is an instance :

> "A Dieu et aux gens detestable
> Est menterie et trahison,
> Pour ce n'est point mis à la table
> Des preux l'image de Jason,
> Qui pour emporter la toison
> De Colcos se veult parjurer.
> Larrecin ne se peult celer." [1]

It was, therefore, a very happy inspiration of the learned bishop of Chalons, chancellor of the order, to substitute for the fleece of the ram that carried Helle another, far more venerable, namely, that which Gideon spread to receive the dew of Heaven. The fleece of Gideon was one of the most

---

[1] To God and to men detestable Is lying and treason, For this reason the image of Jason Is not placed in the gallery of worthies. Who, to carry off the fleece Of Colchos, was willing to commit perjury, Larceny cannot remain hidden.

striking symbols of the Annunciation. Thus the Old Testament judge more or less eclipses the pagan hero, as a patron of the order. Guillaume Fillastre, the successor of Jean Germain as chancellor of the order, discovered four more fleeces in Scripture, each of them denoting a special virtue. But this was plainly overdoing it, and, as far as we can see, was not successful. " Gedeonis signa " remained the most revered appellation of the Golden Fleece.

To describe the solemn pomp of the Golden Fleece, or of the Star, would only be adding new instances to the subject-matter of a preceding chapter. Let it suffice here to point out a single trait common to all the orders of chivalry, in which the original character of a primitive and sacred game is particularly conspicuous, namely, the technical appellations of their officials. The kings-at-arms are called Golden Fleece, Garter. The heralds bear names of countries : Charolais, Zealand. The first of the pursuivants is called " Fusil," after the duke's emblem, the flint-and-steel. The names of the other pursuivants are of a romantic or moral character, as Montreal, Perseverance, or allegorical, as Humble Request, Sweet Thought, Lawful Pursuit, designations borrowed from the *Romaunt of the Rose*. At the feasts of the order, the pursuivants are baptized in these names by sprinkling them with wine. Nicolas Upton, a herald of Humphrey of Gloucester, has described the ceremonial of such a baptism.

The very essence of the conception of an order of chivalry appears in its knightly vows. Every order presupposes vows, but the chivalrous vow exists also outside the orders, under an individual and occasional form. Here the barbarous character, testifying that chivalry has its roots in primitive civilization, comes to the surface. We find parallels in the India of the *Mahâbhârata*, in ancient Palestine, and in the Iceland of the *Sagas*.

What remained, at the end of the Middle Ages, of the cultural value of these chivalrous vows ? We find them very near akin to purely religious vows, serving to accentuate or to fix a lofty moral aspiration. We also find them supplying romantic and erotic needs and degenerating into an amusement and a theme for raillery. It is not easy to determine accurately the degree of sincerity belonging to them. We should not judge them from the impression of silliness and untruthfulness which we derive from the *Vœux du Faisan*, to mention the best known and most historical example. As in the case of tournaments and passages of arms, we only see the dead form of the thing : the cultural significance of the custom has disappeared with the passion animating those to whom these forms were the realization of a dream of beauty.

In the vows we find once more that mixture of asceticism and eroticism which we found underlying the idea of chivalry itself, and so clearly expressed in the tournaments. The Chevalier de la Tour Landry, in his curious book of admonition to his daughters, speaks of a strange order of amorous men and women of noble birth which existed in Poitou and elsewhere, in his youth. They called themselves Galois and Galoises, and had "very savage regulations." In summer they dressed themselves in furs and fur-lined hoods, and lighted a fire on the hearth, whereas in winter they were only allowed to wear a simple coat without fur ; neither mantles, nor hats, nor gloves. During the most severe cold they hid the hearth behind evergreen sprigs, and had only very light bed-clothes. It is not surprising that a great many members died of cold. The husband of a Galoise receiving a Galois under his roof was bound, under penalty of dishonouring himself, to give up his house and his wife to him. Here is a very primitive trait, which the author could hardly have invented, although he may have exaggerated this strange aberration in which we divine a wish to exalt love by ascetic excitement.

The savage spirit of the vows of knights manifests itself very clearly in *Le Vœu du Héron*, a poem of the fourteenth century, of little historical value, describing the feasts given at the court of Edward III at the moment when Robert d'Artois urges the king to declare war on France. The earl of Salisbury is seated at the feet of his lady. When called upon to formulate a vow, he begs her to place a finger on his right eye. Two, if necessary, she replies, and she closes his eye by placing two fingers on it. "Belle, is it well closed ? " asks the knight. "Yes, certainly."

"A dont, dist de le bouche, du cuer le pensement ;
Et je veu et prometh à Dieu omnipotent,
Et à sa douche mère que de beauté resplent,
Qu'il n'est jamais ouvers, pour oré, ne pour vent,
Pour mal, ne pour martire, ne pour encombrement,
Si seray dedans Franche, où il a bonne gent,
Et si aray le fu bouté entièrement
Et serai combatus à grand efforchement
Contre les gens Philype, qui tant a hardement.
. . . Or, aviegne qu'aviegne, car il n'est autrement.
A donc osta son doit la puchelle au cors gent,
Et li iex clos demeure, si ques virent la gent." [1]

The literary motif is not without a real foundation. Froissart actually saw English gentlemen who had covered one eye with a piece of cloth, to redeem a pledge to use only one eye, till they should have achieved some deed of bravery in France.

The extreme of savagery is reached in the vow of the queen, which ends the series in *The Vow of the Heron*. She takes an oath not to give birth to the child of which she is pregnant before the king has taken her to the enemy's country and to kill herself " with a big steel knife," if the confinement announces itself too early.

" I shall have lost my soul and the fruit will perish."

Le Vœu du Héron shows us the literary conception of these vows, the barbarous and primitive character they had in the minds of that time. Their magical element betrays itself in the part which the hair and the beard play in them, as in the case of Benedict XIII, imprisoned at Avignon, who made the very archaic vow not to have his beard shaved before he recovered his liberty.

In making a vow, people imposed some privation upon themselves as a spur to the accomplishment of the actions they were pledged to perform. Most frequently the privation concerns food. The first of the knights whom Philippe de Mézières admitted to his Chivalry of the Passion was a Pole, who during

---

[1] Well then, he said by the mouth the thought of the heart ; And I vow and I promise to Almighty God, And to his sweet mother of resplendent beauty, That it will never be opened, for storm nor for wind, By evil, nor by torture, nor by hindrance, Until I shall be in France, where there are good people, And until I shall have lighted the fire And I shall have báttled with great exertion Against the people of Philip who is so hardy. . . . Now come what may, for it is not otherwise. Then the gentle girl took away her finger And the eye remained shut, as people saw.

nine years had only eaten and drunk standing. Bertrand du Guesclin was dangerously prone to utter vows of this kind. He will not undress till he has taken Montcontour ; he will not eat till he has effected an encounter with the English. It goes without saying that a nobleman of the fourteenth century understood nothing of the magical meaning implied in these fasts. To us this original meaning is clear. It is equally so in the custom of wearing foot-irons as signs of a vow. As early as the eighteenth century, La Curne de Sainte Palaye remarked that the usage of the Chatti, described by Tacitus, corresponded exactly with the fashion which medieval chivalry had preserved. In 1415 Jean de Bourbon vowed, and sixteen knights and squires with him, that each Sunday during two years they would wear on the left leg foot-irons— the knights of gold, the squires of silver—till they should find sixteen adversaries ready to fight them to the death. The " adventurous knight," Jean de Boniface, arriving at Antwerp from Sicily in 1445, wears an " emprise " of the same sort, so does Sir Loiselench in *Le petit Jehan de Saintré*. The propensity to vow to perform some thing, when in danger or in violent emotion, undoubtedly always remains a powerful one. It has very deep psychological roots, and does not belong to any particular religion or civilization. Nevertheless, as a form of chivalrous culture, the vow was dying out at the end of the Middle Ages.

When, at Lille, in 1454, Philip the Good, preparing for his crusade, crowns his extravagant feasts by the celebrated Vows of the Pheasant, it is like the last manifestation of a dying usage, which has become a fantastic ornament, after having been a very serious element of earlier civilization. The old ritual, such as chivalrous tradition and romance taught it, is carefully observed. The vows are taken at the banquet ; the guests swear by the pheasant served up, one " bluffing " the other, just as the old Norsemen vied with each other in fool-hardy vows sworn in drunkenness by the boar served up. There are pious vows, made to God and to the Holy Virgin, to the ladies and to the bird, and others in which the Deity is not mentioned. They contain always the same privations of food or of comfort : not to sleep in a bed on Saturday, not to take animal food on Friday, etc.

One act of asceticism is heaped upon another : one nobleman promises to wear no armour, to drink no wine one day in every week, not to sleep in a bed, not to sit down to meals, to wear the hair-shirt. The method of accomplishing the vowed exploit is minutely specified and registered.

Are we to take all this seriously ? The actors of the play pretend to do so. In connection with the vow of Philippe Pot to fight with his right arm bare, the duke, as though he feared real danger for his favourite, orders this addition to the registered promise : " It is not the pleasure of my very redoubted lord, that Messire Philippe Pot undertakes, in his company, the holy votive journey with his arm bare ; but he desires that he shall travel with him well and sufficiently armed, as beseems." As regards the vow of the duke himself, to fight the Great Turk with his own hand, it provokes general emotion. Among the vows there are conditional ones, betraying the intention of escaping, in case of danger, by a pretext. There are those resembling a fillipeen. And in fact this game, still in fashion some forty years ago, may be regarded as a pale survival of the chivalrous vow.

Yet a vein of mocking pleasantry runs through the superficial pomp. At the Vow of the Heron, Jean de Beaumont takes an oath to serve the lord from whom he may expect the greatest liberality. At those of the Pheasant, Jennet de Rebreviettes swears that unless he wins the favour of his lady before the expedition, he will marry, on his return from the East, the first lady or girl possessing twenty thousand gold pieces, " if she be willing." Yet this same Rebreviettes, in spite of his cynicism, set out as a " poor squire," seeking adventures in the wars against the Moors of Granada.

Thus a blasé aristocracy laughs at its own ideal. After having adorned its dream of heroism with all the resources of fantasy, art and wealth, it bethinks itself that life is not so fine, after all—and smiles.

CHAPTER VII

THE POLITICAL AND MILITARY VALUE OF CHIVALROUS IDEAS

In tracing the picture of the declining Middle Ages, the scholars of our days, generally speaking, take little account of the surviving chivalrous ideas. They are regarded by common consent as a more or less artificial revival of ideas, whose real value had long since disappeared. They would seem to be an ornament of society and no more. The men who made the history of those times, princes, nobles, prelates, or burghers, were no romantic dreamers, but dealt in solid facts. Still, nearly all paid homage to the chivalrous bias, and it remains to consider to what extent this bias modified the course of events. For the history of civilization the perennial dream of a sublime life has the value of a very important reality. And even political history itself, under penalty of neglecting actual facts, is bound to take illusions, vanities, follies, into account. There is not a more dangerous tendency in history than that of representing the past, as if it were a rational whole and dictated by clearly defined interests.

We have, therefore, to estimate the influence of chivalrous ideas on politics and on war at the close of the Middle Ages. Were the rules of chivalry taken into account in the councils of kings and in those of war ? Were resolutions sometimes inspired by the chivalrous point of view ? Without any doubt. If medieval politics were not governed for the better by the idea of chivalry, surely they were so sometimes for the worse. Chivalry during the Middle Ages was, on the one hand, the great source of tragic political errors, exactly as are nationalism and racial pride at the present day. On the other, it tended to disguise well-adjusted calculations under the appearance of generous aspirations. The gravest political error which France could commit was the creation of a quasi-independent Bur-

gundy, and it had a chivalrous reason for its avowed motive :
King John, that knightly muddle-head, wished to reward the
courage shown by his son at Poitiers by an extraordinary
liberality. The stubborn anti-French policy of the dukes of
Burgundy after 1419, although dictated by the interests of
their house, was justified in the eyes of contemporaries by
the duty of exacting an exemplary vengeance for the murder
of Montereau. Burgundian court literature exerts itself to
keep up in all political matters the semblance of chivalrous
inspiration. The surnames of the dukes, that of " Sans
Peur " given to Jean, of " Hardi " to the first Philip, of
" Qui qu'en hongne " which they did not succeed in imposing
on the second Philip, usually called " the Good," are inventions
calculated to place the prince in a nimbus of chivalrous
romance.

Now there was one among the political aspirations of the
epoch where the chivalrous ideal was implied in the nature of
the enterprise itself, namely, the recovery of the Holy Sepulchre. The highest political ideal which all the kings of Europe
were obliged to profess was still symbolized by Jerusalem.
Here the contrast between the real interest of Christendom
and the form the idea took is most striking. The Europe of
1400 was confronted by an Eastern question of supreme
urgency : that of repulsing the Turks who had just taken
Adrianople and wiped out the Serbian kingdom. The imminent danger ought to have concentrated all efforts on the
Balkans. Yet the imperative task of European politics does
not yet disengage itself from the old idea of the crusades.
People only succeeded in seeing the Turkish question as a
secondary part of the sacred duty in which their ancestors
had failed : the conquest of Jerusalem.

The conquest of Jerusalem could not but present itself to
the mind as a work of piety and of heroism—that is to say,
of chivalry. In the councils on Eastern politics the heroic
ideal preponderated more than in ordinary politics, and this it
is which explains the very meagre success of the war against
the Turks. Expeditions which, before all else, required
patient preparation and minute inquiry, tended, more than
once, to be romanticized, so to speak, from the very outset.
The catastrophe of Nicopolis had proved the fatal folly of

undertaking, against a very warlike enemy, an expedition of
great importance as light-heartedly as if it were a question
of going to kill a handful of heathen peasants in Prussia or in
Lithuania.

In the fifteenth century each king still felt virtually bound
to set out and recapture Jerusalem. When Henry V of
England, dying at Paris in 1422, in the midst of his career of
conquest, was listening to the reading of the seven penitential
psalms, he interrupted the officiating priest at the words
*Benigne fac, domine, in bona voluntate tua Sion, ut aedificentur
muri Jerusalem,* and declared that he had intended to go
and conquer Jerusalem, after having re-established peace in
France, " if it had pleased God, his Creator, to let him live to
old age." After that he orders the priest to go on reading,
and dies.

In the case of Philip the Good, the design of a crusade seems
to have been a mixture of chivalrous caprice and political
advertising ; he wished to pose, by this pious and useful project,
as the protector of Christendom, to the detriment of the king
of France. The expedition to Turkey was, as it were, a trump-
card that he did not live to play.

The chivalrous fiction was also at the back of a peculiar
form of political advertisement, to which Duke Philip was
much attached—to wit, the duel between two princes, always
being announced, but never carried out. The idea of having
political differences decided by a single combat between the
two princes concerned, was a logical consequence of the
conception still prevailing, as if political disputes were nothing
but a " quarrel " in the juristic sense of the word. A Burgundian partisan, for instance, serves the " quarrel " of his lord.
What more natural means to settle such a case can be imagined
than the duel of two princes, the two parties to the " quarrel " ?
The solution was satisfactory to both the primitive sense of
right and the chivalrous imagination. In reading the summary
of the carefully arranged preparations for these princely duels,
we ask ourselves, if they were not a conscious feint, either to
impose upon one's enemy, or to appease the grievances of
one's own subjects. Are we not rather to regard them as an
inextricable mixture of humbug and of a chimerical, but, after
all, sincere, craving to conform to the life heroic, by posing

before all the world as the champion of right, who does not hesitate to sacrifice himself for his people ?

How, otherwise, are we to explain the surprising persistence of these plans for princely duels ? Richard II of England offers to fight, together with his uncles, the dukes of Lancaster, York, and Gloucester, against the king of France, Charles VI, and his uncles, the dukes of Anjou, Burgundy and Berry. Louis of Orléans defies the king of England, Henry IV. Henry V of England challenges the dauphin before marching upon Agincourt. Above all, the duke of Burgundy displayed an almost frenzied attachment to this mode of settling a question. In 1425 he challenges Humphrey, duke of Gloucester, in connection with the question of Holland. The motive, as always, is expressly formulated in these terms : " To prevent Christian bloodshed and destruction of the people, on whom my heart has compassion," I wish " that by my own body, this quarrel may be settled, without proceeding by means of wars, which would entail that many noblemen and others, both of your army and of mine, would end their days pitifully."

All was ready for the combat : the magnificent armour and the state dresses, the pavilions, the standards, the banners, the armorial tabards for the heralds, everything richly adorned with the duke's blazons and with his emblems, the flint-and-steel and the Saint Andrew's cross. The duke had gone in for a course of training " both by abstinence in the matter of food and by taking exercise to keep him in breath." He practised fencing every day in his park of Hesdin with the most expert masters. The detailed expenses entailed by this affair are found in the accounts published by de La Borde, but the combat did not take place.

This did not prevent the duke, twenty years later, from again wishing to decide a question touching Luxemburg by a single combat with the duke of Saxony. Towards the close of his life he is still vowing to engage in a hand-to-hand combat with the Grand Turk.

We find this custom of challenges between sovereigns reappearing as late as the hey-day of the Renaissance. To deliver Italy from Cesare Borgia, Francesco Gonzaga offers to fight the latter with sword and dagger. Charles V himself, on two occasions, in 1526 and in 1536, formally proposes to the king of France to end their differences by a single combat. The notion of two princes fighting a duel in order to decide a conflict between their countries had nothing impossible about it at an epoch when the judicial duel was still as firmly rooted in practice and in ideas as it was in the fifteenth century. If a political duel between two real sovereigns never actually took place, at any rate in 1397 a very great lord, accused of a political crime by a nobleman, fought him in due form and was killed. We refer to Othe de Granson, an illustrious knight and admired poet, who perished at Bourg en Bresse by the hand of Gerard d'Estavayer. The latter had made himself the champion of the towns of the Pays de Vaud, which were very hostile to Granson, as he was suspected of complicity in the murder of his lord, Amé VII, of Savoy, surnamed " the Red Count." This judicial duel caused an immense sensation.

If princes had such a chivalrous conception of their duty, it is not astonishing that similar ideas constantly exercised a certain influence on political and military decisions : a negative influence and scarcely of a decisive nature, taking all in all, but nevertheless real. The chivalrous prejudice often caused resolutions to be retarded or precipitated, opportunities to be lost, and profit to be neglected, for the sake of a point of honour ; it exposed commanders to unnecessary dangers. Strategical interests were frequently sacrificed in order to keep up the appearances of the heroic life. Sometimes a king himself would go forth to seek military adventure, like Edward III attacking a convoy of Spanish ships by night. Froissart asserts that the knights of the Star had to swear never to fly more than four acres from the battlefield, through which rule soon afterwards more than ninety of them lost their lives. The article is not found in the statutes of the order, as published by Luc d'Achéry ; nevertheless, such formalism tallies well with the ideas of that epoch. Some days before the battle of Agincourt, the king of England, on his way to meet the French army, one evening passed by mistake by the village which the foragers of his army had fixed upon as night-quarters. He would have had time to return, and he would have done it, if a point of honour had not prevented him. The king, " as the chief guardian of the very laudable ceremonies of honour," had just published an order, according to which knights, while reconnoitring, had to take off their coat-armour, because their honour would not suffer knights to retreat, when accoutred for battle. Now, the king himself had put on his coat-armour, and so, having passed it by, he could not return to the village mentioned. He therefore passed the night in the place he had reached and also made the vanguard advance accordingly, in spite of the dangers that might have been incurred.

Just as a political conflict was regarded as an action at law, so there was also but a difference of degree between a battle and a judicial duel, or the combat of knights in the lists. In his *Arbre des Batailles*, Honoré Bonet places them under the same head, although carefully distinguishing " great general battles " and "particular battles." In the wars of the fifteenth century, and even later, the custom for two captains or two equal groups to appoint meetings for a fight, in sight of the two armies, was still kept up. The Combat of the Thirty has remained the celebrated type of these fights. It was fought in 1351 at Ploërmel, in Brittany, between the French of Beaumanoir and a company of thirty men, English, Germans and Bretons, under a certain Bamborough. Froissart, though full of admiration, cannot help remarking : " Some held it a prowess, and some held it a shame and a great overbearing." The uselessness of these chivalrous spectacles was so evident that those in authority resented them. It was impossible to expose the honour of the kingdom to the hazards of a single combat. When Guy de la Trémoïlle wished to prove in 1386 the superiority of the French by a duel with an English nobleman, Peter Courtenay, the dukes of Burgundy and Berry at the last moment issued a formal prohibition. The authors of the *Jouvencel* disapprove of these competitions of glory. " They are forbidden things and which people should not do. In the first place, those who do it, want to take away the good of others, that is to say, their honour, to procure themselves vain glory, which is of little value ; and, in doing this, he serves none, he spends his money ; . . . in being occupied in doing this, he neglects his part in waging war, the service of his king and the public cause ; and no one should expose his body, unless in meritorious works."

This is the military spirit, which itself has issued from the spirit of chivalry and is now gradually supplanting it. The custom of these fights outlived the Middle Ages. The French and Spanish armies, in the south of Italy, in 1503, feasted their eyes first upon the Combat of the Eleven, without any fatal result, and then upon the famous duel between Bayard and Sotomayor, which was by no means the last of its sort.

Thus, in warfare, the chivalrous point of honour continues to make itself felt, but when an important question arises for decision, strategic prudence carries the day in the majority of cases. Generals still propose to the enemy to come to an understanding as to the choice of the battlefield, but the invitation is generally declined by the party occupying the better position. In vain did the English in 1333 invite the Scotch to come down from their strong position in order to fight them in the plains ; in vain did Guillaume de Hainaut propose an armistice of three days to the king of France, during which a bridge could be built permitting the armies to join battle. Reason, however, is not always victorious. Before the battle of Najera (or of Navarrete), in which Bertrand du Guesclin was taken prisoner, Don Henri de Trastamara desires, at any cost, to measure himself with the enemy in the open field. He voluntarily gives up the advantages offered by the configuration of the ground and loses the battle.

If chivalry had to yield to strategy and tactics, none the less it remained of importance in the exterior apparatus of warfare. An army of the fifteenth century, with its splendid show of rich ornament and solemn pomp, still offered the spectacle of a tournament of glory and honour. The multitude of banners and pennons, the variety of heraldic bearings, the sound of clarions, the war-cries resounding all day long, all this, with the military costume itself and the ceremonies of dubbing knights before the battle, tended to give war the appearance of a noble sport.

After the middle of the century, the drum, of Oriental origin, makes its appearance in the armies of the West, introduced by the lansquenets. With its unmusical hypnotic effect it symbolizes, as it were, the transition from the epoch of chivalry to that of the art of modern warfare ; together with fire-arms it has contributed towards rendering war mechanical.

The chivalrous point of view still presides over the classification of martial exploits by the chroniclers. They take pains to distinguish, according to technical rules, between a pitched battle and an encounter, for it is imperative that every combat has its appropriate place in the records of glory. " And so, from this day forward "—says Monstrelet—" this business was called the encounter of Mons en Vimeu. And it was declared to be no battle, because the parties met by chance and there were hardly any banners unfurled." Henry V solemnly baptizes his great victory, the battle of Agincourt, " inasmuch as all battles should bear the name of the nearest fortress where they are fought."

In spite of the care taken on all hands to keep up the illusion of chivalry, reality perpetually gives the lie to it, and obliges it to take refuge in the domains of literature and of conversation. The ideal of the fine heroic life could only be cultivated within the limits of a close caste. The sentiments of chivalry were current only among the members of the caste and by no means extended to inferior persons. The Burgundian court, which was saturated with chivalrous prejudice, and would not have tolerated the slightest infringement of rules in a " combat à outrance " between noblemen, relished the unbridled ferocity of a judicial duel between burghers, where there was no code of honour to observe. Nothing could be more remarkable in this respect than the interest excited everywhere by the combat of two burghers of Valenciennes in 1455. The old Duke Philip wanted to see the rare spectacle at any cost. One must read the vivid and realistic description given by Chastellain in order to appreciate how a chivalrous writer who never succeeded in giving more than a vaguely fanciful description of a Passage of Arms, made up for it here by giving full rein to the instincts of natural cruelty. Not one detail of the " very beautiful ceremony " escaped him. The adversaries, accompanied by their fencing masters, enter the lists, first Jacotin Plouvier, the plaintiff, next Mahuot. Their heads are cropped close and they are sewn up from head to foot in cordwain dresses of a single piece. They are very pale. After having saluted the duke, who was seated behind lattice-work, they await the signal, seated upon two chairs upholstered in black. The spectators exchange remarks in a low voice on the chances of the combat : How pale Mahuot is as he kisses the Testament! Two servants come to rub them with grease from the neck to the ankles. Both champions rub their hands with ashes and take sugar in their mouths; next they are given quartersticks and bucklers painted with images of saints, which they hold upside down, having, moreover, in their hands " a scroll of devotion."

Mahuot, a small man, begins the combat by throwing sand into Jacotin's face with the point of his buckler. Soon afterwards he falls to the ground under the formidable blows of Jacotin, who throws himself on him, fills his eyes and mouth with sand, and thrusts his thumb into the socket of his eye, to make him let go of a finger which Mahuot has between his teeth. Jacotin wrings the other's arms, jumps upon his back and tries to break it. In vain does Mahuot cry for mercy, and asks to be confessed. " O my lord of Burgundy," he calls out, "I have served you so well in your war of Ghent! O my lord, for God's sake, I beg for mercy, save my life!" . . . Here some pages of Chastellain's chronicle are missing; we learn elsewhere that the dying man was dragged out of the lists and hanged by the executioner.

Did Chastellain end his lively narrative by a moral? It is probable; anyhow, La Marche tells that the nobility were a little ashamed at having been present at such a spectacle. " Because of which God caused a duel of knights to follow, which was irreproachable and without fatal consequences," adds the incorrigible court poet.

As soon as it is a question of non-nobles, the old and deep-rooted contempt for the villein shows us that the ideas of chivalry had availed but little in mitigating feudal barbarism. Charles VI, after the battle of Rosebeke, wishes to see the corpse of Philip of Artevelde. The king does not show the slightest respect for the illustrious rebel. According to one chronicle, he is said to have kicked the body, " treating it as a villein." " When it had been looked at, for some time "— says Froissart—" it was taken from that place and hanged on a tree."

Hard realities were bound to open the eyes of the nobility and show the falseness and uselessness of their ideal. The financial side of a knight's career was frankly avowed. Froissart never omits to enumerate the profits which a successful enterprise procured for its heroes. The ransom of a noble prisoner was the backbone of the business to the warriors of the fifteenth century. Pensions, rents, governor's places, occupy a large place in a knight's life. His aim is " s'avanchier par armes " (to get on in life by arms). Commines rates the courtiers according to their pay, and speaks of " a nobleman of twenty crowns," and Deschamps makes them sigh after the day of payment, in a ballad with the refrain :

"Et quant venra le trésorier ? " [1]

As a military principle, chivalry was no longer sufficient. Tactics had long since given up all thought of conforming to its rules. The custom of making the knights fight on foot was borrowed by the French from the English, though the chivalrous spirit was opposed to this practice. It was also opposed to sea-fights. In the *Debat des Hérauts d'Armes de France et d'Angleterre*, the French herald being asked by his English colleague : Why does the king of France not maintain a great naval force, like that of England ? replies very naïvely :—In the first place he does not need it, and, then, the French nobility prefer wars on dry land, for several reasons, " for (on the sea) there is danger and loss of life and God knows how awful it is when a storm rages and sea-sickness prevails which many people find hard to bear. Again, look at the hard life which has to be lived, which does not beseem nobility."

Nevertheless, chivalrous ideas did not die out without having borne some fruit. In so far as they formed a system of rules of honour and precepts of virtue, they exercised a certain influence on the evolution of the laws of war. The law of nations originated in antiquity and in canon law, but it was chivalry which caused it to flower. The aspiration after universal peace is linked with the idea of crusades and with that of the orders of chivalry. Philippe de Mézières planned his " Order of the Passion " to insure the good of the world. The young king of France—(this was written about 1388, when such great hopes were still entertained of the unhappy Charles VI)—will be easily able to conclude peace with Richard of England, young like himself and also innocent of bloodshed in the past. Let them discuss the peace personally ; let them

[1] And when will the paymaster come ?

tell each other of the marvellous revelations which have already heralded it. Let them ignore all the futile differences which might prevent peace, if negotiations were left to ecclesiastics, to lawyers, and to soldiers. The king of France may fearlessly cede a few frontier towns and castles. Directly after the conclusion of peace the crusade will be prepared. Quarrels and hostilities will cease everywhere; the tyrannical governments of countries will be reformed; a general council will summon the princes of Christendom to undertake a crusade, in case sermons do not suffice to convert the Tartars, Turks, Jews and Saracens.

The share which the ideas of chivalry have had in the development of the law of nations is not limited to these dreams. The notion of a law of nations itself was preceded and led up to by the ideal of a beautiful life of honour and of loyalty. In the fourteenth century we find the formulation of principles of international law blending with the casuistical and often puerile regulations of passages of arms and combats in the lists. In 1352 Sir Geoffroi de Charney (who died at Poitiers bearing the oriflamme) addresses to the king, who has just instituted his order of the Star, a treatise composed of a long list of " demandes," that is to say, questions of casuistry, concerning jousts, tournaments and war. Jousts and tournaments rank first, but the importance of questions of military law is shown by their far greater number. It should be remembered that this order of the Star was the culmination of chivalrous romanticism, founded expressly " in the manner of the Round Table."

Better known than the " demandes " of Geoffroi de Charney is a work that appeared towards the end of the fourteenth century, and which remained in vogue till the sixteenth : *L'Arbre des Batailles* of Honoré Bonet, prior of Selonnet, in Provence. The influence of chivalry on the development of the law of nations nowhere appears more clearly than here. Though the author is an ecclesiastic, the idea which suggests his very remarkable conceptions to him is that of chivalry. He treats promiscuously questions of personal honour and the gravest questions of the law of nations. For example, " by what right can one wage war against the Saracens or other unbelievers," or, " if a prince may refuse the passage through his country to another." What is especially remarkable is the spirit of gentleness and of humanity in which Bonet solves these problems. May the king of France, waging war with England, take prisoner "the poor English, merchants, labourers of the soil and shepherds who tend their flocks in the fields"? The author answers in the negative; not only do Christian morals forbid it, but also "the honour of the age." He even goes so far as to extend the privilege of safe conduct in the enemy's country to the case of the father of an English student wishing to visit his sick son in Paris.

L'Arbre des Batailles was, unfortunately, only a theoretical treatise. We know full well that war in those times was very cruel. The fine rules and the generous exemptions enumerated by the good prior of Selonnet were too rarely observed. Still, if a little clemency was slowly introduced into political and military practice, this was due rather to the sentiment of honour than to convictions based on legal and moral principles. Military duty was conceived in the first place as the honour of a knight.

Taine said: "In the middle and lower classes the chief motive of conduct is self-interest. With an aristocracy the mainspring is pride. Now among the profound sentiments of man there is none more apt to be transformed into probity, patriotism and conscience, for a proud man feels the need of self-respect, and, to obtain it, he is led to deserve it." Is not this the point of view whence we must consider the importance of chivalry in the history of civilization? Pride assuming the features of a high ethical value, knightly self-respect preparing the way for clemency and right. These transitions in the domain of thought are real. In the passage quoted above from *Le Jouvencel* we noticed how chivalric sentiment passes into patriotism. All the best elements of patriotism— the spirit of sacrifice, the desire for justice and protection for the oppressed—sprouted in the soil of chivalry. It is in the classic country of chivalry, in France, that are heard, for the first time, the touching accents of love of the fatherland, irradiated by the sentiment of justice. One need not be a great poet to say these simple things with dignity. No author of those times has given French patriotism such a touching and also such a varied expression as Eustache Deschamps, whom we can only rate as a mediocre poet. Addressing France, he says :

> " Tu as duré et durras sanz doubtance
> Tant com raisons sera de toy amée,
> Autrement, non ; fay donc à la balance
> Justice en toy et que bien soit gardée." [1]

Chivalry would never have been the ideal of life during several centuries if it had not contained high social values. Its strength lay in the very exaggeration of its generous and fantastic views. The soul of the Middle Ages, ferocious and passionate, could only be led by placing far too high the ideal towards which its aspirations should tend. Thus acted the Church, thus also feudal thought. We may apply here Emerson's words : " Without this violence of direction, which men and women have, without a spice of bigot and fanatic, no excitement, no efficiency. We aim above the mark to hit the mark. Every act hath some falsehood of exaggeration in it." That reality has constantly given the lie to these high illusions of a pure and noble social life, who would deny ? But where should we be, if our thoughts had never transcended the exact limits of the feasible ?

[1] You have endured and will, no doubt, endure So long as reason will be loved by you. Not otherwise ; so hold the balance Of justice in yourself, and let it be well kept.

CHAPTER VIII

LOVE FORMALIZED

When in the twelfth century unsatisfied desire was placed by the troubadours of Provence in the centre of the poetic conception of love, an important turn in the history of civilization was effected. Antiquity, too, had sung the sufferings of love, but it had never conceived them save as the expectation of happiness or as its pitiful frustration. The sentimental point of Pyramus and Thisbe, of Cephalus and Procris, lies in their tragic end ; in the heart-rending loss of a happiness already enjoyed. Courtly poetry, on the other hand, makes desire itself the essential motif, and so creates a conception of love with a negative ground-note. Without giving up all connection with sensual love, the new poetic ideal was capable of embracing all kinds of ethical aspirations. Love now became the field where all moral and cultural perfection flowered. Because of his love, the courtly lover is pure and virtuous. The spiritual element dominates more and more, till towards the end of the thirteenth century, the *dolce stil nuovo* of Dante and his friends ends by attributing to love the gift of bringing about a state of piety and holy intuition. Here an extreme had been reached. Italian poetry was gradually to find its way back to a less exalted expression of erotic sentiment. Petrarch is divided between the ideal of spiritualized love and the more natural charm of antique models. Soon the artificial system of courtly love is abandoned, and its subtle distinctions will not be revived, when the Platonism of the Renaissance, latent, already, in the courtly conception, gives rise to new forms of erotic poetry with a spiritual tendency.

In France the evolution of erotic culture was more complicated. The idea of courtly love was not to be supplanted so easily there. The system is not given up ; but the forms are filled by new values. Even before Dante had found the eternal

95

harmony of his *Vita Nuova*, the *Roman de la Rose* had in-
augurated a novel phase of erotic thought in France. The
work, begun before 1240 by Guillaume de Lorris, was finished,
before 1280, by Jean Chopinel. Few books have exercised a
more profound and enduring influence on the life of any period
than the *Romaunt of the Rose*. Its popularity lasted for two
centuries at least. It determined the aristocratic conception
of love in the expiring Middle Ages. By reason of its encyclopedic range it became the treasure-house whence lay society
drew the better part of its erudition.

The existence of an upper class whose intellectual and moral
notions are enshrined in an *ars amandi* remains a rather excep-
tional fact in history. In no other epoch did the ideal of
civilization amalgamate to such a degree with that of love.
Just as scholasticism represents the grand effort of the medieval
spirit to unite all philosophic thought in a single centre, so the
theory of courtly love, in a less elevated sphere, tends to embrace all that appertains to the noble life. The *Roman de la
Rose* did not destroy the system ; it only modified its tendencies
and enriched its contents.

To formalize love is the supreme realization of the aspiration
to the life beautiful, of which we traced above both the ceremonial and the heroic expression. More than in pride and
in strength, beauty is found in love. To formalize love is,
moreover, a social necessity, a need that is the more imperious
as life is more ferocious. Love has to be elevated to the
height of a rite. The overflowing violence of passion demands
it. Only by constructing a system of forms and rules for the
vehement emotions can barbarity be escaped. The brutality
and the licence of the lower classes was always fervently, but
never very efficiently, repressed by the Church. The aristocracy could feel less dependent on religious admonition, because
they had a piece of culture of their own from which to draw
their standards of conduct, namely, courtesy. Literature,
fashion and conversation here formed the means to regulate
and refine erotic life. If they did not altogether succeed, they
at least created the appearance of an honourable life of courtly
love. For, in reality, the sexual life of the higher classes
remained surprisingly rude.

In the erotic conceptions of the Middle Ages two diverging

currents are to be distinguished. Extreme indecency showing itself freely in customs, as in literature, contrasts with an excessive formalism, bordering on prudery. Chastellain mentions frankly how the duke of Burgundy, awaiting an English embassy at Valenciennes, reserves the baths of the town " for them and for all their retinue, baths provided with everything required for the calling of Venus, to take by choice and by election what they liked best, and all at the expense of the duke." Charles the Bold was reproached with his continence, which was thought unbecoming in a prince. At the royal or princely courts of the fifteenth century, marriage feasts were accompanied by all sorts of licentious pleasantries —a usage which had not disappeared two centuries later. In Froissart's narrative of the marriage of Charles VI with Isabella of Bavaria we hear the obscene grinning of the court. Deschamps dedicates to Antoine de Bourgogne an epithalamium of extreme indecency. A certain rhymer makes a lascivious ballad at the request of the lady of Burgundy and of all the ladies.

Such customs seem to be absolutely opposed to the constraint and the modesty imposed by courtesy. The same circles who showed so much shamelessness in sexual relations professed to venerate the ideal of courtly love. Are we to look for hypocrisy in their theory or for cynical abandonment of troublesome forms in their practice ?

We should rather picture to ourselves two layers of civilization superimposed, coexisting though contradictory. Side by side with the courtly style, of literary and rather recent origin, the primitive forms of erotic life kept all their force ; for a complicated civilization like that of the closing Middle Ages could not but be heir to a crowd of conceptions, motives, erotic forms, which now collided and now blended.

The whole of the epithalamic genre may be considered as a heritage of a remote past. In primitive culture marriage and nuptials form but one single sacred rite, converging in the mystery of copulation. Afterwards the Church, by transferring the sacred element of marriage to the sacrament, reserved the mystery for itself, leaving its accessories, to which it objected, to develop freely as popular practices. Thus the epithalamic apparatus, though stripped of its sacred character, nevertheless kept its importance as the main element in the nuptial feasts, thriving there more freely than ever. Licentious expression and gross symbolism were essential to it. The Church was powerless to bridle them. Neither Catholic discipline nor Reformed Puritanism could do away with the quasi-publicity of the marriage-bed, which remained in vogue well into the seventeenth century.

It is therefore from an ethnological point of view, as survivals, that we have to regard the mass of obscenities, equivocal sayings and lascivious symbols which we meet in the civilization of the Middle Ages. They were the remains of mysteries that had degenerated into games and amusements. Evidently the people of that epoch did not feel that, in taking pleasure in them, they were infringing the prescriptions of the courtly code ; they felt themselves on different soil where courtesy was not current.

It would be an exaggeration to say that in erotic literature the whole comic genre was derived from the epithalamium. Certainly the indecent tale, the farce and the lascivious song had long formed a genre of their own of which the forms of expression were liable to but little variation. Obscene allegory predominates ; every trade lent itself to this treatment ; the literature of the time abounds in symbolism borrowed from the tournament, the chase or music ; but most popular of all was the religious travesty of erotic matters. Besides the grossly comic style of the *Cent Nouvelles Nouvelles*, punning with homonymous words like *saint* and *seins*, or using in an obscene sense the words for blessing and confession, eroticecclesiastical allegory took a more refined form. The poets of the circle of Charles d'Orléans compared their amorous sadness to the sufferings of the ascetic and the martyr. They call themselves " les amoureux de l'observance," alluding to the severe reform which the Franciscan order had just undergone. Charles d'Orléans begins one of his pieces :

> "Ce sont ici les dix commandemens,
> Vray Dieu d'amours. . . ." [1]

---

[1] These are the ten commandments, True God of love. . . .

Or, lamenting his dead love, he says :

> " J'ay fait l'obseque de ma dame
> Dedans le moustier amoureux,
> Et le service pour son ame
> A chanté Penser doloreux.
> Mains sierges de soupirs piteux
> Ont esté en son luminaire,
> Aussi j'ay fait la tombe faire
> De regrets. . . ." [1]

All the effects of a sweet and melancholy burlesque are found together in that very tender and pure poem of the end of the century called *L'Amant rendu Cordelier de l'Observance d'Amour*, which describes the reception of an inconsolable lover in the convent of amorous martyrs. It is as though erotic poetry even in this perverse way strove to recover that primitive connection with sacred matters of which the Christian religion had bereft it.

French authors like to oppose " l'esprit gaulois " to the conventions of courtly love, as the natural conception and expression opposed to the artificial. Now the former is no less a fiction than the latter. Erotic thought never acquires literary value save by some process of transfiguration of complex and painful reality into illusionary forms. The whole genre of *Les Cent Nouvelles Nouvelles* and the loose song, with its wilful neglect of all the natural and social complications of love, with its indulgence towards the lies and egotism of sexual life, and its vision of a never-ending lust, implies, no less than the screwed-up system of courtly love, an attempt to substitute for reality the dream of a happier life. It is once more the aspiration towards the life sublime, but this time viewed from the animal side. It is an ideal all the same, even though it be that of unchastity. Reality at all times has been worse and more brutal than the refined æstheticism of courtesy would have it be, but also more chaste than it is represented to be by the vulgar genre which is wrongly regarded as realism.

As an element of literary culture the " genre gaulois " could

---

[1] I have celebrated the obsequies of my lady In the church of love, And the service for her soul Was sung by dolorous Thought. Many tapers of pitiful sighs Have burned in her illumination, Also I had the tomb made Of regrets. . . .

only occupy a secondary place, because erotic poetry is only
fit to beautify life and to serve as a source of inspiration and
imitation, in so far as it takes for its themes, not sexual intercourse itself, but the possibility of happiness, the promise,
desire, languor, expectation. Only thus will it be capable of
expressing all the different shadings of love, and of treating it
equally from the sad and from the merry side. By introducing
into love's domain the concepts of honour, courage, fidelity,
and all the other elements of moral life, it will be of far greater
æsthetic and ethical value. The *Roman de la Rose*, by com-
bining the passionate character of its sensuous central theme
with all the elaborate fancy of the system of courtly love,
satisfied the needs of erotic expression of a whole age.

In this veritable treasure-house of amorous doctrine, ritual
and legend, systematic and complete, the encyclopedic spirit
of the thirteenth century had poured itself out, as it did in the
sterner work of a Vincent of Beauvais. The extraordinary
influence of the book could not but be heightened by its ambiguous nature. The work of two poets of different trends of
thought, it joined—it would be more correct to say it juxta-
posed—the courtly conception of love and sensual cynicism
of the most daring kind. Texts could be found in it for all
purposes.

Guillaume de Lorris had given it charm of form and tenderness of accent. The background of vernal landscape, the
bizarre and yet harmonious imagery of allegorical figures, are
his work. As soon as the lover has approached the wall of
the mysterious garden of love, the allegorical system is unfolded.
Dame Leisure opens the gate for him, Gaiety conducts the
dance, Amor holds by the hand Beauty, who is accompanied
by Wealth, Liberality, Frankness, Courtesy and Youth. After
having locked the heart of his vassal, Amor enumerates to
him the blessings of love, called Hope, Sweet Thought, Sweet
Speech, Sweet Look. Then, when Bel-Accueil, the son of
Courtesy, invites him to come and see the roses, Danger, Male-
bouche, Fear and Shame come to chase him away. The
dramatic struggle commences. Reason comes down from its
high tower, and Venus appears upon the scene. The text of
Guillaume de Lorris ends in the middle of the crisis.

Jean Chopinel, or Clopinel, or de Meun, who finished the

work, adding much more than he found, sacrificed the harmony
of the composition to his fondness for psychological and social
analysis. The conquest of the castle of the roses is drowned
in a continual flood of digressions, speculations and examples.
The sweet breeze of Guillaume de Lorris was followed by the
east wind of chilling scepticism and cruel cynicism of his
successor. The vigorous and trenchant spirit of the second
tarnished the naïve and lightsome idealism of the first. Jean
de Meun is an enlightened man, who believes neither in spectres
nor in sorcerers, neither in faithful love nor in the chastity of
woman, who has an inkling of the problems of mental pathology,
and puts into the mouths of Venus, Nature and Genius the
most daring apology for sensuality.

Venus, requested by her son to come to his aid, swears
not to leave a single woman chaste and makes Amor and the
whole army of assailants take the same vow as regards men.
Nature, occupied in her smithy with her task of preserving
the various species, her eternal struggle against Death, complains that of all creatures, man alone transgresses her commandments by abstaining from procreation. She charges
Genius, her priest, to go and hurl at Love's army, Nature's
anathema on those who despise her laws. In sacerdotal dress,
a taper in his hand, Genius pronounces the sacrilegious ex-
communication, in which the boldest sensualism blends with
refined mysticism. Virginity is condemned, hell is reserved
for those who do not observe the commandments of nature
and of love. For the others the flowered field, where the white
sheep, led by Jesus, the lamb born of the Virgin, crop the
incorruptible grass in endless daylight. At the close Genius
throws the taper into the besieged fortress ; its flame sets the
universe on fire. Venus also throws her torch ; then Shame
and Fear flee, the castle is taken, and Bel-Accueil allows the
lover to pluck the rose.

Here, then, in the *Roman de la Rose*, the sexual motif is again
placed in the centre of erotic poetry, but enveloped by symbolism and mystery and presented in the guise of saintliness. It
is impossible to imagine a more deliberate defiance of the
Christian ideal. The dream of love had taken a form as
artistic as it was passionate. The profusion of allegory satisfied all the requirements of medieval imagination. These

personifications were indispensable for expressing the finer
shades of sentiments. Erotic terminology, to be understood,
could not dispense with these graceful puppets. People used
these figures of Danger, Evil Mouth, etc., as the accepted terms
of a scientific psychology. The passionate character of the
central motif prevented tediousness and pedantry.

In theory, the *Roman de la Rose* does not deny the ideal of
courtesy. The garden of delights is inaccessible except to
the elect, regenerated by love. He who wants to enter must
be free from all hatred, felony, villainy, avarice, envy, sadness,
hypocrisy, poverty and old age. But the positive qualities he
has to oppose to these are no longer ethical, as in the system
of courtly love, but simply of an aristocratic character. They
are leisure, pleasure, gaiety, love, beauty, wealth, liberality,
frankness and courteousness. They are no longer so many
perfections brought about by the sacredness of love, but simply
the proper means to conquer the object desired. For the
veneration of idealized womanhood, Jean Chopinel substituted
a cruel contempt for its feebleness.

Now, whatever influence the *Roman de la Rose* may have
exercised on the minds of men, it did not succeed in completely destroying the older conception of love. Side by side
with the glorification of seduction professed by the *Rose*, the
glorification of the pure and faithful love of the knight maintained its ground, both in lyrical poetry and in the romance
of chivalry, not to speak of the fantasy of tournaments and
passages of arms. Towards the end of the fourteenth century
the question which of the two conceptions of love should be
held by the perfect nobleman provoked a literary dispute such
as French taste loved in later centuries also. The noble
Boucicaut had made himself the champion of true courtesy
by composing with his travelling companions the *Livre des
Cent Ballades*, in which he called on the wits of the court to
decide between the honest and self-denying service of a single
lady, and fashionable flirtation. Knights or poets who, like
Boucicaut, honoured the old ideal of courtesy, were vaunted
as models, Othe de Granson and Louis de Sancerre among
others. Christine de Pisan took part in the dispute by posing
as the intrepid advocate of female honour. Her *Epistre au
Dieu d'Amours* formulated the complaints of women about

all the deceit and insults of men. With serious indignation she denounces the doctrine of the *Roman de la Rose*.

Then the multitude of fervent admirers of Jean de Meun appeared upon the scene. Among them were men of very varying spiritual bent, even ecclesiastics. The debate lasted for years. The nobility and the court took it up as a means of amusement. Boucicaut—encouraged, perhaps, by the praise of Christine de Pisan, for his defence of ideal courtesy— had already founded his " ordre de l'escu vert à la dame blanche," for the defence of oppressed women, when the duke of Burgundy eclipsed him by founding in Paris, at the " hôtel d'Artois," on February 14, 1401, a court of love on a very splendid scale. Philippe le Hardi, the old diplomat, whom one would have supposed to be occupied with affairs of a very different nature, and Louis de Bourbon, had begged the king to institute a court of love to furnish some distraction during an epidemic of the plague which raged at Paris, " to spend part of the time more graciously and in order to find awakening of new joy." The cause of chivalry triumphed in the form of a literary salon. The court was founded on the virtues of humility and of fidelity, " to the honour, praise and commendation and service of all noble ladies." The members were provided with illustrious titles. The two founders and the king were called the Grands Conservateurs. Among the conservators we find Jean sans Peur, his brother Antoine, and his six-years-old son, Philippe. A certain Pierre d'Hauteville, from Hainault, was Prince of Love ; there were also ministers, auditors, knights of honour, knights treasurers, councillors, grand-masters of the chase, squires of love, etc. Burghers and lower clergy were admitted, side by side with princes and prelates. The business of the court much resembled that of a " rhetorical chamber." Refrains were set to be worked up into " ballades couronnées ou chapelées," songs, sirventois, complaints, rondels, lays, virelais, etc. There were debates " in the form of amorous law-suits to defend different opinions." The ladies distributed the prizes, and poems attacking the honour of women were forbidden.

In this pompous and grave apparatus of a graceful amusement one cannot help feeling the effect of Burgundian style beginning to influence the French court itself. It is equally obvious that the royal court, archaic like all courts, must declare in favour of the ancient and severe ideal of love, and that the 700 known members of the club were far from conforming their practice to it. By what is known of their habits, the great lords of that epoch were rather strange protectors of female honour. The most curious fact is that we find there the same persons who, in the debate about love, had defended the *Roman de la Rose* and attacked Christine de Pisan. Evidently it was merely a society amusement.

The intimate circle of Jean de Meun's admirers consisted of men in the service of princes, both priests and laymen. It is identical with that of the first French humanists. One of them, Jean de Montreuil, provost of Lille, secretary to the dauphin and later to the duke of Burgundy, was the author of a good many Ciceronian epistles, and, like his friends, Gontier and Pierre Col, he corresponded with Nicolas de Clemanges, the grave censor of the abuses in the Church. We now find him devoting his talents to the defence of the *Roman de la Rose*, and of its author, Jean de Meun. He asserts that several of the most learned and enlightened men honour the *Roman de la Rose* so much that their appreciation resembles a cult (*paene ut colerent*), and that they would rather do without their shirt than this book. He exhorts his friends to undertake its defence, like himself. " The more I study "—he writes to one of the detractors—" the gravity of the mysteries and the mystery of the gravity of this profound and famous work of Master Jean de Meun, the more I am astonished at your disapprobation." He himself will defend it to his last breath, and many others will serve this cause with words and deeds.

The conviction with which Jean de Montreuil speaks, seems already to indicate that the question of love, after all, involved graver issues than those of a court amusement, and this is further proved by the fact that Jean Gerson, the illustrious chancellor of the university, took part in the quarrel. He hated the *Roman de la Rose* with implacable hatred. The book seemed to him to be the most dangerous pest, the source of all immorality. In his works he reverts again and again to the pernicious influence " of the vicious romaunt of the rose." If he had a copy, which was the only one and worth a thousand pounds, he would rather burn it than sell it to be published.

When Pierre Col had refuted one of Gerson's polemical writings, the latter replied by a treatise against the *Roman de la Rose*, which was more bitter than his former denunciations. He dated it " from my study, on the evening of the 18th of May, 1402.''

Following the example of the author of the *Roman de la Rose*, he gave his treatise the form of an allegoric vision. Awakening, one morning, he feels his soul flying far away, " using the feathers and the wings of various thoughts, from one place to another, to the sacred court of Christianity,'' where he hears the complaints of Chastity addressed to Justice, Conscience and Wisdom about the Fool of love, that is to say, Jean de Meun, who has chased her from the earth, with all her train. The " good guardians '' of Chastity are precisely the evil personages of the Rose : Shame, Fear and Danger, " the good porter, who would not dare, who would not deign to sanction even an impure kiss or dissolute look, or attractive smile or light speech.'' Chastity overwhelms the Fool of love with reproaches. The Fool rails at marriage and monastic life. He teaches " how all young girls should sell their persons early and dearly, without fear and without shame, and that they should make light of deceit and perjury.'' He directs the fancy exclusively to carnal desire, and, to top all perversity, in the speeches of Venus, of Nature, and of Dame Reason, he blends conceptions of Paradise, and of the mysteries of the Faith, with those of sensual pleasure.

There, in truth, was the peril. This imposing work, with its mixture of sensuality, scoffing cynicism and elegant symbolism, infused a voluptuous mysticism into the mind which, to an austere man, was simply an abyss of sin. Had not Gerson's adversary dared to affirm that only the Fool of love could judge of the value of passion ? He who does not know it sees it only as in a glass, to him it remains a riddle. Such was the use he had made for his sacrilegious purposes, of the holy words of Saint Paul ! Pierre Col had not scrupled to affirm that the Song of Solomon was composed in honour of the daughter of Pharaoh. Those who have defamed the *Roman de la Rose*, he declared, have bent their knees before Baal. Nature does not wish that a woman should be content with one single man, and the genius of Nature is God. He carried his blasphemy so far as to show from the Gospel of Saint Luke that formerly a woman's genitals, the rose of the romance, were sacred. Being convinced of the truth of this impious mysticism, he appealed to the friends of the book, forming a cloud of witnesses, and predicted that Gerson himself would fall madly in love, as had happened to other theologians before him.

Gerson did not succeed in destroying the authority, or, at least, the popularity, of the *Roman de la Rose.* In 1444 a canon of Lisieux, Estienne Legris, composed a *Répertoire du Roman de la Rose.* Towards the end of the century Jean Molinet could assert that its sentences were current like proverbs. He has given himself the trouble of "moralizing" the whole book, in giving its allegories a religious meaning. The nightingale calling to love meant the voice of the preacher, the rose meant Jesus. Even in the hey-day of the Renaissance, Clément Marot considered that the work deserved to be modernized, and Ronsard did not consider the figures of Bel-Accueil and Faus Danger too worn for use in his verse.

CHAPTER IX

THE CONVENTIONS OF LOVE

It is from literature that we gather the forms of erotic
thought belonging to a period, but we should try to picture
them functioning as elements of social life. A whole system
of amatory conceptions and usages was current in aristocratic
conversation of those times. What signs and figures of love
which later ages have dropped! Around the god of Love
the bizarre mythology of the *Roman de la Rose* was grouped.
Then there was the symbolism of colours in costume, and of
flowers and precious stones. The meaning of colours, of
which feeble traces still obtain, was of extreme importance
in amorous conversation during the Middle Ages. A manual
of the subject was written about 1458, by the herald Sicily
in his *Le Blason des Couleurs*, laughed at by Rabelais. When
Guillaume de Machaut meets his beloved for the first time,
he is delighted to see her wear a white dress and a sky-blue
hood with a design of green parrots, because green signifies
new love and blue fidelity. Later, he sees her image in a
dream, turning away from him and dressed in green, "signify-
ing novelty," and reproaches her with it in a ballad :

"En lieu de bleu, dame, vous vestez vert." [1]

Rings, veils and bands, all the jewels and presents of court-
ship had their special function, with devices and enigmatic
emblems which sometimes were veritable rebuses. The standard of the dauphin in 1414 bore a gold K, a swan (cygne)
and an L, indicating one of his mother's maids of honour,
who was called la Cassinelle. The "glorieux de court et
transporteurs de noms," at whom Rabelais mocked, represent
"espoir" by a sphere, "mélancholie" by a columbine (anco-
lie). Numerous games served to express the finesses of senti-

---

[1] Instead of in blue, lady, you dress in green.

107

ment, such as The King who does not lie, The Castle of love, Sales of love, Games for sale.   In one of them, for instance, the lady mentions a flower ; the young man has to answer by a rhymed compliment.

> " Je vous vens la passerose.
> —Belle, dire ne vous ose
> Comment Amours vers vous me tire,
> Si l'apercevez tout sanz dire." [1]

The game of Castle of love consisted of a series of allegorical riddles.

> " Du chastel d'Amours vous demant :
> Dites le premier fondement !
> —Amer loyaument.

> " Or me nommez le mestre mur
> Qui joli le font, fort et seur !
> —Celer sagement.

> " Dites moy qui sont li crenel,
> Les fenestres et li carrel !
> —Regart atraiant.

> " Amis, nommez moy le portier !
> —Dangier mauparlant.

> " Qui est la clef qui le puet deffermer ?
> —Prier courtoisement." [2]

Since the times of the troubadours the casuistry of love had occupied a large place in courtly conversation.   It was, so to say, curiosity and backbiting raised to the level of a literary form.   At the court of Louis of Orleans people amuse themselves at meals by " tales, ballads " and " graceful questions."   Poets are especially laid under contribution.   Machaut is requested by a company of ladies and noblemen to reply to a series of " partures of love and of its adventures."   Every love-affair is discussed according to rigorous rules.   " Beau

---

[1] I sell you the hollyhock.—Belle, I dare not tell How Love draws me towards you, But you perceive it, without saying a word.

[2] Of the castle of Love I ask you : Tell me the first foundation !—To love loyally.   Now mention the principal wall Which makes it fine, strong and sure !—To conceal wisely.   Tell me what are the loopholes, The windows and the stones !—Alluring looks.   Friend, mention the porter !—Ill-speaking danger.   Which is the key that can unlock it ?—Courteous request.

sire, which would you prefer : that people spoke ill of your lady and that you found her good, or that she were well spoken of and you should find her bad ? " The strict conception of honour obliged a gentleman to answer : " Lady, I should prefer to hear her well spoken of and that I should find her bad."

Does a lady, neglected by her lover, break faith by choosing another ? May a knight bereft of all hope of seeing his lady, whom a jealous husband keeps locked up, seek a new love ? One step more and love questions will be treated as lawsuits, as in the *Arrestz d'Amour* of Martial d'Auvergne.

The courtly code did not serve exclusively for making verses; it claimed to be applicable to life, or at least to conversation. It is very difficult to pierce the clouds of poetry and to penetrate to the real life of the epoch. How far did courting and flirtation during the fourteenth and fifteenth centuries come up to the requirements of the courtly system or to the precepts of Jean de Meun ? Autobiographical confessions are very rare at that epoch. Even when an actual love-affair is described with the intention of being accurate, the author cannot free himself from the accepted style and technical conceptions. We find an instance of this in the too lengthy narrative of a love-affair of an old poet and a young girl, which Guillaume de Machaut has given us in *Le Livre du Voir-Dit*. He was approaching his sixtieth year, when Peronnelle d'Armentières, of a noble family in Champagne, sent him, in 1362, her first rondel, in which she offered her heart to the celebrated poet, whom she did not know, and invited him to enter with her into a poetical love correspondence. The poor poet, sickly, blind of one eye, gouty, at once kindles. He replies to her rondel and an exchange of letters and of poems begins. Peronnelle is proud of her literary connection ; she does not make a secret of it, and begs the poet to put in writing the true story of their love, inserting their letters and their poetry. Machaut readily complies. " I shall make," he says, " to your glory and praise, something that will be well remembered."

" And, my very sweet heart, are you sorry because we have begun so late ? By God, so am I ; but here is the remedy : let us enjoy life as much as circumstances permit, so that we may make up for the time we have lost ; and that people may speak of our love a hundred years hence, and all well and honourably ; for if there were evil, you would conceal it from God, if you could."

The narrative connecting the letters and the poetry teaches us what degree of intimacy was considered compatible with a decent love-affair. The young lady may permit herself extraordinary liberties, provided everything takes place in the presence of third parties, her sister-in-law, her maid or her secretary. At the first interview, which Machaut has been waiting for with misgivings, because of his unattractive appearance, Peronnelle falls asleep, or pretends to sleep, under a cherry tree, with her head on the poet's knees. The secretary covers her mouth with a green leaf and tells Machaut to kiss the leaf. Just when the latter takes courage to do so, the secretary pulls the leaf away.

She grants him other favours. A pilgrimage to Saint Denis, at the time of the fair, provides them with an opportunity of passing some days together. One afternoon, overcome by the heat of mid-June, they fly from the crowd at the fair to take a few hours' rest. A burgher of the town provides them with a double-bedded room. The blinds are closed and the company lies down. The sister-in-law takes one of the two beds. Peronnelle and her maid occupy the other. She orders the bashful poet to lie down between them, which he does, lying very still for fear of disturbing her. On waking, she orders him to kiss her.

At the end of the trip, she permits him to come and wake her, in order to take leave, and the narrative gives us to understand that she refused him nothing. She gives him the golden key of her honour, to guard that treasure, or what was left of it.

The poet's good fortune ended there. He did not see her again, and, for lack of other adventures, he filled the rest of his book with mythological excursions. At last she lets him know that their relations must end, because of a marriage, probably. He resolves to go on loving and revering her till the end of his days. And after their death, he will pray God, to reserve for her, in the glory of Heaven, the name he gave her : *Toute-belle*.

In the *Voir-Dit* of Machaut religion and love are mixed up with a sort of ingenuous shamelessness. We need not be shocked by the fact that the author was a canon of the church of Reims, for, in the Middle Ages, minor orders, which sufficed for a canon (Petrarch was one), did not absolutely impose celibacy. The fact that a pilgrimage was chosen as an occasion for the lovers to meet was not extraordinary either. At this period pilgrimages served all sorts of frivolous purposes. But what astonishes us is that Machaut, a serious and delicate poet, claims to perform his pilgrimage " very devoutly." At mass he is seated behind her :

> ". . . Quant on dist : Agnus Dei,
> Foy que je doy à Saint Crepais,
> Doucement me donna la pais,[1]
> Entre deux pilers du moustier.
> Et j'en avoie bien mestier,
> Car mes cuers amoureus estoit
> Troublés, quant si tost se partoit." [2]

He says his hours as he is waiting for her in the garden. He glorifies her portrait as his God on earth. Entering the church to begin a novene, he takes a mental vow to compose a poem about his beloved on each of the nine days—which does not prevent him from speaking about the great devotion with which he said his prayers.

We shall revert elsewhere to the astonishing ingenuousness with which, before the Council of Trent, worldly occupations were mixed up with works of the Faith.

As regards the tone of the love-affair of Machaut and Peronnelle, it is soft, cloying, somewhat morbid. The expression of their feelings remains enveloped in arguments and allegories. But there is something touching in the tenderness of the old poet, which prevents him from seeing that " Toute-belle," after all, has but played with him and with her own heart.

To grasp what little we can of actual love relations, apart from literature, we should oppose to the *Voir-Dit*, as a pendant,

---

[1] *Vide* page 37.

[2] When the priest said : Agnus Dei, Faith I owe to Saint Crepais, Sweetly she gave me the pax Between two pillars of the church. And I needed it indeed, For my amorous heart was Troubled that we had to part so soon.

*Le Livre du Chevalier de la Tour Landry pour l'Enseignement
de ses Filles*, written at the same epoch. This time we are
not concerned with an amorous old poet ; we have to do
with a father of a rather prosaic turn of mind, an Angevin
nobleman, who relates his reminiscences, anecdotes and tales
"pour mes filles aprandre à roumancier." This might be
rendered, "to teach my daughters the fashionable conventions
in love matters." The instruction, however, does not turn out
romantic at all. The moral of the examples and admonitions
which the cautious father recommends to his daughters tends
especially to put them on their guard against the dangers of
romantic flirtations. Take heed of eloquent people, always
ready with their "false long and pensive looks and little
sighs, and wonderful emotional faces, and who have more
words at hand than other people." Do not be too encouraging.
He himself, when young, was conducted by his father to a
castle to make the acquaintance of a young lady to whom they
wanted to betroth him. The girl received him very kindly.
He conversed with her on all sorts of subjects, so as to probe
her character somewhat. They got to talk of prisoners, which
gave the knight a chance to pay a neat compliment : "'Ma
demoiselle, it would be better to fall into your hands as a
prisoner than into many another's, and I think your prison
would not be so hard as that of the English.' She replied
that she had recently seen one whom she could wish to be
her prisoner. And then I asked her, if she would make a
bad prison for him, and she said not at all, and that she would
hold him as dear as her own person, and I told her that the
man would be very fortunate in having such a sweet and
noble prison. What shall I say ? She could talk well enough,
and it seemed, to judge from her conversation, that she knew
a good deal, and her eyes had also a very lively and lightsome
expression." When they took leave she begged him two
or three times to came back soon, as if she had known him
for a long time already. "And when we had departed my
lord my father said to me : ' What do you think of her whom
you have seen ? Tell me your opinion.' ' Monseigneur, she
seems to me all well and good, but I shall never be nearer to
her than I am now, if you please.'" Her lack of reserve left
him without any desire to get better acquainted with her.

So they did not get engaged, and of course the author says that he afterwards had reason not to repent it.

It is to be regretted that the chevalier has not given more autobiographical details and fewer moral exhortations, because these personal traits, showing how customs adapted themselves to the ideal, are very rare in the traditions of the Middle Ages.

In spite of his avowed intention to teach his girls "à roumancier," the knight de la Tour Landry thinks, before all things, of a good marriage ; and marriage had little to do with love. He reports to them a "debate" between his wife and himself, on the question, whether it is becoming " d'amer par amours." He thinks that a girl may, in certain cases, for example, "in the hope of marrying," love honourably. His wife thinks otherwise. It is better that a girl should not fall in love at all, not even with her betrothed, otherwise piety would suffer in consequence. " For I have heard many women say who were in love in their youth, that when they were in church, their thoughts and fancies made them dwell more on those nimble imaginations and delights of their love-affairs than on the service of God, and the art of love is of such a nature that just at the holiest moments of the service, that is to say, when the priest holds our Lord on the altar, the most of these little thoughts would come to them." Machaut and Peronnelle might have confirmed this.

It is not easy for us to reconcile the general austerity of the Chevalier de la Tour Landry with the fact that this father does not scruple to instruct his daughters by means of stories which would not have been out of place in the *Cent Nouvelles Nouvelles*. Still, even more recent literature, that of the Elizabethan age, for instance, may remind us how completely the world becomes estranged from the erotic forms of a few centuries back. As for betrothals and marriages, neither the graceful forms of the courtly ideal nor the refined frivolity and open cynicism of the *Roman de la Rose* had any real hold upon them. In the very matter-of-fact considerations on which a match between noble families was based there was little room for the chivalrous fictions of prowess and of service. Thus it came about that the courtly notions of love were never corrected by contact with real life. They could unfold freely in aristocratic conversation, they could offer a literary amusement or a charming game, but no more. The ideal of love, such as it was, could not be lived up to, except in a fashion inherently false.

Cruel reality constantly gave the lie to it. At the bottom of the intoxicating cup of the *Roman de la Rose* the moralist exposed the bitter dregs. From the side of religion maledictions were poured upon love in all its aspects, as the sin by which the world is being ruined. Whence, exclaims Gerson, come the bastards, the infanticides, the abortions, whence hatred, whence poisonings ?—Woman joins her voice to that from the pulpit : all the conventions of love are the work of men : even when it dons an idealistic guise, erotic culture is altogether saturated by male egotism : and what else is the cause of the endlessly repeated insults to matrimony, to woman and her feebleness, but the need of masking this egotism ? One word suffices, says Christine de Pisan, to answer all these infamies : it is not the women who have written the books.

Indeed, medieval literature shows little true pity for woman, little compassion for her weakness and the dangers and pains which love has in store for her. Pity took on a stereotyped and factitious form, in the sentimental fiction of the knight delivering the virgin. The author of the *Quinze Joyes de Mariage*, after having mocked at all the faults of women, undertakes to describe also the wrongs they have to suffer. So far as is known, he never performed this task.

Civilization always needs to wrap up the idea of love in veils of fancy, to exalt and refine it, and thereby to forget cruel reality. The solemn or graceful game of the faithful knight or the amorous shepherd, the fine imagery of courtly allegories, however brutally life belied them, never lost their charm nor all their moral value. The human mind needs these forms, and they always remain essentially the same.

CHAPTER X

THE IDYLLIC VISION OF LIFE

The lasting vogue of the pastoral genre towards the end of the Middle Ages implies a reaction against the ideal of courtesy. Weary of the complicated formalism of chivalrous love, the aristocratic soul renounces the overstrung pretension of heroism in love, and praises rural life as the escape from it. The new, or rather revived, bucolic ideal remains essentially an erotic one. Still there is a strain of bucolic sentiment, the inspiration of which is rather ethical than erotic. We may perhaps distinguish it from the pastoral proper by calling it the idea of the simple life, or of *aurea mediocritas*. It is continually merging into the other.

The negation of the chivalric ideal arises among the nobles themselves. It is in court literature that sarcastic or sentimental criticism of it springs up. The burghers, on the other hand, are always striving to imitate the forms of the noble life. Nothing could be falser than to picture the third estate in the Middle Ages as animated by class hatred, or scorning chivalry. On the contrary, the splendour of the life of the nobility dazzles and seduces them. The rich burghers take pains to adopt the forms and the tone of the nobility. Philip of Artevelde, the leader of the Flemish insurgents, whom one would like to picture as a simple, sober revolutionary, kept a state like a prince's. His going in to dinner is announced by music. His meals are served up on silver plate like that of a count of Flanders ; he goes about dressed in scarlet and miniver, preceded by his unfurled pennon showing a sable scutcheon with three silver hats. The great financier, Jacques Cœur, whom one instinctively thinks of as a modern, took a lively interest, according to Jacques de Lalaing's biographer, in the fantastic and useless projects of that anachronistic knight-errant.

Among those who freed themselves from the chivalric

115

illusion, seeing the misery and the falsehood of it, we must begin with those practical and frigid minds which were, so to say, opposed to it by temperament. Such were Philippe de Commines and his master, Louis XI. In describing the battle of Montlhéry, Commines abstains from all heroic fiction : no fine exploits, no dramatic turns ; he only gives us a realistic picture of comings and goings, of hesitations and fears. He takes pleasure in telling of flights and noting how courage returned with security. He rejects all chivalrous terminology and scarcely mentions honour, which he treats almost as an inevitable evil.

The ideal of chivalry tallies with the spirit of a primitive age, susceptible of gross delusion and little accessible to the corrections of experience. Sooner or later intellectual progress demands a revision of this ideal. It does not disappear, however, it only sheds its too fantastic tendencies. Chivalry, far from being completely disavowed, drops its affectation of a quasi-religious perfection, and will be henceforth only a model of social life. The knight is transformed into the cavalier, who, though still keeping up a very severe code of honour and of glory, will no longer claim to be a defender of the Faith or a protector of the oppressed. The modern gentleman is still ideally linked with the medieval conception of chivalry.

The requirements of moral, æsthetic and social perfection weighed too heavily on the knight. This highly praised chivalry, considered from any point of view whatever, could not conceal its inherent falsity. It was a ridiculous anachronism, a piece of factitious making up. No social utility, no moral value, everywhere vanity and sin. Even as an æsthetic game, the courtly life ended by boring the players. So they turn to another ideal, that of simplicity and of repose. Does this mean that the disillusioned nobles turned to a spiritual life ? Sometimes they did. At all times the lives of many courtiers and soldiers have ended in renunciation of the world. More often, however, they are content themselves to seek elsewhere the sublime life which chivalry failed to give. From the days of antiquity a promise had been held out of an earthly felicity to be found in rural life. Here true peace seemed attainable without strife, simply by flight. Here was a sure refuge from envy and hatred, from the vanity of honours, from oppressive luxury and cruel war. Medieval literature inherited from the classic authors the theme of the praise of the simple life, which may be called the negative side of the bucolic sentiment. Court life and aristocratic pretension are disavowed in favour of solitude, work and study. In the fourteenth century this theme had found its typical expression in France in *Le Dit de Franc Gontier* of Philippe de Vitri, bishop of Meaux, musician and poet, and a friend of Petrarch.

> " Soubz feuille vert, sur herbe delitable
> Lez ru bruiant et prez clere fontaine
> Trouvay fichee une borde portable,
> Ilec mengeoit Gontier o dame Helayne
> Fromage frais, laict, burre fromaigee,
> Craime, matton, pomme, nois, prune, poire,
> Aulx et oignons, escaillongne froyee
> Sur crouste bise, au gros sel, pour mieux boire." [1]

After the meal they kiss " both the mouth and the nose, the soft and the shaggy," then Gontier goes off to fell a tree, while Helayne goes to do the washing.

> " J'oy Gontier en abatant son arbre
> Dieu mercier de sa vie seüre :
> 'Ne sçay,' dit-il, ' que sont pilliers de marbre,
> Pommeaux luisans, murs vestus de paincture ;
> Je n'ay paour de traïson tissue
> Soubz beau semblant, ne qu'empoisonné soye
> En vaisseau d'or. Je n'ay la teste nue
> Devant thirant, ne genoil qui s'i ploye.
>
> 'Verge d'uissier jamais ne me deboute,
> Car jusques la ne m'esprent convoitise,
> Ambicion, ne lescherie gloute.
> Labour me paist en joieuse franchise ;
> Moult j'ame Helayne et elle moy sans faille,
> Et c'est assez. De tombel n'avons cure.'
> Lors je dy : ' Las ! serf de court ne vault maille,
> Mais Franc Gontier vault en or jame pure.' " [2]

---

[1] Under green leaves, on delightful grass Near a noisy brook and a clear fountain I found a portable board, There Gontier took his meal with dame Helayne On fresh cheese, milk, cream and cheese, curds, apple, nut, plum, pear, Garlic and onions, chopped shallots On a brown crust, with coarse salt, to drink the better.

[2] I heard Gontier in felling his tree Thank God for his life of security : " I do not know," he said, " what are pillars of marble, Shining pommels, walls

We observe how here already the motif of the simple life
is coupled with that of natural love.

For later generations the poem of Philippe de Vitri remained
the classic expression of the bucolic sentiment and of the
happiness procured by security and independence, frugality
and health, useful labour and conjugal love, without complications.

Eustache Deschamps imitated him in a number of ballads,
of which one follows its model very closely.

> " En retournant d'une court souveraine
> Ou j'avoie longuement sejourné,
> En un bosquet, dessus une fontaine
> Trouvay Robin le franc, enchapelé ;
> Chapeauls de flours avoit cilz afublé
> Dessus son chief, et Marion sa drue . . ." etc.[1]

He has enlarged the motif in adding to it an indictment of
a knight's or a soldier's life ; there is no worse condition than
that of a warrior ; he commits the seven deadly sins every
day ; avarice and vainglory are the essence of warfare.

> " . . . Je vueil mener d'or en avant
> Estat moien, c'est mon opinion,
> Guerre laissier et vivre en labourant :
> Guerre mener n'est que dampnacion." [2]

Generally, however, he simply praises the golden mean.

> " Je ne requier à Dieu fors qu'il me doint
> En ce monde de lui servir et loer,
> Vivre pour moy, cote entiere ou pourpoint,
> Aucun cheval pour mon labour porter.

---

decorated with paintings ; I have no fear of treason hidden Under fine
appearances, nor that I shall be poisoned In a gold cup. I do not bare
my head Before a tyrant, nor bend my knee.

" No usher's rod ever turns me away, For no covetousness, Ambition, nor
lechery entice me (to court). Labour holds me in joyous liberty ; I love
Helayne dearly, and she loves me without fail, And that is enough. We are
not afraid of the grave." Then I said : " Alas ! a serf of the court is not
worth a doit, But Franc Gontier is worth a sure gem set in gold."

[1] Returning from a sovereign's court Where I had long sojourned, In a bush,
near a fountain I found Robin the free, his head crowned ; With chaplets of
flowers had he adorned His head, and Marion, his beloved . . .

[2] Henceforth I will take up a Middle station, so I am resolved To leave off
fighting and to live by labour ; Waging war is but damnation.

> Et que je puisse mon estat gouverner
> Moiennement, en grace, sanz envie,
> Sanz trop avoir et sanz pain demander,
> Car au jour d'ui est la plus seure vie." [1]

The quest of glory or of gain does but entail misery ; only the poor man is happy, he lives tranquilly and long.

> " . . . Un ouvrier et uns povres chartons
> Va mauvestuz, deschirez et deschaulx
> Mais en ouvrant prant en gré ses travaulx
> Et liement fait son euvre fenir.
> Par nuit dort bien ; pour ce uns telz cueurs loiaulx
> Voit quatre roys et leur regne fenir." [2]

The picture of a working man surviving four kings pleased him so much that he used it several times.

The editor of Deschamps' works, Monsieur Gaston Raynaud, supposes that the poems of this tendency all date from the last period of his life, when, deprived of his functions, forsaken and disappointed, he has at last learned to understand the vanity of court affairs. This is perhaps going too far ; these poems would seem rather to be the expression of sentiments, more or less conventional, current among the nobility itself in the midst of court life.

The theme of contempt for a courtier's life enjoyed great favour with a group of scholars who, towards the end of the fourteenth century, mark the beginning of French humanism, and whose circle was connected with that of the leaders of the great councils of the Church. Pierre d'Ailly himself is the author of a poem forming a companion piece with that of *Franc Gontier* : the tyrant, in contrast with the happy rustic, leading the life of a slave in continuous fear. The theme was admirably fit to be treated in the epistolary style, after the model of Petrarch. Jean de Montreuil tried his hand

---

[1] I only ask of God to give me That I may serve and praise him in this world, Live for myself, my coat or doublet whole, One horse to carry my labour, And that I may govern my estate In mediocre style, in grace, without envy, Without having too much and without begging my bread, For this day is the safest life.

[2] A working man and a poor waggoner, Go about ill dressed, in torn clothes and ill shod, But, labouring, he takes pleasure in his work And merrily finishes it. At night he sleeps well ; and therefore such a loyal heart Sees four kings and their reigns end.

at it; so did Nicolas de Clemanges, three times over. A secretary to the duke of Orleans, the Milanese Ambrose de Miliis, addressed to Gontier Col a Latin letter, in which a courtier dissuades his friend from entering into court service. Translated into French, this letter figures among the works of Alain Chartier, under the title *Le Curial*, and afterwards Robert Gaguin translated it back into Latin.

The theme was even worked out by a certain Charles Rochefort in a long-winded allegorical poem, *L'Abuzé en Court*, afterwards attributed to King René. Towards the end of the fifteenth century, Jean Meschinot still rhymes as follows:

> " La cour est une mer, dont sourt
> Vagues d'orgueil, d'envie orages. . . .
> Ire esmeut debats et outrages,
> Qui les nefs jettent souvent bas :
> Traison y fait son personnage.
> Nage aultre part pour tes ebats." [1]

In the sixteenth century the old motif had lost nothing of its freshness.

For the most part the praises of a frugal life and of hard work in the fields are not based on the delights of simplicity and labour in themselves, nor on the security and independence they seemed to confer ; the positive content of the ideal is the longing for natural love. The pastoral is the idyllic form assumed by erotic thought. Just like the dream of heroism which is at the bottom of the ideas of chivalry, the bucolic dream is somewhat more than a literary genre. It is a craving to reform life itself. It does not stop at describing the life of shepherds with its innocent and natural pleasures. People want to imitate it, if not in real life, at least in the illusion of a graceful game. Weary of factitious conceptions of love, the aristocracy sought a remedy for them in the pastoral ideal. Facile and innocent love amid the delights of nature seemed to be the lot of country people, theirs to be the truly enviable form of happiness. The villein, in his turn, becomes an ideal type.

---

[1] The court is a sea, whence come Waves of pride, thunderstorms of envy. Wrath stirs up quarrels and outrages, Which often cause the ships to sink ; Treason plays its part there, Swim elsewhere for your amusement.

The antique form of bucolic life still satisfied the aspirations of the waning Middle Ages. No need is felt to correct the pastoral fiction in accordance with real life. The new enthusiasm for nature does not mean a truly deep sense of reality, not even a sincere admiration for work; it is only an attempt to adorn courteous manners by an array of artificial flowers, playing at shepherd and shepherdess just as people had played at Lancelot and Guinevere.

In the *Pastourelle*, the short poem relating the facile adventure of the knight with the country girl, pastoral fancy is still in touch with reality. In the pastoral proper, however, the lover or poet thinks himself a shepherd too, all contact with reality is lost, all things are transferred to a sunlit landscape full of the singing of birds and playing of reed-pipes, where even sadness assumes a sweet sound. The faithful shepherd continues to resemble the faithful knight only too closely; after all, it is courtly love transposed into another key.

However artificial it might be, pastoral fancy still tended to bring the loving soul into touch with nature and its beauties. The pastoral genre was the school where a keener perception and a stronger affection towards nature were learned. The literary expression of the sentiment of nature was a by-product of the pastoral. Out of the simple words of exultation at the joys caused by sunshine and shade, birds and flowers, the loving description of scenery and rural life gradually develops. A poem like *Le Dit de la Pastoure* of Christine de Pisan marks the transition of the pastoral to a new genre.

The bucolic idyll, then, offered itself as a new style for courtly amusement, a supplement to chivalry, as it were. Once received as such, it becomes another mask. The pastoral travesty serves for all sorts of diversions; the domains of pastoral fancy and of chivalric romanticism mingle. Tournaments are held in the apparel of an eclogue, like the " Pas d'armes de la bergère " of King René. These pastoral representations, even if they did not really deceive people, at least seem to have been regarded as important. Among his " Marvels of the World " Chastellain mentions King René's playing at shepherd.

" J'ay un roi de Cécille
Vu devenir berger
Et sa femme gentille
De ce mesme mestier,
Portant la pannetière,
La houlette et chappeau,
Logeans sur la bruyère
Auprès de leur trouppeau." [1]

On another occasion, pastoral fancy had to supply a literary form for political satire. It is hard to imagine a more bizarre product than *Le Pastoralet*, a very long poem by a partisan of Burgundy, who, in this pretty disguise, relates the murder of Louis of Orleans for the purpose of exculpating Jean sans Peur and of venting his spleen on the house of Orleans. The two hostile dukes represented by Tristifer and Léonet in an environment of country dances and ornaments of flowers, Tristifer-Orleans robbing the shepherds of their bread and cheese, apples and nuts, shepherd's reeds and bells, and threatening them with his large crook, even the battle of Agincourt described in pastoral guise . . . one would be inclined to think this style rather flamboyant, if we did not remember that Ariosto uses the same machinery for exculpating his patron, the Cardinal d'Este, who was hardly less guilty than Jean sans Peur.

The pastoral element is never absent from court festivities. It was admirably fitted both for masquerades and for political allegories. Here the bucolic conception coalesced with another of Scriptural origin : the prince and his people symbolized by the shepherd and his sheep, the duties of the ruler compared to those of the shepherd. Meschinot sings :

" Seigneur, tu es de Dieu bergier ;
Garde ses bestes loyaument,
Mets les en champ ou en vergier,
Mais ne les perds aucunement,
Pour ta peine auras bon paiement
En bien le gardant, et se non,
A male heure reçus ce nom." [2]

---

[1] I have seen a king of Sicily Turn shepherd And his gentle wife Take to the same trade, Carrying the shepherd's pouch, The crook and hat, Dwelling on the heath Near their flock.

[2] Lord, you are God's shepherd ; Guard his animals loyally, Lead them to the field or the orchard, But lose them by no means, You will have good pay-

Represented in actual mummery, these ideas naturally took the outward appearance of the pastoral proper. At the marriage feasts of Charles the Bold and Margaret of York at Bruges in 1468, an " entremets " glorified the princesses of yore as " noble shepherdesses who formerly tended and guarded the sheep of the ' pays de par deça ' (the provinces ' over here ')." At Valenciennes, in 1493, the revival of the land after the devastations of war was represented, " all in pastoral style." Even in war the pastoral game was kept up. The stone-mortars of the duke of Burgundy before Granson are called " the shepherd and the shepherdess." Philippe de Ravestein takes the field with four-and-twenty noblemen ; they are all dressed up as shepherds and carry shepherds' pouches and crooks.

As the *Roman de la Rose* had done, because of its contrast with the chivalric ideal, so the bucolic ideal in its turn gave rise to an elegant quarrel. A number of variations had been made on the theme of Franc Gontier : every one had declared that he was sighing for a diet of cheese, apples, onions, brown bread and fresh water, for a woodcutter's work with its liberty and carelessness. But aristocratic life still looked very little like it and sceptics were aware of the inherent falsity of the factitious ideal. Villon unmasked it. In *Les contrediz Franc Gontier* he opposed to the idealized country man and his love under the roses, the fat canon, free from care, tasting good wines and the joys of love in a comfortable room, supplied with an ample hearth and a soft bed. The brown bread and the water of Franc Gontier ?

> " Tous les oyseaulx d'ici en Babiloine
> A tel escot une seule journée
> Ne me tiendroient, non une matinée." [1]

---

ment for your trouble Of guarding them well, and if you do not, You received this name in an evil hour.

[1] All the birds from here to Babylon With such a fare a single day Would not keep me, no not one morning.

CHAPTER XI

THE VISION OF DEATH

No other epoch has laid so much stress as the expiring Middle Ages on the thought of death. An everlasting call of *memento mori* resounds through life. Denis the Carthusian, in his *Directory of the Life of Nobles*, exhorts them : " And when going to bed at night, he should consider how, just as he now lies down himself, soon strange hands will lay his body in the grave." In earlier times, too, religion had insisted on the constant thought of death, but the pious treatises of these ages only reached those who had already turned away from the world. Since the thirteenth century, the popular preaching of the mendicant orders had made the eternal admonition to remember death swell into a sombre chorus ringing throughout the world. Towards the fifteenth century, a new means of inculcating the awful thought into all minds was added to the words of the preacher, namely, the popular woodcut. Now these two means of expression, sermons and woodcuts, both addressing themselves to the multitude and limited to crude effects, could only represent death in a simple and striking form. All that the meditations on death of the monks of yore had produced, was now condensed into a very primitive image. This vivid image, continually impressed upon all minds, had hardly assimilated more than a single element of the great complex of ideas relating to death, namely, the sense of the perishable nature of all things. It would seem, at times, as if the soul of the declining Middle Ages only succeeded in seeing death under this aspect.

The endless complaint of the frailty of all earthly glory was sung to various melodies. Three motifs may be distinguished. The first is expressed by the question : where are now all those who once filled the world with their splendour ?

The second motif dwells on the frightful spectacle of human beauty gone to decay. The third is the death-dance : death dragging along men of all conditions and ages.

Compared with the two others, the first of these themes is but a graceful and elegiac sigh. After having taken shape in Greek poetry, it was adopted by the Fathers, and pervaded the literature of all Christendom, and that of Islam also. Byron, too, used it in *Don Juan.* The Middle Ages cultivated it with special predilection. We find it in the heavy rhythm of the erudite poetry of the twelfth century :

> "Est ubi gloria nunc Babylonia ? nunc ubi dirus
> Nabugodonosor, et Darii vigor, illeque Cyrus ? . . .
> Nunc ubi Regulus ? aut ubi Romulus, aut ubi Remus ?
> Stat rosa pristina nomine, nomina nuda tenemus." [1]

Franciscan poetry of the thirteenth century (if the following lines are not of an older date) still preserves an echo of these rhyming hexameters :

> "Dic ubi Salomon, olim tam nobilis
> Vel Sampson ubi est, dux invincibilis,
> Et pulcher Absalon, vultu mirabilis,
> Aut dulcis Jonathas, multum amabilis ? " [2]

Deschamps composed at least four of his ballads on this theme. Gerson worked it out in a sermon ; Denis the Carthusian in his treatise, *De quatuor hominum novissimis* (on the four last things of man) ; Chastellain in a long poem entitled *Le Pas de la Mort.* Olivier de la Marche, in his *Parement et Triumphe des Dames* composed on it a lament over all the princesses who died in his time. Villon gives it a new accent of soft tenderness in his *Ballade des Dames du Temps jadis*, with the refrain :

> "Mais où sont lex neiges d'antan ? "

And then he sprinkles it with irony in the *Ballad of the*

[1] Where is now your glory, Babylon, where is now the terrible Nebuchadnezzar, and strong Darius and the famous Cyrus ? Where is now Regulus, or where Romulus, or where Remus ? The rose of yore is but a name, mere names are left to us.

[2] Say where is Solomon, once so noble, Or Samson where is he, the invincible chief, And fair Absalom of the wonderful face, Or sweet Jonathan, the most amiable ?

Lords by adding to the series of kings, popes and princes of his time the words :

"Helas ! et le bon roy d'Espaigne
Duquel je ne sçay pas le nom." [1]

However, the wistfulness of remembrance and the thought of frailty in itself do not satisfy the need of expressing, with violence, the shudder caused by death. The medieval soul demands a more concrete embodiment of the perishable : that of the putrefying corpse.

Ascetic meditation had, in all ages, dwelt on dust and worms. The treatises on the contempt of the world had, long since, evoked all the horrors of decomposition, but it is only towards the end of the fourteenth century that pictorial art, in its turn, seizes upon this motif. To render the horrible details of decomposition, a realistic force of expression was required, to which painting and sculpture only attained towards 1400. At the same time, the motif spread from ecclesiastical to popular literature. Until far into the sixteenth century, tombs are adorned with hideous images of a naked corpse with clenched hands and rigid feet, gaping mouth and bowels crawling with worms. The imagination of those times relished these horrors, without ever looking one stage further, to see how corruption perishes in its turn, and flowers grow where it lay.

A thought which so strongly attaches to the earthly side of death can hardly be called truly pious. It would rather seem a kind of spasmodic reaction against an excessive sensuality. In exhibiting the horrors awaiting all human beauty, already lurking below the surface of corporeal charms, these preachers of contempt for the world express, indeed, a very materialistic sentiment, namely, that all beauty and all happiness are worthless *because* they are bound to end soon. Renunciation founded on disgust does not spring from Christian wisdom.

It is noteworthy that the pious exhortations to think of death and the profane exhortations to make the most of youth almost meet. A painting in the monastery of the Celestines at Avignon, now destroyed, attributed by tradition

[1] Alas! and the good king of Spain, Whose name I do not know.

to the founder, King René himself, represented the body of a dead woman, standing, enveloped in a shroud, with her head dressed and worms gnawing her bowels. In the inscription at the foot of the picture the first lines read :

> " Une fois sur toute femme belle
> Mais par la mort suis devenu telle,
> Ma chair estoit très belle, fraische et tendre,
> Or, est-elle toute tournée en cendre.
> Mon corps estoit très plaisant et très gent,[1]
> Je me souloye souvent vestir de soye,
> Or en droict fault que toute nue je soys.
> Fourrée estois de gris et de menu vair,
> En grand palais me logeois à mon vueil,
> Or suis logée en ce petit cercueil.
> Ma chambre estoit de beaux tapis ornée,
> Or est d'aragnes ma fosse environnée." [2]

Here the *memento mori* still predominates. It tends imperceptibly to change into the quite worldly complaint of the woman who sees her charms fade, as in the following lines of the *Parement et Triumphe des Dames* by Olivier de la Marche.

> " Ces doulx regards, ces yeulx faiz pour plaisance,
> Pensez y bien, ilz perdront leur clarté,
> Nez et sourcilz, la bouche d'eloquence
> Se pourriront . . .
> Se vous vivez le droit cours de nature
> Dont LX ans est pour ung bien grant nombre,
> Vostre beaulté changera en laydure,
> Vostre santé en maladie obscure,
> Et ne ferez en ce monde que encombre.
> Se fille avez, vous luy serez ung umbre,
> Celle sera requise et demandée,
> Et de chascun la mère habandonnée." [3]

---

[1] It seems that two lines are missing after the lines 5 and 8.

[2] Once I was beautiful above all women But by death I became like this, My flesh was very beautiful, fresh and soft, Now it is altogether turned to ashes. My body was very pleasing and very pretty, I used frequently to dress in silk, Now I must rightly be quite nude. I was dressed in grey fur and miniver, I lived in a great palace as I wished, Now I am lodged in this little coffin. My room was adorned with fine tapestry, Now my grave is enveloped by cobwebs.

[3] These sweet looks, these eyes made for pleasance, Remember, they will lose their lustre, Nose and eyelashes, the eloquent mouth Will putrefy. . . . If you live your natural lifetime, Of which sixty years is a great

All pious purpose has disappeared in the ballads of Villon, where the old courtesan, " la belle heaulmière," calls to mind her irresistible beauty of former times and is deeply grieved at its sad decline.

> " Qu'est devenu ce front poly,
>   Ces cheveulx blons, sourcils voultiz,
>   Grant entrœil, le regart joly,
>   Dont prenoie les plus soubtilz ;
>   Ce beau nez droit, grant ne petiz,
>   Ces petites joinctes oreilles,
>   Menton fourchu, cler vis traictiz
>   Et ces belles levres vermeilles ?
>
> .   .   .   .
>
>   Le front ridé, les cheveux gris,
>   Les sourcilz cheuz, les yeuls estains. . . ." [1]

This inability to free oneself from the attachment to matter manifests itself in yet other forms. A result of the same sentiment is to be found in the extreme importance ascribed in the Middle Ages to the fact that the bodies of certain saints had never decayed—that of Saint Rosa of Viterbo, for example. The Assumption of the Holy Virgin exempting her body from earthly corruption was on that account regarded as the most precious of all graces. On various occasions attempts were made to retard decomposition. The features of the corpse of Pierre de Luxembourg were touched up with paint to preserve them intact until the burial. The body of a heretic preacher of the sect of the Turlupins, who died in prison, before sentence was passed, was preserved in lime for a fortnight, that it might be burned at the same time with a living heretical woman.

The importance attached to being buried in the soil of one's own country gave rise to usages which the Church had to

deal, Your beauty will change into ugliness, Your health into obscure malady, And you will only be in the way here below.   If you have a daughter, you will be a shadow to her, She will be in request and asked for, And the mother will be abandoned by all.

[1] What has become of this smooth forehead, Fair hair, curving eyelashes, Large space between the eyes, pretty looks, Wherewith I caught the most subtle ones That fine straight nose, neither large nor small, These tiny ears close to the head, The dimpled chin, well-shaped bright face, And those beautiful vermilion lips ? . . .   The forehead wrinkled, hair grey, The eyelashes come off, lack-lustre eyes. . . .

interdict strictly as being contrary to the Christian religion. In the twelfth and thirteenth centuries, when a prince or a person of rank died far from his country, the body was often cut up and boiled so as to extract the bones, which were sent home in a chest, whereas the rest was interred, not without ceremony, however, on the spot. Emperors, kings and bishops have undergone this strange operation. Pope Boniface VIII forbade it as *detestandae feritatis abusus, quam ex quodam more horribili nonnulli fideles improvide prosequuntur.*[1] Yet his successors sometimes granted dispensations. Numbers of Englishmen who fell in France in the Hundred Years' War enjoyed this privilege, notably Edward of York and the earl of Suffolk, who died at Agincourt; Henry V himself; William Glasdale, who perished at Orleans at the time of its relief; a nephew of Sir John Fastolfe, and others.

At the close of the Middle Ages the whole vision of death may be summed up in the word *macabre*, in its modern meaning. Of course, this meaning is the outcome of a long process. But the sentiment it embodies, of something gruesome and dismal, is precisely the conception of death which arose during the last centuries of the Middle Ages. This bizarre word appeared in French in the fourteenth century, under the form *macabré*, and, whatever may be its etymology, as a proper name. A line of the poet Jean Le Fèvre, " Je fis de Macabré la dance," which may be dated 1376, remains the birth-certificate of the word for us.

Towards 1400 the conception of death in art and literature took a spectral and fantastic shape. A new and vivid shudder was added to the great primitive horror of death. The macabre vision arose from deep psychological strata of fear ; religious thought at once reduced it to a means of moral exhortation. As such it was a great cultural idea, till in its turn it went out of fashion, lingering on in epitaphs and symbols in village cemeteries.

The idea of the death-dance is the central point of a whole group of connected conceptions. The priority belongs to the motif of the three dead and three living men, which is found

[1] An abuse of abominable savagery, practised by some of the faithful in a horrible way and inconsiderately.

in French literature from the thirteenth century onward.
Three young noblemen suddenly meet three hideous dead
men, who tell them of their past grandeur and warn them
of their own near end. Art soon took hold of this suggestive
theme. We can see it still in the striking frescoes of the
Campo santo of Pisa. The sculpture of the portal of the church
of the Innocents at Paris, which the duke of Berry had carved
in 1408, but which has not been preserved, represented the
same subject. Miniature painting and woodcuts spread it
broadcast.

The theme of the three dead and three living men
connects the horrible motif of putrefaction with that of the
death-dance. This theme, too, seems to have originated in
France, but it is unknown whether the pictorial representation
preceded the scenic or the reverse. The thesis of Monsieur
Emile Mâle, according to which the sculptural and pictorial
motifs of the fifteenth century were supposed as a rule to be
derived from dramatic representations, has not been able to
keep its ground, on critical examination. It may be, however,
that we should make an exception in favour of the death-
dance. Anyhow, the Dance of the Dead has been acted as
well as painted and engraved. The duke of Burgundy had
it performed in his mansion at Bruges in 1449. If we could
form an idea of the effect produced by such a dance, with
vague lights and shadows gliding over the moving figures,
we should no doubt be better able to understand the horror
inspired by the subject, than we are by the aid of the pictures
of Guyot Marchant or Holbein.

The woodcuts with which the Parisian printer, Guyot
Marchant, ornamented the first edition of the *Danse Macabré*
in 1485 were, very probably, imitated from the most celebrated
of these painted death-dances, namely, that which, since 1424,
covered the walls of the cloister of the churchyard of the
Innocents at Paris. The stanzas printed by Marchant were
those written under these mural paintings ; perhaps they
even hail back to the lost poetry of Jean Le Fèvre, who in
his turn seems to have followed a Latin model. The woodcuts of 1485 can give but a feeble impression of the paintings
of the Innocents, of which they are not exact copies, as the
costumes prove. To have a notion of the effect of these

THE BISHOP AND THE SQUIRE.

FROM THE DEATH DANCE, BY GUYOT MARCHANT, PARIS, 1485.

THE MADONNA OF MELUN. BY JEHAN FOUCQUET.

frescoes, one should rather look at the mural paintings of the church of La Chaise-Dieu, where the unfinished condition of the work heightens the spectral effect.

The dancing person whom we see coming back forty times to lead away the living, originally does not represent Death itself, but a corpse : the living man such as he will presently be. In the stanzas the dancer is called " the dead man " or " the dead woman." It is a dance of the dead and not of Death ; the researches of Monsieur Gédéon Huet have made it probable that the primitive subject was a roundabout dance of dead people, come forth from their graves, a theme which Goethe revived in his *Totentanz*. The indefatigable dancer is the living man himself in his future shape, a frightful double of his person. " It is yourself," said the horrible vision to each of the spectators. It is only towards the end of the century that the figure of the great dancer, of a corpse with hollow and fleshless body, becomes a skeleton, as Holbein depicts it. Death in person has then replaced the individual dead man.

While it reminded the spectators of the frailty and the vanity of earthly things, the death-dance at the same time preached social equality as the Middle Ages understood it, Death levelling the various ranks and professions. At first only men appeared in the picture. The success of his publication, however, suggested to Guyot the idea of a dance macabre of women. Martial d'Auvergne wrote the poetry ; an unknown artist, without equalling his model, completed the pictures by a series of feminine figures dragged along by a corpse. Now it was impossible to enumerate forty dignities and professions of women. After the queen, the abbess, the nun, the saleswoman, the nurse, and a few others, it was necessary to fall back on the different states of feminine life : the virgin, the beloved, the bride, the woman newly married, the woman with child. And here the sensual note reappears, to which we referred above. In lamenting the frailty of the lives of women, it is still the briefness of joy that is deplored, and with the grave tone of the *memento mori* is mixed the regret for lost beauty.

Nothing betrays more clearly the excessive fear of death felt in the Middle Ages than the popular belief, then widely spread, according to which Lazarus, after his resurrection, lived in continual misery and horror at the thought that he should have again to pass through the gate of death. If the just had so much to fear, how could the sinner soothe himself ? And then what motif was more poignant than the calling up of the agony of death ? It appeared under two traditional forms : the *Ars moriendi* and the *Quator hominum novissima*, that is, the four last experiences awaiting man, of which death was the first. These two subjects were largely propagated in the fifteenth century by the printing-press and by engravings. The Art of Dying, as well as the Last Four Things, comprised a description of the agony of death, in which it is easy to recognize a model supplied by the ecclesiastical literature of former centuries.

Chastellain, in a long-winded poem, *Le Pas de la Mort*, has assembled all the above motifs ; he gives successively the image of putrefaction—the lament : Where are the great ones of the earth ?—an outline of a death-dance—and the art of dying. Being prolix and heavy, he needs a great many lines to express what Villon presents in half a stanza. But in comparing them we recognize their common model. Chastellain writes :

> " Il n'a membre ne facture
> Qui ne sente sa pourreture.
> Avant que l'esperit soit hors,
> Le cœur qui veult crevier au corps
> Haulce et soulière la poitrine
> Qui se veult joindre à son eschine.
> —La face est tainte et apalie,
> Et les yeux treilliés en la teste.
> La parole luy est faillie,
> Car la langue au palais se lie.
> Le poulx tressault et sy halette.
>
> . . . .
>
> Les os desjoindent à tous lez ;
> Il n'a nerf qu'au rompre ne tende." [1]

---

[1] There is not a limb nor a form, Which does not smell of putrefaction. Before the soul is outside, The heart which wants to burst in the body Raises and lifts the chest Which nearly touches the backbone.—The face is discoloured and pale, And the eyes veiled in the head. Speech fails him, For the tongue cleaves to the palate. The pulse trembles and he pants. . . . The bones are disjointed on all sides ; There is not a tendon which does not stretch as to burst.

And Villon :

> " La mort le fait fremir, pallir,
> Le nez courber, les vaines tendre,
> Le col enfler, la chair mollir,
> Joinctes et nerfs croistre et estendre. . . ." [1]

And again the sensual thought mingles with it :

> " Corps femenin, qui tant es tendre,
> Poly, souef, si precieux,
> Te fauldra il ces maulx attendre ?
> Oy, ou tout vif aller es cieulx." [2]

Nowhere else were all the images tending to evoke the horror of death assembled so strikingly as in the churchyard of the Innocents at Paris. There the medieval soul, fond of a religious shudder, could take its fill of the horrible. Above all other saints, the remembrance of the saints of that spot, and of their bloody and pitiful martyrdom, was fitted to awake the crude compassion which was dear to the epoch. The fifteenth century honoured the Holy Innocents with special veneration. Louis XI presented to the church " a whole Innocent," encased in a crystal shrine. The cemetery was preferred to every other place of burial. A bishop of Paris had a little of the earth of the churchyard of the Innocents put into his grave, as he could not be laid there. The poor and the rich were interred without distinction. They did not rest there long, for the cemetery was used so much, twenty parishes having a right of burial there, that it was necessary, in order to make room, to dig up the bones and sell the tombstones after a very short time. It was believed that in this earth a human body was decomposed to the bone in nine days. Skulls and bones were heaped up in charnel-houses along the cloisters enclosing the ground on three sides, and lay there open to the eye by thousands, preaching to all the lesson of equality. The noble Boucicaut, among others, had contributed to the construction of these " fine charnel-houses." Under the cloisters the death-dance exhibited its

---

[1] Death makes him shudder and turn pale, The nose to curve, the veins to swell, The neck to inflate, the flesh to soften, Joints and tendons to grow and swell.

[2] O female body, which is so soft, Smooth, suave, precious, Do these evils await you ? Yes, or you must go to heaven quite alive.

images and its stanzas. No place was better suited to the simian figure of grinning death, dragging along pope and emperor, monk and fool. The duke of Berry, who wished to be buried there, had the history of the three dead and the three living men carved at the portal of the church. A century later, this exhibition of funeral symbols was completed by a large statue of Death, now in the Louvre, and the only remnant of it all.

Such was the place which the Parisians of the fifteenth century frequented as a sort of lugubrious counterpart of the Palais Royal of 1789. Day after day, crowds of people walked under the cloisters, looking at the figures and reading the simple verses, which reminded them of the approaching end. In spite of the incessant burials and exhumations going on there, it was a public lounge and a rendezvous. Shops were established before the charnel-houses and prostitutes strolled under the cloisters. A female recluse was immured on one of the sides of the church. Friars came to preach and processions were drawn up there. A procession of children only (12,500 strong, thinks the Burgher of Paris) assembled there, with tapers in their hands, to carry an Innocent to Notre Dame and back to the churchyard. Even feasts were given there. To such an extent had the horrible become familiar.

The desire to invent a visible image of all that appertained to death entailed the neglecting of all those aspects of it which were not suited to direct representation. Thus the cruder conceptions of death, and these only, impressed themselves continually on the minds. The macabre vision does not represent the emotions of tenderness or of consolation. The elegiac note is wanting altogether. At bottom the macabre sentiment is self-seeking and earthly. It is hardly the absence of the departed dear ones that is deplored; it is the fear of one's own death, and this only seen as the worst of evils. Neither the conception of death the consoler, nor that of rest long wished for, of the end of suffering, of the task performed or interrupted, have a share in the funeral sentiment of that epoch. The soul of the Middle Ages did not know the " divine depth of sorrow." Or, rather, it knew it only in connection with the Passion of Christ.

In all these sombre lamentations about death the accents of true tenderness are extremely rare. They could, however, hardly be wanting in relation to the death of children. And, indeed, Martial d'Auvergne, in his death-dance of women, makes the little girl, when led away by death, say to her mother : " Take good care of my doll, my knuckle-bones and my fine dress." But this touching note is only heard exceptionally. The literature of the epoch knew child-life so little ! When Antoine de la Salle, in *Le Reconfort de Madame du Fresne*, wishes to console a mother for the death of her twelve-years-old son, he can think of nothing better than citing a still more cruel loss : the heart-rending case of a boy given as a hostage and put to death. To overcome grief, the only advice he can offer is to abstain from all earthly attachments. A doctrinaire and dry consolation ! La Salle, however, adds a second short story. It is a version of the popular tale of the dead child, who came back to beg its mother to weep no more, that its shroud might dry. And here suddenly from this simple story—not of his own invention—there arises a poetical tenderness and beneficent wisdom, which we look for in vain in the thousands of voices repeating in various tones the awful *memento mori*. Folk-tale and folk-song, no doubt, in these ages preserved many sentiments which higher literature hardly knew.

The dominant thought, as expressed in the literature, both ecclesiastical and lay, of that period, hardly knew anything with regard to death but these two extremes : lamentation about the briefness of all earthly glory, and jubilation over the salvation of the soul. All that lay between—pity, resignation, longing, consolation—remained unexpressed and was, so to say, absorbed by the too much accentuated and too vivid representation of Death hideous and threatening. Living emotion stiffens amid the abused imagery of skeletons and worms.

CHAPTER XII

RELIGIOUS THOUGHT CRYSTALLIZING INTO IMAGES

Towards the end of the Middle Ages two factors dominate religious life : the extreme saturation of the religious atmosphere, and a marked tendency of thought to embody itself in images.

Individual and social life, in all their manifestations, are imbued with the conceptions of faith. There is not an object nor an action, however trivial, that is not constantly correlated with Christ or salvation. All thinking tends to religious interpretation of individual things ; there is an enormous unfolding of religion in daily life. This spiritual wakefulness, however, results in a dangerous state of tension, for the presupposed transcendental feelings are sometimes dormant, and whenever this is the case, all that is meant to stimulate spiritual consciousness is reduced to appalling commonplace profanity, to a startling worldliness in other-worldly guise. Only saints are capable of an attitude of mind in which the transcendental faculties are never in abeyance.

The spirit of the Middle Ages, still plastic and naïve, longs to give concrete shape to every conception. Every thought seeks expression in an image, but in this image it solidifies and becomes rigid. By this tendency to embodiment in visible forms all holy concepts are constantly exposed to the danger of hardening into mere externalism. For in assuming a definite figurative shape thought loses its ethereal and vague qualities, and pious feeling is apt to resolve itself in the image.

Even in the case of a sublime mystic, like Henry Suso, the craving for hallowing every action of daily life verges in our eyes on the ridiculous. He is sublime when, following the usages of profane love, he celebrates New Year's Day and May Day by offering a wreath and a song to his betrothed,

Eternal Wisdom, or when, out of reverence for the Holy Virgin, he renders homage to all womankind and walks in the mud to let a beggar woman pass. But what are we to think of what follows ? At table Suso eats three-quarters of an apple in the name of the Trinity and the remaining quarter in commemoration of " the love with which the heavenly Mother gave her tender child Jesus an apple to eat " ; and for this reason he eats the last quarter with the paring, as little boys do not peel their apples. After Christmas he does not eat it, for then the infant Jesus was too young to eat apples. He drinks in five draughts because of the five wounds of the Lord, but as blood and water flowed from the side of Christ, he takes his last draught twice. This is, indeed, pushing the sanctification of life to extremes.

In so far as it concerns individual piety, this tendency to apply religious conceptions to all things and at all times is a deep source of saintly life. As a cultural phenomenon this same tendency harbours grave dangers. Religion penetrating all relations in life means a constant blending of the spheres of holy and of profane thought. Holy things will become too common to be deeply felt. The endless growth of observances, images, religious interpretations, signifies an augmentation in quantity at which serious divines grew alarmed, as they feared the quality would deteriorate proportionately. The warning which we find recurring in all reformist writings of the time of the schism and of the councils is—the Church is being overloaded.

Pierre d'Ailly, in condemning the novelties which were incessantly introduced into the liturgy and the sphere of belief, is less concerned about the piety of their character than about the steady increase itself. The signs of the ever-ready divine grace multiplied endlessly ; a host of special benedictions sprang up side by side with the sacraments ; in addition to relics we find amulets ; the bizarre gallery of saints became ever more numerous and variegated. However emphatically divines insisted upon the difference between sacraments and *sacramentalia*, the people would still confound them. Gerson tells how he met a man at Auxerre, who maintained that All Fools' Day was as sacred as the day of the Virgin's Conception. Nicolas de Clemanges wrote a treatise, *De novis festivitatibus non instituendis,* in which he denounced the apocryphal nature of some among these new institutions. Pierre d'Ailly, in *De Reformatione,* deplores the ever-increasing number of churches, of festivals, of saints, of holy-days ; he protests against the multitude of images and paintings, the prolixity of the Service, against the introduction of new hymns and prayers, against the augmentation of vigils and fasts. In short, what alarms him is the evil of superfluity.

There are too many religious orders, says d'Ailly, and this leads to a diversity of usages, to exclusiveness and rivalry, to pride and vanity. In particular he desired to impose restrictions on the mendicant orders, whose social utility he questions : they live to the detriment of the inmates of leper houses and hospitals, and other really poor and wretched people, who are truly entitled to beg (*ac aliis vere pauperibus et miserabilibus indigentibus quibus convenit jus et verus titulus mendicandi*). Let the sellers of indulgences be banished from the Church, which they soil with their lies and make ridiculous. Convents are built on all sides, but sufficient funds are lacking. Where is this to lead ?

Pierre d'Ailly does not question the holy and pious character of all these practices in themselves, he only deplores their endless multiplication ; he sees the Church weighed down under the load of particulars.

Religious customs tended to multiply in an almost mechanical way. A special office was instituted for every detail of the worship of the Virgin Mary. There were particular masses, afterwards abolished by the Church, in honour of the piety of Mary, of her seven sorrows, of all her festivals taken collectively, of her sisters—the two other Marys—of the archangel Gabriel, of all the saints of our Lord's genealogy. A curious example of this spontaneous accretion of religious usage is found in the weekly observance of Innocents' Day. The 28th of December, the day of the massacre at Bethlehem, was taken to be ill-omened. This belief was the origin of a custom, widely spread during the fifteenth century, of considering as a black-letter day, all the year through, the day of the week on which the preceding Innocents' Day fell. Consequently, there was one day in every week on which people abstained from setting out upon a journey and beginning a

new task, and this day was called Innocents' Day, like the
festival itself. Louis XI observed this usage scrupulously.
The coronation of Edward IV of England was repeated, as it
had taken place on a Sunday, because the 28th of December
of the previous year had been a Sunday too. René de Lorraine
had to give up his plan of fighting a battle on the 17th of
October, 1476, as his lansquenets refused to encounter the
enemy " on Innocents' Day."

This belief, of which we find some traces appearing in England as late as the eighteenth century, called forth a treatise
from Gerson against superstition in general. His penetrating
mind had realized some of the danger with which these excres-
cences of the creed menaced the purity of religious thought.
He was aware of their psychological basis ; according to him,
these beliefs proceed *ex sola hominum phantasiatione et melan-
cholica imaginatione* ; it is a disorder of the imagination caused
by some lesion of the brain, which in its turn is due to diabolic
illusions.

The Church was constantly on her guard lest dogmatic
truth should be confounded with this mass of facile beliefs, and
lest the exuberance of popular fancy should degrade God. But
was she able to stand against this strong need of giving a concrete form to all the emotions accompanying religious thought ?
It was an irresistible tendency to reduce the infinite to the
finite, to disintegrate all mystery. The highest mysteries of
the creed became covered with a crust of superficial piety.
Even the profound faith in the eucharist expands into childish
beliefs—for instance, that one cannot go blind or have a stroke
of apoplexy on a day on which one has heard mass, or that one
does not grow older during the time spent in attending mass.
While herself offering so much food to the popular imagination,
the Church could not claim to keep that imagination within
the limits of a healthy and vigorous piety.

In this respect the case of Gerson is characteristic. He
composed a treatise, *Contra vanam curiositatem*, by which he
means the spirit of research which desires to scrutinize the
secrets of nature. But whilst protesting against it, he himself
becomes guilty of a curiosity which to us seems out of place
and deplorable. Gerson was the great promoter of the adoration of Saint Joseph. His veneration for this saint makes

him desirous of learning all that concerns him. He routs out all particulars of the married life of Joseph : his continence, his age, the way in which he learned of the Virgin's pregnancy. He is indignant at the caricature of a drudging and ridiculous Joseph, which the arts were inclined to make of him. In another passage Gerson indulges in a speculation on the bodily constitution of Saint John the Baptist : *Semen igitur materiale ex qua corpus compaginandum erat, nec durum nimis nec rursus fluidum abundantius fuit.*

Whether the Virgin had taken an active part in the supernatural conception, or, again, whether the body of Christ would have decomposed, if it had not been for the resurrection, were what the popular preacher Olivier Maillard called " beautiful theological questions " to discuss before his auditors. The mixture of theological and embryological speculation to which the controversy about the immaculate conception of the Virgin gave rise shocked the minds of that period so little that grave divines did not scruple to treat the subject from the pulpit.

This familiarity with sacred things is, on the one hand, a sign of deep and ingenuous faith ; on the other, it entails irreverence whenever mental contact with the infinite fails. Curiosity, ingenuous though it be, leads to profanation. In the fifteenth century people used to keep statuettes of the Virgin, of which the body opened and showed the Trinity within. The inventory of the treasure of the dukes of Burgundy makes mention of one made of gold inlaid with gems. Gerson saw one in the Carmelite monastery at Paris ; he blames the brethren for it, not, however, because such a coarse picture of the miracle shocked him as irreverent, but because of the heresy of representing the Trinity as the fruit of Mary.

All life was saturated with religion to such an extent that the people were in constant danger of losing sight of the distinction between things spiritual and things temporal. If, on the one hand, all details of ordinary life may be raised to a sacred level, on the other hand, all that is holy sinks to the commonplace, by the fact of being blended with everyday life. In the Middle Ages the demarcation of the sphere of religious thought and that of worldly concerns was nearly obliterated. It occasionally happened that indulgences figured among the prizes of a lottery. When a prince was making a solemn entry, the altars at the corners of the streets, loaded with the precious reliquaries of the town and served by prelates, might be seen alternating with dumb shows of pagan goddesses or comic allegories.

Nothing is more characteristic in this respect than the fact of there being hardly any difference between the musical character of profane and sacred melodies. Till late in the sixteenth century profane melodies might be used indiscriminately for sacred use, and sacred for profane. It is notorious that Guillaume Dufay and others composed masses to the theme of love-songs, such as " Tant je me déduis,"[1] " Se la face ay pale,"[2] " L'omme armé."[3] There was a constant interchange of religious and profane terms. No one felt offended by hearing the Day of Judgment compared to a settling of accounts, as in the verses formerly written over the door of the audit office at Lille.

> "Lors ouvrira, au son de buysine
> Sa générale et grant chambre des comptes."[4]

A tournament, on the other hand, is called " des armes grantdisime pardon " (the great indulgence conferred by arms) as if it were a pilgrimage. By a chance coincidence the words *mysterium* and *ministerium* were blended in French into the form " mistère," and this homonymy must have helped to efface the true sense of the word " mystery " in everyday parlance, because even the most commonplace things might be called " mistère."

While religious symbolism represented the realities of nature and history as symbols or emblems of salvation, on the other hand religious metaphors were borrowed to express profane sentiments. People in the Middle Ages, standing in awe of royalty, do not shrink from using the language of adoration in praising princes. In the lawsuit about the murder of Louis of Orleans, the counsel for the defence makes the shade of the duke say to his son : " Look at my wounds and observe that

---

[1] So much I enjoy myself.
[2] If my face is pale.   [3] The armed man.
[4] Then to the sound of the trumpet God shall open His general and grand audit office.

five of them are particularly cruel and mortal." The bishop of Chalons, Jean Germain, in his *Liber de virtutibus Philippi ducis Burgundiae*, in his turn does not scruple to compare the victim of Montereau to the Lamb. The Emperor Frederick III, when sending his son Maximilian to the Low Countries to marry Mary of Burgundy, is compared by Molinet to God the Father. The same author makes the people of Brussels say, when they wept with tenderness on seeing the emperor entering their town with Maximilian and Philip le Beau: "Behold the image of the Trinity, the Father, the Son and the Holy Ghost." He offers a wreath of flowers to Mary of Burgundy, a worthy image of Our Lady, " secluse la virginité." [1] "Non point que je veuille déifier les princes!" [2] Molinet adds.

Although we may consider such formulæ of adulation empty phrases, they show none the less the depreciation of sacred imagery resulting from its hackneyed use. We can hardly blame a court poet, when Gerson himself ascribes to the royal auditors of his sermons guardian angels of a higher rank in the celestial hierarchy than those of other men.

The step from familiarity to irreverence is taken when religious terms are applied to erotic relations. The subject has been dealt with above. The author of the *Quinze Joyes de Mariage* chose his title to accord with the joys of the Virgin. The defender of the *Roman de la Rose* used sacred terms to designate the *partes corporis inhonestas et peccata immunda atque turpia*. No instance of this dangerous association of religious with amatory sentiments could be more striking than the Madonna ascribed to Foucquet, making part of a diptych which was formerly preserved at Melun and is now partly at Antwerp and partly at Berlin ; Antwerp possessing the Madonna and Berlin the panel representing the donor, Etienne Chevalier, the king's treasurer, together with Saint Stephen. In the seventeenth century Denis Godefroy noted down a tradition, then already old, according to which the Madonna had the features of Agnès Sorel, the royal mistress, for whom Chevalier felt a passion that he did not trouble to conceal. However this may be, the Madonna is, in fact, represented here according to the canons of contemporary fashion : there is the bulging

[1] Save the virginity.   [2] Not that I want to deify princes.

shaven forehead, the rounded breasts, placed high and wide apart, the high and slender waist. The bizarre inscrutable expression of the Madonna's face, the red and blue cherubim surrounding her, all contribute to give this painting an air of decadent impiety in spite of the stalwart figure of the donor. Godefroy observed on the large frame of blue velvet E's done in pearls linked by love-knots of gold and silver thread. There is a flavour of blasphemous boldness about the whole, unsurpassed by any artist of the Renaissance.

The irreverence of daily religious practice was almost unbounded. Choristers, when chanting mass, did not scruple to sing the words of the profane songs that had served as a theme for the composition : *baisez-moi, rouges nez.*[1]

A startling piece of impudence is recorded of the father of the Frisian humanist Rodolph, Agricola, who received the news that his concubine had given birth to a son on the very day when he was elected abbot. " To-day I have twice become a father. God's blessing on it ! " said he.

At the end of the fourteenth century people took the increasing irreverence to be an evil of recent date, which, indeed, is a common phenomenon at all times. Deschamps deplores it in the following lines :

> " On souloit estre ou temps passé
> En l'église benignement,
> A genoux en humilité
> Delez l'autel moult closement,
> Tout nu le chief piteusement,
> Maiz au jour d'uy, si come beste,
> On vient à l'autel bien souvent
> Chaperon et chapel en teste." [2]

On festal days, says Nicolas de Clemanges, few people go to mass. They do not stay till the end, and are content with touching the holy water, bowing before Our Lady, or kissing the image of some saint. If they wait for the elevation of the Host, they pride themselves upon it, as if they had conferred a

---

[1] " Kiss me," " Red noses."

[2] In bygone times people used to be Gentle in church, On their knees in humility Close beside the altar, With meekly uncovered head, But at present, like beasts, They too often come to the altar With hood and hat on their heads.

benefit on Christ. At matins and vespers the priest and his
assistant are the only persons present. The squire of the village
makes the priest wait to begin mass till he and his wife have
risen and dressed. The most sacred festivals, even Christmas
night, says Gerson, are passed in debauchery, playing at
cards, swearing and blaspheming. When the people are
admonished, they plead the example of the nobility and the
clergy, who behave in like manner with impunity. Vigils
likewise, says Clemanges, are kept with lascivious songs and
dances, even in church ; priests set the example by dicing as they
watch. It may be said that moralists paint things in too dark
colours ; but in the accounts of Strassburg we find a yearly
gift of 1,100 litres of wine granted by the council to those who
" watched in prayer " in church during the night of Saint
Adolphus.

Denis the Carthusian wrote a treatise, *De modo agendi processiones*, at the request of an alderman, who asked him how one
might remedy the dissoluteness and debauchery to which the
annual procession, in which a greatly venerated relic was borne,
gave rise. " How are we to put a stop to this ? " asks the alderman. " You may be sure that the town council will not easily
be persuaded to abolish it, for the procession brings large
profits to the town, because of all the people who have to be
fed and lodged. Besides, custom will have it so." " Alas, yes,"
sighs Denis ; " he knows too well how processions were disgraced
by ribaldry, mockery and drinking." A most vivid picture of
this evil is found in Chastellain's description of the degradation
into which the procession of the citizens of Ghent, with the
shrine of Saint Liévin, to Houthem, had fallen. Formerly,
he says, the notabilities were in the habit of carrying the holy
body " with great and deep solemnity and reverence " ; at
present there is only " a mob of roughs, and boys of bad
character " ; they carry it singing and yelling, " with a hundred
thousand gibes, and all are drunk." They are armed, " and
commit many offences where they pass, as if they were let
loose and unchained ; that day everything appears to be given
up to them under the pretext of the body they carry."

We have already mentioned how much disturbance was
caused during church services by people vying with each other
in politeness. The usage of making a trysting-place of the

church by young men and young women was so universal that only moralists were scandalized by it. The virtuous Christine de Pisan makes a lover say in all simplicity :

> "Se souvent vais ou moustier,
> C'est tout pour veoir la belle
> Fresche comme rose nouvelle." [1]

The Church suffered more serious profanation than the little love services of a young man who offered his fair one the " pax," or knelt by her side. According to the preacher Menot, prostitutes had the effrontery to come there in search of customers. Gerson tells that even in the churches and on festival days obscene pictures were sold *tanquam idola Belphegor*, which corrupted the young, while sermons were ineffective to remedy this evil.

As to pilgrimages, moralists and satirists are of one mind ; people often go " pour folle plaisance." The Chevalier de la Tour Landry naïvely classes them with profane pleasures, and he entitles one of his chapters, " Of those who are fond of going to jousts and on pilgrimages."

On festal days, exclaims Nicolas de Clemanges, people go to visit distant churches, not so much to redeem a pledge of pilgrimage as to give themselves up to pleasure. Pilgrimages are the occasions of all kinds of debauchery ; procuresses are always found there, people come for amorous purposes. It is a common incident in the *Quinze Joyes de Mariage*; the young wife, who wants a change, makes her husband believe that the baby is ill, because she has not yet accomplished her vow of pilgrimage, made during her confinement. The marriage of Charles VI with Isabella of Bavaria was preceded by a pilgrimage. It is far from surprising that the serious followers of the *devotio moderna* called the utility of pilgrimages in question. Those who often go on pilgrimages, says Thomas à Kempis, rarely become saints. One of his friends, Frederick of Heilo, wrote a special treatise, *Contra peregrinantes*.

The excesses and abuses resulting from an extreme familiarity with things holy, as well as the insolent mingling of pleasure with religion, are generally characteristic of periods

[1] If I often go to church, It is all for seeing the fair one Fresh as a new-blown rose.

of unshaken faith and of a deeply religious culture. The same
people who in their daily life mechanically follow the routine
of a rather degraded sort of worship will be capable of rising
suddenly, at the ardent word of a preaching monk, to unparal-
leled heights of religious emotion. Even the stupid sin of
blasphemy has its roots in a profound faith. It is a sort of
perverted act of faith, affirming the omnipresence of God and
His intervention in the minutest concerns. Only the idea of
really daring Heaven gives blasphemy its sinful charm. As
soon as an oath loses its character of an invocation of God,
the habit of swearing changes its nature and becomes mere
coarseness. At the end of the Middle Ages blasphemy is
still a sort of daring diversion which belongs to the nobility.
"What!" says the nobleman to the peasant in a treatise
by Gerson, "you give your soul to the devil, you deny God
without being noble?" Deschamps, on his part, notices
that the habit of swearing tends to descend to people of low
estate.

> "Si chétif n'y a qui ne die :
> Je renie Dieu et sa mère." [1]

People make a pastime of coining new and ingenious oaths,
says Gerson : he who excels in this impious art is honoured as
a master. Deschamps tells us that all France swore first after
the Gascon and the English fashion, next after the Breton,
and finally after the Burgundian. He composed two ballads
in succession made up of all the oaths then in vogue strung
together, and ended with a pious phrase. The Burgundian
oath was the worst of all. It was, *Je renie Dieu* (I deny
God), which was softened down to *Je renie de bottes* (boots).
The Burgundians had the reputation of being abominable
swearers ; for the rest, says Gerson, the whole of France, for
all her Christianity, suffers more than any other country from
the effects of this horrible sin, which causes pestilence, war and
famine. Even monks were guilty of mild swearing. Gerson
and d'Ailly expressly call upon the authorities to combat the
evil by renewing the strict regulations everywhere, but imposing light penalties which may be really exacted. And a
royal decree of 1397, in fact, re-established the old ones of 1269

---

[1] There is none so mean but says, I deny God and His mother.

and 1347, but unfortunately also renewed the old penalties of lip-slitting and cutting out of tongues, which bore witness, it is true, to a holy horror of blasphemy, but which it was not possible to enforce. In the margin of the register containing the ordinance, someone has noted : " At present, 1411, all these oaths are in general use throughout the kingdom without being punished."

Gerson, with his long experience as a confessor, knew the psychological nature of the sin of blasphemy very well. On the one hand, he says, there are the habitual swearers, who, though culpable, are not perjurers, as it is not their intention to take an oath. On the other, we find young men of a pure and simple nature who are irresistibly tempted to blaspheme and to deny God. Their case reminds us of John Bunyan's, whose disease took the form of " a propensity to utter blasphemy, and especially to renounce his share in the benefits of the redemption." Gerson counsels these young men to give themselves up less to the contemplation of God and the saints, as they lack the mental strength required.

It is impossible to draw the line of demarcation between an ingenuous familiarity and conscious infidelity. As early as the fifteenth century people liked to show themselves *esprits forts* and to deride piety in others. The word " papelard," meaning a hypocrite, was in frequent use with lay writers of the time. " De jeune angelot vieux diable " (a young saint makes an old devil), said the proverb, or, in solemn Latin metre, *Angelicus juvenis senibus sathanizat in annis.* " It is by such sayings," Gerson exclaims, " that youth is perverted. A brazen face, scurrilous language and curses, immodest looks and gestures, are praised in children. Well, what is to be expected in old age of a *sathanizing* youth ? "

The people, he says, do not know how to steer a middle course between overt unbelief and the foolish credulity, of which the clergy themselves set the example. They give credence to all revelations and prophecies, which are often but fancies of diseased people or lunatics, and yet when a serious divine, who has been honoured by genuine revelations, is occasionally mistaken, he is called impostor and " papelard," and the people henceforth refuse to listen to any divine because all are considered hypocrites.

We not unfrequently find individual expressions of avowed unbelief. " Beaux seigneurs," says Captain Bétisac to his comrades when about to die, " I have attended to my spiritual concerns and, in my conscience, I believe I have greatly angered God, having for a long time already erred against the faith, and I cannot believe a word about the Trinity, nor that the Son of God has humbled Himself to such an extent as to come down from Heaven into the carnal body of a woman ; and I believe and say that when we die there is no such thing as a soul. . . . I have held this opinion ever since I became self-conscious, and I shall hold it till the end." The provost of Paris, Hugues Aubriot, is a violent hater of the clergy ; he does not believe in the sacrament of the altar, he makes a mock of it ; he does not keep Easter, he does not go to confession. Jacques du Clercq relates that several noblemen, in full possession of their faculties, refused extreme unction. Perhaps we should regard these isolated cases of unbelief less as wilful heresy than as a spontaneous reaction against the incessant and pressing call of the faith, arising from a culture overcharged with religious images and concepts. In any case, they should not be confounded either with the literary and superficial paganism of the Renaissance, nor with the prudent epicurean-ism of some aristocratic circles from the thirteenth century downward, nor, above all, with the passionate negation of ignorant heretics who had passed the boundary-line between mysticism and pantheism.

The naïve religious conscience of the multitude had no need of intellectual proofs in matters of faith. The mere presence of a visible image of things holy sufficed to establish their truth. No doubts intervened between the sight of all those pictures and statues—the persons of the Trinity, the flames of hell, the innumerable saints—and belief in their reality. All these conceptions became matters of faith in the most direct manner ; they passed straight from the state of images to that of convictions, taking root in the mind as pictures clearly outlined and vividly coloured, possessing all the reality claimed for them by the Church, and even a little more.

Now, when faith is too directly connected with a pictured representation of doctrine, it runs the risk of no longer making

qualitative distinctions between the nature and the degree of
sanctity of the different elements of religion. The image by
itself does not teach the faithful that one should adore God and
only venerate the saints. Its psychological function is limited
to creating a deep conviction of reality and a lively feeling of
respect. It therefore became the task of the Church to warn
incessantly against want of discrimination in this respect, and
to preserve the purity of doctrine by explaining precisely
what the image stood for. In no other sphere was the danger
of luxuriance of religious thought caused by a vivid imagination more obvious.

Now, the Church did not fail to teach that all honours
rendered to the saints, to relics, to holy places, should have
God for their object. Although the prohibition of images in
the second commandment of the Decalogue was abrogated by
the new law, or limited to God the Father alone, the Church
purposed, nevertheless, to maintain intact the principle of *non
adorabis ea neque coles* : Images were only meant to show simple-
minded people what to believe. They are the books of the
illiterate, says Clemanges ; a thought which Villon has expressed
in the touching lines which he puts into his mother's mouth :

> " Femme je suis pourette et ancienne,
>   Qui riens ne sçai ; oncques lettre ne leuz ;
>   Au moustier voy dont suis paroissienne
>   Paradis paint, où sont harpes et luz,
>   Et ung enfer où dampnez sont boulluz :
>   L'ung me fait paour, l'autre joye et liesse . . ." [1]

The medieval Church was, however, rather heedless of the
danger of a deterioration of the faith caused by the popular
imagination roaming unchecked in the sphere of hagiology.
An abundance of pictorial fancy, after all, furnished to the
simple mind quite as much matter for deviating from pure
doctrine as any personal interpretation of Holy Scripture. It
is remarkable that the Church, so scrupulous in dogmatic
matters, should have been so confiding and indulgent towards
those who, sinning out of ignorance, rendered more homage

---

[1] I am a poor old woman who knows nothing ; I never could read. In
my parish church I see Paradise painted, where are harps and lutes, And a
hell, where the damned are boiled. The one frightens me, the other brings
joy and mirth.

to images than was lawful. It suffices, says Gerson, that they
meant to do as the Church requires.

Thus towards the end of the Middle Ages an ultra-realistic
conception of all that related to the saints may be noticed in the
popular faith. The saints had become so real and such familiar
characters of current religion that they became bound up with
all the more superficial religious impulses. While profound
devotion still centred on Christ and His mother, quite a host
of artless beliefs and fancies clustered about the saints. Everything contributed to make them familiar and life-like. They
were dressed like the people themselves. Every day one met
" Messires " Saint Roch and Saint James in the persons of
living plague patients and pilgrims. Down to the Renaissance
the costume of the saints always followed the fashion of the
times. Only then did Sacred Art, by arraying the saints in
classical draperies, withdraw them from the popular imagination and place them in a sphere where the fancy of the
multitude could no longer contaminate the doctrine in its
purity.

The distinctly corporeal conception of the saints was accentuated by the veneration of their relics, not only permitted by
the Church but forming an integral part of religion. It was
inevitable that this pious attachment to material things should
draw all hagiolatry into a sphere of crude and primitive ideas,
and lead to surprising extremes. In the matter of relics the
deep and straightforward faith of the Middle Ages was never
afraid of disillusionment or profanation through handling holy
things coarsely. The spirit of the fifteenth century did not
differ much from that of the Umbrian peasants, who, about
the year 1000, wished to kill Saint Romuald, the hermit, in
order to make sure of his precious bones ; or of the monks of
Fossanuova, who, after Saint Thomas Aquinas had died in
their monastery, in their fear of losing the relic, did not shrink
from decapitating, boiling and preserving the body. During
the lying in state of Saint Elizabeth of Hungary, in 1231, a
crowd of worshippers came and cut or tore strips of the linen
enveloping her face ; they cut off the hair, the nails, even the
nipples. In 1392, King Charles VI of France, on the occasion
of a solemn feast, was seen to distribute ribs of his ancestor,
Saint Louis ; to Pierre d'Ailly and to his uncles Berry and

Burgundy he gave entire ribs ; to the prelates one bone to divide between them, which they proceeded to do after the meal.

It may well be that this too corporeal and familiar aspect, this too clearly outlined shape, of the saints has been the very reason why they occupy so little space in the sphere of visions and supernatural experience. The whole domain of ghost-seeing, signs, spectres and apparitions, so crowded in the Middle Ages, lies mainly apart from the veneration of the saints. Of course, there are exceptions, such as Saint Michael, Saint Katherine and Saint Margaret appearing to Joan of Arc ; and other instances might be added. But, generally speaking, popular phantasmagoria is full of angels, devils, shades of the dead, white women, but not of saints. Stories of apparitions of particular saints are, as a rule, suspect of having already undergone some ecclesiastical or literary interpretation. To the agitated beholder a phantom has no name and hardly a shape. In the famous vision of Frankenthal, in 1446, the young shepherd *sees* fourteen cherubim, all alike, who *tell* him they are the fourteen " Holy Martyrs," to whom Christian iconography attributed such distinct and marked appearances. Where a primitive superstition does attach to the veneration of some saint, it retains something of the vague and formless character that is essential to superstition, as in the case of Saint Bertulph at Ghent, who can be heard rapping the sides of his coffin in S. Peter's abbey " moult dru et moult fort " (very frequently and very loudly) as a warning of impending calamity.

The saint, with his clearly outlined figure, his well-known attributes and features as they were painted or carved in the churches, was wholly lacking in mystery. He did not inspire terror as do vague phantoms and the haunting unknown. The dread of the supernatural is due to the undefined character of its phenomena. As soon as they assume a clear-cut shape they are no longer horrible. The familiar figures of the saints produced the same sort of reassuring effect as the sight of a policeman in a foreign city. The complex of ideas connected with the saints constituted, so to say, a neutral zone of calm and domestic piety, between the ecstasy of contemplation and of the love of Christ on the one hand, and the horrors of demonomania on the other. It is perhaps not too bold to assert that the veneration of the saints, by draining off an overflow of religious effusion and of holy fear, acted on the exuberant piety of the Middle Ages as a salutary sedative.

The veneration of the saints has its place among the more outward manifestations of faith. It is subject to the influences of popular fancy rather than of theology, and they sometimes deprive it of its dignity. The special cult of Saint Joseph towards the end of the Middle Ages is characteristic in this respect. It may be looked upon as the counterpart of the passionate adoration of the Virgin. The curiosity with which Joseph was regarded is a sort of reaction from the fervent cult of Mary. The figure of the Virgin is exalted more and more and that of Joseph becomes more and more of a caricature. Art portrays him as a clown dressed in rags ; as such he appears in the diptych by Melchior Broederlam at Dijon. Literature, which is always more explicit than the graphic arts, achieves the feat of making him altogether ridiculous. Instead of admiring Joseph as the man most highly favoured of all, Deschamps represents him as the type of the drudging husband.

> " Vous qui servez a femme et a enfans
> Aiez Joseph toudis en remembrance ;
> Femme servit toujours tristes, dolans,
> Et Jhesu Crist garda en son enfance ;
> A piè trotoit, son fardel sur sa lance ;
> En plusieurs lieux est figuré ainsi,
> Lez un mulet, pour leur faire plaisance,
> Et si n'ot oncq feste en ce monde ci." [1]

And again, still more grossly :

> " Qu'ot Joseph de povreté
> De durté
> De maleurté
> Quant Dieux nasqui !
> Maintefois l'a comporté
> Et monté
> Par bonté
> Avec sa mère autressi,

---

[1] You who serve a wife and children Always bear Joseph in mind ; He served his wife, gloomily and mournfully, And he guarded Jesus Christ in his infancy ; He went on foot with his bundle slung on his staff ; In several places he is pictured thus, Beside a mule to give them pleasure, And so he had never any amusement in this world.

Sur sa mule les ravi :
Je le vi
Paint ainsi ;
En Egipte en est alé.

" Le bonhomme est painturé
Tout lassé,
Et troussé
D'une cote et d'un barry :
Un baston au coul posé,
Vieil, usé
Et rusé.
Feste n'a en ce monde cy,
Mais de lui
Va le cri :
C'est Joseph le rassoté." [1]

This shows how familiarity led to irreverence of thought. Saint Joseph remained a comic type, in spite of the very special reverence paid to him. Doctor Eck, Luther's adversary, had to insist that he should not be brought on the stage, or at least that he should not be made to cook the porridge, " *ne ecclesia Dei irrideatur.*" The union of Joseph and Mary always remained the object of a deplorable curiosity, in which profane speculation mingled with sincere piety. The Chevalier de la Tour Landry, a man of prosaic mind, explains it to himself in the following manner : " God wished that she should marry that saintly man Joseph, who was old and upright, for God wished to be born in wedlock, to comply with the current legal requirements, to avoid gossip."

An unpublished work of the fifteenth century [2] represents the mystic marriage of the soul with the celestial spouse as if it were a middle-class wedding. " If it pleases you," says Jesus to the Father, " I shall marry and shall have a large bevy of children and relations." The Father fears a misalliance, but

---

[1] What poverty Joseph suffered What hardships What misery When God was born ! Many a time he has carried him, And placed him In his goodness With his mother, too, On his mule, and took them with him : I saw him Painted thus ; He went into Egypt.

The good man is painted Quite exhausted, And dressed in A frock and a striped garment, A stick across his shoulder, Old, spent And broken. For him there was no amusement in this world, But of him People say—That is Joseph, the fool.

[2] *Le Livre de Crainte Amoureuse,* by Jean Berthelemy, Bibliothèque Nationale, MS. français, 1875.

the Angel succeeds in persuading him that the betrothed-elect is worthy of the Son ; on which the Father gives his consent in these terms :

> " Prens la, car elle est plaisant
> Pour bien amer son doulx amant ;
> Or prens de nos biens largement,
> Et luy en donne habondamment." [1]

There is no doubt of the seriously devout intention of this treatise. It is only an instance of the degree of triviality entailed by unbridled exuberance of fancy.

Every saint, by the possession of a distinct and vivid outward shape, had his own marked individuality, quite contrary to the angels, who, with the exception of the three famous archangels, acquired no definite appearance. This individual character of each saint was still more strongly accentuated by the special functions attributed to many of them. Now this specialization of the kind of aid given by the various saints was apt to introduce a mechanical element into the veneration paid to them. If, for instance, Saint Roch is specially invoked against the plague, almost inevitably too much stress came to be laid on his part in the healing, and the idea required by sound doctrine, that the saint wrought the cure only by means of his intercession with God, came in danger of being lost sight of. This was especially so in the case of the " Holy Martyrs " (les saints auxiliaires), whose number is usually given as fourteen, and sometimes as five, eight, ten, fifteen. Their veneration arose and spread towards the end of the Middle Ages.

> " Ilz sont cinq sains, en la genealogie,
> Et cinq sainctes, a qui Dieu octria
> Benignement a la fin de leur vie,
> Que quiconques de cuer les requerra
> En tous perilz, que Dieu essaucera
> Leurs prieres, pour quelconque mesaise.
> Saiges est donc qui ces cinq servira,
> Jorges, Denis, Christofle, Gille et Blaise." [2]

---

[1] Take her, for she is pleasing and fit To love her sweet bridegroom ; Now take plenty of our possessions, And give them to her in abundance.

[2] There are five saints in the genealogy, And five female saints to whom God granted Benignantly at the end of their lives, That whosoever shall invoke

The Church had sanctioned the popular belief expressed by Deschamps in these verses by instituting an office of the Fourteen Auxiliary Saints. The binding character of their intercession is clearly there expressed : " O God, who hast distinguished Thy chosen saints, George, etc., etc., with special privileges before all others, that all those who in their need invoke their help, shall obtain the salutary fulfilment of their prayer, according to the promise of Thy grace." So there had been a formal delegation of divine omnipotence. The people could, therefore, not be blamed if, with regard to these privileged saints it forgot the pure doctrine a little. The instantaneous effect of prayer addressed to them contributed still more to obscure their part as intercessors ; they seemed to be exercising divine power by virtue of a power of attorney. Hence it is very natural that the Church abolished this special office of the Fourteen Auxiliary Saints after the Council of Trent. The extraordinary function attributed to them had given rise to the grossest superstition, such as the belief that it sufficed to have looked at a Saint Christopher, painted or carved, to be protected for the rest of the day from a fatal end. This explains the countless number of the saints' images at the entrances of churches.

As for the reason why this group was singled out among all the saints, it should be noticed that the greater number of them appear in art with some very striking attribute. Saint Achatius wore a crown of thorns ; Saint Giles was accompanied by a hind, Saint George by a dragon ; Saint Christopher was of gigantic stature ; Saint Blaise was represented in a den of wild beasts ; Saint Cyriac with a chained devil ; Saint Denis carrying his head under his arm; Saint Erasmus being disembowelled by means of a windlass ; Saint Eustace with a stag carrying a cross between its antlers ; Saint Pantaleon with a lion ; Saint Vitus in a cauldron ; Saint Barbara with her tower ; Saint Katherine with her wheel and sword ; Saint Margaret with a dragon. It may well be that the special favour with which the Fourteen Auxiliary Saints were regarded was due, at least partially, to the very impressive character of their images.

their help with all his heart In all dangers, that He will hear their prayers, In all disorders whatsoever. He therefore is wise who serves these five, George, Denis, Christopher, Giles and Blaise.

The names of several saints were inseparably bound up with
divers disorders, and even served to designate them. Thus
various cutaneous diseases were called Saint Anthony's evil.
Gout went by the name of Saint Maur's evil. The terrors of the
plague called for more than one saintly protector ; Saint Sebastian, Saint Roch, Saint Giles, Saint Christopher, Saint Valen-
tine, Saint Adrian, were all honoured in this capacity by offices,
processions and fraternities. Now here lurked another menace
to the purity of the faith. As soon as the thought of the
disease, charged with feelings of horror and fear, presented
itself to the mind, the thought of the saint sprang up at the
same instant. How easily, then, did the saint himself become
the object of this fear, so that to him was ascribed the heavenly
wrath that unchained the scourge. Instead of unfathomable
divine justice, it was the anger of the saint which seemed the
cause of the evil and required to be appeased. Since he healed
the evil, why should he not be its author ? On these lines the
transition from Christian ethic to heathen magic was only too
easy. The Church could not be held responsible, unless we are
to blame her carelessness regarding the adulteration of the
pure doctrine in the minds of the ignorant.

There are numerous testimonies to show that the people
sometimes really regarded certain saints as the authors of
disorders, though it would be hardly fair to consider as such
those oaths which almost attributed to Saint Anthony the part
of an evil fire-demon. " Que Saint Antoine me arde " (May
Saint Anthony burn me !), "Saint Antoine arde le tripot,"
" Saint Antoine arde la monture " (Saint Anthony burn the
brothel ! Saint Anthony burn the beast !)—these are lines
by Coquillart. So also Deschamps makes some poor fellow
say :

> " Saint Antoine me vent trop chier
> Son mal, le feu ou corps me boute ; " [1]

and thus apostrophizes a gouty beggar : " You cannot walk ?
All the better, you save the toll : Saint Mor ne te fera fremir "
(Saint Maur will not make you tremble).

Robert Gaguin, who was not at all hostile to the veneration

---

[1] Saint Anthony sells me his evil all too dear, He stokes the fire in my
body.

of the saints, in his *De validorum per Franciam mendicantium varia astucia*, describes beggars in these terms : " One falls on the ground expectorating malodorous spittle and attributes his condition to Saint John. Others are covered with ulcers through the fault of Saint Fiacrius, the hermit. You, O Damian, prevent them from making water, Saint Anthony burns their joints, Saint Pius makes them lame and paralysed."

In one of his Colloquies Erasmus makes fun of this belief. One of the interlocutors asks whether in Heaven the saints are more malevolent than they were on earth. " Yes," answers the other, " in the glory of Paradise the saints do not choose to be insulted. Who was sweeter than Saint Corneille, more compassionate than Saint Anthony, more patient than Saint John the Baptist, during their lives ? And now what horrible maladies they send if they are not properly honoured ! " Rabelais states that the lower class of preachers themselves represented Saint Sebastian to their congregation as the author of the plague and Saint Eutropius of dropsy. Henri Estienne has written of the same superstitions in the like manner. That they existed is thus clearly established.

The emotional constituents of the veneration of the saints had fastened so firmly on the forms and colours of their images that mere æsthetic perception was constantly threatening to obliterate the religious element. The vivid impression presented by the aspect of the images with their pious or ecstatic looks, rich gilding, and sumptuous apparel, all admirably reproduced by a very realistic art, left hardly any room for doctrinal reflection. Effusions of piety went out ardently towards those glorious beings, without a thought being given to the limits fixed by the Church. In the popular imagination the saints were living and were as gods. There is nothing surprising, therefore, in the fact that strict pietists like the Brethren of the Common Life and the Windesheim canons saw a certain danger to popular piety in the development of the veneration of the saints. It is very remarkable, however, that the same idea occurs to a man like Eustache Deschamps, a superficial poet and a commonplace mind, and for that very reason so faithful a mirror of the general aspirations of his time.

"Ne faictes pas les dieux d'argent,
D'or, de fust, de pierre ou d'arain,
Qui font ydolatrer la gent. . . .
Car l'ouvrage est forme plaisant ;
Leur painture dont je me plain,
La beauté de l'or reluisant,
Font croire à maint peuple incertain
Que ce soient dieu pour certain,
Et servent par pensées foles
Telz ymages qui font caroles
Es moustiers ou trop en mettons ;
C'est tresmal fait ; a brief paroles,
Telz simulacres n'aourons.

. . . .

Prince, un Dieu croions seulement
Et aourons parfaictement
Aux champs, partout, car c'est raisons,
Non pas faulz dieux, fer n'ayment,
Pierres qui n'ont entendement :
Telz simulacres n'aourons." [1]

Perhaps we may consider the diligent propagation of the cult of guardian angels towards the end of the Middle Ages as a sort of unconscious reaction against the motley crowd of popular hagiology. Too large a part of the living faith had crystallized in the veneration of the saints, and thus there arose a craving for something more spiritual as an object of reverence and a source of protection. In addressing itself to the angel, vaguely conceived and almost formless, piety restored contact with the supernatural and with mystery. Once more it is Jean Gerson, the indefatigable worker for the purity of faith, whom we find perpetually recommending the cult of the guardian angel. But here also he had to combat unbridled curiosity, which threatened to submerge piety under a mass of commonplace details. And it was just in connection with this subject of angels, which was more or less unbroken ground,

---

[1] Do not make gods of silver, Of gold, of wood, of stone or of bronze, That lead people to idolatry. . . . Because the work has a pleasant shape ; Their colouring of which I complain, The beauty of shining gold, Make many ignorant people believe That these are God for certain, And they serve by foolish thoughts Such images as stand about In churches where they place too many of them That is very ill done ; in short Let us not adore such counterfeits. . . .
Prince, let us only believe in one God And let us adore him to perfection In the fields, everywhere, for this is right, No false gods, of iron or of stone, Stones which have no understanding : Let us not adore such counterfeits.

that numbers of delicate questions obtruded themselves. Do they never leave us ? Do they know beforehand whether we shall be saved or lost ? Had Christ a guardian angel ? Will the Antichrist have one ? Can the angel speak to our soul without visions ? Do the angels lead us to good as devils lead us to evil ?—Leave these subtle speculations to divines, concludes Gerson ; let the faithful keep to simple and wholesome worship.

A hundred years after Gerson wrote, the Reformation attacked the cult of the saints, and nowhere in the whole contested area did it meet with less resistance. In strong contrast with the belief in witchcraft and demonology, which fully maintained their ground in Protestant countries, both among the clergy and the laity, the saints fell without a blow being struck in their defence. This was possibly due to the fact that nearly everything connected with the saints had become *caput mortuum*. Piety had depleted itself in the image, the legend, the office. All its contents had been so completely expressed that mystic awe had evaporated. The cult of the saints was no longer rooted in the domain of the unimaginable. In the case of demonology, these roots remained as terribly strong as ever.

When, therefore, Catholic Reform had to re-establish the cult of the saints, its first task was to prune it ; to cut down the whole luxuriant growth of medieval imagination and establish severer discipline, so as to prevent a reflorescence.

CHAPTER XIII

TYPES OF RELIGIOUS LIFE

In studying the history of religious life, we must beware of drawing the lines of demarcation too sharply. When we see side by side the most striking contrasts of passionate piety and mocking indifference, it is so easy to explain them by opposing, as if they made up distinct groups, the worldly to the devout, the intellectuals to the ignorant, the reformers to the conservatives. But, in so doing, we fail to take sufficient account of the marvellous complexity of the human soul and of the forms of culture. To explain the astonishing contrasts of religious life towards the end of the Middle Ages, we must start with the recognition of a general lack of balance in the religious temper, rendering both individuals and masses liable to violent contradictions and to sudden changes.

The general aspect presented by religious life in France towards the end of the Middle Ages is that of a very mechanical and frequently very lax practice, chequered by spasmodic effusions of ardent piety. France was a stranger to that special form of pietism which sequesters itself in small circles of fervent devotees, such as we find springing up in the Netherlands : the " devotio moderna," dominated by the figure of Thomas à Kempis. Still, the religious needs which gave birth to this movement were not wanting in France, only the devotees did not form a special organization. They found a refuge in the existing orders, or they remained in secular life, without being distinguished from the mass of believers. Perhaps the Latin soul endures more easily than that of Northern peoples the conflicts with which life in the world confronts the pious.

Of all the contradictions which religious life of the period presents, perhaps the most insoluble is that of an avowed contempt of the clergy, a contempt seen as an undercurrent throughout the Middle Ages, side by side with the very great respect shown for the sanctity of the sacerdotal office. The soul of the masses, not yet completely Christianized, had never altogether forgotten the aversion felt by the savage for the man who may not fight and must remain chaste. The feudal pride of the knight, the champion of courage and of love, was at one, in this, with the primitive instinct of the people. The worldliness of the higher ranks of the clergy and the deterioration of the lower grades did the rest. Hence it was that nobles, burghers and villeins had for a long time past been feeding their hatred with spiteful jests at the expense of the incontinent monk and the guzzling priest. Hatred is the right word to use in this context, for hatred it was, latent, but general and persistent. The people never wearied of hearing the vices of the clergy arraigned. A preacher who inveighed against the ecclesiastical state was sure of being applauded. As soon as a homilist broaches this subject, says Bernardino of Siena, his hearers forget all the rest ; there is no more effective means of reviving attention when the congregation is dropping off to sleep, or suffering from heat or cold. Everybody instantly becomes attentive and cheerful.

Contempt and gibes are levelled especially at the mendicant orders. The types of unworthy priests in the *Cent Nouvelles Nouvelles*, like the starving chaplain who reads mass for three doits, or the confessor pledged to absolve the family of everything every year, in return for his board and lodging, are all of them mendicant friars. In a series of New Year's wishes Molinet rhymes thus :

> " Prions Dieu que les Jacobins
> Puissent manger les Augustins,
> Et les Carmes soient pendus
> Des cordes des Frères Menus." [1]

At the same time, the restoration of the mendicant orders caused a revival of popular preaching, which gave rise to those vehement outbursts of fervour and penitence which stamped so powerfully the religious life of the fifteenth century.

There is in this special hatred for the begging friars an

---

[1] Let us pray God that the Jacobins May eat the Augustinians, And that the Carmelites may be hanged With the cords of the Minorites.

indication of a most important change of ideas. The formal and dogmatic conception of poverty as extolled by Saint Francis of Assisi, and as observed by the mendicant orders, was no longer in harmony with the social sentiment which was just arising. People were beginning to regard poverty as a social evil instead of an apostolic virtue. Pierre d'Ailly opposed to the mendicant orders the " true poor "—*vere pauperes*. England, which, earlier than other nations, became alive to the economic aspect of things, gave, towards the end of the fourteenth century, the first expression to the sentiment of the sanctity of productive labour in that strangely fantastic and touching poem, *The Vision of William concerning Piers Plowman.*

Still, this general abuse of priests and monks goes hand in hand with a profound veneration for their sacred function. Ghillebert de Lannoy saw a priest at Rotterdam appease a tumult by raising the *Corpus Domini.*

The sudden transitions and the violent contrasts of the religious life of the ignorant masses reappear in that of cultured individuals. Often enlightenment comes like a thunderclap, as it did in the case of Saint Francis suddenly hearing the words of the Gospel as a compulsory command. A knight hears the baptismal ritual read : he has perhaps heard it twenty times before, but suddenly the miraculous virtue of these words pierces into his soul, and he promises himself henceforth to chase away the devil by the mere recollection of the baptism. Jean de Bueil is on the point of witnessing a duel, the adversaries are both going to swear to their good right on the Host. Suddenly the captain, seized by the thought that one of them must needs forswear himself and will be lost irrevocably, exclaims : " Do not swear ; only fight for a wager of 500 crowns, without taking an oath."

As for the great lords, the basic unsoundness of their life of arrogant pomp and disordered enjoyment contributed to give a spasmodic character to their piety. They are devout by starts, for life is far too distracting. Charles V of France sometimes gives up the chase at the most exciting moments to hear mass. Ann of Burgundy, the wife of Bedford, now scandalizes the Parisians by splashing a procession by her mad riding, now leaves a court fête at midnight to attend the matins of the Celestines. She brought upon herself a premature death by visiting the sick of the Hôtel Dieu.

Among the princes and the lords of the fifteenth century, more than one presents the type of an almost inconceivable mixture of devotion and debauchery. Louis of Orleans, an insane lover of luxury and pleasure, addicted even to the sin of necromancy, has his cell in the common dormitory of the Celestines, where he shares the privations and duties of monastic life, rising at midnight and sometimes hearing five or six masses a day.

The coexistence in one person of devotion and worldliness is displayed in a striking fashion in Philip the Good. The duke, famous for his " moult belle compagnie " of bastards, his extravagant feasts, his grasping policy, and for a pride not less violent than his temper, is at the same time strictly devout. He was in the habit of remaining in his oratory for a long time after mass, and living on bread and water four days a week, as well as on all the vigils of Our Lady and the apostles. He is often still fasting at four o'clock in the afternoon. He gives alms on a great scale and in secret. After the surprise of Luxemburg, he remains engrossed in his hours and special prayers of thanksgiving so long that his escort, awaiting him on horseback, grow impatient, for the fight was not yet quite over. On being warned of the danger, the duke replies : " If God has granted me victory, He will keep it for me."

Gaston Phébus, count of Foix, King René, Charles of Orleans, represent so many different types of a very worldly and often frivolous temperament, coupled with a devotional spirit which one shrinks from stigmatizing as hypocrisy or bigotry. It has rather to be regarded as a kind of reconciliation, hardly conceivable to the modern mind, between two moral extremes. Its possibility in the Middle Ages depends on the absolute dualism of the two conceptions, which then dominated all thinking and living.

Men of the fifteenth century often couple with austere devotion the love of bizarre splendour. The craving to decorate faith with the magnificence of forms and colours is displayed in other forms besides works of religious art ; it is sometimes found in the forms of spiritual life itself. When

Philippe de Mézières plans his Order of the Passion, which was to save Christendom, he imagines a whole phantasmagoria of colours. The knights, according to their ranks, will be dressed in red, green, scarlet and azure, with red crosses and hoods of the same colour. The grand-master will be all in white. If he saw but little of this splendour, as his order was never established, he was at least able to satisfy his artistic taste in the monastery of the Celestines at Paris, which was the refuge of his last years. If the rules of the order, which he followed as a lay-brother, were very severe, the convent-church, on the other hand, a mausoleum of the princes of the time, was most sumptuous, all sparkling with gold and precious stones ; it was reputed the most beautiful of Paris.

It is but a step from luxurious piety to theatrical displays of hyperbolic humility. Olivier de la Marche remembered to have seen in his youth the entry of Jacques de Bourbon, the titular king of Naples, who had renounced the world because of the exhortations of Saint Colette. The king, miserably dressed, was carried in a sort of hand-barrow, " not differing from the barrows in which dung and ordure are usually carried." An elegant cortège followed closely. " And I have heard it recounted and said "—says La Marche—" that in all the towns where he came, he made similar entries out of humility."

The minute directions given by a number of saintly persons concerning their burial bear witness to the same excessive humility. The blessed Pierre Thomas, improving upon the example of Saint Francis of Assisi, leaves orders to wrap him up in a sack, with a cord round his neck, and so place him on the ground to die. " Bury me," he says, " at the entrance of the choir, that every one may walk over my body, even dogs and goats." Philippe de Mézières, his disciple and friend, tries to go even further in fantastic humility. In his dying hour a heavy iron chain is to be placed round his neck. When he has given up the ghost, he is to be dragged by his feet, naked, into the choir, where he is to remain on the ground, his arms crossed, tied by three ropes to a plank. Thus " this fine treasure for the worms " is to wait till people come to carry it to the grave. The plank is to take the place of the " sumptuous coffin, ornamented with his vain and worldly coat of arms, which would have been displayed at the interment of the unhappy pilgrim, if God had so much hated him that he had let him die at the court of princes of this world." Dragged along once more, his " carrion " is to be thrown, quite naked, into the grave.

One is not surprised to hear that this lover of precise specification made several wills. In the later ones details of this kind are wanting ; and at his death, which occurred in 1405, he was honourably buried in the frock of the Celestines, and two epitaphs, probably of his own composition, were carved on his tombstone.

The ideal of sanctity has always been incapable of much variation. The fifteenth century, in this respect, brings no new aspiration. Consequently, the Renaissance exercised hardly any influence on the conception of saintly life. The saint and the mystic remain almost wholly untouched by the changing times. The types of saints of the Counter-Reformation are still those of the later Middle Ages, who in their turn did not essentially differ from those of the preceding centuries. Both before and after the great turning of the tide, two types of saints stand out conspicuously : the men of fiery speech and energetic action, like Ignatius de Loyola, Francis Xavier, Charles Borromeo, who belong to the same class as Bernardino of Siena, John Capistrano and the blessed Vincent Ferrer, in earlier times ; and the men absorbed in tranquil rapture, or practising extravagant humility, the poor in spirit, like Saint Francis of Paula and the blessed Pierre of Luxemburg in the fifteenth century, and Aloysius Gonzaga in the sixteenth.

It would not be unreasonable to compare to the romanticism of chivalry, as an element of medieval thought, a romanticism of saintliness, in the sense of a tendency to give the colours of fancy and the accents of enthusiasm to an ideal form of virtue and of duty. It is remarkable that this romanticism of saintliness always aims far more at miracles and excesses of humility and of asceticism, than at brilliant achievements in the service of religious policy. The Church has sometimes canonized the great men of action who have revived or purified religious culture, but popular imagination has been more impressed, in all ages, by the supernatural and by irrational excess.

It is not without interest to note some traits showing us the attitude of the aristocracy, refined and fastidious and engrossed in the chivalrous ideas, towards the ideal of saintly life. The princely families of France have produced later saints than Saint Louis. Charles of Blois, descended, by his mother, from the house of Valois, found himself charged, by his marriage with the heiress of Brittany, with a war of succession, which filled the greater part of his life. On marrying Jeanne de Penthièvre, he had promised to adopt the arms and the battle-cry of the duchy, which meant : to fight Jean de Montfort, the pretender supported by England. The count of Blois waged the war like the best of knights and captains of his time. He passed nine years in captivity in England, and perished at Aurai in 1364, battling side by side with Bertrand du Guesclin and Beaumanoir.

Now this prince, whose career was altogether military, had led, from his youth onward, the life of an ascetic. As a child he plunged into the study of edifying books, a taste which his father did his best to moderate, judging it unsuitable to a future warrior. Later he used to sleep on straw near the conjugal bed. After his death he was found to have worn a hair-shirt under his armour. He confessed every evening, saying that no Christian ought to go to sleep in the state of sin. As a prisoner in London he was in the habit of entering the cemeteries to kneel down and say the *de profundis*. The Breton squire whom he asks to say the responses refused, saying : " No ; there lie those who have killed my parents and friends and have burnt their houses." On being released, he resolved to undertake a pilgrimage, barefooted, in the snow, from La Roche-Derrien, where he had been captured, to the shrine of Saint Yves at Tréguier. The people, hearing this, covered the road with straw and blankets, but the count made a detour and hurt his feet, so that for weeks he was unable to walk.

Directly after his death his royal relations, especially his son-in-law, Louis d'Anjou, a son of the king, took steps to have him canonized. The proceedings, which took place at Angers in 1371, ended in his beatification.

If we are to trust Froissart, this Charles of Blois would seem to have had a bastard. " There was killed in good style the aforesaid Lord Charles of Blois, with his face to the enemy, and a bastard son of his called Jehans de Blois, and several other knights and squires of Brittany." Was Froissart mistaken ? Or are we to suppose that the mingling of piety and sensuality, which is so evident in the figures of Louis of Orleans and of Philip the Good, reappears in him in a still more astonishing degree ?

No such question arises in the case of the blessed Pierre de Luxembourg, another ascetic sprung from court circles. This scion of the house of Luxemburg, which in its several branches held the imperial dignity and a preponderant place at the courts of France and Burgundy, is a striking representative of the type called by William James " the under-witted saint," a narrow mind, which can only live in a carefully isolated sphere of devotion. He died in his eighteenth year, in 1387, having been loaded from his childhood with ecclesiastical dignities, being bishop of Metz at fifteen and a cardinal soon after. His personality as it disengages itself from the narratives of the witnesses in the proceedings for his canonization is almost pitiful. He is of a consumptive disposition and has overgrown his strength. Even as a child he was wholly given up to austerity and devotion. He reprimands his brother when he laughs, because the Gospel does tell us that the Lord wept, but not that he laughed. " Sweet, courteous and debonair "—says Froissart—" virgin as to the body, a very great giver of alms. The greater part of the day and the night he spent in prayer. And in all his life there was nothing but humility." At first his noble parents tried to dissuade him from a life of religion. When he said he wished to go forth and preach, he was told : " You are much too tall, everybody would recognize you at once. You could not endure the cold, and as to preaching the crusade, how could you do that ? " " I see," said Pierre—and here the very recesses of his narrow mind seem lighted up for a moment—" I see very well, that you want to lead me from the right road to the bad ; but assuredly, if I once enter on it, I shall do so much that the whole world will talk of me."

When once his ascetic aspirations had overcome all attempts

to extirpate them, his parents were clearly proud of having such a young saint in the family. Imagine, amidst the un-bridled luxury of the courts of Berry and Burgundy, this sickly boy, horribly dirty and covered with vermin, as the witnesses attest. He is ever occupied with his sins and notes them down every day in a pocket-book. If he is prevented from doing this by a journey or some other reason, he makes up for this neglect by writing for hours. At night he is seen writing up or reading his pocket-books by the light of a candle. He rises at midnight and awakes the chaplains in order to confess ; sometimes he knocks in vain—they turn a deaf ear to his nocturnal call. If he obtains a hearing, he reads out his lists of sins from his little scraps. Towards the end of his life, he is shriven twice a day and will not allow his confessor to leave him for a moment. After his death a whole chest was found filled with these little lists of sins.

The Luxembourgs and their friends immediately took steps to get him canonized. The request was made at Avignon by the king himself, and supported both by the University of Paris and the Chapter of Notre Dame. The greatest lords of France appeared as witnesses at the trial in 1389 : André de Luxembourg, Louis de Bourbon, Enguerrand de Coucy. Though the canonization was not obtained because of the pope's negligence (the beatification only took place in 1527), the veneration of Pierre de Luxembourg was at once established, and miracles multiplied at Avignon, on the spot where he lay buried. The king founded a Celestine monastery there after the model of the one at Paris, which was the favourite sanctuary of the high nobility, and which Pierre had also frequented in his youth. The foundation-stone was laid by the dukes of Orleans, Berry and Burgundy.

There is another case which may serve to illustrate the intercourse of princes with saints : Saint Francis of Paula at the court of Louis XI. The very peculiar type of piety which this king presents is too well known to be described here at large. Louis XI, " who bought the grace of God and of the Virgin Mary for more money than ever king did," dis-plays all the qualities of the crudest fetishism. His passion for relics, pilgrimages and processions seems to us almost totally devoid of really pious sentiment, and even of respect.

He used to handle the holy objects as if they were expensive medicines. At the approach of death he sent to all parts of the world for extraordinary relics. The pope sent him the corporal of Saint Peter. The Great Turk actually offered him a collection of relics which were still at Constantinople. On the table beside his bed was the "Sainte Ampoule," the vase in which the holy oil for coronation was kept, and which had never left Reims before. According to Commines, the king wanted to try its miraculous virtue by having his whole body anointed. The cross of Saint Laud was specially sent for from Angers to take an oath upon, for Louis made a difference between oaths taken on one relic and on another. These are traits reminding us of the Merovingian times.

In him the fervent venerator of relics blends with the collector of curiosities. He corresponds with Lorenzo de Medici about the ring of Saint Zanobi and about an *Agnus Dei*, that is to say, one of these figures cut out of the fibrous trunk of an Asiatic fern, which were also called *Agnus Scythicus*, or Tartarian lamb, and to which rare medicinal virtues were attributed. At Plessis lès Tours the holy persons, summoned thither to say prayers for the king, rub shoulders with musicians of all sorts. "At that time the king had a great number of players of deep-toned and sweet instruments brought to him, whom he lodged at Saint-Cosme, near Tours, where they assembled, as many as a hundred and twenty, among whom there were many shepherds from the country of Poitou. Who often played before the king's mansion (but they did not see him), that the king might enjoy the aforesaid instruments as a pleasure and pastime and to prevent him from sleeping. And, on the other hand, he also sent for a great number of male and female bigots and devout people like hermits and saintly creatures, to pray God incessantly to allow that he should not die and that He might let him live longer."

Saint Francis of Paula, the Calabrian hermit, who surpassed the Minorite friars in humility by founding the order of the Minims, was literally a purchase of the royal collector. After having failed with the king of Naples, Louis's diplomacy succeeded, by the pope's intervention, in securing the miraculous man. A noble escort bore him from Italy, sorely against his will. His ferocious asceticism reminds us of the barbarous saints of the tenth century, Saint Nil and Saint Romuald. He flies at the sight of a woman. Since his youth he has never touched a piece of money. He sleeps upright or in a leaning position ; he lets his hair and beard grow. He does not eat animal food and accepts only roots. The king, who is already ill, took pains to procure the proper food for his rare saint. "Monsieur de Genas, I beg you to send me lemons and sweet oranges, and muscatel pears, and parsnips,[1] and it is for the holy man who eats neither flesh nor fish ; and you will do me a very great pleasure." At court he was known only as "the holy man," so that Commines appears not to have known his name, although he often saw him. The mockers and suspicious persons also called him "holy man." The king himself, at the instigation of Jacques Coitier, his physician, begun by setting spies on the man of God and by putting him to the proof. Commines is prudently reserved about him. Although declaring that he had never seen a man "of such saintly life, nor one in whom the Holy Spirit seemed more to speak through his mouth," he concludes : "He is still alive, so that he may well change, for the better or for the worse, so that I shall be silent, as many mocked at the arrival of this hermit, whom they called 'holy man.' " It is noteworthy that learned theologians like Jan Standonck and Jean Quentin, having come from Paris to speak to him about the founding of a monastery of Minims at Paris, went back full of admiration.

It is a significant fact that the princes of the fifteenth century often ask the advice of great visionaries and extravagant ascetics in political matters. Thus Saint Colette is consulted by Philip the Good and by his mother, Marguerite of Bavaria, and acts as an intermediary in the controversies between the houses of France, Savoy and Burgundy. Her canonization was demanded with pious insistence by the house of Burgundy.

More important still was the public part played by Denis the Carthusian. He also was frequently in touch with the house of Burgundy. Obsessed by the fear of imminent

---

[1] Perhaps the king wrote by mistake, *pastenargues* for *pastèques* = water-melons.

catastrophes, such as the conquest of Rome by the Turks, he urges the duke to undertake a crusade. He dedicates to him a treatise on princely government. He advises the duke of Guelders in the conflict with his son. Numbers of noblemen, clerks and burghers come to consult him in his cell at Ruremonde, where he is constantly engaged in resolving doubts, difficulties and questions of conscience.

Denys le Chartreux, or of Rickel, is the most complete type of religious enthusiast at the end of the Middle Ages. His mental range and many-sided energy are hardly conceivable. To mystic transports, ferocious asceticism, continual visions and revelations he unites immense activity as a theological writer. His works fill forty-five quarto volumes. All medieval divinity meets in him as the rivers of a continent flow together in an estuary. *Qui Dionysium legit nihil non legit,*[1] said sixteenth-century theology. He sums up, he concludes, but he does not create. All that his great predecessors have thought is reproduced by him in a simple and easy style. He wrote all his books himself, and revised, corrected, subdivided and illuminated them. At the end of his life, he deliberately laid down his pen. *Ad securae taciturnitatis portum me transferre intendo.*[2]

He never knew repose. Every day he recites the psalter almost entirely, and, at any rate, half. He prays continually, while dressing or while engaged in any other occupation. When others go to sleep again after matins, he remains awake. Big and strong, he exposes his body with impunity to all kinds of privations. I have a head of iron, he would say, and a stomach of brass. He feeds, for choice, on tainted victuals.

The enormous amount of theological meditation and speculation which he achieved, was not the fruit of a peaceful and balanced life of study ; it was carried out in the midst of intense emotions and violent shocks. Visions and revelations are with him ordinary experiences. Ecstasies come to him on all sorts of occasions, especially when he hears music, sometimes in the midst of noble company, who are listening to his wise advice. As a child he rose when the moon was

---

[1] He who reads Denis reads everything.
[2] I am now going to enter the haven of secure taciturnity.

shining brightly, thinking it was time to go to school. He
is a stammerer. He sees the room of a dying woman full
of demons who knock the stick out of his hand. He constantly
converses with the dead. When asked if he often sees apparitions of deceased persons, he answers: "yes, hundreds of
times." Although constantly occupied with his supernatural
experiences, he does not like to speak about them, and is
ashamed of the ecstasies which earned him among the laudatory
surnames of the great theologians that of *Doctor ecstaticus*.

The great figure of Denis the Carthusian no more escaped
suspicion and raillery than the miracle-worker of Louis XI.
The slander and abuse of the world pursued him all his life.
The mental attitude of the fifteenth century towards the
highest religious manifestations of the age is made up equally
of enthusiasm and distrust.

CHAPTER XIV

RELIGIOUS SENSIBILITY AND RELIGIOUS IMAGINATION

Ever since the gentle mysticism of Saint Bernard, in the twelfth century, had started the strain of pathetic tenderness about the Passion of Christ, the religious sensibility of the medieval soul had been increasing. The mind was saturated with the concepts of Christ and the cross. In early childhood the image of the cross was implanted on the sensitive heart, so grand and forbidding as to overshadow all other affections by its gloom. When Jean Gerson was a child, his father one day stood with his back against a wall, his arms outspread, saying : " Thus, child, was your God crucified, who made and saved you." This image of his father, he tells us, remained engraved on his mind, expanding as he grew older, even in his old age, and he blessed his pious father for it, who had died on the day of the Exaltation of the Cross. Saint Colette, when four years old, every day heard her mother in prayer lament and weep about the Passion, sharing the pain of contumely, blows, and torments. This recollection fixed itself in the supersensitive heart of Colette with such intensity, that she felt, all her life through, the most severe oppression of heart every day at the hour of the crucifixion ; and at the reading of the Passion she suffered more than a woman in childbed.

A preacher sometimes paused to stand in silence, with his arms extended in the form of the cross, for a quarter of an hour.

The soul is so imbued with the conception of the Passion that the most remote analogy suffices to make the chord of the memory of Christ vibrate. A poor nun carrying wood to the kitchen imagines she carries the cross ; a blind woman doing the washing takes the tub for the manger and the washhouse for the stable.

This extreme religious sensibility shows itself by copious weeping. Devotion, says Denis the Carthusian, is a sort of tenderness of heart, which easily moves to tears of piety. We should pray God to have " the daily baptism of tears." They are the wings of prayer and, according to Saint Bernard, the wine of angels. We should give ourselves up to the grace of meritorious tears, get ready for them and let ourselves be carried away by them all the year round, but especially during Lent, so that we may say with the psalmist : *Fuerunt mihi lacrimae meae panis die ac nocte.*[1] Sometimes they come so easily, that we pray sobbing and groaning. If they do not come, we should not force them ; we should then content ourselves with the tears of the heart. In the presence of others we should avoid these signs of extraordinary devotion.

Vincent Ferrer shed so many tears every time he consecrated the Host that the whole congregation also wept, insomuch that a general wailing was heard as if in the house of one dead.

Popular devotion in France did not take a special form as we notice in the Netherlands, where it was standardized, so to say, in the pietistic movement of the Brethren of the Common Life and the regular canons of the Congregation of Windesheim. This was the circle whence proceeded the " Imitation of Christ." The regulations which the Dutch devout bound themselves to obey, gave their piety a conventional form and preserved them from dangerous excesses of fervour. French devotion, although very similar, kept more of its passionate and spasmodic character, and led more easily to fantastic aberrations, in those cases where it did not speedily wear itself out.

Nowhere do we notice its character better than in the writings of Gerson. The chancellor of the university was the great dogmatic and moral censor of his time. His prudent, scrupulous, slightly academic mind was admirably fitted to distinguish between true piety and exaggerated religious manifestations. This was, indeed, his favourite occupation. Benevolent, sincere and pure, he had that meticulous carefulness in point of good style and form which so often reminds us of his modest origin in the case of a man who has raised himself by his own talents from humble circumstances to an aristocratic mentality. He

[1] My tears have been my meat day and night.

was a born psychologist and had a fine sense of style, which is near akin to the craving for orthodoxy.

At the Council of Constance, Gerson defended the Dutch Brethren of the Common Life against whom a Dominican of Groningen brought a charge of heresy. He was, nevertheless, fully aware of the dangers threatening the Church from a too exuberant popular devotion. It may therefore appear strange that he often disapproved of manifestations of piety in his own country, which reappear in that very " devotio moderna " of the Netherlands, over which he threw the mantle of his authority. The explanation is that the devout in France had no safe sheepfold of organization and of discipline to keep them within the limits of what the Church could tolerate.

The world, said Gerson, is approaching its end, and, like an old dotard, is exposed to all sorts of fancies, dreams and illusions which lead many a one to stray outside the pathway of truth. Mysticism is brought into the streets. Many people take to it, without suitable direction, and indulge in too rigid fasts, too protracted vigils, and too abundant tears, all of which disturb their brains. In vain they are advised to be moderate and to take heed lest they fall into the devil's snares. At Arras, he tells us, he visited a woman who won the admiration of the multitude by going completely without food during several consecutive days, against her husband's wishes. He talked to her and only found in her a vain and arrogant obstinacy ; for, after her fasts, she ate with insatiable voracity. Her face betrayed imminent insanity. He also cites the case of an epileptic woman who thought that each twinge of pain in her corns was a sign that a soul descended to hell.

Gerson set little store by visions and revelations which were recent and universally spoken of, including even those of Bridget of Sweden and Catherine of Siena. He had heard so many stories of this sort that he had lost all belief in them. Someone or other would always be asserting that it had been revealed to him that he would be pope. A certain man, in particular, believed himself predestined, first, to become pope, then to be the Antichrist, so that he had thought of killing himself in order to save Christendom from such an evil.

There is nothing more dangerous, says Gerson, than ignorant devotion. The poor devout, learning that the heart of Mary exulted in her God, strain themselves to exult also ; they call up all sorts of images without being able to distinguish between truth and delusion, and they take them all for miraculous proofs of their excellent devotion.

Contemplative life has great dangers, he continues ; it has made numbers of people melancholy or mad. Gerson perceived the connection between fasting and hallucinations, and had a glimpse of the rôle played by fasting in the practice of magic.

Now, where was a man of Gerson's psychological subtlety to draw the line of demarcation in the manifestations of piety, between what is holy and laudable and what is inadmissible ? The dogmatic point of view did not meet the case. It was easy for him, a theologian by profession, to point out deviations from dogma. But he felt that, as regards manifestations of piety, considerations of an ethical sort should guide our judgment, that it was a question of degree and of taste. There is no virtue, says Gerson, which is more neglected in these miserable times of schism than discretion.

The Church in the Middle Ages tolerated many religious extravagances, provided they did not lead up to novelties of a revolutionary sort, in morals or in doctrine. So long as it spent itself in hyperbolic fancies or in ecstasies, superabundant emotion was not a source of danger. Thus, many saints were conspicuous for their fanatical reverence for virginity, taking the form of a horror of all that relates to sex. Saint Colette is an instance of this. She is a typical representative of what has been called by William James the theopathic condition. Her supersensibility is extreme. She can endure neither the light nor the heat of fire, only the light of candles. She has an immoderate horror of flies, ants and slugs, and of all dirt and stenches of all kinds. Her abomination of sexual functions inspires her with repugnance for those saints who have passed through the matrimonial state, and leads her to oppose the admission of non-virginal persons to her congregation. The Church has ever praised such a disposition, judging it to be edifying and meritorious.

On the other hand, the same sentiment became dangerous, as soon as the fanatics of chastity, not content with shutting themselves up in their own sphere of purity, wanted to apply their principles to ecclesiastical and social life. The Church was

repeatedly obliged to disown the violent assailants of the validity
of the sacraments administered by priests living in fornication,
for the double reason that sound catholic doctrine has always
separated the sacredness of the office from the personal dignity
of the bearer, and that she knew herself to be not strong enough
to uproot the evil. Jean de Varennes had been a learned
divine and a celebrated preacher. Chaplain to the youthful
Cardinal of Luxemburg at Avignon, he seemed destined for
the highest ecclesiastical career, when he suddenly threw up
all his benefices, with the exception of a canonry of Notre Dame
of Reims, gave up the great style of his life and went to Saint
Lié, his birthplace, where he began to lead a saintly life and
to preach. " And he was much visited by people who came
to see him from all countries on account of the simple, very
noble and most honest life he led." Soon he is called " the
holy man of Saint Lié " ; he is regarded as a future pope,
a miraculous being, a messenger of God. All France talks
of him.

Now, in the person of Jean de Varennes the passion of sexual
purity assumes a revolutionary aspect. He reduces all the
evils of the Church to the one evil of lust. His extremist
programme for the re-establishment of chastity is not aimed
only at the clergy. As to fornicating priests, he denies the
efficacy of the sacraments they administer : an ancient and
redoubtable thesis which the Church had encountered more
than once. According to him, it was not permissible for a
priest to live in the same house with his sister or with an
elderly woman. Moreover, he attacks immorality in general.
He ascribes twenty-three different sins to the matrimonial state.
He demands that adultery shall be punished according to the
Ancient Law ; Christ Himself would have ordered the stoning
of the adulterous woman, if He had been sure of her fault.
He asserts that no woman in France is chaste, and that no
bastard can live a good life and be saved. In his vehement
indignation he preaches resistance to the ecclesiastical authorities, to the archbishop of Reims in particular. " A wolf, a
wolf ! " he cried to the people, who understood but too well
who the wolf was, and repeated joyously : " Hahay, aus leus,
mes bones gens, aus leus." The archbishop had Jean de
Varennes locked up in a horrible prison.

This severity towards all revolutionary tendencies of a doctrinal kind contrasts with the indulgence shown by the Church for the extravagances of religious imagination, notably for ultra-sensuous fancies about divine love. It required the psychological perspicacity of a Gerson to be aware that there also the Faith was menaced by a moral and doctrinal danger.

The spiritual state called *dulcedo Dei*, the sweetness of the delights of the love of Christ, was towards the end of the Middle Ages one of the most active elements of religious life. The followers of the " devotio moderna " in the Netherlands had systematized it, and thereby made it more or less innocuous. Gerson, who distrusted it, has analysed it in his treatise, *De diversis diaboli tentationibus*, and elsewhere. "The day," he said, " would be too short if I were to enumerate the innumerable follies of the loving, nay, the raving, *amantium, immo et amentium.*" He knew the peril by experience. For he can have only meant himself when he described the case of one of his acquaintances who had carried on a spiritual friendship with a nun, at first without any trace of carnal inclination, and without suspecting any sin, till a separation revealed to him the amorous nature of this relation. So that he drew the inference from it, *Amor spiritualis facile labitur in nudum carnalem amorem,*[1] and considered himself warned.

The devil, he says, sometimes inspires us with feelings of immense and marvellous sweetness which is very like devotion, so that we make the quest of this delight our object and want to love God only to attain it. Many have deceived themselves by immoderately cultivating such feelings ; they have taken the mad excitement of their hearts for divine ardour, and were thus miserably led astray. Others strive to attain insensibility or complete passiveness, to become a perfect tool for God.

It is this sensation of absolute annihilation of the individual, tasted by the mystics of all times, which Gerson, as a supporter of a moderate and prudent mysticism, could not tolerate. A female visionary told him that in the contemplation of God her mind had been annihilated, really annihilated, and then created anew. " How do you know ? " he asked her. " I experienced it," she had answered. The logical absurdity of this reply had sufficed him to prove the reprehensible nature of these fancies.

---

[1] Spiritual love easily falls into sheer carnal love.

It was dangerous to let such sensations express themselves by explicit formulas ; the Church could only tolerate them in the form of images. Catherine of Siena might say that her heart had been changed into the heart of Christ. But Marguerite Porete, an adherent of the sect of the Brethren of the Free Spirit, who also believed that her soul had been annihilated in God, was burnt at Paris.

What the Church dreaded above all in the idea of the annihilation of the personality was the consequence, accepted by the extremist mystics of all religions, that the soul absorbed in God, and therefore, having no will, can no longer sin, even in following its carnal appetites. How many poor ignorant people had been dragged by such doctrines into the most abominable licence. Every time Gerson touches the question of the dangers of spiritual love, he remembers the excesses of the Bégards and of the Turlupins ; he fears a truly satanic impiety, like that of the nobleman he mentions as having confessed to a Carthusian that the sin of lust did not prevent him from loving God ; on the contrary, it inflamed him to seek for and taste more eagerly the sweetness of divine love.

So long as the transports of mysticism were translated into passionate imaginings of a symbolic nature, however vivid their colours might be, they caused but a relative danger. On becoming crystallized in images, they lost some of their noxiousness. In this way the exuberant imagery of the time, to a certain extent, diverted the most dangerous tendencies of the religious life of the epoch, however bizarre it may appear to us. Jan Brugman, a popular Dutch preacher, might with impunity compare Jesus, taking human form, to a drunkard, who forgets himself, sees no danger, who gives away all he has. " Oh, was He not truly drunk, when love urged Him to descend from the highest heavens to this lowest valley of the earth ? " He sees Him in heaven, going about to pour out drinks for the prophets, " and they drank till they were fit to burst, and David with his harp, leaped before the table, just as if he were the Lord's fool."

Not only the grotesque Brugman, the serene Ruysbroeck, too, likes to represent divine love under the image of drunkenness. Hunger also served as a figure to express the relations of the soul with Christ. Ruysbroeck, in *The Adornment of the Spiritual*

Marriage, says : " Here begins an eternal hunger which is never appeased ; it is an inner craving and hankering of the loving power and the created spirit for an uncreated good. . . . Those that experience it are the poorest of men ; for they are eager and greedy and they have an insatiable hunger. Whatever they eat and drink, they never become satiated by it, for this hunger is eternal." The metaphor may be inverted, so that the hunger is Christ's, as in *The Mirror of Eternal Salvation*. " His hunger is immensely great ; He consumes us entirely to the bottom, for He is a greedy glutton with a voracious hunger ; He devours even the marrow of our bones. . . . First He prepares His repast and in His love He burns up all our sins and our faults. Next, when we are purified and roasted by the fire of love, He opens his mouth like a voracious being who wishes to swallow all."

A little insistence on the details of the metaphor will make it ridiculous. " You will eat Him," says *Le Livre de Crainte Amoureuse* of Jean Berthelemy, in speaking of the Eucharist, " roasted at the fire, well baked, not at all overdone or burnt. For just as the Easter lamb was properly baked and roasted between two fires of wood or of charcoal, thus was gentle Jesus on Good Friday placed on the spit of the worthy cross, and tied between the two fires of His very fearful death and passion, and of the very ardent charity and love which He felt for our souls and our salvation ; He was, as it were, roasted and slowly baked to save us."

The infusion of divine grace is described under the image of the absorption of food, and also of being bathed. A nun feels quite deluged in the blood of Christ and faints. All the red and warm blood of the five wounds flowed through the mouth of Saint Henry Suso into his heart. Catherine of Siena drunk from the wound in His side. Others drunk of the Virgin's milk, like Saint Bernard, Henry Suso, Alain de la Roche.

The Breton, Alain de la Roche, a Dominican, born about 1428, is a very typical representative of this religious imagery, both ultra-concrete and ultra-fantastic. He was the zealous promoter of the use of the rosary, with a view to which he founded the Universal Brotherhood of the Psalter of Our Lady. The description of his numerous visions is characterized at the same time by an excess of sexual imagination and by the absence of all genuine emotion. The passionate tone which, in the grand mystics, makes these too sensuous images of hunger and thirst, of blood and voluptuousness, bearable, is altogether lacking. The symbolism of spiritual love has become with him a mere mechanical process. It is the decadence of the medieval spirit. We shall return to it shortly.

Now, whereas the celestial symbolism of Alain de la Roche seems artificial, his infernal visions are characterized by a hideous actuality. He sees the animals which represent the various sins equipped with horrible genitals, and emitting torrents of fire which obscure the earth with their smoke. He sees the prostitute of apostasy giving birth to apostates, now devouring them and vomiting them forth, now kissing them and petting them like a mother.

This is the reverse side of the suave fancies of spiritual love. Human imagination contained, as the inevitable complement of the sweetness of celestial visions, a black mass of demonological conceptions which also sought expression in language of ardent sensuality. Alain de la Roche forms the link between the placid and gentle pietism of the " devotio moderna " and the darkest horror produced by the medieval spirit on the wane : the delusion of witchcraft, at that time fully developed into a fatally consistent system of theological zeal and judicial severity. A faithful friend of the regulars of Windesheim and the Brethren of the Common Life, in whose house he died at Zwolle in 1475, he was at the same time the preceptor of Jacob Sprenger, a Dominican like himself, not only one of the two authors of the *Malleus maleficarum*, but also the propagator in Germany of the Brotherhood of the Rosary, founded by Alain.

CHAPTER XV

SYMBOLISM IN ITS DECLINE

Thus religious emotion always tended to be transmuted into images. Mystery seemed to become graspable by the mind when invested with a perceptible form. The need of adoring the ineffable in visible shapes was continually creating ever new figures. In the fourteenth century, the cross and the lamb no longer sufficed for the effusions of overflowing love offered to Jesus ; to these is added the adoration of the name of Jesus, which occasionally threatens to eclipse even that of the cross. Henry Suso tattoos the name of Jesus over his heart and compares himself to the lover who wears the name of his beloved embroidered on his coat. Bernardino of Siena, at the end of a moving sermon, lights two candles and shows the multitude a board a yard in length, bearing on an azure ground the name Jesus in golden letters, surrounded by the sun's rays. The people filling the church kneel down and weep with emotion. The custom spreads, especially with the Franciscan preachers. Denis the Carthusian is represented in art holding such a board in his uplifted hands. The sun as a crest above the arms of Geneva is derived from this usage. The ecclesiastical authorities regarded the matter with suspicion ; there was some talk of superstition and of idolatry ; there were tumults for and against ; Bernardino was summoned before the *curia*, and the usage was forbidden by Pope Martin V. About the same time a very similar form of adoring Christ under a visible sign was successfully introduced into the ritual, namely, that of the monstrance. To this also the Church objected at first ; the use of the monstrance was originally forbidden except during the week of the Corpus Christi. In taking, instead of the original form of a tower, that of a radiant sun, the monstrance became very like the board, bearing Jesus' name, of which the Church disapproved.

The abundance of images in which religious thought threatened to dissolve itself would have only produced a chaotic phantasmagoria, if symbolic conception had not worked it all into a vast system, where every figure had its place.

Of no great truth was the medieval mind more conscious than of Saint Paul's phrase : *Videmus nunc per speculum in aenigmate, tunc autem facie ad faciem.*[1] The Middle Ages never forgot that all things would be absurd, if their meaning were exhausted in their function and their place in the phenomenal world, if by their essence they did not reach into a world beyond this. This idea of a deeper significance in ordinary things is familiar to us as well, independently of religious convictions : as an indefinite feeling which may be called up at any moment, by the sound of raindrops on the leaves or by the lamplight on a table. Such sensations may take the form of a morbid oppression, so that all things seem to be charged with a menace or a riddle which we must solve at any cost. Or they may be experienced as a source of tranquillity and assurance, by filling us with the sense that our own life, too, is involved in this hidden meaning of the world. The more this perception converges upon the absolute One, whence all things emanate, the sooner it will tend to pass from the insight of a lucid moment to a permanent and formulated conviction. " By cultivating the continuous sense of our connection with the power that made things as they are, we are tempered more towardly for their reception. The outward face of nature need not alter, but the expressions of meaning in it alter. It was dead and is alive again. It is like the difference between looking on a person without love, or upon the same person with love. . . . When we see all things in God, and refer all things to Him, we read in common matters superior expressions of meaning."[2]

Here, then, is the psychological foundation from which symbolism arises. In God nothing is empty of sense : *nihil vacuum neque sine signo apud Deum*, said Saint Irenæus. So the conviction of a transcendental meaning in all things seeks to formulate itself. About the figure of the Divinity a majestic system of correlated figures crystallizes, which all

[1] For now we see through a glass darkly ; but then face to face.
[2] W. James: *Varieties of Religious Experience*, p. 474.

have reference to Him, because all things derive their meaning from Him. The world unfolds itself like a vast whole of
symbols, like a cathedral of ideas. It is the most richly
rythmical conception of the world, a polyphonous expression
of eternal harmony.

In the Middle Ages the symbolist attitude was much more
in evidence than the causal or the genetic attitude. Not
that this latter mode of conceiving the world, as a process of
evolution, was wholly absent. Medieval thought, too, sought
to understand things by means of their origin. But, destitute
of experimental methods, and neglecting even observation
and analysis, it was reduced, in order to state genetic relations,
to abstract deduction. All notions of one thing proceeding
from another took the naïve form of procreation or ramifi-
cation. The image of a tree or a pedigree sufficed to represent
any relations of origin and cause. An *arbor de origine juris
et legum*, for example, classified all law in the form of a tree
with numerous branches. Owing to its primitive methods,
the evolutionist thought of the Middle Ages was bound to
remain schematic, arbitrary and sterile.

From the causal point of view, symbolism appears as a
sort of short-circuit of thought. Instead of looking for the
relation between two things by following the hidden detours of
their causal connections, thought makes a leap and discovers
their relation, not in a connection of cause or effects, but in
a connection of signification or finality. Such a connection
will at once appear convincing, provided only that the two
things have an essential quality in common which can be
referred to a general value. Expressed in terms of experimental psychology : all mental association based on a casual
similitude whatever will immediately set up the idea of an
essential and mystic connection. This may well seem a rather
meagre mental function. Moreover, it reveals itself as a very
primitive function, when envisaged from an ethnological point
of view. Primitive thought is characterized by a general
feebleness of perception of the exact demarcation between
different concepts, so that it tends to incorporate into the
notion of a definite something all the notions connected with
it by any relation or similitude whatsoever. With this
tendency the symbolizing function is closely related.

It is, however, possible to view symbolism in a more favourable light by abandoning for a while the point of view of modern science. Symbolism will lose this appearance of arbitrariness and abortiveness when we take into account the fact that it is indissolubly linked up with the conception of the world which was called Realism in the Middle Ages, and which modern philosophy prefers to call, though less correctly, Platonic Idealism.

Symbolic assimilation founded on common properties presupposes the idea that these properties are essential to things. The vision of white and red roses blooming among thorns at once calls up a symbolic assimilation in the medieval mind : for example, that of virgins and martyrs, shining with glory, in the midst of their persecutors. The assimilation is produced because the attributes are the same : the beauty, the tenderness, the purity, the colours of the roses, are also those of the virgins, their red colour that of the blood of the martyrs. But this similarity will only have a mystic meaning if the middle-term connecting the two terms of the symbolic concept expresses an essentiality common to both ; in other words, if redness and whiteness are something more than names for a physical difference based on quantity, if they are conceived as essences, as realities. The mind of the savage, of the child, and of the poet never sees them otherwise.

Now, beauty, tenderness, whiteness, being realities, are also entities ; consequently all that is beautiful, tender or white must have a common essence, the same reason of existence, the same significance before God.

In pointing out these very strong links between symbolism and realism (in the scholastic sense), we should be careful not to think too much of the quarrel about the universals. We know very well that the realism which declared *universalia ante rem*, and attributed essentiality and pre-existence to general ideas, did not dominate medieval thought without a struggle. Undoubtedly there were also nominalists. But it does not seem too bold to affirm that radical nominalism has never been anything but a reaction, an opposition, a countercurrent vainly disputing the ground with the fundamental tendencies of the medieval spirit. As philosophical formulæ, realism and nominalism had early made each other the necessary concessions. The new nominalism of the fourteenth century, that of the Occamites or Moderns, merely removed certain inconveniences of an extreme realism, which it left intact by relegating the domain of faith to a world beyond the philosophical speculations of reason.

Now, it is in the domain of faith that realism obtains, and here it is to be considered rather as the mental attitude of a whole age than as a philosophic opinion. In this larger sense it may be considered inherent in the civilization of the Middle Ages and as dominating all expressions of thought and of the imagination. Undoubtedly Neo-Platonism strongly influenced medieval theology, but was not the sole cause of the general " realist " trend of thought. Every primitive mind is realist, in the medieval sense, independently of all philosophic influence. To such a mentality everything that receives a name becomes an entity and takes a shape which projects itself on the heavens. This shape, in the majority of cases, will be the human shape.

 All realism, in the medieval sense, leads to anthropomorphism. Having attributed a real existence to an idea, the mind wants to see this idea alive, and can only effect this by personifying it. In this way allegory is born. It is not the same thing as symbolism. Symbolism expresses a mysterious connection between two ideas, allegory gives a visible form to the conception of such a connection. Symbolism is a very profound function of the mind, allegory is a superficial one. It aids symbolic thought to express itself, but endangers it at the same time by substituting a figure for a living idea. The force of the symbol is easily lost in the allegory.

So allegory in itself implies from the outset normalizing, projecting on a surface, crystallizing. Moreover, medieval literature had taken it in as a waif of decadent Antiquity. Martianus Capella and Prudentius had been the models. Allegory seldom loses an air of elderliness and pedantry. Still, the use of it supplied a very earnest craving of the medieval mind. How else can we explain the preference which this form enjoyed so long ?

These three modes of thought together—realism, symbolism and personification—have illuminated the medieval mind with a flood of light. The ethic and æsthetic value of the symbolical interpretation of the world was inestimable. Embracing all nature and all history, symbolism gave a conception of the world, of a still more rigorous unity than that which modern science can offer. Symbolism's image of the world is distinguished by impeccable order, architectonic structure, hierarchic subordination. For each symbolic connection implies a difference of rank or sanctity : two things of equal value are hardly capable of a symbolic relationship with each other, unless they are both connected with some third thing of a higher order.

Symbolist thought permits of an infinity of relations between things. Each thing may denote a number of distinct ideas by its different special qualities, and a quality may also have several symbolic meanings. The highest conceptions have symbols by the thousand. Nothing is too humble to represent and to glorify the sublime. The walnut signifies Christ ; the sweet kernel is His divine nature, the green and pulpy outer peel is His humanity, the wooden shell between is the cross. Thus all things raise the thoughts to the eternal ; being thought of as symbols of the highest, in a constant gradation, they are all transfused by the glory of divine majesty. Every precious stone, besides its natural splendour, sparkles with the brilliance of its symbolic values. The assimilation of roses and virginity is much more than a poetic comparison, for it reveals their common essence. As each notion arises in the mind the logic of symbolism creates a harmony of ideas. The special quality of each of them is lost in this ideal harmony and the rigour of rational conception is tempered by the presentment of some mystic unity.

A consistent concord reigns between all the spiritual domains. The Old Testament is the prefiguration of the New, profane history reflects the one and the other. About each idea other ideas group themselves, forming symmetrical figures, as in a kaleidoscope. Eventually all symbols group themselves about the central mystery of the Eucharist ; here there is more than symbolic similitude, there is identity : the Host is Christ and the priest in eating it becomes truly the sepulchre of the Lord.

The world, objectionable in itself, became acceptable by its symbolic purport. For every object, each common trade had a mystical relation with the most holy, which ennobled it. Bonaventura identified the handicrafts symbolically with the eternal generation and incarnation of the Word, and with the covenant between God and the soul. Even profane love is attached by symbolic connection to divine love. In this way all individual suffering is but the shadow of divine suffering, and all virtue is as a partial realization of absolute goodness. Symbolism, in thus detaching personal suffering and virtue from the sphere of the individual in order to raise them to that of the universal, constituted a salutary counterpoise to the strong religious individualism, bent on personal salvation, which is characteristic of the Middle Ages.

Religious symbolism offered one cultural advantage more. To the letter of formulated dogma, rigid and explicit in itself, the flowering imagery of symbols formed, as it were, a musical accompaniment, which by its perfect harmony allowed the mind to transcend the deficiencies of logical expression.

Symbolism opened up all the wealth of religious conceptions to art, to be expressed in forms full of colour and melody, and yet vague and implicit, so that by these the profoundest intuitions might soar towards the ineffable.

In the later Middle Ages the decline of this mode of thought had already long set in. The representation of the Universe in a grand system of symbolical relations had long been complete. Still, the symbolizing habit maintained itself, adding ever new figures that were like petrified flowers. Symbolism at all times shows a tendency to become mechanical. Once accepted as a principle, it becomes a product, not of poetical enthusiasm only, but of subtle reasoning as well, and as such it grows to be a parasite clinging to thought, causing it to degenerate.

Symbolic assimilation is often only based on an equality of number. An immense perspective of ideal series of relationships is opened up in this way, but they amount to nothing more than arithmetical exercises. Thus the twelve months signified the apostles, the four seasons the evangelists, the year Christ. A regular cluster was formed of systems of seven. With the seven virtues correspond the seven supplications of the Lord's Prayer, the seven gifts of the Holy Spirit, the seven beatitudes and the seven penitential psalms. All these groups of seven are again connected with the seven moments of the Passion and the seven sacraments. Each of them is opposed to one of the seven deadly sins, which are represented by seven animals and followed by seven diseases.

A director of consciences like Gerson, from whom these examples are borrowed, is inclined to lay the stress on the moral and practical value of these symbolisms. In a visionary like Alain de la Roche the æsthetic element prevails. His symbolic speculations are very highly elaborated and somewhat factitious. In order to obtain a system in which the numbers fifteen and ten enter, representing the cycles of 150 Aves and of 15 Paters, which he prescribed to his Brotherhood of the Rosary, he adds the eleven celestial spheres and the four elements and then multiplies by the ten categories (substance, quality, etc.). As the product he obtained 150 natural habits. In the same way the multiplication of the ten commandments by fifteen virtues gives 150 moral habits. To arrive at the figure of fifteen virtues, he counts, besides the three theological virtues and the four cardinal virtues, seven capital virtues, which makes fourteen ; there remain two other virtues : religion and penitence ; that makes sixteen, which is one too many ; but as temperance of the cardinal series is identical with abstinence of the capital series, we finally obtain the number fifteen. Each of these fifteen virtues is a queen having her nuptial bed in one of the divisions of the Pater Noster. Each of the words of the Ave signifies one of the fifteen perfections of the Virgin, and at the same time a precious stone, and is able to drive away a sin, or the animal which represents that sin. They represent other things as well : the branches of a tree which carries all the blessed ones ; the steps of a staircase. To quote but two examples : the word *Ave* signifies the innocence of the Virgin and the diamond ; it drives away pride, or the lion, which represents pride. The word *Maria* denotes her wisdom and the carbuncle ; it drives away envy, symbolized by a black dog.

Sometimes Alain gets a little entangled in his very complicated system of symbolisms.

Symbolism was, in fact, played out. Finding symbols and allegories had become a meaningless intellectual pastime, shallow fancifulness resting on a single analogy. The sanctity of the object still gives it some small spiritual value. As soon as the craze of symbolism spreads to profane or simply moral matters, decadence is manifest. Froissart, in *Li Orloge amoureus*, compares all the details of love to the various parts of a timepiece. Chastellain and Molinet vie with each other in political symbolism. The three estates represent the qualities of the Virgin. The seven electors of the Empire signify the virtues ; the five towns of Artois and Hainault, which in 1477 remained faithful to the house of Burgundy, are the five wise virgins. In reality this is symbolism turned upside down ; it uses things of the higher order as symbols of things of the lower order, for these authors in effect raise terrestrial things to the higher level by employing sacred conceptions merely to adorn them.

The *Donatus moralisatus*, sometimes, but erroneously, ascribed to Gerson, mixed up Latin grammar with theology : the noun-substantive is the man, the pronoun means that he is a sinner. The lowest grade of this kind of mental activity is represented by works like *Le Parement et Triumphe des Dames* of Olivier de la Marche, in which each article of female costume symbolizes a virtue—a theme also developed by Coquillart.

> " De la pantouffle ne nous vient que santé
> Et tout prouffit sans griefve maladie,
> Pour luy donner tiltre d'auctorité
> Je luy donne le nom d'humilité." [1]

In the same way shoes mean care and diligence, stockings perseverance, the garter resolution, etc.

It is clear that to the men of the fifteenth century this genre did not appear so silly as it does to us, otherwise they would not have cultivated it with so much gusto. We are thus led to conclude that, to the mind of the declining Middle Ages, symbolism and allegory had not yet lost all their living significance. The tendency to symbolize and to personify was so spontaneous that nearly every thought, of itself, took a figurative shape. Every idea being considered as an entity, and every quality as an essence, they were at once invested by the imagination with a personal form. Denis the Carthusian, in his revelations, sees the Church in fully as personal a

---

[1] The slipper only gives us health And all profit without serious illness. To give it a title to authority I give it the name of humility.

shape as when it was represented in an allegory on the stage. One of his revelations deals with the future reformation of the Church, such as fifteenth-century theology was hoping for : a Church cleansed from the evils that stained it. The spiritual beauty of this purified Church was revealed to his vision in the form of a superb and precious garment, with marvellous colours and ornaments. Another time he sees the persecuted Church : ugly, anæmic, enfeebled. God warns him that the Church is going to speak, and Denis then hears the inner voice as though it proceeded from the person of the Church *quasi ex persona Ecclesiae*. The figurative form that thinking assumes here is so direct and so sufficient to evoke the desired associations, that no need is felt to explain the allegory in detail. The idea of a splendid garment is fully adequate to express spiritual purity ; thought here has resolved itself into an image, just as it can resolve itself into a melody.

Let us recall once more the allegorical personages of the *Roman de la Rose*. To us it requires an effort to picture to ourselves Bel-Accueil, Doulce Mercy, Humble Requeste. To the men of the Middle Ages, on the other hand, these figures had a very vivid æsthetic and sentimental value, which put them almost on a level with those divinities which the Romans conceived out of abstractions, like Pavor and Pallor, Concordia, etc. To the minds of the declining Middle Ages, Doux Penser, Honte, Souvenirs, and the rest, were endowed with a quasi-divine existence. Otherwise the *Roman de la Rose* would have been unreadable. One of the figures passed even from its original meaning to still more concrete signification : Danger in amorous parlance meant the jealous husband.

Allegory is often called in to express a thought of particular importance. Thus the bishop of Chalons, wishing to address a very serious political remonstrance to Philip the Good, gives it an allegorical form and presents it to the duke at Hesdin on Saint Andrew's Day, 1437. " Haultesse de Signourie," chased out of the Empire, having first fled to France, next to the court of Burgundy, is inconsolable, and complains of being harrowed there, too, by " Carelessness of the prince, Feebleness of counsel, Envy of servants, Exaction of the subjects," to drive away which it will be necessary to oppose " Vigilance of the prince," etc., to them. In short, the whole political argument has taken the form of a *tableau vivant* instead of a newspaper leader, as it would take with us. Evidently this was the way to create an impression, and it follows that allegory still had a suggestive force which we find it very hard to realize.

The " Burgher of Paris " in his diary is a prosaic man, who takes little trouble to ornament his style. Nevertheless, when he comes to the most horrible events he has to relate, that is to say, to the Burgundian murders in Paris, in June, 1418, he at once rises to allegory. " Then arose the goddess of Discord, who lived in the tower of Evil Counsel, and awoke Wrath, the mad woman, and Covetousness and Rage and Vengeance, and they took up arms of all sorts and cast out Reason, Justice, Remembrance of God and Moderation most shamefully." His narrative of the atrocities committed is entirely composed in the symbolic fashion. " Then Madness the enraged, and Murder and Slaughter killed, cut down, put to death, massacred all they found in the prisons . . . and Covetousness tucked up her skirts into her belt with Rapine, her daughter, and Larceny, her son. . . . Afterwards the aforesaid people went by the guidance of their goddesses, that is to say, Wrath, Covetousness and Vengeance, who led them through all the public prisons of Paris, etc."

Why does the author use allegory here ? To give his narrative a more solemn tone than the one he uses for the daily events which he generally notes down in his diary. He feels the necessity of regarding these atrocious events as something more than the crimes of a few individual malefactors ; allegory is his way of expressing his sense of tragedy.

It is just when allegory chafes us most that it fully reveals its dominion over the medieval mind. We can bear it more or less in a tableau vivant where conventional figures are draped in a fantastical and unreal apparel. The fifteenth century dresses up its allegorical figures, as well as its saints, in the costume of the time and has the faculty of creating new personages for each thought it wants to express. To tell the moral tale of a giddy young man, who is led to ruin by the life at court, Charles de Rochefort, in *L'Abuzé en Court*, invents a whole new series of personages, like those of the *Rose*, and these dim creations, Fol cuidier, Folle bombance (Foolish credulity,

Foolish show), and the rest, are represented in the miniatures illustrating the work like noblemen of the age. Time himself does not require a beard or a scythe, and appears in doublets and hose. The very commonplace aspect of these allegories is precisely what shows their vitality.

We can understand that a human shape is ascribed to virtues or to sentiments, but the spirit of the Middle Ages does not hesitate to extend this process to notions which, to us, have nothing personal. The personification of Lent was a widely known type from 1300 onward. We find it in the poem, *La Bataille de Karesme et de Charnage*, a theme which Peter Breughel was to take up much later and illustrate with his mad fancy. A current proverb said : *Quaresme fait ses flans la nuit de Pasques.*[1] In certain towns of North Germany a doll, called Lent, was suspended in the choir of the church and taken down during mass on the Wednesday before Easter.

Was there a difference between the idea which people formed of saints and that of purely symbolic personages ? Undoubtedly, the former were acknowledged by the Church, they had a historical character and statues of wood and stone, but the latter were in touch with living fancy, and, after all, we may ask ourselves if to popular imagination Bel-Accueil or Faux Semblant did not appear as real as Saint Barbara and Saint Christopher.

On the other hand, there is no real contrast between medieval allegory and Renaissance mythology. There is rather a fusion. The mythological figures are older than the Renaissance. Venus and Fortune, for instance, had never completely died, and allegory, on the other hand, kept its vogue for a long time after the fifteenth century, nowhere stronger than in English literature. In the poetry of Froissart, Doux Semblant, Refus, Dangier and Escondit are seen contending, as it were, with mythological figures like Atropos, Clotho, Lachesis. At first the latter are less vivid and coloured than the allegories ; they are dull and shadowy and there is nothing classic about them. Gradually Renaissance sentiment brings about a complete change. The Olympians and the nymphs get the better of the allegorical personages, who fade away, in proportion as the poetic glory of Antiquity is more intensely felt.

[1] Lent bakes his cakes on Easter-night.

Symbolism, with its servant allegory, ultimately became an intellectual pastime. The symbolic mentality was an obstacle to the development of causal thought, as causal and genetic relations must needs look insignificant by the side of symbolic connections. Thus the sacred symbolism of the two luminaries and the two swords for a long time barred the road to historic and juridical criticism of papal authority. For the symbolizing of Papacy and Empire as the Sun and the Moon, or as the two swords brought by the Disciples, was to the medieval mind far more than a striking comparison ; it revealed the mystic foundation of the two powers, and established directly the precedence of Saint Peter. Dante, in order to investigate the historical foundation of the pope's primacy, had first to deny the appropriateness of the symbolism.

The time was not distant when people were bound to awake to the dangers of symbolism ; when arbitrary and futile allegories would become distasteful and be rejected as trammels of thought. Luther branded them in an invective which is aimed at the greatest lights of scholastic theology : Bonaventura, Guillaume Durand, Gerson and Denis the Carthusian. " These allegorical studies," he exclaims, " are the work of people who have too much leisure. Do you think I should find it difficult to play at allegory-making about any created thing whatsoever ? Who is so feeble-witted that he could not try his hand at it ? "

Symbolism was a defective translation into images of secret connections dimly felt, such as music reveals to us. *Videmus nunc per speculum in aenigmate.* The human mind felt that it was face to face with an enigma, but none the less it kept on trying to discern the figures in the glass, explaining images by yet other images. Symbolism was like a second mirror held up to that of the phenomenal world itself.

CHAPTER XVI

THE EFFECTS OF REALISM

All that was thinkable had taken image-shape : conception had become almost entirely dependent on imagination. Now, a too systematic idealism (this is what realism meant in the Middle Ages) gives a certain rigidity to the conception of the world. Ideas, being conceived as entities and of importance only by virtue of their relation with the Absolute, easily range themselves as so many fixed stars on the firmament of thought. Once defined, they only lend themselves to classification, subdivision and distinction according to purely deductive norms. Apart from the rules of logic, there is never a corrective at hand to indicate a mistake in the classification, and this causes the mind to be deluded as to the value of its own operations and the certainty of the system.

If the medieval mind wants to know the nature or the reason of a thing, it neither looks into it, to analyse its structure, nor behind it, to inquire into its origin, but looks up to heaven, where it shines as an idea. Whether the question involved is political social or moral, the first step taken is always to reduce it to its universal principle. Even quite trifling and ordinary things are regarded in this light. Thus a point is debated in the University of Paris : May examination fees be levied for intermediate degrees ? The chancellor thinks so ; Pierre d'Ailly intervenes to defend the opposite view. Now, he does not start from arguments based on law or tradition, but from an application of the text : *Radix omnium malorum cupiditas*,[1] and so he sets himself to prove by an entirely scholastic exposition that the aforesaid exaction is simoniacal, heretical, and contrary to natural and divine law. This is what so often disappoints and wearies us moderns in reading medieval demonstrations : they are directed

[1] The root of all evil is covetousness.

195

heavenwards, and lose themselves from the very start in moral generalities and Scriptural cases.

This profound and systematic idealism betrays itself everywhere. There is an ideal and clearly defined conception of every trade, dignity or estate, to which the individual who belongs to it has to conform as best he may. Denis the Carthusian, in a series of treatises, *De vita et regimine episcoporum, archidiaconorum*, etc., etc., pointed out to all—bishops, canons, priests, scholars, princes, nobles, knights, merchants, husbands, widows, girls, friars—the ideal form of their professional duties, and the way to sanctify their calling or condition by living up to that ideal. His exposition of moral precepts, however, remains abstract and general ; he never brings us into contact with the realities of the occupations or walks in life of which he speaks.

This tendency to reduce all things to a general type has been considered a fundamental weakness in the mentality of the Middle Ages, owing to which the power to discern and describe individual traits was never attained. Starting from this premise, the well-known summary of the Renaissance as the coming of individualism would be justified. But at bottom this antithesis is inexact and misleading. Whatever the faculty of seeing specific traits may have been in the Middle Ages, it must be noted that men disregarded the individual qualities and fine distinctions of things, deliberately and of set purpose, in order always to bring them under some general principle. This mental tendency is a result of their profound idealism. People feel an imperious need of always and especially seeing the general sense, the connection with the absolute, the moral ideality, the ultimate significance of a thing. What is important is the impersonal. The mind is not in search of individual realities, but of models, examples, norms.

Every notion concerning the world or life had its fixed place in a vast hierarchic system of ideas, in which it is linked with ideas of a higher and more general order, on which it depends like a vassal on his lord. The proper business of the medieval mind is discrimination, displaying severally all concepts as if they were so many substantial things. Hence the faculty of detaching a conception from the ideal complex to which it belongs in order to regard it as a thing by itself. When

Foulques de Toulouse is blamed for giving an alms to an Albigensian woman, he answers : " I do not give it to the heretic, but to the poor woman." Margaret of Scotland, queen of France, having kissed Alain Chartier, the poet, whom she found asleep, exculpates herself in these terms : " I did not kiss the man, but the precious mouth whence have issued and gone forth so many good words and virtuous sayings." It is the same turn of mind which, in the field of high theological speculation, distinguishes in God between an antecedent will, desiring the salvation of all, and a consequent will, extending only to the elect.

Without the brake of empirical observation, the habit of always subordinating and subdividing becomes automatic and sterile, mere numbering, and nothing else. No subject lent itself better to it than the category of virtues and of sins. Every sin has its fixed number of causes, species, noxious effects. There are, according to Denis the Carthusian, twelve follies, deceiving the sinner ; each of them is illustrated, fixed and represented by Scripture texts and by symbols, so that the whole argument displays itself like a church portal ornamented with sculptures. The enormity of sin should be considered from seven points of view : that of God, that of the sinner, of matter, of circumstances, of the intention, of the nature of the sin and of its consequences. Next, every one of these seven points is subdivided, in its turn, into eight, or into fourteen. There are six infirmities of the mind which incline us to sin, etc. This systematizing of morality has its striking analogies in the sacred books of Buddhism.

Now, this everlasting classification, this anatomy of sin, would be apt to weaken the consciousness of sin which it should enhance, if it were not attended with an effort of the imagination directed to the gravity of the fault and the horrors of the chastisements. All moral conceptions are exaggerated, overcharged to excess, because they are always placed in direct connection with divine majesty. In every sin, even the least, the universe is concerned. No human soul can be fully conscious of the enormity of sin. All the saints and the just, the celestial spheres, the elements, the lower creatures and inanimate objects, cry for vengeance on the sinner. Denis strives to over-stimulate the fear of sin and of hell by detailed descriptions and terrifying images. Dante has touched with beauty the darkness of hell : Farinata and Ugolino are heroic, and Lucifer is majestic. But this monk, devoid of all poetic grace, draws a picture of devouring torment and nothing more ; his very dullness makes the horror of it. " Let us imagine," he says, " a white-hot oven, and in this oven a naked man, never to be released from such a torment. Does not the mere sight of it appear insupportable ? How miserable this man would seem to us ! Let us think how he would sprawl in the oven, how he would yell and roar : in short, how he would *live*, and what would be his agony and his sorrow when he understood that this unbearable punishment was never to end."

The horrible cold, the loathsome worms, the stench, hunger and thirst, the darkness, the chains, the unspeakable filth, the endless cries, the sight of the demons, Denis calls up all this before us like a nightmare. Still more oppressive is the insistence on psychic suffering : the mourning, the fear, the empty feeling of everlasting separation from God, the inexpressible hatred of God, the envy of the bliss of the elect ; the confusion of all sorts of errors and delusions in the brain. And the thought that this is to last in all eternity is by ingenious comparisons wrought up to the fever-point of horror.

The treatise *De quatuor hominum novissimis*, from which these details are borrowed, was the customary reading during meal-time at the convent of Windesheim. A truly bitter condiment ! But medieval man always preferred drastic treatment. He was like an invalid who has been treated too long with heroic medicines, only the most powerful stimulants produced an effect on him. In order to make some virtue shine in all its splendour, the Middle Ages present it in an exaggerated form, which a sedater moralist would perhaps regard as a caricature. Saint Giles praying God not to allow his wound caused by an arrow to heal is their pattern of patience. Temperance finds its models in saints who always mix ashes with their food, chastity in those who tested their virtue by sleeping beside a woman. If it is not some extravagant act, it is the extreme youth of the saint which marks him out as a model, Saint Nicholas refusing his mother's milk on feast-days, or Saint Quiricus (a martyr, either three years or nine months old) refusing to be consoled by the prefect, and thrown into the abyss.

Here, again, it is the dominant idealism which makes people only relish the excellence of virtue in an extra strong dose. Virtue is conceived as an idea ; its beauty shines more brightly in the hyperbolic perfection of its essence than in the imperfect practice of everyday life.

Nothing shows better the primitive character of the hyper-idealist mentality, called realism in the Middle Ages, than the tendency to ascribe a sort of substantiality to abstract concepts. Though philosophic realism did never admit these materialist tendencies, and strove to avoid such consequences, it cannot be denied that medieval thought frequently yielded to the inclination to pass from pure idealism to a sort of magic idealism, in which the abstract tends to become concrete. Here the ties which bind the Middle Ages to a very remote cultural past are very clearly displayed.

It was about 1300 that the doctrine of the treasure of the works of supererogation of Christ and the saints took a fixed form. The idea itself of such a treasure, the common possession of all the faithful, in so far as they are members of the mystic body of Christ, which is the Church, was by that time very ancient. But the way in which it was applied, in the sense that the superabundant good works constitute an inexhaustible reserve, which the Church can dispose of by retail, does not appear before the thirteenth century. Alexandre de Halès was the first to use the word *thesaurus* in the technical sense, which it has kept ever since. The doctrine did not fail to excite resistance. In the end, however, it prevailed and was officially formulated in 1343 in the bull *Unigenitus* of Clement VI. There the treasure has altogether the form of a capital confided by Christ to Saint Peter, and still increasing every day. For, in proportion as men are more drawn to justice by the distribution of this treasure, the merits, of which it is composed, will go on accumulating.

The material conception of ethical categories made itself felt more with regard to sin than to virtue. The Church, it is true, has always explicitly taught that sin is not a thing or an entity. But how could it have prevented the error, when everything concurred to insinuate it into men's minds ? The primitive instinct which see sins as stuff which soils or corrupts, which one should, therefore, wash away, or destroy, was strengthened by the extreme systematizing of sin, by their figurative representation, and even by the penitentiary technique of the Church itself. In vain did Denis the Carthusian remind the people that it was but for the sake of comparison that he calls sin a fever, a cold and corrupted humour—popular thought undoubtedly lost sight of the restrictions of dogmatists. The terminology of the law, less anxious than theology as to doctrinal purity, did not hesitate, in England, to connect with felony the notion of a corruption of the blood : this is the realistic conception in its spontaneous form.

On one special point the dogma itself demanded this perfectly realist conception : that is to say, with regard to the blood of the Redeemer. The faithful are bound to conceive it as absolutely material. A drop of the precious blood, said Saint Bernard, would have sufficed to save the world, but it was shed abundantly, as Saint Thomas Aquinas expresses it in a hymn :

> " Pie Pelicane, Jesu domine,
> Me immundum munda tuo sanguine,
> Cuius una stilla salvum facere
> Totum mundum quit ab omni scelere." [1]

---

[1] Pious pelican, Lord Jesus, cleanse me, impure one, by your blood, of which one drop can save all the world from all iniquity.

Compare Marlowe's *Faustus* : " See, where Christ's blood streams in the firmament ! One drop of blood will save me."

CHAPTER XVII

RELIGIOUS THOUGHT BEYOND THE LIMITS OF IMAGINATION

The imagination was continually striving, and in vain, to express the ineffable by giving it shape and figure. To call up the absolute, recourse is always had to the terminology of extension in space, and the effort always fails. From the pseudo-Dionysius the Areopagite onward, mystic authors have piled up terms of immensity and infinity. It is always infinite extension which has to serve for rendering the eternal accessible to reason. Mystics exert themselves to find suggestive images. Imagine, says Denis the Carthusian, a mountain of sand, as large as the universe ; that every hundred thousand years a grain be taken from it. The mountain will disappear at last. But after such an inconceivable space of time the sufferings of hell will not have diminished, and will not be nearer to the end than when the first grain was removed. And yet, if the damned knew that they would be set free when the mountain had disappeared, it would be a great consolation to them.

If, to inculcate fear and horror, the imagination disposed of resources of appalling wealth, the expression of celestial joys, on the other hand, always remained extremely primitive and monotonous. Human language cannot provide a vision of absolute bliss. It has at its disposal only inadequate superlatives, which can do nothing but strengthen the idea arithmetically. What was the use of producing terms of height, or extension, or the inexhaustible ? People never could progress beyond imagery, the reduction of the infinite to the finite, and the consequent weakening of the feeling of the absolute. Every sensation in expressing itself lost a little of its immediate force, every attribute ascribed to God robbed Him of a little of His majesty.

Thus begins the tremendous struggle of the spirit which yearns to rise above all imagery. It is the same at all epochs and with all races. Mystics, it has been said, have neither birthday nor native land. But the support of imagination cannot be given up all at once. The insufficiency of all modes of expression is gradually accepted. First the brilliant imagery of symbolism is abandoned, and the too concrete formulas of dogma are avoided. But still the contemplation of the absolute Being ever remains linked up with notions of extension or of light. Next these notions change into their negative opposites—silence, the void, obscurity. And as these latter formless conceptions, too, in their turn, prove insufficient, a constant joining of each to its contrary is tried. Finally, nothing remains to express the idea of divinity but pure negation.

Of course, these successive stages in the abandoning of imagery have not actually followed in strict chronological order. All had been reached already by Denis the Areopagite. In the following passage of Denis the Carthusian we find the greater number of these modes of expression united. In a revelation he hears the voice of God who is angry. "On hearing this answer the monk, collected within himself, and finding himself as transported into a region of immense light, most sweetly, in an intense tranquillity, by a secret call without external sound invoked the most secret and truly hidden, the incomprehensible God : O most over-lovable God, Thou in Thyself art the light and the region of light, in which Thy elect sweetly come to rest, repose, sleep. Thou art like a desert most over-vast, even and intraversable, where the truly pious heart, entirely purified of all individual affection, illumined from on high and inflamed by sacred ardour, deviates without erring and errs without deviating, happily fails and unfailingly convalesces."

We here find first the image of light, next that of sleep, then that of the desert, and, lastly, the opposites which cancel one another. The mystic imagination found a very impressive concept in adding to the image of the desert, that is to say, extension of surface—that of the abyss, or extension of depth. The sensation of giddiness is added to the feeling of infinite space. The German mystics, as well as

Ruysbroeck, have made a very plastic use of this striking image.

Master Eckhart spoke of " the abyss without mode and without form of the silent and waste divinity." The fruition of bliss, says Ruysbroeck, " is so immense that God Himself is as swallowed up with all the blessed . . . in an absence of modes, which is a not-knowing, and in an eternal loss of self." And elsewhere : " The seventh degree, which follows next . . . is attained when, beyond all knowledge and all knowing, we discover in ourselves a bottomless not-knowing ; when beyond all names given to God and to creatures, we come to expire and pass over in eternal namelessness, where we lose ourselves . . . and when we contemplate all these blessed spirits which are essentially sunken away, merged and lost in their super-essence, in an unknown darkness without mode."

Always the hopeless attempt to dispense with images and to attain " the state of void, that is mere absence of images," which only God can give. " He deprives us of all images and brings us back to the initial state where we find only wild and waste absoluteness, void of all form or image, for ever corresponding with eternity."

The contemplation of God, says Denis the Carthusian, is more adequately rendered by negations than by affirmations. " For, when I say : God is goodness, essence, life, I seem to indicate what God is, as if what He is had anything in common with, or any resemblance to, a creature, whereas it is certain, that He is incomprehensible and unknown, inscrutable and ineffable, and separated from all He works by an immeasurable and wholly incomparable difference and excellence." It is for this reason that the " uniting wisdom " was called by the Areopagite : unreasonable, insane and foolish.

But whether Denis or Ruysbroeck speak of light changed into darkness (a motif inspired by the Old Testament and which the pseudo-Areopagite had developed), or again of ignorance, forlornness or of death, they never get beyond images.

Without metaphors it is impossible to express a single thought. All effort to rise above images is doomed to fail. To speak of our most ardent aspirations only in negative terms does not satisfy the cravings of the heart, and where philosophy no longer finds expression, poetry comes in again. Mysticism has always rediscovered the road from the giddy heights of sublime contemplation to the flowery meadows of symbolism. The sweet lyricism of the older French mystics, Saint Bernard and the Victorines, will always come to the aid of the seer, when all the resources of expression have been exhausted. In the transports of ecstasy the colours and figures of allegory reappear. Henry Suso sees his betrothed, Eternal Wisdom : " She soared high above him in a sky with clouds, she was bright like the morning star and shone like the radiant sun ; her crown was eternity, her robe beatitude, her speech sweetness, her kiss absolute delight ; she was remote and near, high aloft and below ; she was present and yet hidden ; she let herself be approached and yet no one could grasp her."

The Church has always feared the excesses of mysticism, and with reason. For the fire of contemplative rapture, consuming all forms and images, must needs burn all formulas, concepts, dogmas, and sacraments too. However, the very nature of mystic transport implied a safeguard for the Church. To be uplifted to the clarity of ecstasy, to wander on the solitary heights of contemplation stripped of forms and images, tasting union with the only and absolute principle, was to the mystic never more than the rare grace of a single moment. He had to come down from the mountain-tops. The extremists, it is true, with their following of " enfants perdus," did deviate into pantheism and eccentricities. The others, however— and it is among these that we find the great mystics—never lost their way back to the Church awaiting them with its wise and economic system of mysteries fixed in the liturgy. It offered to everybody the means to get into touch at a given moment with the divine principle in all security and without danger of individual extravagances. It economized mystic energy, and that is why it has always outlived unbridled mysticism and the dangers it compassed.

" Unitive wisdom is unreasonable, insane and foolish." The path of the mystic leading into the infinite leads to unconsciousness. By denying all positive connection between the Deity and all that has form and a name, the operation of transcendency is really abolished : " All creatures "—says Eckhart—" are mere nothing ; I do not say that they are little or aught : they are nothing. That which has no entity, is not. All creatures have no being, for their being depends on the presence of God." Intensive mysticism signifies return to a pre-intellectual mental life. All that is culture is obliterated and annulled.

If, notwithstanding, mysticism has, at all times, borne abundant fruit for civilization, it is because it always rises by degrees, and because in its initial stages it is a powerful element of spiritual development. Contemplation demands a severe culture of moral perfection as a preparatory condition. The gentleness, the curbing of desires, the simplicity, the temperance, the laboriousness practised in mystical circles, create about them an atmosphere of peace and of pious fervour. All the great mystics have praised humble labour and charity. In the Netherlands these concomitant features of mysticism —moralism, pietism—became the essence of a very important spiritual movement. From the preparatory phases of intensive mysticism of the few issued the extensive mysticism of the " devotio moderna " of the many. Instead of the solitary ecstasy of the blessed moment comes a constant and collective habit of earnestness and fervour, cultivated by simple townspeople in the friendly intercourse of their Fraterhouses and Windesheim convents. Theirs was mysticism by retail. They had " only received a spark." But in their midst the spirit lived which gave the world the work in which the soul of the declining Middle Ages found its most fruitful expression for the times to come : *The Imitation of Jesus Christ*. Thomas à Kempis was no theologian and no humanist, no philosopher and no poet, and hardly even a true mystic. Yet he wrote the book which was to console the ages. Perhaps here the abundant imagination of the medieval mind was conquered in the highest sense.

Thomas à Kempis leads us back to everyday life.

CHAPTER XVIII

THE FORMS OF THOUGHT AND PRACTICAL LIFE

The specific forms of the thought of an epoch should not only be studied as they reveal themselves in theological and philosophic speculations, or in the conceptions of creeds, but also as they appear in practical wisdom and everyday life. We may even say that the true character of the spirit of an age is better revealed in its mode of regarding and expressing trivial and commonplace things than in the high manifestations of philosophy and science. For all scholarly speculation, at least in Europe, is affiliated in a very complicated way to Greek, Hebrew, even Babylonian and Egyptian origins, whereas in everyday life the spirit of a race or of an epoch expresses itself naïvely and spontaneously.

The mental habits and forms characteristic of the high speculation of the Middle Ages nearly all reappear in the domain of ordinary life. Here, too, as we might expect, primitive idealism, which the schools called realism, is at the bottom of all mental activity. To take every idea by itself, to give it its formula, to treat it as an entity, next to combine the ideas, to classify them, to arrange them in hierarchic systems, always to build cathedrals with them, such, in practical life also, is the way in which the medieval mind proceeds.

All that acquires a fixed place in life is considered as having a reason for existence in the divine scheme. The most commonplace customs share this honour with the most exalted things. A very plain instance of this may be found in the treatment of rules of court etiquette, which we have touched upon already in another connection. Aliénor de Poitiers and Olivier de la Marche considered them wise laws, judiciously instituted by ancient kings and binding for all centuries to come. Aliénor speaks of them as of sacred monuments of the wisdom of ages : " And then I have heard it said by the

206

ancients who knew . . ." etc. She sees with sorrow signs of decline. For a good many years the ladies of Flanders have been putting the bed of a woman newly delivered of a child before the fire, " at which people mocked a good deal," because formerly this was never done. What are we coming to ? " But at present everybody does what he pleases : because of which we may well be afraid that all will go badly."—La Marche gravely asks the following question : Why has the " fruit-master," also the " wax-department " (le mestier de la cire), that is to say, illumination, among his attributes ?— He answers, not less gravely : Because wax is extracted from flowers whence the fruit comes too : " so that this matter is very well ordained thus."

In matters of utility or of ceremony medieval authority creates a special organ for every function, because it regards the function as an idea and considers it as an actual thing. The " grand sergeanty " of the king of England comprised a dignitary whose office it was to hold the king's head when he crossed the Channel and was suffering with sea-sickness. A certain John Baker held this office in 1442, and after his death it passed to his two daughters.

Of the same nature is the custom, very ancient and very primitive, of giving a proper name to inanimate objects. We witnessed a revival of this usage when the big guns during the late war got names. During the Middle Ages it was much more frequent. Like the swords of the heroes in the *chansons de geste*, the stone mortars in the wars of the fourteenth and fifteenth centuries had names of their own : " Le Chien d'Orléans, la Gringade, la Bourgeoise, Dulle Griete." A few very celebrated diamonds are still known by proper names : this, too, is a survival of a widely spread custom. Several jewels of Charles the Bold had their names : " le sancy, les trois frères, la hôte, la balle de Flandres." If, at the present time, ships still have names, but bells and most houses have not, the reason lies in the fact that the ship preserves a sort of personality, also expressed in the English usage of making ships feminine. In the Middle Ages this tendency to personify things was much stronger ; every house and every bell had its name.

In the minds of the Middle Ages every event, every case,

fictitious or historic, tends to crystallize, to become a parable, an example, a proof, in order to be applied as a standing instance of a general moral truth. In the same way every utterance becomes a dictum, a maxim, a text. For every question of conduct Scripture, legends, history, literature, furnish a crowd of examples or of types, together making up a sort of moral clan, to which the matter in question belongs. If it is desired to make someone to pardon an offence, all the Biblical cases of pardon are enumerated to him ; if to dissuade him from marrying, all the unhappy marriages of antiquity are cited. In order to free himself from blame for the murder of the duke of Orleans, Jean sans Peur compares himself to Joab and his victim to Absalom, rating himself as less guilty than Joab, because he had not acted in open defiance of a royal warning. "Ainsy avoit le bon duc Jehan attrait ce fait à moralité." [1]

In the Middle Ages everyone liked to base a serious argument on a text, so as to give it a foundation. In 1406, at the national council of Paris, where the question of the schism was debated, the twelve propositions for and against renouncing obedience to the pope of Avignon, all started from a Biblical quotation. Profane orators, too, no less than preachers, choose their text.

All the traits indicated are found united in striking fashion in the famous plea delivered on the 8th of March, 1408, at the hôtel de Saint Pol before a princely audience, by Master Jean Petit, divine, preacher and poet, in order to clear the duke of Burgundy of the charge of the murder which the latter repented of having confessed. It is a real masterpiece of political wickedness, built up with perfect art and in a severe style on the text : *Radix omnium malorum cupiditas* (the root of all evil is covetousness). The whole is cunningly arranged in a scheme of scholastic distinctions and complementary Biblical texts, illustrated by Scriptural and historical examples and animated by a fiendish verve. After having enumerated twelve reasons obliging the duke of Burgundy to honour, love and avenge the king of France, Maître Petit draws two applications from his text : covetousness makes apostates and it makes traitors. Apostasy and treason are divided and

[1] Thus good duke John had drawn the moral inference of the case.

subdivided, and then illustrated by three examples. Lucifer, Absalom and Athalia rise up before the imagination of the hearers as the archetypes of a traitor. Eight truths are brought forward to justify tyrannicide. Referring to one of the eight, he says : " I shall prove this truth by twelve reasons in honour of the twelve apostles." And he cites three sentences of the doctors, three of the philosophers, three of the jurists and three from Scripture. From the eight truths eight corollaries are derived, completed by a ninth. By the aid of allusions or insinuations he revives all the old suspicions which hung over the memory of the ambitious and debauched prince : his responsibility for the disaster of the " bal des ardents," where the young king's company, disguised as wild men, miserably perished by fire, while the king himself narrowly escaped ; his plans of murder and poisoning, hatched in the Celestine monastery, in the course of his conversations with " the sorcerer," Philippe de Mézières. The notorious leaning of the duke towards necromancy furnished an opportunity for describing very picturesque scenes of horror. Maître Petit is even familiar with the demons whom Orleans consulted ; he knows their names and the way in which they were dressed. He goes so far as to ascribe a sinister meaning to the delirious utterances of the mad king.

All this makes up the major term of the syllogism. The minor follows it, point by point. Grounding themselves on the general propositions which had raised the case to the plane of fundamental ethics and had artfully roused a sentiment of shuddering horror, the direct accusations burst out in a flood of passionate hatred and defamation. The pleading lasted for four hours, and at the end Jean sans Peur pronounced the words : " I avouch you " (Je vous avoue). The justification was written out in four costly copies for the duke and his nearest relations, ornamented with gilding and miniatures, and bound in pressed leather. It was also for sale.

The tendency to give each particular case the character of a moral sentence or of an example, so that it becomes something substantial and unchallengeable, the crystallization of thought, in short, finds its most general and natural expression in the proverb. In the thought of the Middle Ages proverbs have performed a very living function. There were hundreds in current use in every nation. The greater number are striking and concise. Their tone is often ironical, their accent always that of bonhomie and resignation. The wisdom we glean from them is sometimes profound and beneficent. They never preach resistance. "Les grans poissons mangent les plus petis." "Les mal vestus assiet on dos ou vent." "Nul n'est chaste si ne besongne." "Au besoing on s'aide du diable." "Il n'est si ferré qui ne glice." [1] To the laments of moralists about the depravation of man the proverbs oppose a smiling detachment. The proverb always glozes over iniquity. Now it is naïvely pagan and now almost evangelical. A people which has many proverbs in current use will be less given to talking nonsense, and so will avoid many confused arguments and empty phrases. Leaving arguments to cultured people, it is content with judging each case by referring to the authority of some proverb. The crystallization of thought in proverbs is therefore not without advantage to society.

Proverbs in their crude simplicity were thoroughly in accordance with the general spirit of the literature of the epoch. The level reached by authors was but little higher than that of the proverbs. The dicta of Froissart often read like proverbs gone wrong. "It is thus with feats of arms : sometimes one loses, another time one wins." "There is nothing of which one does not tire." It is therefore safer, instead of hazarding moral sentences of one's own, to use well-established proverbs like Geffroi de Paris, who lards his rhyming chronicle with them. The literature of the time is full of ballads of which each stanza ends with a proverb, as, for instance, the *Ballade de Fougères* of Alain Chartier, the *Complaincte de Eco* of Coquillart, and several poems by Jean Molinet, not to mention Villon's well-known ballad which was entirely composed of them. The 171 stanzas of the *Passe Temps d'Oysiveté*, by Robert Gaguin, nearly all end in some phrase looking like a proverb, although the greater number are not found in the best-known collections. Did Gaguin invent them, then ? In that case we should have a still more curious indication of the vital function of the proverb at this

---

[1] The big fishes eat the smaller. The badly dressed are placed with their back to the wind. None is chaste if he has no business. At need we let the devil help us. No horse is so well shod that it never slips.

epoch, if we see them here arising in an individual mind, *in statu nascendi*, as it were.

In political speeches and in sermons, proverbs are in frequent use. Gerson, Jean de Varennes, Jean Petit, Guillaume Fillastre, Olivier Maillard, take pains to strengthen their arguments by the most common ones. " Qui de tout se tait, de tout a paix.—Chef bien peigné porte mal bacinet.—Qui commun sert, nul ne l'en paye."[1]

Related to the proverb, in so far as it is a crystallized form of thought, is the motto, which the declining Middle Ages cultivated with marked predilection. It differs from it in that it is not, like the proverb, a wise adage of general application, but a personal maxim or exhortation. To adopt a motto is, so to say, to choose a text for the sermon of one's life. The motto is a symbol and a token. Marked in golden letters on every article of the wardrobe and of the equipment, it must have exercised a suggestive influence of no mean importance. The moral tone of these mottoes is mostly that of resignation, like that of the proverbs, or that of hope. The motto should be mysterious. " Quand sera ce ?—Tost ou tard vienne.—Va oultre.—Autre fois mieulx.—Plus deuil que joye."[2] The greater number refer to love. " Aultre naray.— Vostre plaisir.—Souvienne vous.—Plus que toutes."[3] When of such a nature they were worn on armour and caparisons. Those engraved in rings have a more intimate note : " Mon cuer avez.—Je le desire.—Pour toujours.—Tout pour vous."[4]

A complement to mottoes is found in the emblem, like the knotty stick of Louis of Orleans with the motto " Je l'envie," a gambling term meaning " I challenge," to which Jean sans Peur replied with a plane and the words " Ic houd," that is to say, " accepted." Another instance is the flint-and-steel of Philip the Good. With the emblem and the motto we enter the sphere of heraldic thought, of which the psychology is yet to be written. To the men of the Middle Ages the coat of arms

---

[1] He who is silent about all things, is troubled by nothing.—A well-groomed head wears the helmet badly.—He who serves the common weal, is paid by none for his trouble.

[2] When will it be ?—Soon or late it may come.—Onward.—Better next time.—More sorrow than joy.

[3] I shall have no other.—Your pleasure.—Remember.—More than all.

[4] You have my heart.—I desire it.—For ever.—All for you.

was undoubtedly more than a matter of vanity or of genealogical interest. Heraldic figures in their minds acquired a value almost like that of a *totem*. Whole complexes of pride and ambition, of loyalty and devotion, were condensed in the symbols of lions, lilies or crosses, which thus marked and expressed intricate mental contexts by means of an image.

The spirit of casuistry, which was greatly developed in the Middle Ages, is another expression of the same tendency to isolate each thing as a special entity. It is another effect of the dominant idealism. Every question which presents itself must have its ideal solution, which will become apparent as soon as we have ascertained, by the aid of formal rules, the relation of the case in question to the eternal verities. Casuistry reigns in all the departments of the mind : alike in morals and in law, and in matters of ceremony, of etiquette, of tournaments and the chase, and, above all, of love. We have already spoken of the influence which chivalrous casuistry exercised on the origins of the laws of war. Let us quote some more examples from the *Arbre des Batailles* of Honoré Bonet. Should a member of the clergy aid his father or his bishop ? Is one bound to make good borrowed armour which one has lost during a battle ? May one fight a battle on festal days ? Is it better to fight fasting or after a meal ?

No subject lent itself better to the distinction of casuistry than that of prisoners of war. To take noble and rich prisoners was, at that time, the main point of the military profession. In what circumstances may one escape from captivity ? What is a safe conduct worth ? To whom does an escaped and recaptured prisoner belong ? May a prisoner on parole fly, if his victor puts him in chains ? Or may he do so, if his captor forgot to ask his parole ? In *Le Jouvencel* two captains dispute for a prisoner before the commander-in-chief. " I seized him first," says one, " by the arm and by the right hand, and tore his glove from him." " But to me," says the other, " he gave that same hand with his parole."

Besides idealism, a strong formalism is at the bottom of all the traits enumerated. The innate belief in the transcendental reality of things brings about as a result that every notion is strictly defined and limited, isolated, as it were, in a plastic form, and it is this form which is all-important. Mortal sins are distinguished from venial sins according to fixed rules. In law, culpability is established in the first place by the formal nature of the deed. The ancient judicial adage, " The deed judges the man," had lost nothing of its force. Although jurisprudence had been long ago freed from the extreme formalism of primitive law, which knew no difference between the intentional and the involuntary deed and did not punish an attempt that had miscarried, yet traces of a severe formalism existed in great number at the close of the Middle Ages. Thus, there was a rule of long standing that a slip of the tongue in the formula of an oath rendered it null and void, the oath being a sacred thing. In the thirteenth century an exception was made in favour of foreign merchants who only knew the language of the country imperfectly, and it was conceded that their incorrect language in taking the oath should not lose them their rights.

The extreme sensibility to everything touching honour is an effect of the general formalism. A nobleman is blamed for having the caparison of his horse ornamented with his armorial bearings, because, if the horse, " a brute beast," should stumble at the joust, the coat of arms would be dragged through the sand and the whole family dishonoured.

The formal element occupied a large place in everything connected with vengeance, expiations, reparations for wounded honour. The right of vengeance, a very vital element in the customs of France and the Netherlands in the fifteenth century, was exercised more or less according to fixed rules. It is not always furious anger which urges people to acts of violence in pursuit of vengeance ; amends for offended honour are sought according to a well-regulated plan. It is, above all, a question of shedding blood, not of killing ; sometimes care is taken to wound the victim only in the face, the arms, or the thighs.

The satisfaction sought for, being formal, is symbolic. In political reconciliations in the fifteenth century, symbolic actions have a very large share : demolition of houses which recall the crime, erection of commemorative crosses or chapels, injunctions to block up a doorway, etc., not to mention expiatory processions and masses for the dead. After his reconciliation with his brother at Rouen in 1469, Louis XI's first care is to have the ring which the bishop of Lisieux gave to Charles in marrying him to Normandy as its duke, broken on an anvil in the presence of the notables.

The chronicle of Jean de Roye records a striking instance of this craving for symbols and forms. One Laurent Guernier had been hanged by mistake at Paris in 1478 ; he had obtained a reprieve, but his pardon arrived too late. A year later his brother obtained permission to have the body honourably buried. " And before this bier went four town criers of the aforesaid town sounding their rattles, and on their breasts were the arms of the aforesaid Guernier, and around that bier were four tapers and eight torches, carried by men dressed in mourning and bearing the aforesaid crest. And in this way it was carried, passing through the aforesaid city of Paris . . . as far as the gate of Saint Anthony, where the aforesaid corpse was placed on a cart draped in black to take it to Provins to be buried. And one of the aforesaid criers who walked before the aforesaid corpse, cried : ' Good people, say your pater nosters for the soul of the late Laurent Guernier, in his life an inhabitant of Provins, who was lately found *dead under an oak-tree* ! ' "

The mentality of the declining Middle Ages often seems to us to display an incredible superficiality and feebleness. The complexity of things is ignored by it in a truly astounding manner. It proceeds to generalizations unhesitatingly on the strength of a single instance. Its liability to wrong judgment is extreme. Inexactitude, credulity, levity, inconsistency, are common features of medieval reasoning. All these defects are rooted in its fundamental formalism. To explain a situation or an event, a single motive suffices, and, for choice, the most general motive, the most direct or the grossest. To Burgundian party-feeling, for example, there could be but a single ground which could have urged the duke of Burgundy to compass the murder of the duke of Orleans : he wished to avenge the (assumed) adultery of the queen with Orleans. In every controversy people would disregard all the features of the case save a few, whose significance they exaggerated at pleasure. Thus the presentment of a fact, in the minds of the epoch, is always like a primitive woodcut, with strong and simple lines and very clearly marked contours.

So much for "simplistic" habits of mind. As to ill-considered generalization, it manifests itself on every page of the literature of that time. From a single case of impartiality reported of the English of olden time, Olivier de la Marche concludes that at that period the English were virtuous, and because of that had been able to conquer France. The importance of a particular case is exaggerated, because it is seen in an ideal light. Moreover, every case can be paralleled in sacred history, and so be exalted to higher significance. In 1404 a procession of students at Paris was assaulted : two were wounded, the clothes of a third were torn. This was enough for the chancellor of the University, carried away by the heat of his indignation, and by a simple consonance, " Les enfants, les jolis escoliers comme agneaux innocens,"[1] to launch into comparison of the incident to the massacre of Bethlehem.

If for every particular case an explanation is so easily admitted, and, once admitted, takes root in the mind without meeting with resistance, then the danger of wrong judgments is extremely great. Nietzsche said that abstaining from wrong judgments would make life impossible, and it is probable that the intense life which we sometimes envy past centuries, was partly due to the facility of false judgments. In our own day too, in times which require the utmost exertion of national force, the nerves need the help of false judgment. The men of the Middle Ages lived in a continual mental crisis. They could not for a moment dispense with false judgments of the grossest kind. If, in the fifteenth century, the cause of the dukes of Burgundy could persuade so many Frenchmen first to breach of fealty and next to hostility to their country, this political sentiment can only be explained by a whole tissue of emotional conceptions and confused ideas.

It is in this light that the general and constant habit of ridiculously exaggerating the number of enemies killed in battle should be considered. Chastellain gives a loss of five nobles on the side of the duke at the battle of Gavre, as against twenty or thirty thousand of the Ghent rebels.

What are we to say, lastly, of the curious levity of the authors of the close of the Middle Ages, which often impresses us as an absolute lack of mental power ? It sometimes seems

---

[1] The children, the pretty scholars, like innocent lambs.

as if they were content to present to their readers a series of vague pictures, and felt no need whatever of really hard thinking. Superficial description of outward circumstances—this is all we get from writers like Froissart and Monstrelet. Compared with Herodotus, to say nothing of Thucydides, their narrative is disjointed, empty, without pith or meaning. They do not distinguish the essential from the accidental. Their lack of precision is deplorable. Monstrelet was present at the interview of the duke of Burgundy with Joan of Arc, when a prisoner : he does not remember what was said. Thomas Basin himself, who conducted the process of rehabilitation, says in his chronicle that Joan was born at Vaucouleurs instead of Domremy, and that she was conducted to Tours by Baudricourt himself, whom he calls lord of the town instead of captain, while he is mistaken by three months as to the date of her first interview with the dauphin. Olivier de la Marche, master of the ceremonies and an impeccable courtier, constantly muddles the genealogy of the ducal family and goes so far as to make the marriage of Charles with Margaret of York take place after the siege of Neuss in 1475, though he was present at the wedding festivities in 1468. Even Commines is not exempt from surprising inexactitudes.

The credulity and the lack of critical spirit are too general and too well known to make it necessary to cite examples. It goes without saying that here the degree of erudition makes a great difference. Basin and Molinet treated the popular belief that Charles the Bold would come back as a fable. Ten years after the battle of Nancy, people were still lending money which was to be reimbursed on his return.

> " J'ay veu chose incongneue :
> Ung mort ressusciter,
> Et sur sa revenue
> Par milliers achapter.
> L'un dit : il est en vie,
> L'autre : ce n'est que vent.
> Tous bons cueurs sans envie
> Le regrettent souvent." [1]

---

[1] I have seen an unknown thing : A dead man coming to life, And on his return Buy for thousands. The one says : he is alive. The other : it is but wind. All good hearts, void of envy, Regret his loss often.

A mentality, dominated like that of the declining Middle Ages by a lively imagination, by naïve idealism and by strong feeling, easily believes in the reality of every concept which presents itself to the mind. When once an idea has received a name and a form, its truth is presumed ; it glides, so to say, into the system of spiritual figures and shares in their credibility.

On the one hand, their clear outlines and frequently anthropomorphic character give ideas a marked degree of fixity and immobility ; on the other hand, the *meaning* of a conception runs a constant risk of being lost in the too vivid *form*. The principal person of the long allegorical and satirical poem of Eustache Deschamps, *Le Miroir de Mariage*, is called Franc Vouloir. Folly and Desire advise him to marry, Repertory of Science dissuades him. Now, if we ask ourselves what Deschamps wanted to express by the abstraction Franc Vouloir, it appears that the idea oscillates between the careless liberty of the bachelor and free will in a philosophic sense. The personification has more or less absorbed the idea which gave it birth. As undecided as the character of the central figure is the moral tone of the poem. The pious praise of the spiritual marriage and of the contemplative life contrasts strangely with the customary and rather vulgar mockery of women and of female virtue. The author sometimes puts exalted truths into the mouth of Folly and Desire, though their part is that of the devil's advocate. It is very hard to decide what was the personal conviction of the poet, and to what degree he was serious.

To distinguish clearly the serious element from pose and playfulness, is a problem that crops up in connection with nearly all the manifestations of the mentality of the Middle Ages. We saw it arise in connection with chivalry, and with the forms of love and of piety. We always have to remember that in more primitive cultural phases than ours, the line of demarcation between sincere conviction and "pretending" often seems to be wanting. What would be hypocrisy in a modern mind, is not always so in a medieval one.

The general want of balance, characterizing the soul of this epoch, in spite of the clear-cut form of its ideas, is especially felt in the domain of superstition. On the subject of sorcery, doubt and rationalistic interpretations alternate with the blindest credulity. We can never tell precisely to what degree this belief was sincere. Philippe de Mézières, in the *Songe du Vieil Pelerin*, tells that he himself learned the magic arts from a Spaniard. During more than ten years he did not succeed in forgetting his infamous knowledge. " A sa volenté ne povoit pas bien extirper de son cuer les dessusdits signes et l'effect d'iceulx contre Dieu."[1] At last, " through the grace of God, by dint of confessing and resisting, he was delivered from this great folly, which is an enemy to the Christian soul."

During the horrible campaign of persecution against sorcerers in 1461, known as the " Vauderie d'Arras," both the people and the magistrates gravely doubted the reality of the alleged crimes. Outside the town of Arras, says Jacques du Clercq, " not one person in a thousand believed that it was true that they practised the aforesaid sorcery. Such things were never before heard of happening in these countries." Nevertheless, the town suffered severely in consequence : people would no longer shelter its merchants or give them credit, for fear that, accused of witchcraft, on the morrow, perhaps, they might lose all their possessions by confiscation. One of the inquisitors, who claimed to be able to discover the guilty at sight, and went so far as to declare that it was impossible for a man to be wrongly accused of sorcery, afterwards went mad. A poem full of hatred accused the persecutors of having got up the whole affair out of covetousness, and the bishop himself called the persecution " a thing intended by some evil persons." Philip the Good, having asked the advice of the Faculty of Louvain, several of its members declared that the sorcery was not real. Upon which the duke, who, in spite of the archaic turn of his mind, was not superstitious, sent the king-at-arms of the Golden Fleece to Arras. Then the executions and the imprisonments ceased. Later on, all the processes were annulled, which fact the town celebrated by a joyful feast with representations of edifying " moralities."

[1] He could not voluntarily extirpate from his mind the aforesaid signs and their effect against God.

The opinion that the rides through the air and the orgies of the witches' sabbath were but delusions which the devil suggested to the poor foolish women, was already rather widely spread in the fifteenth century. Froissart, describing the striking case of a Gascon nobleman and his familiar demon called Horton (he surpasses himself here in exactness and vividness of narrative), treats it as an " error." But it is an error caused by the devil, so the rationalizing interpretation, after all, goes only half-way. Gerson alone goes so far as to suggest the notion of a cerebral lesion, the others confine themselves to the hypothesis of diabolical illusions. Martin Lefranc, provost of the church of Lausanne, in the *Champion des Dames,* which he dedicated to Philip the Good in 1440, defended this opinion.

> " Je ne croiray tant que je vive
> Que femme corporellement
> Voit par l'air comme merle ou grive,
> —Dit le Champion prestement.—
>
> .   .   .   .
>
> Quant la pourelle est en sa couche,
> Pour y dormir et reposer,
> L'ennemi qui point ne se couche
> Se vient encoste allé poser.
> Lors illusions composer
> Lui scet sy tres soubtillement
> Qu'elle croit faire ou proposer
> Ce qu'elle songe seulement.
> Force la vielle songera
> Que sur un chat ou sur un chien
> A l'assemblée s'en ira ;
> Mais certes il n'en sera rien :
> Et sy n'est baston ne mesrien
> Qui le peut ung pas enlever." [1]

In general the mental attitude towards supernatural facts

[1] As long as I live I shall not believe That a woman can bodily Travel through the air like blackbird or thrush, Said the Champion forthwith. . . . When the poor woman lies in her bed, In order to sleep and to rest there, The enemy who never lies down to sleep Comes and remains by her side. Then to call up illusions Before her he can so subtly, That she thinks she does or proposes to do What she only dreams. Perhaps the gammer will dream That on a cat or on a dog She will go to the meeting ; But certainly nothing will happen ; And there is neither a stick nor a beam Which could lift her a step.

was a vacillating one. Rational interpretation, timid credulity, or the suspicion of diabolical ruses, have the upper hand by turns. The Church did its best to combat superstitions. Friar Richard, the popular preacher at Paris, has the mandrakes brought to him to be burned, " which many foolish people kept in safe places, having such great faith in this ordure, that, indeed, they firmly believed, that so long as they had it (provided it were very neatly wrapped up in silk or linen folds) they would never be poor so long as they lived."

Dogmatic theology was always studious to inculcate the exact distinction between matters of faith and of superstition. Benedictions and conjurations, says Denis the Carthusian in his treatise *Contra vitia superstitionum*, have no effect in themselves. They operate only in so far as they are pronounced as humble prayers, with pious intention and placing one's hope in God. Since popular belief, nevertheless, attributes magical virtue to them, it would be better that the clergy forbade these practices altogether.

Unhappily, the zeal of the Church for the purity of the faith did not affect demonomania. Its own doctrine prevented it from uprooting belief in it. For it kept to the norm, fixed by the authority of Saint Augustine and Saint Thomas : *Omnia quae visibiliter fiunt in hoc mundo, possunt fieri per daemones.*[1] Conjurations, says Denis, continuing the argument we have just cited, often take effect in spite of the absence of a pious intention, because then the devil has taken a hand in it. This ambiguity left room for a good deal of uncertainty. The fear of sorcery and the blind fury of persecution continued to darken the mental atmosphere of the age. The official confirmation of both the theory and the practice of persecution was effected in the last quarter of the fifteenth century by the *Malleus maleficarum*, the Hammer for Witches, by two German Dominicans, which appeared in 1487, and by the bull, *Summis desiderantes*, of Pope Innocent VIII, of 1484.

So towards the end of the Middle Ages this dark system of delusion and cruelty grew slowly to completion. All the deficiencies of medieval thinking and its inherent tendencies

[1] All that happens visibly in this world, can be done by demons.

to gross error had contributed to its building. The fifteenth century transmitted it to the coming age like a horrible disease, which for a long time neither classical culture nor Protestant reformation nor the Catholic revival were able or even willing to cure.

CHAPTER XIX

ART AND LIFE

If a man of culture of 1840 had been asked to characterize French civilization in the fifteenth century in a few words, his answer would probably have been largely inspired by impressions from Barante's *Histoire des Ducs de Bourgogne* and Hugo's *Notre Dame de Paris*. The picture called up by these would have been grim and dark, scarcely illuminated by any ray of serenity and beauty.

The experiment repeated to-day would yield a very different result. People would now refer to Joan of Arc, to Villon's poetry, but above all to the works of art. The so-called primitive Flemish and French masters—Van Eyck, Rogier van der Weyden, Foucquet, Memling, with Claus Sluter, the sculptor, and the great musicians—would dominate their general idea of the epoch. The picture would altogether have changed its colour and tone. The aspect of mere cruelty and misery as conceived by romanticism, which derived its information chiefly from the chronicles, would have made room for a vision of pure and naïve beauty, of religious fervour and profound mystic peace.

It is a general phenomenon that the idea which works of art give us of an epoch is far more serene and happy than that which we glean in reading its chronicles, documents, or even literature. Plastic art does not lament. Even when giving expression to sorrow or pain it transports them to an elegiac sphere, where the bitter taste of suffering has passed away, whereas the poets and historians, voicing the endless griefs of life, always keep their immediate pungency and revive the harsh realities of bygone misery.

Now, our perception of former times, our historical organ, so to say, is more and more becoming visual. Most educated people of to-day owe their conception of Egypt, Greece, or the

222

Middle Ages, much more to the sight of their monuments, either in the original or by reproductions, than to reading. The change of our ideas about the Middle Ages is due less to a weakening of the romantic sense than to the substitution of artistic for intellectual appreciation.

Still, this vision of an epoch resulting from the contemplation of works of art is always incomplete, always too favourable, and therefore fallacious. It has to be corrected in more than one sense. Confining ourselves to the period in question, we first have to take into consideration the fact that, proportionately, far more of the written documents than of the monuments of art have been preserved. The literature of the declining Middle Ages, with some few exceptions, is known to us fairly completely. We have products of all genres : the most elevated and the most vulgar, the serious and the comic, the pious and the profane. Our literary tradition reflects the whole life of the epoch. Written tradition, moreover, is not confined to literature : official records, in infinite number, enable us to augment almost indefinitely the accuracy of our picture.

Art, on the contrary, is by its very nature limited to a less complete and less direct expression of life. Moreover, we only possess a very special fraction of it. Outside ecclesiastical art very little remains. Profane art and applied art have only been preserved in rare specimens. This is a serious want, because these are just the forms of art which would have most clearly revealed to us the relation of artistic production to social life. The modest number of altar-pieces and tombs teaches us too little in this respect ; the art of the epoch remains to us as a thing apart from the history of the time. Now, really to understand art, it is of great importance to form a notion of the function of art in life ; and for that it does not suffice to admire surviving masterpieces, all that has been lost asks our attention too.

Art in those times was still wrapped up in life. Its function was to fill with beauty the forms assumed by life. These forms were marked and potent. Life was encompassed and measured by the rich efflorescence of the liturgy : the sacraments, the canonical hours of the day and the festivals of the ecclesiastical year. All the works and all the joys of life, whether dependent on religion, chivalry, trade or love, had their marked form.

The task of art was to adorn all these concepts with charm and colour ; it is not desired for its own sake, but to decorate life with the splendour which it could bestow. Art was not yet a means, as it is now, to step out of the routine of every-day life to pass some moments in contemplation; it had to be enjoyed as an element of life itself, as the expression of life's significance. Whether it served to sustain the flight of piety or to be an accompaniment to the delights of the world, it was not yet conceived as mere beauty.

Consequently, we might venture the paradox that the Middle Ages knew only applied art. They wanted works of art only to make them subservient to some practical use. Their purpose and their meaning always preponderated over their purely æsthetic value. We should add that the love of art for its own sake did not originate in an awakening of the craving for beauty, but developed as a result of superabundant artistic production. In the treasuries of princes and nobles, objects of art accumulated so as to form collections. No longer serving for practical use, they were admired as articles of luxury and of curiosity ; thus the taste for art was born which the Renaissance was to develop consciously.

In the great works of art of the fifteenth century, notably in the altar-pieces and tombs, the nature of the subject was far more important than the question of beauty. Beauty was required because the subject was sacred or because the work was destined for some august purpose. This purpose is always of a more or less practical sort. The triptych served to intensify worship at the great festivals and to preserve the memory of the pious donors. The altar-piece of the Lamb by the brothers Van Eyck was opened at high festivals only. Religious pictures were not the only ones which served a practical purpose. The magistrates of the towns ordered representations of famous judgments to decorate the law courts, in order to solemnly exhort the judges to do their duty. Such are the judgment of Cambyses, by Gerard David, at Bruges ; that of the Emperor Otto, by Dirk Bouts, at Louvain ; and the lost pictures by Rogier van der Weyden, once at Brussels.

The following example may serve to illustrate the importance attached to the subjects represented. In 1384 an interview took place at Lelinghem for the purpose of bringing about an armistice between France and England. The duke of Berry had the naked walls of the old chapel, where the negotiating princes were to meet, covered with tapestry representing battles of antiquity. But John of Gaunt, duke of Lancaster, as soon as he saw them on entering, demanded that these pictures of war should be removed, because those who aspire to peace ought not to have scenes of combat and of destruction before their eyes. The tapestries were replaced by others representing the instruments of the Passion.

The importance of the subject is closely connected with the artistic value in the case of portraits, which even now preserve some moral significance, as souvenirs or heirlooms, because the sentiments determining their use are as vital as ever. In the Middle Ages portraits were ordered for all sorts of purposes, but rarely, we may be certain, to obtain a masterpiece of art. Besides gratifying family affection and pride, the portrait served to enable betrothed persons to make acquaintance. The embassy sent to Portugal by Philip the Good in 1428, to ask for the hand of a princess, was accompanied by Jan van Eyck, with orders to paint her portrait. Court chroniclers liked to keep up the fiction that the royal fiancé had fallen in love with the unknown princess on seeing her portrait—for instance, Richard II of England when courting the little Isabelle of France, aged six. Sometimes it is even said that a selection was made by comparing portraits of different parties. When a wife had to be found for the young Charles VI, according to the *Religieux de Saint Denis*, the choice lay between a Bavarian, an Austrian and a Lorraine duchess. A painter of talent was sent to the three courts ; three portraits were submitted to the king, who chose the young Isabella of Bavaria, judging her by far the most beautiful.

Nowhere was the practical use of works of art weightier than in connection with tombs, by far the most important domain of the sculpture of the epoch. The wish to have an effigy of the deceased was so strong that it claimed satisfaction even before the construction of the tomb. At the burial of a man of rank, he is represented either by a living man or by an effigy. At the funeral service of Bertrand du Guesclin, at Saint Denis, " four men-at-arms, armed cap-à-pie, mounted on four chargers, well appointed and caparisoned, representing the dead man

as he was alive," entered the church. An account of the Polig-
nacs of 1375 relating to a funeral ceremony shows the item :
" Six shillings to Blaise for representing the dead knight at the
funeral." At royal interments a figure of leather, in state dress,
represented the deceased. Great pains were taken to obtain
a good likeness. Sometimes there is more than one of these
effigies in the cortège. Visitors to Westminster Abbey know
these figures. Perhaps the origin of making funeral masks,
which began in France in the fifteenth century, is to be found
here.

As all art was more or less applied art, the distinction between artists and craftsmen did not arise. The great masters
in the service of the courts of Flanders, of Berry, or of Burgundy,
each of them an artist of a very marked personality, did not
confine themselves to painting pictures and to illuminating
manuscripts ; they were not above colouring statues, painting
shields and staining banners, or designing costumes for tournaments and ceremonies. Thus Melchior Broederlam, court
painter to the first duke of Burgundy, after holding the same
position in the household of his father-in-law, the count of
Flanders, puts the finishing touches to five sculptured chairs
for the palace of the counts. He repairs and paints some
mechanical apparatus at the castle of Hesdin, used for wetting
the guests with water by way of a surprise. He does work on
a carriage for the duchess. He directs the sumptuous decoration of the fleet which the duke had assembled at Sluys in
1387 for an expedition against the English, which, however,
did not take place. So, too, at wedding festivities and funeral
ceremonies court painters were laid under contribution. Statues
were painted in Jan van Eyck's workshop. He himself made
a sort of map of the world for Duke Philip, on which the towns
and the countries were painted with marvellous delicacy. Hugo
van der Goes designed posters advertising a papal indulgence
at Ghent. When the Archduke Maximilian was a prisoner at
Bruges in 1488, the painter Gerard David was sent for, to
decorate with pictures the wickets and shutters of his prison.

Of all the handiwork of the masters of the fifteenth century,
only a portion of a very special nature has survived : some
tombs, some altar-pieces and portraits, numerous miniatures,
also a certain number of objects of industrial art, comprising

vessels used in religious worship, sacerdotal dress and church furniture, but of secular work, except woodwork and chimneys, scarcely anything is left. How much more should we know of the art of the fifteenth century if we could compare the bathing and hunting pieces of Jan van Eyck and Rogier van der Weyden with their *pietàs* and madonnas. It is not only profane pictures we lack. There are whole departments of applied art of which we can hardly even form a conception. For this we lack the power to compare with the priestly vestments that have been preserved, the court costumes with their precious stones and tiny bells, that have perished : we lack the actual sight of the brilliantly decorated war-ships of which miniatures give us but a conventional and clumsy representation. Froissart, who, as a rule, is little susceptible to impressions of beauty, fairly exults in his descriptions of the splendours of a decked-out fleet, with its streamers, gay with blazonry, floating from the mast-heads, and some reaching to the water. The ship of Philippe le Hardi, decorated by Broederlam, was painted azure and gold ; large heraldic shields surrounded the pavilion of the castle ; the sails were studded with daisies and the initials of the duke and the duchess, and bore the motto *Il me tarde.* The nobles vied with each other in lavishing money on the decoration of their vessels. Painters had a good time of it, says Froissart ; there were not enough of them to go round, and they got whatever prices they asked. According to him, many nobles had their ship-masts entirely covered with gold-leaf. Guy de Trémouille spent £2,000 on decorations. " And all this was paid by the poor people of France. . . ."

These lost products of decorative art would have revealed to us, above all, extravagant sumptuousness. This trait is characteristic of the epoch ; it is to be found equally in the works which we do possess, but as we study these only for the sake of their beauty, we pay little attention to this element of splendour and of pomp, which no longer interests us, but which was just what people of that time prized most.

Burgundo-French culture of the expiring Middle Ages tends to oust beauty by magnificence. The art of this period exactly reflects this spirit. All that we cited above as characteristic of the mental processes of the epoch : the craving to give a definite form to every idea, and the overcrowding of the mind with figures and forms systematically arranged—all this reappears in art. There, too, we find the tendency to leave nothing without form, without figure, without ornament. The flamboyant style of architecture is like the postlude of an organist who cannot conclude. It decomposes all the formal elements endlessly ; it interlaces all the details ; there is not a line which has not its counter-line. The form develops at the expense of the idea, the ornament grows rank, hiding all the lines and all the surfaces. A *horror vacui* reigns, always a symptom of artistic decline.

All this means that the border-line between pomp and beauty is being obliterated. Decoration and ornament no longer serve to heighten the natural beauty of a thing ; they are overgrowing it and threaten to stifle it. The further we get away from pure plastic art, the more this rankness of formal decorative motifs is accentuated. This may be very clearly observed in sculpture. In the creation of isolated figures this overgrowth of forms does not occur : the statues of Moses' well and the " plourants " of the tombs are as sober as the figures of Donatello. But where sculpture is performing a decorative function we at once find the overgrowth. In looking at the tabernacle of Dijon, every one will be struck by a lack of harmony between the sculpture of Jacques de Baerze and the painting of Broederlam. The picture, painted for its own sake, is simple and sober ; the reliefs, on the contrary, in which the purpose is decorative, are complicated and overloaded. We notice the same contrast between painting and tapestry. Textile art, even when representing scenes and figures, remains limited by its technique to decorative conception and expression ; hence we find the same craving for excessive ornamentation.

In the art of costume, the essential qualities of pure art, that is to say, measure and harmony, vanish altogether, because splendour and adornment are the sole objects aimed at. Pride and vanity introduce a sensual element incompatible with pure art. No epoch ever witnessed such extravagance of fashion as that extending from 1350 to 1480. Here we can observe the unhampered expansion of the æsthetic sense of the time. All the forms and dimensions of dress are ridiculously exaggerated. The female head-dress assumes the conical shape of the " hennin," a form evolved from the little coif, keeping the hair under the kerchief. High and bombed foreheads are in fashion, with the temples shaved. Low-necked dresses make their appearance. The male dress had features still more bizarre—the immoderate length of the points of the shoes, called " poulaines," which the knights at Nicopolis had to cut off, to enable them to flee ; the laced waists ; the balloon-shaped sleeves standing up at the shoulders ; the too long " houppelandes " and the too short doublets ; the cylindrical or pointed bonnets ; the hoods draped about the head in the form of a cock's comb or a flaming fire. A state costume was ornamented by hundreds of precious stones.

The taste for unbridled luxury culminated in the court fêtes. Every one has read the descriptions of the Burgundian festivities at Lille in 1454, at which the guests took the oath to undertake the crusade, and at Bruges in 1468, on the occasion of the marriage of Charles the Bold with Margaret of York. It is hard to imagine a more absolute contrast than that of these barbarous manifestations of arrogant pomp and the pictures of the brothers Van Eyck, Dirk Bouts and Rogier van der Weyden, with their sweet and tranquil serenity. Nothing could be more insipid and ugly than the " entremets," consisting of gigantic pies enclosing complete orchestras, full-rigged vessels, castles, monkeys and whales, giants and dwarfs, and all the boring absurdities of allegory. We find it difficult to regard these entertainments as something more than exhibitions of almost incredible bad taste.

Yet we must not exaggerate the distance separating the two extreme forms of the art of the fifteenth century. In the first place, it is important to realize the function of festivals in the society of that time. They still preserved something of the meaning they have in primitive societies, that of the supreme expression of their culture, the highest mode of a collective enjoyment and an assertion of solidarity. At epochs of great renovations of society, like that of the French Revolution, we see that festivals resume this social and æsthetic function.

Modern man is free, when he pleases, to seek his favourite distractions individually, in books, music, art or nature. On the other hand, at a time when the higher pleasures were neither numerous nor accessible to all, people felt the need of such collective rejoicings as festivals. The more crushing the misery of daily life, the stronger the stimulants that will be needed to produce that intoxication with beauty and delight without which life would be unbearable. The fifteenth century, profoundly pessimistic, a prey to continual depression, could not forgo the emphatic affirmation of the beauty of life, afforded by these splendid and solemn collective rejoicings. Books were expensive, the country was unsafe, art was rare ; the individual lacked the means of distraction. All literary, musical and artistic enjoyment was more or less closely connected with festivals.

Now festivals, in so far as they are an element of culture, require other things than mere gaiety. Neither the elementary pleasures of gaming, drinking and love, nor luxury and pomp as such, are able to give them a framework. The festival requires style. If those of modern times have lost their cultural value, it is because they have lost style. In the Middle Ages the religious festival, because of its high qualities of style founded on the liturgy itself, for a long time dominated all the forms of collective cheerfulness. The popular festival, which had its own elements of beauty in song and dance, was linked up with those of the Church. It is towards the fifteenth century that an independent form of civil festival with a style of its own disengages itself from the ecclesiastical one. The "rhetoricians" of Northern France and the Netherlands are the representatives of this evolution. Till then only princely courts had been able to equip secular festivals with form and style, thanks to the resources of their wealth and the social conception of courtesy.

Nevertheless, the style of the courtly festival could not but remain greatly inferior to that of religious festivals. In the latter worship and rejoicing in common were always the expression of a sublime thought, which lent them a grace and dignity that even the excesses of their frequently burlesque details could not affect. On the other hand, the ideas glorified by the secular feast were nothing more than those of chivalry and of courtly love. The ritual of chivalry, no doubt, was rich enough to give these festivities a venerable and solemn style. There were the accolade, the vows, the chapters of the orders, the rules of the tournaments, the formalities of homage, service and precedence, all the dignified proceedings of kings-at-arms and heralds, all the brightness of blazonry and armour. But this did not suffice to satisfy all aspirations. The court fêtes were expected to visualize in its entirety the dream of the heroic life. And here style failed. For in the fifteenth century the apparatus of chivalrous fancy was no longer anything but vain convention and mere literature.

The staging of the amazing festivities of Lille or of Bruges is, so to say, applied literature. The ponderousness of material representation destroyed the last remainder of charm which literature with the lightness of its airy reveries had hitherto preserved. The unfaltering seriousness with which these monstrous pageants were organized is truly Burgundian. The ducal court seems to have lost, by its contact with the North, some qualities of the French spirit. For the preparation of the banquet of Lille, which was to crown and conclude a series of banquets which the nobles provided, each in his turn, vying with each other in magnificence, Philip the Good appointed a committee, presided over by a knight of the Golden Fleece, Jean de Lannoy. The most trusted counsellors of the duke— Antoine de Croy, the chancellor Nicolas Rolin himself— were frequently present at the sessions of the committee, of which Olivier de la Marche was a member. When the latter in his memoirs comes to this chapter, a feeling of awe still comes over him. " Because great and honourable achievements deserve a lasting renown and perpetual remembrance . . .," thus he begins the narrative of these memorable things. It is needless to reprint it here, as it belongs to the *loci communes* of historical literature.

Even from across the sea people came to view the gorgeous spectacle. Besides the guests, a great number of noble spectators were present at the feast, disguised for the most part. First every one walked about to admire the fixed show-pieces ; later came the " entremets," that is to say, representations of " personages " and tableaux vivants. Olivier himself played the important part of Holy Church, making his appearance in a tower on the back of an elephant, led by a gigantic Turk. The tables were loaded with the most extravagant decorations. There were a rigged and ornamented carack, a meadow surrounded by trees with a fountain, rocks and a statue of Saint Andrew, the castle of Lusignan with the fairy Mélusine, a bird-

shooting scene near a windmill, a wood in which wild beasts
walked about, and, lastly, a church with an organ and singers,
whose songs alternated with the music of the orchestra of
twenty-eight persons, which was placed in a pie.

The problem for us is to determine the quality of taste or
bad taste to which all this bears witness. It goes without saying that the mythological and allegorical tenor of these " entremets " cannot interest us. But what was the artistic execution
worth ? What people looked for most was extravagance and
huge dimensions. The tower of Gorcum represented on the
table of the banquet of Bruges in 1468 was 46 feet high. La
Marche says of a whale, which also figured there : " And certainly
this was a very fine entremets, *for* there were more than forty
persons in it." People were also much attracted by mechanical
marvels : living birds flying from the mouth of a dragon conquered by Hercules, and such-like curiosities, in which, to us,
any idea of art is altogether lacking. The comic element was
of a very low class : boars blow the trumpet in the tower of
Gorcum ; elsewhere goats sing a motet, wolves play the flute,
four large donkeys appear as singers—and all this in honour of
Charles the Bold, who was a good musician.

I would not, however, suggest that there may not have been
many an artistic masterpiece among these pretentious and ridiculous curiosities. Let us not forget that the men who enjoyed
these Gargantuan decorations were the patrons of the brothers
Van Eyck and of Rogier van der Weyden—the duke himself,
Rolin, the donor of the altars of Beaune and of Autun, Jean
Chevrot, who commissioned Rogier to paint " The Seven Sacraments," now at Antwerp. What is more, it was the painters
themselves who designed these show-pieces. If the records do
not mention Jan van Eyck or Rogier as having contributed
to similar festivities, they do give the names of the two Mar-
mions and Jacques Daret. For the fête of 1468 the services of
the whole corporation of painters were requisitioned ; they were
summoned in haste from Ghent, Brussels, Louvain, Tirlemont,
Mons, Quesnoy, Valenciennes, Douai, Cambray, Arras, Lille,
Ypres, Courtray, Oudenarde, to work at Bruges. It is impossible to believe that their handiwork was ugly. The thirty
vessels decorated with the arms of the duke's domains, the
sixty images of women dressed in the costume of their country,

" carrying fruit in baskets and birds in cages. . . ." I should
be ready to give more than one mediocre church-picture to see
them.

We may go further, at the risk of being thought paradoxical,
and affirm that we have to take this art of show-pieces, which
has disappeared without leaving a trace, into account, if we
would thoroughly understand the art of Claus Sluter.

Of all the forms of art, sepulchral sculpture is most fettered
by the exigencies of its purpose. The sculptors charged with
making the ducal tombs were not left free to create beautiful
things ; they had to exalt the glory of the deceased prince.
The painter can always give free rein to his imagination ; he
is never obliged to limit himself strictly to commissioned work.
It is probable, on the other hand, that the sculptor of this
epoch rarely worked except on specified tasks. The motifs of
his art, moreover, are limited in number and fixed by a rigorous
tradition. It is true that painters and sculptors are equally
servants of the ducal household ; Jan van Eyck, as well as
Sluter and his nephew, Claus de Werve, bore the title of
" varlet de chambre," but for the two latter, the service is far
more real than for the painters. The two great Dutchmen
whom the irresistible attraction of French art life drew for
good from their native country were completely monopolized
by the duke of Burgundy. Claus Sluter inhabited a house
at Dijon which the duke placed at his disposal ; there he
lived as a gentleman, but at the same time as a servant of
the court. His nephew and successor, Claus de Werve, is
the tragic type of an artist in the service of princes : kept
back at Dijon year after year, to finish the tomb of Jean sans
Peur, for which the financial means were never forthcoming,
he saw his artistic career, so brilliantly begun, ruined by fruitless waiting.

Thus the art of the sculptor at this epoch is a servile art.
On the other hand, sculpture is generally little influenced by
the taste of an epoch, because its means, its material and its
subjects are limited and little subject to change. When a great
sculptor appears, he creates everywhere and always that *opti-
mum* of purity and simplicity which we call classic. The
human form and its drapery are susceptible of few variations.
The masterpieces of carving of the different ages are very much

alike, and, for us, Sluter's work shares this eternal identity of sculpture.

Nevertheless, on examining it more closely, we notice that especially the art of Sluter bears the marks of being influenced by the taste of the time (not to call it Burgundian taste) as far as the nature of sculpture permits. Sluter's works have not been preserved as they were, and as the master intended them to be. We must picture the well of Moses as it was in 1418, when the papal legate granted an indulgence to whosoever should come to visit it in a pious spirit. It must be remembered that the well is but a fragment, a part of a calvary with which the first duke of Burgundy of the house of Valois intended to crown the well of his Carthusian monastery of Champmol. The principal part, that is to say, the crucified Christ with the Virgin, Saint John and Mary Magdalen, had almost completely disappeared before the French Revolution. There remains only the pedestal, surrounded by the statues of the six prophets who predicted the death of the Saviour, with a cornice supported by angels. The whole composition is in the highest degree a representation, " une œuvre parlante," a show, closely related as such to the tableaux vivants or the " personnages " of the princely entries and of the banquets. There, too, the subjects were borrowed, for choice, from the prophecies relating to the coming of Christ. Like these " personnages," the figures surrounding the well hold scrolls containing the text of their predictions. It rarely happens in sculpture that the written word is of such importance. We can only fully realize the marvellous art here displayed in *hearing* these sacred and solemn words. *Immolabit eum universa multitudo filiorum Israel ad vesperum* ; this is Moses' sentence. *Foderunt manus meas et pedes meos, dinumeraverunt omnia ossa mea* ; this is David's. Jeremiah says : *O vos omnes qui transitis per viam, attendite et videte si est dolor sicut dolor meus.*[1] Isaiah, Daniel, Zachariah, all announce the death of the Lord. It is like a threnody of six voices rising up to the cross. Now in this feature lies the

---

[1] Exodus xii. 6 : " And the whole assembly of the congregation of Israel shall kill it in the evening." Psalm xxii. 16, 17 : " They pierced 'My hands and My feet. They told all My bones." Lamentations of Jeremiah i. 12 : " All ye that pass by, behold, and see if there be any sorrow like unto My sorrow."

essence of the work. The gestures of the hands by which the attention is directed to the texts are so emphatic, and there is an expression of such poignant grief on the faces, that the whole is in some danger of losing the *ataraxia* which marks great sculpture. It appeals too directly to the spectator. Compared with the figures of Michelangelo, those of Sluter are too expressive, too personal. If more had come down to us of the calvary supported by the prophets than the head and the torso of Christ, of a stark majesty, this expressive character would be still more evident.

The spectacular character of the calvary of Champmol also came into prominence in the luxurious decorations of the work. We must picture it in all its polychrome splendour, for Jean Malouel, the artist, and Herman of Cologne, the gilder, were not sparing of vivid colours and brilliant effects. The pedestals were green, the mantles of the prophets were gilt, their tunics red and azure with golden stars. Isaiah, the gloomiest of all, wore a dress of gold-cloth. The open spaces were filled with golden suns and initials. The pride of blazonry displayed itself not only round the columns below the figures, but on the cross itself, which was entirely gilt. The extremities of the arms of the cross, shaped like capitals, bore the coats of arms of Burgundy and Flanders. Can one ask for better proof of the spirit in which the duke conceived this great monument of his piety ? As a crowning " bizarrerie," a pair of spectacles of gilded brass, the work of Hannequin de Hacht, were placed on Jeremiah's nose.

This serfdom of a great art controlled by the will of a princely patron is tragic, but it is at the same time exalted by the heroic efforts of the great sculptor to shake off his shackles. The figures of the " plourants " around the sarcophagus had for a long time been an obligatory motif in Burgundian sepulchral art. These weeping figures were not meant to express grief in general ; the sculptor was bound to give a faithful representation of the funeral cortège with the dignitaries present at the burial. But the genius of Sluter and his pupils succeeded in transforming this motif into the most profound expression of mourning known in art, a funeral march in stone.

Is it so certain, after all, that we are right in thinking of the artist as struggling with the lack of taste and refinement of his

patron ? It is quite possible that Sluter himself considered
Jeremiah's spectacles a very happy find. In the men of that
epoch artistic taste was still blended with the passion for what
is rare or brilliant. In their simplicity they could enjoy the
bizarre as if it were beauty. Objects of pure art and articles
of luxury and curiosity were equally admired. Long after the
Middle Ages the collections of princes contained works of art
mixed up indiscriminately with knick-knacks made of shells
and of hair, wax statues of celebrated dwarfs and such-like
articles. At the castle of Hesdin, where side by side with art
treasures the " engins d'esbatement " (contrivances for amusement) usual in princely pleasure-grounds were found in abundance, Caxton saw a room ornamented with pictures representing the history of Jason, the hero of the Golden Fleece. The
artist is unknown, but was probably a distinguished master.
To heighten the effect, a " machinerie " was annexed which
could imitate lightning, thunder, snow and rain, in memory of
the magic arts of Medea.

In the shows at the entries of princes inventive fancy stuck
at nothing. When Isabella of Bavaria made her entry into
Paris in 1389, there was a white deer with gilt antlers, and a
wreath round its neck, stretched out on a "lit de justice,"
moving its eyes, antlers, feet, and at last raising a sword. At
the moment when the queen crossed the bridge to the left of
Notre Dame, an angel descended " by means of well-constructed
engines " from one of the towers, passed through an opening
of the hangings of blue taffeta with golden fleurs-de-lis which
covered the bridge, and put a crown on her head. Then the
angel " was pulled up again as if he had returned to heaven
of his own accord." Philip the Good and Charles VIII were
treated to similar descents. Lefèvre de Saint Remy greatly
admired the spectacle of four trumpeters and twelve nobles on
artificial horses, " sallying forth and caracoling in such a way
that it was a fine thing to see."

Time the destroyer has made it easy for us to separate pure
art from all these gewgaws and bizarre trappings, which have
completely disappeared. This separation which our æsthetic
sense insists upon, did not exist for the men of that time.
Their artistic life was still enclosed within the forms of social
life. Art was subservient to life. Its social function was to

enhance the importance of a chapel, a donor, a patron, or a festival, but never that of the artist. Fully to realize its position and scope in this respect is now hardly possible. Too little of the material surroundings in which art was placed, and too few of the works of art themselves, have come down to us. Hence the priceless value of the few works by which private life, outside courts and outside the Church, is revealed to us. In this respect no painting can compare with the portrait of Jean Arnolfini and of his wife, by Jan van Eyck, in the National Gallery. The master, who, for once, need not portray the majesty of divine beings nor minister to aristocratic pride, here freely followed his own inspiration : it was his friends whom he was painting on the occasion of their marriage. Is it really the merchant of Lucca, Jean Arnoulphin, as he was called in Flanders, who is represented ? Jan van Eyck painted this face twice (the other portrait is at Berlin) ; we can hardly imagine a less Italian-looking physiognomy, but the description of the picture in the inventory of Margaret of Austria, " Hernoul le fin with his wife in a chamber," leaves little room for doubt. However this may be, the persons represented were friends of Van Eyck ; he himself witnesses to it by the ingenious and delicate way in which he signs his work, by an inscription over the mirror : *Johannes de Eyck fuit hic*, 1434.

" Jan van Eyck was here." Only a moment ago, one might think. The sound of his voice still seems to linger in the silence of this room. All that tenderness and profound peace, which only Rembrandt was to recapture, emanate from this picture. That serene twilight hour of an age, which we seemed to know and yet sought in vain in so many of the manifestations of its spirit, suddenly reveals itself here. And here at last this spirit proves itself happy, simple, noble and pure, in tune with the lofty church music and the touching folk-songs of the time.

So perhaps we imagine a Jan van Eyck escaping from the noisy gaiety and brutal passions of court life, a Jan van Eyck of the simple heart, a dreamer. It does not require a great effort of fancy to call up the " varlet de chambre " of the duke, serving the great lords against his will, suffering all the disgust of a great artist obliged to belie his sublime ideal of art by contributing to the mechanical devices of a festival.

Nothing, however, justifies us in forming such a conception

of his personality. This art, which we admire, bloomed in the
atmosphere of that aristocratic life, which repels us. The little
we know of the lives of fifteenth-century painters shows them
to us as men of the world and courtiers. The duke of Berry
was on good terms with his artists. Froissart saw him in
familiar conversation with André Beauneveu in his marvellous
castle of Mehun sur Yevre. The three brothers of Limburg,
the great illuminators, come to offer the duke, as a New Year's
present, a surprise in the shape of a new illuminated manuscript,
which turned out to be " a dummy book, made of a block of
white wood painted to look like a book, in which there were
no leaves and nothing was written." Jan van Eyck, without
doubt, moved constantly in court circles. The secret diplomatic missions entrusted to him by the duke required a man
of the world. He passed, moreover, for a man of letters,
reading classic authors and studying geometry. Did he not,
by an innocent whim, disguise in Greek letters his modest
device, *Als ik kan* (As I can) ?

The intellectual and moral life of the fifteenth century seems
to us to be divided into two clearly separated spheres. On the
one hand, the civilization of the court, the nobility and the rich
middle classes : ambitious, proud and grasping, passionate and
luxurious. On the other hand, the tranquil sphere of the
" devotio moderna," of the *Imitation of Christ*, of Ruysbroeck
and of Saint Colette. One would like to place the peaceful
and mystic art of the brothers Van Eyck in the second of these
spheres, but it belongs rather to the other. Devout circles
were hardly in touch with the great art that flourished at this
time. In music they disapproved of counterpoint, and even
of organs. The rule of Windesheim forbade the embellish-
ment of the singing by modulations, and Thomas à Kempis
said : " If you cannot sing like the nightingale and the lark,
then sing like the crows and the frogs, which sing as God meant
them to." The music of Dufay, Busnois, Okeghem, developed
in the chapels of the courts. As to painting, the writers of
the " devotio moderna " do not speak of it ; it was outside
their range of thought. They wanted their books in a simple
form and without illuminations. They would probably have
regarded the altar-piece of the Lamb as a mere work of pride,
and actually did so regard the tower of Utrecht Cathedral.

The great artists generally worked for other circles than those of the devout townspeople. The art of the brothers Van Eyck and of their followers, though it sprang up in municipal surroundings and was fostered by town circles, cannot be called a bourgeois art. The court and the nobility exercised too powerful an attraction. Only the patronage of princes permitted the art of miniature to raise itself to the degree of artistic refinement which characterizes the work of the brothers of Limburg and the artists of the Hours of Turin. The employers of the great painters were, besides the princes themselves, the great lords, temporal or spiritual, and the great upstarts with whom the Burgundian epoch abounds, all gravitating towards the court. The ground for the difference between Franco-Flemish and Dutch art in this period lies in the fact that the latter still preserves some traits of simple soberness recalling the little out-of-the-way towns, such as Haarlem, where it was born. And even Dirk Bouts went south and painted at Louvain and Brussels.

Among the patrons of fifteenth-century art may be named Jean Chevrot, bishop of Tournay, whom a scutcheon designates as the donor of that work of touching and fervent piety, now at Antwerp, "The Seven Sacraments." Chevrot is the type of the court prelate ; as a trusted counsellor of the duke, he was full of zeal for the affairs of the Golden Fleece and for the crusade. Another type of donor is represented by Pierre Bladelin, whose austere face is seen on the Middelburg altarpiece, now at Berlin. He was the great capitalist of those times; from the post of receiver of Bruges, his native town, he rose to be paymaster-general of the duke. He introduced control and economy into the ducal finances. He was appointed treasurer of the Golden Fleece and knighted. He was sent to England to ransom Charles of Orleans. The duke wished to charge him with the administration of the finances of the expedition against the Turks. He employed his wealth, which was the wonder of his contemporaries, on works of embankment and the founding of a new town in Flanders, to which he gave the name of Middelburg, after the town in Zeeland of that name.

Other notable donors—Judocus Vydt, the canon Van de Paele, the Croys, the Lannoys—belonged to the very rich, noble or burgher, ancient or new, of their time. Most famous of all is Nicolas Rolin, the chancellor, "sprung from little people," jurist, financier, diplomat. The great treaties of the dukes, from 1419 to 1435, are his work. "He used to govern everything quite alone and manage and bear the burden of all business by himself, be it of war, be it of peace, be it of matters of finance." By methods which were not above suspicion he amassed enormous wealth, which he spent on all sorts of pious and charitable foundations. Nevertheless, people spoke with hatred of his avarice and pride, and had no faith in the devotional feelings which inspired his pious works. This man whom we see in the Louvre kneeling so devoutly in the picture painted for him by Jan van Eyck for Autun, his native town, and again in that by Rogier van der Weyden, destined for his hospital of Beaune, passed for a mind only set on earthly things. "He always harvested on earth," says Chastellain, "as though the earth was to be his abode for ever, in which his understanding erred and his prudence abased him, when he would not set bounds to that, of which his great age showed him the near end." This is corroborated by Jacques du Clercq in these terms : "The aforesaid chancellor was reputed one of the wise men of the kingdom, to speak temporally ; for as to spiritual matters, I shall be silent."

Are we, then, to look for a hypocritical expression in the face of the donor of La Vierge au Chancelier Rolin ? Let us remember, before condemning him, the riddle presented by the religious personality of so many other men of his time, who also combined rigid piety with excesses of pride, of avarice and of lust. The depths of these natures of a past age are not easily sounded.

In the piety interpreted by the art of the fifteenth century, the extremes of mysticism and of gross materialism meet. The faith pictured here is so direct that no earthly figure is too sensual or too heavy to express it. Van Eyck may drape his angels and divine personages with ponderous and stiff brocades, glittering with gold and precious stones ; to call up the celestial sphere he has no need of the flowing garments and sprawling limbs of the baroque style.

Yet neither this art nor this faith is primitive. By using the term primitive to designate the masters of the fifteenth century we run the risk of a misunderstanding. They are

PORTRAIT OF THE CHANCELLOR ROLIN. BY ROGIER VAN DER
WEYDEN.

[See page 2:0

"APRIL." BY THE BROTHERS VAN LIMBURG. FROM THE CALENDAR OF THE
"TRES RICHES HEURES DU DUC DE BERRY."

[See page 270.

primitive in a purely chronological sense, in so far as, for us, they are the first to come, and no older painting is known to us. But if to this designation we attach the meaning of a primitive spirit, we are egregiously mistaken. For the spirit which this art denotes is the same which we pointed out in religious life : a spirit rather decadent than primitive, a spirit involving the utmost elaboration, and even decomposition, of religious thought through the imagination.

In very early times the sacred figures had been seen as endlessly remote : awful and rigid. Then, from the twelfth century downward, the mysticism of Saint Bernard introduced a pathetic element into religion, which contained immense possibilities of growth. In the rapture of a new and overflowing piety people tried to share the sufferings of Christ by the aid of the imagination. They were no longer satisfied with the stark and motionless figures, infinitely distant, which romanesque art had given to Christ and His Mother. All the forms and colours which imagination drew from mundane reality were now lavished by it upon the celestial beings. Once let loose, pious fancy invaded the whole domain of faith and gave a minutely elaborate shape to every holy thing.

At first verbal expression had been in advance of pictorial and plastic art. Sculpture was still adhering to the formal rigidity of preceding ages, when literature undertook to describe all the details, both physical and mental, of the drama of the cross. A sort of pathetic naturalism arose, for which the *Meditationes vitae Christi*, early attributed to Saint Bonaventura, supplied the model. The nativity, the childhood, the descent from the cross, each received a fixed form, a vivid colouring. How Joseph of Arimathea mounted the ladder, how he had to press the hand of the Lord in order to draw out the nail, was all described in minute detail.

In the meantime, towards the end of the fourteenth century, pictorial technique had made so much progress that it more than overtook literature in the art of rendering these details. The naïve, and at the same time refined, naturalism of the brothers Van Eyck was a new form of pictorial expression ; but viewed from the standpoint of culture in general, it was but another manifestation of the crystallizing tendency of thought which we noticed in all the aspects of the mentality of the declining Middle Ages.   Instead of heralding the advent of the Renaissance, as is generally assumed, this naturalism is rather one of the ultimate forms of development of the medieval mind.   The craving to turn every sacred idea into precise images, to give it a distinct and clearly outlined form, such as we observed in Gerson, in the *Roman de la Rose*, in Denis the Carthusian, controlled art, as it controlled popular beliefs and theology.   The art of the brothers Van Eyck closes a period.

CHAPTER XX

THE ÆSTHETIC SENTIMENT

The study of the art of an epoch remains incomplete unless we try to ascertain also how this art was appreciated by contemporaries : what they admired in it, and by what standards they gauged beauty. Now, there are few subjects about which tradition is so defective as the æsthetic sentiment of past ages. The faculty and the need of expressing in words the sentiment of beauty have only been developed in recent times. What sort of admiration for the art of their time was felt by the men of the fifteenth century ? Speaking generally, we may assert that two things impressed them especially : first, the dignity and sanctity of the subject ; next, the astonishing mastery, the perfectly natural rendering of all the details. Thus we find, on the one hand, an appreciation which is rather religious than artistic ; on the other hand, a naïve wonder, hardly entitled to rank as artistic emotion. The first to leave us critical observations on the painting of the brothers Van Eyck and Rogier van der Weyden was a Genoese man of letters, of the middle of the fifteenth century, Bartolomeo Fazio. Most of the pictures he speaks of are lost. He praises the beautiful and chaste figure of a Virgin, the hair of the archangel Gabriel, " surpassing real hair," the holy austerity expressed by the ascetic face of Saint John the Baptist, and a Saint Jerome who " seems to be alive." He admires the perspective of the cell of Jerome, a ray of light falling through a fissure, drops of sweat on the body of a woman in a bath, an image reflected by a mirror, a burning lamp, a landscape with mountains, woods, villages, castles, human figures, the distant horizon, and, once again, the mirror. The terms he uses to vent his enthusiasm betray merely a naïve curiosity, losing itself in the unlimited wealth of details, without arriving at a judgment on the beauty of the whole. Such is the

243

appreciation of a medieval work by a mind which is still medieval.

A century later, after the triumph of the Renaissance, it is just this minuteness in the execution of details which is condemned as the fundamental fault of Flemish art. According to the Portuguese artist, Francesco de Holanda, Michelangelo spoke about it as follows :

" Flemish painting pleases all the devout better than Italian. The latter evokes no tears, the former makes them weep copiously. This is not a result of the merits of this art ; the only cause is the extreme sensibility of the devout spectators. The Flemish pictures please women, especially the old and very young ones, and also monks and nuns, and lastly men of the world who are not capable of understanding true harmony. In Flanders they paint, before all things, to render exactly and deceptively the outward appearance of things. The painters choose, by preference, subjects provoking transports of piety, like the figures of saints or of prophets. But most of the time they paint what are called landscapes with plenty of figures. Though the eye is agreeably impressed, these pictures have neither art nor reason ; neither symmetry nor proportion ; neither choice of values nor grandeur. In short, this art is without power and without distinction ; it aims at rendering minutely many things at the same time, of which a single one would have sufficed to call forth a man's whole application."

It was the medieval spirit itself which Michelangelo judged here. Those whom he called the devout are people of the medieval spirit. For him the ancient beauty has become a thing for the small and the feeble. Not all his contemporaries thought as he did. In the North many continued to venerate the art of their ancestors, among them Dürer and Quentin Metsys, and Jan Scorel, who is said to have kissed the altarpiece of the Lamb. But Michelangelo here truly represents the Renaissance as opposed to the Middle Ages. What he condemns in Flemish art are exactly the essential traits of the declining Middle Ages : the violent sentimentality, the tendency to see each thing as an independent entity, to get lost in the multiplicity of concepts. To this the spirit of the Renaissance is opposed, and, as always happens, only realizes its new conception of art and of life by temporally misjudging the beauties and the truths of the preceding age.

The consciousness of æsthetic pleasure and its expression are of tardy growth. A fifteenth-century scholar like Fazio, trying to vent his artistic admiration, does not get beyond the language of commonplace wonder. The very notion of artistic beauty is still wanting. The æsthetic sensation caused by the contemplation of art is lost always and at once either in pious emotion or a vague sense of well-being.

Denis the Carthusian wrote a treatise, *De venustate mundi et pulchritudine Dei*. The difference of the two words of the title at once indicates his point of view : true beauty only appertains to God, the world can only be *venustus*—pretty. All the beauties of creation, he says, are but brooks flowing from the source of supreme beauty. A creature may be called beautiful in so far as it shares in the beauty of the divine nature, and thereby attains some measure of harmony with it. As a starting-point of æsthetics, this is large and sublime, and might well serve as a basis for the analysis of all particular manifestations of beauty. Denis did not invent his fundamental idea : he founds himself on Saint Augustine and the pseudo-Areopagite, on Hugues de Saint Victor and Alexandre de Halès. But as soon as he tries really to analyse beauty, the deficiency of observation and expression is apparent. He borrows even his examples of earthly beauty from his predecessors, especially from Hugues and Richard de Saint Victor : a leaf, the troubled sea with its changing hues, etc. His analysis is very superficial. Herbs are beautiful, because they are green; precious stones, because they sparkle; the human body, the dromedary and the camel, because they are appropriate to their purpose ; the earth, because it is long and large ; the heavenly bodies, because they are round and light. Mountains are admirable for their enormous dimensions, rivers for the length of their course, fields and woods for their vast surface, the earth for its immeasurable mass.

Medieval theory reduced the idea of beauty to that of perfection, proportion and splendour. Three things, says Saint Thomas, are required for beauty : first, integrity or perfection, because what is incomplete is ugly on that account ; next, true proportion or consonance ; lastly, brightness, because we call beautiful whatever has a brilliant colour. Denis the Carthusian tries to apply these standards, but he hardly succeeds : applied æsthetics are seldom successful. When the idea of beauty is so highly intellectualized, it is not surprising that the mind passes at once from earthly beauty to that of the angels and of the empyrean, or to that of abstract conceptions. There was no place, in this system, for the notion of artistic beauty, not even in connection with music, the effects of which, one would have supposed, could not fail to suggest the idea of beauty of a specific character.

Musical sensation was immediately absorbed in religious feeling. It would never have occurred to Denis that he might admire in music or painting any other beauty than that of holy things themselves.

One day, on entering the church of Saint John at Bois-le-Duc, while the organ was playing, he was instantly transported by the melody into a prolonged ecstasy.

Denis was one of those who objected to introducing the new polyphonous music into the church. Breaking the voice (*fractio vocis*), he says, seems to be the sign of a broken soul ; it is like curled hair in a man or plaited garments in a woman : vanity, and nothing else. He does not mean that there are not devout people whom melody stimulates into contemplation, therefore the Church is right in tolerating organs ; but he disapproves of artistic music which only serves to charm those who hear it, and especially to amuse the women. Certain people who practised singing in melodic parts assured him they experienced a certain pleasurable pride, and even a sort of lasciviousness of the heart (*lascivia animi*). In other words, to describe the exact nature of musical emotion the only terms he can find are those denoting dangerous sins.

From the earlier Middle Ages onward many treatises on the æsthetics of music were written, but these treatises, constructed according to the musical theories of antiquity, which were no longer understood, teach us little about the way in which the men of the Middle Ages really enjoyed music. In analysing musical beauty, fifteenth-century writers do not get beyond the vagueness and naïveness which also characterized their admiration of painting. Just as, in giving expression

to the latter, they only praise the lofty character of the treatment and the perfect rendering of nature, so in music only
sacred dignity and imitative ingenuity are appreciated. To the
medieval spirit, musical emotion quite naturally took the form
of an echo of celestial joy. " For music "—says the honest
rhetorician Molinet, a great lover of music, like Charles the
Bold—" is the resonance of the heavens, the voice of the angels,
the joy of paradise, the hope of the air, the organ of the
Church, the song of the little birds, the recreation of all gloomy
and despairing hearts, the persecution and driving away of
the devils." The ecstatic character of musical emotion, of
course, did not escape them. " The power of harmony "—
says Pierre d'Ailly—" is such that it withdraws the soul from
other passions and from cares, nay, from itself."

The high valuation of the imitative element in art entailed
graver dangers for music than for painting. Composition of
the fourteenth and fifteenth centuries really suffered from the
craze for naturalistic music, such as the *caccia* (whence English
" catch "), originally representing a hunt with baying and
yelping hounds and blowing horns. At the beginning of the sixteenth century, a pupil of Josquin de Prés, Jannequin, composed
several " Inventions " of this stamp, representing, amongst
others, the battle of Marignano, the street-cries of Paris,
the singing of birds and the chattering of women. Fortu-
nately, the musical inspiration of the epoch was far too rich
and alive to be enslaved by such an artificial theory ; the
masterpieces of Dufay, Binchois or Okeghem are free from
imitative tricks.

Substituting for beauty the notions of measure, order and
appropriateness offered a very defective explanation of it.
One other means at least satisfied deeper æsthetic instincts :
the reduction of beauty to the sensation of light and splendour. To define the beauty of spiritual things, Denis the
Carthusian always compares them to light. Wisdom, science,
art, are so many luminous essences, illuminating the mind
by their brightness.

This tendency to explain beauty by light sprang from a
strongly marked predilection of the medieval mind. When
we leave definitions of the idea of beauty aside, and examine
the æsthetic sense of the epoch in its spontaneous expres-

sions, we notice that nearly always when men of the Middle
Ages attempt to express æsthetic enjoyment, their emotions
are caused by sensations of luminous brightness or of lively
movement.

Froissart, for example, is not, as a rule, very susceptible
to impressions of pure beauty. His endless narratives leave
him no time for that. There are one or two spectacles, however, which never fail to enrapture him : that of vessels on
the sea with their pavilions and streamers, with their rich
decoration of many-coloured blazons, sparkling in the sunshine ; or the play of reflected sunlight on the helmets and
cuirasses, on the points of the lances, the gay colours of the
pennons and banners, of a troop of cavaliers on the march.
Eustache Deschamps has expressed his sense of the beauty
of mills in movement and of a ray of sunlight scintillating in
a dewdrop. La Marche was struck by the beauty of reflected
sunlight on the blonde hair of a cavalcade of German and
Bohemian noblemen. These displays of æsthetic sentiment
are important, because in the fifteenth century they are
extremely rare.

This fondness for all that glitters reappears in the general
gaudiness of dress, especially in the excessive number of
precious stones sewed on the garments. After the Middle
Ages this sort of ornament will be replaced by ribbons and
rosettes. Transferred to the domain of hearing, this partiality
for brilliant things is shown by the naïve pleasure taken in
tinkling or clicking sounds. La Hire wore a red mantle covered
all over with little silver bells like cow-bells. At an entry
in 1465, Captain Salazar was accompanied by twenty men-
at-arms, the harness of whose horses was ornamented with
large silver bells. The horses of the counts of Charolais
and of Saint Pol were adorned in the same way, also those of
the lord of Croy, at the entry of Louis XI into Paris in 1461.
At festivals jingling florins or nobles were often sewn on to
the dress.

To determine the taste in colours characteristic of the
epoch would require a comprehensive and statistical research,
embracing the chromatic scale of painting as well as the colours
of costume and decorative art. Perhaps costume would
prove to be the best clue to the nature of the taste for colour,

because there it exhibits itself most spontaneously. Now, we have very few specimens of the materials used at that time, except in church vestments. Descriptions of costumes for tournaments and festivals, on the other hand, are very numerous. The following summary aims only at giving a provisional impression, based on an examination of these descriptions. It is necessary to observe that they refer to garments of state and of luxury, differing, as to colour, from ordinary costume, but showing the æsthetic sense more freely. When we consult the accounts published by Monsieur Couderc of a great Parisian tailor of the fifteenth century, we find that the quiet colours, grey, black and violet, occupy a large place, whereas in festal garments the most violent contrasts and the most vivid colours abound. Red predominates ; at some princely entries all the accoutrements were in red. White comes next in popularity. Every combination of colours was allowed : red with blue, blue with violet. In an " entremets " described by La Marche a lady appeared in violet-coloured silk on a hackney covered with a housing of blue silk, led by three men in vermilion-tinted silk and in hoods of green silk.

Black was already a favourite colour, even in state apparel, especially in velvets. Philip the Good, in his later years, constantly dressed in black, and had his suite and horses arrayed in the same colour. King René, who was always in quest of what was refined and distinguished, combined grey and white with black. Together with grey and violet, black was far more in vogue than blue and green, whereas yellow and brown are, as yet, almost completely wanting. Now, the relative rarity of blue and of green must not be simply ascribed to an æsthetic predilection. The symbolic meaning attached to blue and green was so marked and peculiar as to make them almost unfit for usual dress. They were the special colours of love. Blue signified fidelity ; green, amorous passion.

> "Il te fauldra de vert vestir,
> C'est la livrée aux amoureux. . . ." [1]

---

[1] You will have to dress in green, It is the livery of lovers. . .

Thus says a song of the fifteenth century. Deschamps says of the lovers of a lady :

> "Li uns se vest pour li de vert,
> L'autre de bleu, l'autre de blanc,
> L'autre s'en vest vermeil com sanc,
> Et cilz qui plus la veult avoir
> Pour son grant dueil s'en vest de noir." [1]

Although other colours also had their meaning in amorous symbolism, a man exposed himself specially to raillery by dressing in blue or in green, above all in blue, for a suggestion of hypocrisy was mixed up with it.   Christine de Pisan makes a lady say to her lover who draws attention to his blue dress :

> "Au bleu vestir ne tient mie le fait
> N'a devises porter, d'amer sa dame,
> Mais au servir de loyal cuer parfait
> Elle sans plus, et la garder de blasme.
> . . . Là gist l'amour, non pas au bleu porter,
> Mais puet estre que plusieurs le meffait
> De faulseté cuident couvrir soubz lame
> Par bleu porter. . . ." [2]

That is probably why, by a very curious transition, blue, instead of being the colour of faithful love, came to mean infidelity too, and next, besides the faithless wife, marked the dupe.   In Holland the blue cloak designated an adulterous woman, in France the " cote bleue " denotes a cuckold.   At last blue was the colour of fools in general.

Whether the dislike of brown and yellow sprang from an æsthetic aversion or from their symbolic signification remains undecided.   Perhaps an unfavourable meaning was attributed to them, because they were thought ugly.

> "Gris et tannée puis bien porter
> Car ennuyé suis d'espérance." [3]

---

[1] Some dress themselves for her in green, Another in blue, another in white, Another dresses himself in vermilion like blood, And he who desires her most Because of his great sorrow, dresses in black.

[2] To wear blue is no proof Nor to wear mottoes, of love for one's lady, But to serve her with a perfectly loyal heart And no others, and to keep her from blame. . . . Love lies in that, not in wearing blue.   But it may be that many think To cover the offence of falsehood under a tombstone, By wearing blue. . . .

[3] I may well wear grey and tan For hope has only brought me pain.

Grey and brown were both colours of sadness, yet grey was much in demand for festal apparel, whereas brown was very rare.

Yellow meant hostility. Henry of Wurtemberg passed before Philip of Burgundy with all his retinue dressed in yellow, " and the duke was informed that it was meant for him."

After the middle of the fifteenth century, there seems to be a temporary diminution of black and white in favour of blue and yellow. In the sixteenth century, at the same time when artists begin to avoid the naïve contrasts of primary colours, the habit of using bizarre and daring combinations of colours for costume vanishes too.

In so far as art is concerned, it might be supposed that this change was due to the influence of Italy, but the facts do not confirm this. Gerard David, who carries on most directly the tradition of the primitive school, already shows this refinement of colour-sentiment. It must therefore be regarded as a tendency of a more general character. Here is a domain in which the history of art and that of civilization have still a great deal to learn from each other.

CHAPTER XXI

VERBAL AND PLASTIC EXPRESSION COMPARED

I

With each attempt to draw a sharp line of demarcation between the Middle Ages and the Renaissance, this border-line has receded further and further backward. Ideas and forms which one had been accustomed to regard as character-istic of the Renaissance proved to have existed as early as the thirteenth century. Accordingly, the word Renaissance has been so much extended by some as to include even Saint Francis of Assisi. But the term, thus understood, loses its genuine meaning. On the other hand, the Renaissance, when studied without preconceived ideas, is found to be full of elements, which were characteristic of the medieval spirit in its full bloom. Thus it has become nearly impossible to keep up the antithesis, and yet we cannot do without it, because Middle Ages and Renaissance by the usage of half a century have become terms which call up before us, by means of a single word, the difference between two epochs, a difference which we feel to be essential, though hard to define, just as it is impossible to express the difference of taste between a strawberry and an apple.

To avoid the inconvenience inherent in the unsettled nature of the two terms Middle Ages and Renaissance, the safest way is to reduce them, as much as possible, to the meaning they originally had—for instance, not to speak of Renaissance in reference to Saint Francis of Assisi or the ogival style.

Nor should the art of Claus Sluter and the brothers Van Eyck be called Renaissance. Both in form and in idea it is a product of the waning Middle Ages. If certain historians of art have discovered Renaissance elements in it, it is be-cause they have confounded, very wrongly, realism and Renaissance. Now this scrupulous realism, this aspiration to render exactly all natural details, is the characteristic feature of the spirit of the expiring Middle Ages. It is the same tendency which we encountered in all the fields of the thought of the epoch, a sign of decline and not of rejuvenation. The triumph of the Renaissance was to consist in replacing this meticulous realism by breadth and simplicity.

The art and literature of the fifteenth century in France and in the Netherlands are almost exclusively concerned with giving a finished and ornate form to a system of ideas which had long since ceased to grow. They are the servants of an expiring mode of thought. Now, the literature and the art of a period in which artistic creation is almost limited to mere paraphrasing of ideas fully thought out, will differ widely from each other in their value for future ages. Let us consider roughly, for a moment, the impression left upon us, on the one hand, by the literature of the fifteenth century, and on the other hand by its painting. Villon and Charles d'Orléans apart, most of the poets will appear superficial, monotonous and tiresome. Always allegories with insipid personages and hackneyed moralizing, always the same themes repeated to satiety : the sleeper in the orchard, who, in a dream, sees a symbolic lady ; the walk at daybreak in the month of May ; the " debate " on a love case ; in short, an exasperating shallowness, cloying romanticism, vapid imagery. We shall rarely glean a thought there which is worth being remembered, or an expression which dwells in our memory. The artists, on the other hand, are not only very great, like Van Eyck, Foucquet, or the unknown who painted " The Man with the Glass of Wine," but nearly all, even the mediocre ones, arrest our attention by each detail of their work and hold us by their originality and freshness. Yet their contemporaries admired the poets much more than the artists. Why was the flavour lost in the one case and preserved in the other ?

The explanation is that words and images have a totally different æsthetic function. If the painter does nothing but render exactly, by means of line and colour, the external aspect of an object, he yet always adds to this purely formal reproduction something inexpressible. The poet, on the contrary, if he only aims at formulating anew an already expressed concept, or describing some visible reality, will exhaust the whole treasure of the ineffable. Unless rhythm or accent save it by their own charms, the effect of the poem will depend solely on the echo which the subject, the thought in itself, awakens in the soul of the hearer. A contemporary will be thrilled by the poet's word, for the thought which the latter expresses also forms an integral part of his own life, and it will appear the more striking to him in so far as its form is more brilliant. A happy selection of terms will suffice to make the expression of it acceptable and charming to him. As soon, however, as this thought is worn out and no longer responds to the preoccupations of the soul of the period, nothing of value is left to the poem except its form. No doubt, that is of extreme value. Sometimes it is so fresh and so touching that it makes us forget the insignificance of the contents. A new beauty of form was already revealing itself in the literature of the fifteenth century ; still, in the greater number of its productions, the form as well was worn out and the qualities of rhythm and tone are poor. In such a case, without novelty of thought or form, nought remains but an interminable post-lude on hackneyed themes, a poetry without a future.

The painter of the same epoch and of the same mentality as the poet will have nothing to fear from time. For the inexpressible which he has put into his work will always be there as fresh as on the first day. Let us consider the portraits of Jan van Eyck, the somewhat pointed and pinched face of his wife, the aristocratic, impassible and morose head of Baudouin de Lannoy, the suffering and resigned visage of the Arnolfini at Berlin, the enigmatic candour of " Leal Souvenir " in the National Gallery. In each of these physiognomies the personality was probed to the last inch. It is the profoundest character-drawing possible. These characters were not analysed by the artist, but *seen* as a whole and then revealed to us by his picture. He could not have described them in words, even though he had been, at the same time, the greatest poet of his age. Painting, even when it professes no more than to render the outward appearance of things, preserves its mystery for all time to come.

Hence the art and the literature of the fifteenth century, though born of the same inspiration and the same spirit, in-

PORTRAIT OF GIOVANNI ARNOLFINI.   BY JAN VAN EYCK.

"LEAL SOUVENIR." BY JAN VAN EYCK.

evitably produce on us quite different effects. Apart from this fundamental difference, it may be shown, by the comparison of particular specimens, that the literary and the pictorial expression have far more traits in common than might be supposed from our general appreciation of the one and the other.

Let us take the brothers Van Eyck as being the most eminent representatives of the art of the epoch. Who are the men of letters to be matched with them, in order to compare their inspiration, their modes of expression ? We have to look for them in the same environment whence came the great painters, that is to say, as we demonstrated above, in the environment of the court, the nobility and the rich middle classes. There we may assume an affinity of spirit to exist. The literature which may be matched with the art of the brothers Van Eyck is that which the patrons of painting protected and admired.

At first sight the comparison seems to bring to light an essential difference. Whereas the subject-matter of the artists is almost entirely religious, the profane genre preponderates in literature. Still, we must remember that the profane element occupied a much larger place in painting than might be supposed from what has been preserved. On the other hand, we run some risk of overrating a little the preponderance of profane literature. The history of literature, being naturally concerned with the tale, the romance, the satire, the song, historical writings, might easily lead us to forget that pious works always occupied the first and the largest place in the libraries of the time. In order to make a fair comparison between fifteenth-century painting and literature, we must begin by imagining side by side with the surviving altarpieces and portraits all sorts of worldly and even frivolous paintings, such as hunting or bathing scenes. The above-named Fazio mentions a picture by Rogier van der Weyden representing a woman in a sweating-bath, with two laughing young men peeping through a chink.

Art and letters in the fifteenth century share the general and essential tendency of the spirit of the expiring Middle Ages : that of accentuating every detail, of developing every thought and every image to the end, of giving concrete form to every concept of the mind. Erasmus tells us that he once heard a preacher in Paris preach during forty days on the Parable of the Prodigal Son, so that he devoted all Lent to it. He described his journeys on his setting out and on his return, the bill of fare of his meals at the inns, the mills he passed, his dicing, etc., torturing the texts of prophets and evangelists to find some that might seem to give some support to his twaddle. " And because of that the ignorant multitude and the fat big-wigs considered him almost a god."

To realize the place conceded to the minute execution of details, it suffices to examine some paintings by Jan van Eyck. Let us first take the Madonna of the chancellor Rolin, at the Louvre. In any other artist the laborious exactness with which the materials of the dresses are painted, also the marble of the tiles and the columns, the reflections of the window-panes, and the chancellor's breviary, would give an impression of pedantry. Even in him the exaggerated finish of the details, as in the ornaments of the capitals, on which a whole series of Biblical scenes is represented, is hurtful to the general effect. But it is especially in the marvellous perspective opened behind the figures of the Virgin and the donor that his passion for details is given rein. " The dumbfounded spectator," as Monsieur Durand-Gréville says in describing this picture, " discovers between the head of the divine child and the Virgin's shoulder, a town full of pointed gables and elegant belfries, with a big church with numerous buttresses, and a vast square, cut across all its length by a staircase on which come and go and run countless little touches of the brush, which are so many living figures ; his eye is next attracted by a curved bridge swarming with groups of people who pass and repass ; it follows the meanderings of a river on which tiny barks make ripples ; and in the midst of which, on an island smaller than the nail of a child's finger, rises up a lordly castle with numerous turrets, surrounded by trees ; it traces on the left a quay planted with trees, and covered with foot-passengers ; it goes even further, passing beyond the green hill-tops, rests for a moment on the distant line of snowy mountains, to lose itself, at last, in the infinite space of a sky, which is hardly blue, where floating vapours are vaguely discerned."

Are not unity and harmony lost in this aggregation of details,

THE MADONNA OF THE CHANCELLOR ROLIN. BY JAN VAN EYCK.

THE ANNUNCIATION. BY JAN VAN EYCK.

as Michelangelo affirmed of Flemish art in general ? Having recently seen the picture again, I can no longer deny it, as I formerly did on the strength of recollections many years old.

Another work of the master, which lends itself particularly to the analysis of endless detail, is the " Annunciation " in the Hermitage, at Petrograd. If the triptych of which this picture formed the right wing ever existed as a whole, it must have been a superb creation. Van Eyck here developed all the virtuosity of a master conscious of his power to overcome all difficulties. Of all his works it is the most hieratic and, at the same time, the most refined. He followed the iconographic rules of the past in using as a background for the apparition of the angel the ample space of a church and not the intimacy of a bedchamber, as he did in the altar-piece of the Lamb, where the scene is full of grace and tenderness. Here, on the contrary, the angel salutes Mary by a ceremonious bow ; he is not represented with a spray of lilies and a narrow diadem ; he carries a sceptre and a rich crown, and about his lips there is the stiff smile of the sculpture of Ægina. The splendour of the colours, the glitter of the pearls, the gold and the precious stones, surpass those of all the other angelic figures painted by Van Eyck. His coat is green and gold, his mantle of brocade is red and gold, his wings are covered with peacock feathers. The book of the Virgin and the cushion before her are executed with painstaking and minute care. In the church there is a profusion of anecdotal details. The tiles of the pavement are ornamented with the signs of the zodiac and scenes from the lives of Samson and of David. The wall of the apse is decorated with the figures of Isaac and of Jacob in the medallions between the arches, and that of Christ on the celestial globe between two seraphim in a window, besides other mural paintings representing the finding of the child Moses and the giving of the tables of the Law, all explained by legible inscriptions. Only the decoration of the wooden ceiling, though still discernible, remains indistinct.

This time unity and harmony are not lost in the accumulation of details. The twilight of the lofty edifice envelops all with mysterious shade, so that the eye can only with difficulty distinguish the anecdotal details.

It is the privilege of the painter that he can give the rein to his craving for endless elaboration of details (perhaps one ought to say, that he can comply with the most impossible demands of an ignorant donor) without sacrificing the general effect. The sight of this multitude of details fatigues us no more than the sight of reality itself. We only notice them if our attention has been directed to them, and we soon lose sight of them, so that they serve only to heighten effects of colouring or perspective.

When the same boundless passion for details is displayed in literature, the effect is quite different. In the first place, literature proceeds in another way ; it sets itself to enumerate all the ideas and all the objects which the mind of the poet associates with his subject. Most of the authors of the fifteenth century are singularly prolix. They do not know the value of omission, they fill the canvas of their composition with all the details that present themselves, but without giving, as does painting, an accurate image of their particular features —they confine themselves to enumerating them. It is a strictly quantitative method, whereas that of painting is qualitative.

Another difference between the two modes of expression proceeds from the fact that the relation between the essential and the accidental is not the same in both. In painting we can hardly distinguish between principal and accessory elements. Everything is essential. The principal subject may be of no interest to the spectator or in his opinion badly rendered, without the work losing its charm, on that account. Unless the religious sentiment preponderates over æsthetic appreciation, the spectator before the altar-piece of the Lamb will regard with as much, perhaps with more profound emotion, the flowery field of the principal scene, the procession of adorers of the Lamb, the towers behind the trees in the background, as the central figures of the composition in their august divinity. His glance will stray from the rather uninteresting figures of God, the Virgin, and Saint John the Baptist, to those of Adam and Eve, to the portraits of the donors, to the charming perspective of the sunlit street and the little brass kettle with the towel. He will hardly ask if the mystery of the Eucharist has here found its most appropriate expression, so much will he be enchanted by the touching intimacy and the incredible perfection of all these details, purely accessory in the eyes of those who ordered and who executed the masterpiece.

Now, in the expression of details the artist is absolutely free. Whereas he is tied down by rigid convention in the composition of his principal theme he may give a free rein to his imagination in all other respects. He may paint the materials, the vegetation, the horizons, the faces, just as his genius prompts him ; the wealth of detail will no more overload his picture than flowers weigh down a dress which they adorn.

In the poetry of the fifteenth century the relation of the essential to the accident is reversed. The poet is generally free as regards his principal subject ; something novel is expected from him. As to accessories, however, he is tied down by tradition ; there is a conventional way of expressing each detail, from which, though he may be unconscious of it, he can hardly deviate ; the flowers, the delights of nature, sorrows and joys, all these are sung in a fashion which varies but little. Moreover, the salutary limitation which the dimension of his picture imposes upon the artist does not exist for the poet, as a rule. Hence, to be worthy of this liberty the poet should be relatively greater than the artist. Even mediocre painters may delight posterity, whereas the mediocre poet is forgotten.

To make the effect of the abuse of details in a fifteenth-century poem felt, it would be necessary to quote it entirely. As this is impossible, we must content ourselves with considering a few fragmentary specimens.

Alain Chartier in his day was held to be a great poet. He was compared to Petrarch, and even Clement Marot placed him in the first rank. We may, therefore, fairly compare his work with that of the greatest painters of his time, and set the description of nature with which his *Livre des Quatre Dames* opens against the landscape of the altar-piece of the Lamb.

One spring morning the poet goes out for a walk, to drive away his persistent melancholy.

"Pour oublier melencolie,
Et pour faire chiere plus lie,
Ung doulx matin aux champs issy,
Au premier jour qu'amours ralie
Les cueurs en la saison jolie. . . ." [1]

All this is conventional and without any special grace of rhythm or of accent. Then follows the description of a spring morning :

"Tout autour oiseaulx voletoient,
Et si très-doulcement chantoient
Qu'il n'est cueur qui n'en fust joyeulx.
Et en chantant en l'air montoient,
Et puis l'un l'autre surmontoient
A l'estrivée à qui mieulx mieulx.
Le temps n'estoit mie nueux,
De bleu estoient vestuz les cieux,
Et le beau soleil cler luisoit." [2]

The mention of these delights would not have lacked charm if the author had known where to stop. But he was not so discreet ; having gone through all the singing birds, he continues his enumeration at a jog-trot :

"Les arbres regarday flourir,
Et lièvres et connins courir.
Du printemps tout s'esjouyssoit.
Là sembloit amour seignourir.
Nul n'y peult vieillir ne mourir,
Ce me semble, tant qu'il y soit.
Des erbes ung flair doulx issoit,
Que l'air sery adoulcissoit,
Et en bruiant par la valee
Ung petit ruisselet passoit,
Qui les pays amoitissoit,
Dont l'eaue n'estoit pas salee.
Là buvoient les oysillons,
Après ce que des grisillons,

---

[1] To forget melancholy, And to cheer myself, One sweet morning I went out into the fields On the first day on which love joins Hearts in the beautiful season.

[2] All around birds were flying, And they sang so very sweetly That there is no heart that would not be gladdened by it. And while singing they rose up in the air, And then passed and repassed each other, Vying with each other as to which should rise highest. The weather was not cloudy at all. The heavens were clad in blue. And the beautiful sun was shining brightly.

Des mouschettes et papillons
Ilz avoient pris leur pasture.
Lasniers, aoutours, esmerillons
Vy, et mouches aux aguillons,
Qui de beau miel paveillons
Firent aux arbres par mesure.
De l'autre part fut la closture
D'ung pré gracieuz, ou nature
Sema les fleurs sur la verdure,
Blanches, jaunes, rouges et perses.
D'arbres flouriz fut la ceinture,
Aussi blancs que se neige pure
Les couvroit, ce sembloit paincture,
Tant y eut de couleurs diverses." [1]

A brook brawls over pebbles, fishes swim in it, a grove
spreads its twigs on the bank, forming a green curtain. And
then the birds reappear : ducks, turtle-doves, pheasants and
herons ; all the birds from here to Babylon, as Villon would
say.

The artist and the poet, both striving to render the beauty
of nature, both dominated by the tendency to fasten on each
detail, nevertheless arrive, because of the diversity of their
methods, at a very different result. Unity and simplicity in
the picture, in spite of the mass of details, monotony and form-
lessness in the poem.

But are we right in comparing poetry with painting, with
respect to expressive power ? Should we not rather take
prose, less tied down to obligatory motifs, freer in its choice of
means to give an exact vision of reality ?

One of the fundamental traits of the mind of the declining
Middle Ages is the predominance of the sense of sight, a predominance which is closely connected with the atrophy of

[1] I saw the trees blossom, And hares and rabbits run. Everything rejoiced
at the spring. Love seemed to hold sway there. None could age or die, It
seemed to me, so long as he was there. From the herbs arose a sweet smell,
Which the clear air made sweeter still, And purling through the valley A little
brook passed Moistening the lands Of which the water was not salt. There
drank the little birds After they had fed upon crickets, Little flies and butter-
flies. I saw there lanners, hawks and merlins, And flies with a sting (wasps)
Who made pavilions of fine honey In the trees by measure. In another part
was the enclosure Of a charming meadow, where nature Strewed flowers
on the verdure White, yellow, red and violet. It was encircled by blossoming
trees As white as if pure snow Covered them, it looked like a painting, So many
various colours there were.

thought. Thought takes the form of visual images. Really to impress the mind a concept has first to take a visible shape. The insipidity of allegory could be borne, because the satisfaction of the mind lay in the vision. This constant need of expressing the visible was far better fulfilled by pictorial than by literary means. And again better by prose than by poetry, because it conforms more easily to the visualizing turn of mind. The prose of the fifteenth century in general is superior to its poetry, because prose, like painting, could attain a high degree of direct and powerful realism, which was denied to poetry by its stage of development and by its proper nature.

There is one author, especially, who, by the eminent clearness of his vision of external things, reminds us of Van Eyck, namely, Georges Chastellain. He was a Fleming from the Alost district. Though he calls himself " a loyal Frenchman," " a Frenchman by birth," it is highly probable that Flemish was his mother-tongue. La Marche calls him " a born Fleming, though writing in the French language." He himself likes to lay stress on his rusticity ; he speaks of " his coarse speech," he calls himself " a Flemish man, a man of the cattle-breeding marshes, rude, ignorant, stammering of tongue, greasy of mouth and of palate and quite bemired with other defects, proper to the nature of the land." His Flemish birth explains the heaviness of his flowery speech, his pompous and turgid grandiloquence ; in short, his truly " Burgundian " style, which makes him almost unbearable to the French reader. It is a formal style, of somewhat elephantine character. But it is also to his Flemish cast of mind that Chastellain owes his lucid and penetrating vision and the richness of his colouring.

There are undeniable affinities between Chastellain and Jan van Eyck. In his best moments Chastellain equals Van Eyck at his worst, and that is saying a good deal. Let us recall the group of singing angels of the altar-piece of the Lamb. Those heavy dresses of red and gold brocade, loaded with precious stones, those too expressive grimaces, the somewhat puerile decoration of the lectern—all this in painting is the equivalent of the showy Burgundian prose. It is a rhetorician's style transferred to painting. Now, whereas this rhetorical element occupies but a small place in painting, it is the principal thing in Chastellain's prose, where the clear observation and the vivid realism are too often drowned in the flood of flowery phrases and stilted terms.

Only, when Chastellain describes an event which grips his visualizing mind, he evinces an imaginative strength, which makes him very interesting. He has no more ideas than his contemporaries and colleagues ; his arsenal, like theirs, is stocked with nothing but moral, pious and chivalrous commonplaces ; his speculations never go below the surface. But his powers of observation are remarkably keen and his descriptions very lively.

The portrait he drew of Duke Philip has all the vigour of a Van Eyck. He delights in the description of scenes of action and passion, displaying a degree of true and simple realism which would have made this chronicler an excellent novelist. Take, for instance, his narrative of a quarrel between the duke and his son Charles, which took place in 1457. His visual perception is nowhere so vivid as here ; all the outward circumstances of the event are rendered with perfect clearness. A few rather long quotations are indispensable.

The difference arose in connection with a vacancy in the household of the young count of Charolais. The old duke wanted, contrary to his promise, to give the place to a member of the family of Croy, then in high favour. Charles, who did not share his father's feelings for that family, had destined it for one of his friends.

"Le duc donques par un lundy qui estoit le jour Saint-Anthoine, après sa messe, aiant bien désir que sa maison demorast paisible et sans discention entre ses serviteurs, et que son fils aussi fist par son conceil et plaisir, après que jà avoit dit une grant part de ses heures et que la cappelle estoit vuide de gens, il appela son fils à venir vers luy et lui dist doucement : 'Charles de l'estrif qui est entre les sires de Sempy et de Hémeries pour le lieu de chambrelen, je vueil que vous y mettez cès et que le sire de Sempy obtiengne le lieu vacant.' Adont dist le conte : 'Monseigneur, vous m'avez baillié une fois vostre ordonnance en laquelle le sire de Sempy n'est point, et monseigneur, s'il vous plaist, je vous prie que ceste-là je la puisse garder.'—'Déa,' ce dit le duc lors, 'ne vous chailliez des ordonnances, c'est à moy à croistre et à diminuer, je vueil que le sire de Sempy y soit mis.'—'Hahan!' ce dist le conte (car ainsi jurait tousjours), 'monseigneur, je vous prie, pardonnez-moy, car je ne le pourroye faire, je me tiens à ce que vous m'avez ordonné. Ce a fait le seigneur de Croy, qui m'a brassé cecy, je le vois bien.'—'Comment,' ce dist le duc, ' me désobéy-rez-vous ? ne ferez-vous pas ce que je veuil ? '—'Monsei-gneur, je vous obéyray volentiers, mais je ne feray point cela.' Et le duc, à ces mots, enfelly de ire, respondit : ' Hà ! garsson, désobéyras-tu à ma volenté ? va hors de mex yeux,' et le sang, avecques les paroles, lui tira à cœur, et devint pâle et puis à coup enflambé et si espoentable en son vis, comme je l'oys recorder au clerc de la chapelle qui seul estoit emprès luy, que hideur estoit à le regarder." . . .[1]

The duchess, who was present at this dispute, was so much frightened by her husband's look, that she tried to lead her son out of the oratory, and pushed him before her, to get out of range of his father's wrath. But they had to turn several corners before coming to the door of which the clerk had the key. "Caron, open the door for us," says the duchess, but the clerk falls at her feet, praying her to persuade her son to ask pardon, before leaving the chapel. In answer to his mother's urgent request, Charles answers in a loud voice : "Déa, madame, monseigneur m'a deffendu ses yeux et est

---

[1] The duke then, on a Monday, which was Saint Anthony's day, after mass, being very desirous that his house should remain peaceful and without dissensions between his servants, and that his son, too, should do his will and pleasure, after he had already said a great part of his hours, and the chapel was empty of people, called his son to come to him and said to him gently : " Charles, the quarrel which is going on between the lords of Sempy and of Hémeries, about this place of chamberlain, I wish that you put a stop to it, and that the lord of Sempy obtains the vacancy." Then said the count : " Monseigneur, you once gave me your orders in which the lord of Sempy is not mentioned, and monseigneur, if you please, I pray you, that I may keep to them."—" Déa," this said the duke then, " do not trouble yourself about orders, it belongs to me to augment and to diminish, I wish that the lord of Sempy be placed there."—" Hahan ! " this said the count (for he always swore like that), "monseigneur, I beg you, forgive me, for I could not do it, I abide by what you have ordered me. This was done by my lord of Croy, who played me this trick, I can see that."—" How," this said the duke," will you disobey me ? will you not do what I wish ? "—" Monseigneur, I shall gladly obey you. But I shall not do this." And the duke, at these words, choking with anger, replied : " Hà ! boy, will you disobey my will ? Go out of my sight," and the blood with these words rushing to his heart, he turned pale and then all at once flushed and there came such a horrible expression on his face, as I heard from the clerk of the chapel, who alone was with him, that it was hideous to look at him. ; . .

indigné sur moy, par quoy, après avoir eu celle deffense, je ne m'y retourneray point si tost, ains m'en yray à la garde de Dieu, je ne scay où."[1] Then is heard the voice of the duke, who has remained in his seat, paralysed with fury . . . and the duchess in an agony of fear says to the clerk : "My friend, open the door quickly, quickly, we must be gone, or we are lost."

On returning to his apartments, the old duke, beside himself with anger, fell into a fit of mental aberration ; about nightfall he left Brussels alone, on horseback, insufficiently dressed and without warning anyone. "Les jours pour celle heurre d'alors estoient courts, et estoit jà basse vesprée quant ce prince droit-cy monta à cheval, et ne demandoit riens autre fors estre emmy les champs seul et à par luy. Sy porta ainsy l'aventure que ce propre jour-là, après un long et âpre gel, il faisoit un releng, et par une longue épaisse bruyne, qui avoit couru tout ce jour là, vesprée tourna en pluie bien menue, mais trés-mouillant et laquelle destrempoit les terres et rompoit glasces avecques vent qui s'y entrebouta."[2]

Both this passage, and the preceding one, are assuredly not lacking in simple and natural force. In the description which follows of the nocturnal ride of the duke, as he wanders through the fields and woods, Chastellain has mixed his pompous rhetoric with this spontaneous naturalism, which produces a very bizarre effect. Starving and tired, the old duke, having lost his way, vainly calls for help. He narrowly escapes falling into a river which he takes for a road. He is wounded by falling with his horse. He listens in vain for the crowing of a cock, or the barking of a dog, which might have indicated some habitation to him. At last he perceives a glimmer and tries to get to it ; loses sight of it, finds it again and reaches it at last. "Mais plus l'approchoit, plus sambloit hideuse chose

---

[1] Faith, madam, monseigneur has forbidden me to come into his sight and is indignant at me, so that, after this prohibition, I shall not return to him so soon, but under God's care, I shall go away, I do not know where.

[2] The days were short at that time, and it was already evening when that prince here mounted his horse, and asked nothing but to be alone out in the fields. It so happened that on that day after a long and sharp frost it had begun to thaw, and because of a lasting thick fog which had been about all day, in the evening a fine but very penetrating rain began to fall, which soaked the fields and broke the ice as did the wind which joined in.

et espoentable, car feu partoit d'une mote d'en plus de mille
lieux, avecques grosse fumière, dont nul ne pensast à celle
heure fors que ce fust ou purgatoire d'aucune âme ou autre
illusion de l'ennemy. . . ." [1] Upon this he stops, but suddenly remembers that charcoal-burners are in the habit of
lighting such kilns in the depths of woods. However he does
not find a house anywhere near, and begins roaming about
once more. At last the barking of a dog directs him to the
hovel of a poor man, where he finds rest and food.

Other episodes furnished Chastellain with themes for striking
descriptions, such as the judicial duel between the two burghers
of Valenciennes, mentioned above ; the nocturnal quarrel at
the Hague, between the envoys of Friesland and some Burgundian noblemen whose sleep they disturb by playing at
" touch and go " in the room above on their pattens ; the riot
at Ghent in 1467, at the entry of the new Duke Charles, which
coincided with the fair of Houthem, whither the people were
in the habit of taking the shrine of Saint Liévin in a procession.
In all these pages we admire the author's faculty of observation. A number of spontaneous details betray his strongly
visual perception. The duke facing the rebels sees before
him " a multitude of faces in rusty helmets, framing the grinning beards of villains, biting their lips." The lout who forces
his way to the window, by the duke's side, wears a gauntlet of
blackened iron with which he strikes the window-sill to command silence.

The gift of finding the right and simple word accurately to
describe things seen is, at bottom, the same visual power
which enables Van Eyck to give his portraits their perfect
expression. Only, in literature, this realism remains enslaved
by conventional forms and suffocated under a heap of arid
rhetoric.

In this respect painting was greatly in advance of literature.
It was already expert in the technique of rendering the effects
of light. Miniature-painters especially were occupied with
the problem of fixing the light-effect of a moment. In painting,

---

[1] But the more he approached it, the more it seemed a hideous and frightful
thing, for fire came out of a mound in more than a thousand places with thick
smoke, and, at that hour, anybody would think that it was the purgatory of
some soul or some other illusion of the devil.

the effect of a light in the dark was first successfully achieved by Geertgen of Sint Jan of Haarlem, in his "Nativity," but long before this the illuminators had tried to render the light of the torches reflected on the cuirasses in the scene of the apprehension of Christ. The master who illuminated the *Cuer d'Amours espris* by King René had already succeeded in painting a sunrise and the most mysterious twilights, the master of the "Heures d'Ailly" a sun breaking through the clouds after a thunderstorm. On the other hand, the literary means for rendering the effects of light were still primitive. But, perhaps, we should seek in another direction the literary equivalent of this faculty for fixing the impression of a moment. It would rather seem to lie in the current use, in the literature of the fourteenth and fifteenth centuries, of *oratio recta*. At no other epoch has the effect of direct speech been so eagerly sought. The endless dialogues of which Froissart makes use, even to make a political situation clear, are often empty enough, nay, even tedious ; still sometimes the impression of something immediate and instantaneous is produced in a very vivid manner, for instance in the following dialogue, which we should think of as being shouted. " Lors il entendi les nouvelles que leur ville estoit prise. ' Et de quel gens ? ' demande-il. Respondirent ceulx qui à luy parloient : ' Ce sont Bretons ! '—' Ha,' dist-il, ' Bretons sont mal gent, ils pilleront et ardront la ville et puis partiront.' ' Et quel cry crient-ils ? ' dist le chevalier.—' Certes, sire, ils crient La Trimouille ! ' "[1]

To quicken the movement of the dialogue Froissart is rather too fond of the trick of making one interlocutor repeat with astonishment the last words of the other.—" ' Monseigneur, Gaston est mort.'—' Mort ? ' dist le conte.—' Certes, mort est-il pour vray, monseigneur.' "[2]

And elsewhere : " Si luy demanda, en cause d'amours et de lignaige, conseil.—' Conseil,' respondi l'archevesque, ' certes,

[1] Then he heard the news that their town was taken. "And by what people?" he asks. Those with whom he was speaking answered, "They are Bretons !" "Ha," says he, "Bretons are bad people, they will pillage and burn and afterwards depart." "And what war-cry do they cry ?" said the knight. "Sure, my lord, they cry La Trimouille !"

[2] "My lord, Gaston is dead." "Dead ?" said the count. "Indeed, he is dead in sooth, my lord."

beaux nieps, c'est trop tard. Vous voulés clore l'estable quand
le cheval est per du.' " [1]
Poetry, too, used the trick of short alternating sentences a
good deal.

> "Mort, je me plaing—De qui ?—De toy.
> —Que t'ay je fait ?—Ma dame as pris.
> —C'est vérité.—Dy moy pour quoy.
> —Il me plaisoit—Tu as mespris." [2]

Here the means have become the object. The virtuosity of
these jerky dialogues was carried to an extreme in the ballad
of Jean Meschinot, in which France accuses Louis XI. In
each of the thirty lines, questions and answers alternate,
sometimes more than once. Still, this bizarre form does not
destroy the effect of the political satire. This is the first
stanza :

> "Sire . . .—Que veux ?—Entendez . . .—Quoy ?—Mon cas.
> —Or dy.—Je suys . . .—Qui ?—La destruicte France !
> —Par qui ?—Par vous.—Comment ?—En tous estats.
> —Tu mens.—Non fais.—Qui le dit ?—Ma souffrance.
> —Que souffres tu ?—Meschief—Quel ?—A oultrance.
> —Je n'en croy rien.—Bien y pert.—N'en dy plus !
> —Las ! si feray.—Tu perds temps.—Quelz abus !
> —Qu'ay-je mal fait ?—Contre paix—Et comment ?
> —Guerroyant . . .—Qui ?—Vos amys et congnus.
> —Parle plus beau—Je ne puis, bonnement." [3]

With Froissart the sober and accurate description of outward circumstances sometimes acquires tragic force, just
because it leaves out all psychological speculation, as for
instance in the episode of the death of the young Gaston

---

[1] So he asked him for counsel in matters of love and lineage. The archbishop answered, "Counsel, sure, good nephew, it is too late for that. You
want to shut the stable when the horse is lost."

[2] Death I complain. Of whom ? Of you. What have I done to you ?
You have taken my lady. That is so. Tell me why ? It pleased me.
You mistook.

[3] Sire . . . What do you want ? Listen . . . To what ? To my case.
Speak out. I am . . . Who ? Devastated France ! By whom ? By you.
How ? In all estates. You lie. I do not. Who says so ? My sufferings. What
do you suffer ? Misery. Which ? The extremity of misery. I do not
believe a word of it. Evidently. Do not say any more about it. Alas !
I must. It is no use. What a shame ! What have I done ill ? You have
sinned against peace. And how ? By warring. With whom ? With your
friends and kinsmen. Speak more pleasingly. I cannot, in truth.

MINIATURE FROM "LE CUER D'AMOURS ESPRIS."

By an Unknown Master, in a MS. in the State Library, Vienna.

"SEPTEMBER." BY THE BROTHERS VAN LIMBURG, FROM THE CALENDAR OF
THE "TRES RICHES HEURES DU DUC DE BERRY."

Phébus, killed by his father in a fit of anger. Froissart's soul was a photographic plate. Under the uniform surface of his own style we may discern the qualities of the various story-tellers who communicated to him the endless number of his items of news. For example, all that was told him by his travelling companion, the knight Espaing du Lyon, has been admirably rendered.

In short, whenever the literature of the period works by means of direct observation, without conventional trammels, it approaches painting, without however rivalling it. There-fore we should not look for the equivalents of painted landscapes or interiors in literary descriptions of nature. Painting of the fifteenth century produced marvels of perspective, because there the masters could let themselves go, as landscapes were accessory and did not suffer from the same severe restrictions as the principal subject. Notice the contrast between the principal scene and the background of the " Adoration of the Magi " in the " Très riches heures de Chantilly." The figures in the foreground are affected and bizarre, the scene is over-crowded, whereas the view of Bourges in the distance attains a perfect serenity and harmony.

In literature, on the other hand, the feeling for nature was not free, neither was the manner of expressing it. Love of nature had taken the form of the pastoral and was therefore controlled by sentimental and æsthetic convention. The poems in which the beauty of flowers and the song of birds are sung proceed from an inspiration quite different from that which gave birth to painted landscapes. Literature in describing nature moves on another plane than painting.

Nevertheless it is in the pastoral that we can trace the development of the literary feeling for nature. Side by side with the poems of Alain Chartier, cited above, we may place those of the royal shepherd René singing in a disguised form his love for Jeanne de Laval, in the pastoral poem of *Regnault et Jehanneton*. There we find ingenuous gaiety and freshness ; the king even tried, not without success, to render the effect of night closing in, but all this is far from being great art, like that of the calendars in the breviaries.

The pictures of the months in the calendar of the " Très riches heures de Chantilly " enable us to compare the expression of the same motif in art and in literature, and that strongly in favour of the former. The reader will remember the glorious castles which ornament the background of the miniatures of the brothers of Limburg ; September with the vintage in progress and the castle of Saumur, rising like a vision behind it, the steeples of the towers with their high weather-vanes, the pinnacles and the graceful chimneys, all shooting up like tall white flowers against the deep blue of the sky ; or December and the sombre towers of Vincennes looming threateningly behind the leafless woods. What means or methods had a poet like Eustache Deschamps at his disposal to rival scenes like these when he produced a sort of literary counterpart to them in a series of poems, in praise of seven castles of Northern France ? The description of architectural forms at which he tried his hand in the lines devoted to the castle of Bièvre was by no means successful. So he limited himself to enumerating the delights which these castles provided ; thus, speaking of Beauté, he says :

> " Son filz ainsné, daulphin de Viennois,
> Donna le nom à ce lieu de Beauté.
> Et c'est bien drois, car moult est delectables :
> L'en y oit bien le rossignol chanter ;
> Marne l'ensaint, les haulz bois profitables
> Du noble parc puet l'en veoir branler. . . .
> Les prez sont pres, les jardins deduisables,
> Les beaus preaulx, fontenis bel et cler,
> Vignes aussi et les terres arables,
> Moulins tournans, beaus plains à regarder." [1]

What a difference between the effect of these lines and that of the miniature ! And yet the method is the same : it is an enumeration of the things seen (or, in the case of the poet, things heard). But the view of the artist embraces a definite and limited space, in which he not merely has to collect a number of things, but also to harmonize and blend them into a single whole. In the miniature of February Paul

---

[1] His eldest son, the dauphin of Viennois, Gave this spot the name of Beauty. And justly, for it is very delectable : One hears the nightingale sing there ; The river Marne surrounds it, the lofty pleasant woods Of the noble park may be seen waving on the wind. Meadows are near, pleasuregardens, The fine lawns, beautiful and clear fountains, Also vineyards and arable lands, Turning mills, plains beautiful to view.

of Limburg assembled all the peculiarities of winter : peasants warming themselves before the hearth, the wash drying, crows on the snow, the sheepfold and beehives, the barrels and the cart, and the wintry landscape in the background with the tranquil village and the solitary house on the hill. All this mass of details is worked into the peaceful harmony of the landscape, and the unity of the picture is perfect. The poet, on the other hand, suffers his gaze to roam at will, but never concentrates it ; and there is no framework to compel him to give unity to his work.

In an epoch of pre-eminently visual inspiration, like the fifteenth century, pictorial expression easily surpasses literary expression. Although representing only the visible forms of things, painting nevertheless expresses a profound inner sense, which literature when it limits itself to describing externals wholly fails to do.

The poetry of the fifteenth century often gives us the impression of being almost devoid of new ideas. The inability to invent new fiction is general. The authors rarely go beyond the touching up, embellishing or modernizing of old subject-matter. What may be called a stagnation of thought prevails, as though the mind, exhausted after building up the spiritual fabric of the Middle Ages, had sunk into inertia. The poets themselves are aware of this feeling of fatigue. Deschamps laments :

> "Hélas ! on dit que je ne fais mès rien,
> Qui jadis fis mainte chose nouvelle ;
> La raison est que je n'ay pas merrien
> Dont je fisse chose bonne ne belle." [1]

In the fifteenth century the old romances of chivalry are recast from verse into very prolix prose. This " unrhyming " —" dérimage "—is another sign of the general stagnation of fancy. Nevertheless it marks at the same time an important broadening in the general conception of literature. In the more primitive stages of literature verse is the primary mode of expression. As late as the thirteenth century every subject, even natural history or medicine, seemed to lend itself

---

[1] Alas ! it is said that I no longer make anything, I who formerly made many new things ; The reason is that I have no subject-matter Of which to make good or fine things.

to treatment in verse, because the principal mode of assimilating a written work was still hearing it recited and getting it by heart. Even the "chansons de geste," it seems, were chanted to a uniform melody. Individual and expressive declamation, as we understand it, was unknown in the Middle Ages. The growing predilection for prose means that reading was superseding recitation. Another custom, dating from the same epoch, testifies to this transition, namely the division of a work into small chapters with summaries, whereas formerly scarcely any division had been thought necessary. In fifteenth-century literature prose was, to a certain degree, the more refined and artistic form.

The superiority of prose is, however, purely formal; it lacks novelty of thought just as much as poetry. Froissart is the type of this extreme shallowness of thought and facility of expression. The simplicity of his ideas is surprising. Only three or four motives or sentiments are known to him : fidelity, honour, cupidity, courage, and these in their simplest forms. He uses no allegorical or mythological figures, never touches on theology, and even moral reflections are almost wholly absent. He goes on narrating, without effort, correctly, and yet he remains empty, because he has but the mechanical exactitude of a cinematograph. His moral reflections, when they do occur, are so commonplace as to be almost bewildering. Certain conceptions are, with him, always accompanied by fixed judgments. He cannot speak of Germans without recalling their cupidity and their barbarous treatment of prisoners. Even the quotations from Froissart which are currently presented to us as piquant prove when read in their context to lack the point attributed to them. On reading his appreciation of the first Duke of Burgundy of the house of Valois, " sage, froid et imaginatif, et qui sur ses besognes veoit au loin," [1] we think we have lighted upon a penetrating and concise analysis of character. Only, Froissart applied these terms to almost everybody !

The poverty and sterility of Froissart's mind, as compared with Chastellain's, for example, is all the more evident, as his style is wholly devoid of rhetorical qualities. Now it is rhetoric which in the literature of the fifteenth century signal-

[1] Wise, frigid and imaginative, and far-sighted in business.

izes the coming of the new spirit. For readers of that age lack
of novelty in the matter was made up for by the æsthetic
enjoyment of an ornate style. Everything seemed to them to
be new when garbed in far-fetched and turgid phrases. It
is an error to suppose that only literature cultivated this
stylistic ornamentation, and that art was exempt from it.
Art also displays the same pursuit of novelty and rich variety
of expression. In the pictures of the brothers Van Eyck
there are parts which might be called "rhetorician-like" :
for example, the figure of Saint George presenting Canon van
de Paele to the Virgin at Bruges. The magnificent helmet,
the gilt armour, in which a naïve classicism is apparent, the
dramatic gesture of the saint, all this is closely akin to Chastellain's grandiloquence. The same tendency recurs in the
figure of the archangel Michael in the small triptych of Dresden
and in the group of angels singing and playing, on the altar-
piece of the Lamb. It is also present in the work of the
brothers of Limburg : for instance, in the bizarre magnificence
of their "Adoration of the three Magi."

Unless the ornate form be so charming and so novel as to
suffice in itself for giving life to a piece of verse, the poetry of
the fifteenth century is happiest when it is not aspiring to
express an important thought, nor aiming at elegance of style.
When it is content to call up a simple image or scene, or to
express a simple sentiment, it is not without vigour. Hence
it is more successful in short pieces than in long-winded com-
positions and grave subjects. In the roundel and the ballad,
constructed on a single airy theme, all grace depends on tone,
rhythm and vision ; in fact, the more the artistic song of the
time approaches the popular song, the greater is its charm.

The end of the fourteenth century is a turning-point in the
relations between music and lyrical poetry. The song of the
preceding period was intimately linked with musical recitation.
The common type of the lyrical poet of the Middle Ages is
always the poet-composer. Guillaume de Machaut used to
compose the melodies of his poems. He also fixed the customary lyrical forms of his time : roundels, ballads, etc. He
invented the "débat," the contention of different parties on
a moot point. His roundels and ballads are very airy, simple
in form and thought ; they have little colour ; all these are

merits, for a poem that is sung should not be too expressive. Here is an example:

> "Au departir de vous mon cuer vous lais
> Et je m'en vois dolans et esplourés.
> Pour vous servir, sans retraire jamais,
> Au departir de vous mon cuer vous lais.
> Et par m'ame, je n'arai bien ne pais,
> Jusqu'au retour, einsi desconfortés.
> Au departir de vous mon cuer vous lais
> Et je m'en vois dolans et esplourés." [1]

In Eustache Deschamps we no longer find composer and poet united. Hence his ballads are much more vivid and highly coloured than Machaut's, therefore often more interesting and yet of an inferior poetical style.

The roundel, because of its very structure, preserved the airy and fluent character of a song to be set to music, even after poets ceased to be composers.

> "M'aimerez-vous bien,
> Dictes, par vostre ame?
> Mais que je vous ame
> Plus que nulle rien,
> M'aimerez-vous bien?
> Dieu mit tant de bien
> En vous, que c'est basme
> Pour ce je me clame
> Vostre. Mais combien
> M'aimerez-vous bien?" [2]

These lines are by Jean Meschinot. The simple and pure talent of Christine de Pisan lends itself admirably to these fugitive effects. She versified with the facility characteristic of the epoch, without much variety of form or thought, in a subdued tone and with a slight touch of melancholy. Her poems remind us of those ivory tablets of the fourteenth century, which always represent the same motifs: a hunting scene, episodes of the *Roman de la Rose* or of Tristram and

---

[1] On parting from you I leave you my heart And I go away lamenting and weeping. To serve you without ever retracting. And by my soul, I shall indeed have no peace Till my return, being thus discomforted.

[2] Do you love me indeed? Tell me, by your soul. If I love you More than anything, Will you love me indeed? God put so much goodness In you that it is balm; Therefore I proclaim myself Yours. But how much Will you love me?

Yseult, yet always retain a certain freshness and impeccable, though conventional, gracefulness. When in Christine courtly sweetness goes hand in hand with the simplicity of the popular song, we hear an accent of the most exquisite purity.

We print the dialogue of two lovers who meet after a separation.

> " Tu soies le très bien venu,
>   M'amour, or m'embrace et me baise
>   Et comment t'es tu maintenu
>   Puis ton départ ? Sain et bien aise
>   As tu esté toujours ? Ça vien
>   Costé moy, te sié et me conte
>   Comment t'a esté, mal ou bien,
>   Car de ce vueil savoir le compte.
>
> —Ma dame, a qui je suis tenu
>   Plus que aultre, a nul n'en desplaise,
>   Sachés que desir m'a tenu
>   Si court qu'oncques n'oz tel mesaise,
>   Ne plaisir ne prenoie en rien
>   Loings de vous. Amours, qui cuers dompte,
>   Me disoit : ' Loyauté me tien,
>   Car de ce vueil savoir le compte.'
>
> —Dont m'as tu ton serment tenu,
>   Bon gré t'en sçay, par saint Nicaise ;
>   Et puis que sain es revenu
>   Joye arons assez ; or t'apaise
>   Et me dis se scez de combien
>   Le mal qu'en as eu a plus monte
>   Que cil qu'a souffert le cuer mien,
>   Car de ce vueil savoir le compte.
>
> —Plus mal que vous, si com retien,
>   Ay eu, mais dites sanz mesconte,
>   Quans baisiers en aray je bien ?
>   Car de ce vueil savoir le compte." [1]

---

[1] You are most welcome, My love ; now embrace me and kiss me. And how have you been Since your departure ? Healthy and at ease Have you always been ? Here, come Beside me ; sit down and tell me How you have been, well or not, For of this I want to have an account.
—Lady, to whom I am bound More than to any other, may it displease no one, Know that desire so curbed me That I never had such discomfort Nor did I take pleasure in anything Far from you. Love, who tames hearts, Said to me : " Remain faithful to me, For of this I want to have an account."
—So you kept your oath to me, I thank you much for it by saint Nicaise ;

Here is a girl deploring the absence of her lover :

> " Il a au jour d'ui un mois
> Que mon ami s'en ala.
>
> Mon cuer remaint morne et cois,
> Il a au jour d'ui un mois.
>
> ' A Dieu,' me dit, ' je m'en vois ' ;
> Ne puis a moy ne parla,
> Il a au jour d'ui un mois." [1]

Here are words of consolation, addressed to a lover :

> " Mon ami, ne plourez plus ;
> Car tant me faittes pitié
> Que mon cuer se rent conclus
> A vostre doulce amistié.
> Reprenez autre maniere ;
> Pour Dieu, plus ne vous doulez,
> Et me faittes bonne chiere :
> Je vueil quanque vous voulez." [2]
>
> . . . .

What gives these verses their abiding womanly charm is their
spontaneous tenderness, their simplicity devoid of all pomp and
pretension. Christine was content to follow the inspiration of
her heart. But this is also the reason why her poems so often
show the defect, characteristic of the poetry and music of all
epochs of feeble inspiration, that of exhausting all their vigour
in the opening lines. How many poems do we find with a fresh
and striking theme, which begin like a blackbird's song, only
to lose themselves in thin rhetoric after the first stanza ! The
poet (or in music, the composer), after stating his theme, had

---

And as you came back safe and sound We shall have joy enough ; now be
appeased And tell me if you know by how much The grief you had from it
exceeds That which my heart has suffered, For of this I want to have an
account.

—More grief than you, as I think, I had, but tell me without miscalculation,
How many kisses shall I have for it ? For of this I want to have an account.

[1] It is a month to-day Since my lover departed. My heart remains gloomy
and silent. It is a month to-day. " Good-bye," he said, " I am going " ;
Since then he has not spoken to me. It is a month to-day.

[2] Friend, weep no more ; For I am so touched with pity That my heart
gives itself up To your sweet friendship. Change your bearing ; For God's
sake, be sad no longer. And show me a cheerful face : I am willing whatever
you will.

come to the end of his inspiration. We are constantly disillusioned in this way by most of the fifteenth-century poets. Here is an example taken from the ballads of Christine de Pisan :

> " Quant chacun s'en revient de l'ost
> Pour quoy demeures tu derriere ?
> Et si scez que m'amour entiere
> T'ay baillée en garde et depost." [1]

One expects the motif of the dead lover who reappears. But we are deceived : after two more insignificant stanzas the poem finishes. What freshness there is in the first lines of Froissart's *Debat dou Cheval et dou Levrier :*

> " Froissart d'Escoce revenoit
> Sus un cheval qui gris estoit,
> Un blanc levrier menoit en lasse.
> ' Las,' dist le levrier, ' je me lasse,
> Grisel, quant nous reposerons ?
> Il est heure que nous mengons.' " [2]

After this the charm is lost ; the author, in short, had no other inspiration than a moment's vision of the two animals conversing.

The motifs are occasionally of incomparable grandeur and suggestive force, but the development remains most feeble. The theme of Pierre Michault in his *Danse aux Aveugles* was masterly ; the everlasting dance of the human race about the thrones of the three blind deities, Love, Fortune, and Death. He only succeeded in working it up into very mediocre poetry. An anonymous poem, entitled *Exclamacion des Os Sainct Innocent*, begins by making the charnel-houses of the famous churchyard speak :

> " Les os sommes des povres trespassez.
> Cy amassez par monceaulx compassez,
> Rompus, cassez, sans reigle ne compas. . . ." [3]

---

[1] When everybody comes back from the army Why do you stay behind ? Yet you know that I pledged you My loyal love to keep.

[2] Froissart came back from Scotland On a horse which was grey, He led a white greyhound in a leash. "Alas," said the greyhound, "I am tired, Grisel, when shall we rest ? It is time we were feeding."

[3] We are the bones of the poor dead, Here heaped up by measured mounds, Broken, fractured, without rule or measure.

What an exordium for a weird lament ! Yet what follows is a most commonplace *memento mori*.

All these themes have only been realized visually. Such vision may supply an artist with material for a most grand conception and consummate execution ; it is insufficient for a poet.

CHAPTER XXII

VERBAL AND PLASTIC EXPRESSION COMPARED

II

The superiority of painting to literature in point of expressiveness is not, however, absolute and complete. There are regions where it does not exist, and these we must now consider.

The whole domain of the comic is much more open to literature than to plastic art. Unless it stoops to caricature, art can only express the comic in a slight degree. In art the comic tends at once to become serious again ; we do not laugh on looking at Breughel, although we admire in him the same force of droll fancy which makes us laugh in reading Rabelais. Only where the comic forms but a slight accessory can pictorial expression rival the written word. We can observe it in what is called genre painting, which may be considered the most attenuated form of the comic.

The disproportionate refinement of details which we noticed above as being characteristic of the paintings of the epoch tends insensibly to change into the pleasure of relating petty curious facts. Whereas in the room of Arnolfini the minutiæ do not injure the solemn intimacy of the picture in the least, they have become mere curiosities in the master of Flémalle. His Joseph on the " Altar of Merode " is occupied with making mouse-traps. With him all the details are " genre," with an almost imperceptible flavour of the comic about them. Between his manner of painting an opened window-shutter, a sideboard, a chimney, and that of Van Eyck, there is all the difference between purely pictorial vision and " genre " painting.

Now here comes to light a clear advantage of speech over pictorial representation. As soon as something more than mere vision has to be expressed, literature, thanks to its faculty of expressing moods explicitly, takes the lead. Let us remember again Deschamps' ballads, celebrating the beauty of the castles, which we compared with and found inferior to the perfect miniatures of the brothers of Limburg. These poems of Deschamps lack power and splendour ; he has not succeeded in reproducing the vision of these glorious halls. But now compare the ballad in which he paints himself, lying ill in his poor little castle of Fismes, kept awake by the cries of barn-owls, starlings, crows and sparrows, nesting in his tower.

> " C'est une estrange melodie
> Qui ne semble pas grant deduit
> A gens qui sont en maladie.
> Premiers les corbes font sçavoir
> Pour certain si tost qu'il est jour :
> De fort crier font leur pouoir,
> Le gros, le gresle, sanz sejour ;
> Mieulx vauldroit le son d'un tabour
> Que telz cris de divers oyseaulx,
> Puis vient la proie ; vaches, veaulx,
> Crians, muyans, et tout ce nuit,
> Quant on a le cervel trop vuit,
> Joint du moustier la sonnerie,
> Qui tout l'entendement destruit
> A gens qui sont en maladie." [1]

At night the owls come with their sinister screeching, evoking thoughts of death :

> " C'est froit hostel et mal reduit
> A gens qui sont en maladie." [2]

This trick of the mere enumeration of a multitude of details loses its wearisome character, as soon as the faintest trace of humour is mixed up with it. In the middle of a very prolix allegorical poem, *L'Espinette amoureuse*, Froissart diverts us

---

[1] It is a strange melody, Which is not felt as a great amusement By people who are ill. First the ravens let us know For certain as soon as it is day : They cry aloud with all their might In deep and shrill tones, without interruption. Even the sound of a drum would be better Than those cries of various birds. Next come the cattle going to pasture, cows, calves, Bellowing, lowing, and all this is noxious When one has an empty brain, With the bells of the church chiming in, And destroying altogether the understanding Of people who are ill.

[2] It is a cold hostelry and ill refuge for people who are ill.

by the enumeration of some sixty games at which he used to play at Valenciennes as a boy. The descriptions of burgher customs or of the female toilet, long though they be, do not fatigue us, because they contain a satirical element which was lacking in the poetical descriptions of the beauty of spring. From the "genre" to the burlesque is but a step. But here again painting may rival literature in expressive power. Before 1400 art had already attained some mastery of this element of burlesque vision which was to reach its full growth in Pieter Breughel in the sixteenth century. We find it in the figure of Joseph in the "Flight into Egypt" by Broederlam at Dijon and, again, in the three soldiers asleep in the picture of the "Three Marys at the Sepulchre," at one time attributed to Hubert Van Eyck. Of the artists of the epoch none took more pleasure in effects of bizarre jocularity than Paul of Limburg. A spectator of the "Purification of the Virgin" wears a kind of bent wizard's cap, a yard long, and immoderately wide sleeves. The font displays three monstrous masks, shooting out their tongues. In the framework of the "Visitation," we see a soldier in a tower fighting with a snail, and a man wheeling away on a barrow a pig playing the bagpipes.

The literature of the epoch is bizarre in nearly every page, and very fond of burlesque. A vision worthy of Breughel is called up by Deschamps in the ballad of the watchman on the tower of Sluys; he sees the troops for the expedition against England collecting on the beach; they appear to him like an army of rats and mice.

"Avant, avant! tirez-vous ça.
Je voy merveille, ce me semble.
—'Et quoy, guette, que vois-tu là ?'
Je voy dix mille rats ensemble
Et mainte souris qui s'assemble
Dessus la rive de la mer. . . ." [1]

On another occasion, sitting at table, absent-minded and gloomy, Deschamps suddenly began to notice the way in which the courtiers were eating: some chewing like pigs;

[1] Forward, forward, come here. I see a marvellous thing, it seems to me.— And what, watchman, do you see there?—I see ten thousand rats together And a multitude of mice collecting On the seashore. . . .

some gnawing like mice, or using their teeth like a saw ; others whose beards moved up and down or who made such horrible faces that they looked like devils.

As soon as literature sets to work to depict the life of the masses, it shows this realism full of vitality and good humour, which was to develop abundantly, but not till later, in painting. The peasant receiving in his hovel the duke of Burgundy, who has lost his way, reminds us, by the portrait which Chastellain draws of him, of Breughel's types. The Pastoral deviates from its central theme, which is sentimental and romantic, to find in the description of shepherds eating, dancing, and courting, matter for a naïve naturalism with a spice of burlesque.

Wherever the eye suffices for communicating the sense of the comic, however airy it may be, art is able to express it as well as, or better than, literature. Apart from this, pictorial art can never render the comic. Line and colour are impotent wherever the comic effect lies in a point of wit. Literature is incontestably sovereign both in the low-comedy genre of the farce and the fabliaux, and in the higher domain of irony.

It is especially in erotic poetry that irony developed ; by adding its acrid flavour it refined the erotic genre ; it purified it at the same time by introducing into it an element of a serious nature. Outside the pale of love-poetry irony was still heavy and clumsy. It is worth remarking that a French writer of the fourteenth or fifteenth century, speaking ironically, often takes care to inform his reader of the fact. Deschamps praises his age ; all is well, peace and justice reign everywhere :

> " L'en me demande chascun jour
> Qu'il me semble du temps que voy,
> Et je respons : c'est tout honour,
> Loyauté, verité et foy,
> Largesce, prouesce et arroy,
> Charité et biens qui s'advance
> Pour le commun ; mais, par ma loy,
> Je ne di pas quanque je pence." [1]

---

[1] People ask me every day What I think of the present times, And I answer : it is all honour, Loyalty, truth and faith, Liberality, heroism and order, Charity and advancement Of the common weal ; but, by my faith, I do not say what I think.

Another ballad, of the same tenor, has the refrain : "Tous ces poins a rebours retien" ; [1] a third ends with the words :

> "Prince, s'il est par tout generalment
> Comme je say, toute vertu habonde ;
> Mais tel m'orroit qui diroit : ' Il se ment ' . . . ." [2]

A wit of the end of the fifteenth century entitles an epigram : "Soubz une meschante paincture faicte de mauvaises couleurs et du plus meschant peinctre du monde, par manière d'yronnie par maître Jehan Robertet." [3] When dealing with love, on the other hand, irony had already often attained a high degree of refinement. In this region it blended with the gentle despondency and the languishing tenderness which renewed the erotic poetry of the fifteenth century. For the first time we hear the poet voice his melancholy with a smile about his own misfortune, such as Villon giving himself the air of " l'amant remis et renié " [4] or Charles of Orleans singing his little songs of disillusion. Nevertheless the figure " Je riz en pleurs " [5] is not Villon's invention. Long before him the scripture word, *risus dolore miscebitur et extrema gaudii luctus occupat*,[6] had given a text for poetical application. Othe de Granson, for example, had said :

> "Veillier ou lit et jeuner à la table
> Rire plourant et en plaignant chanter." [7]

And again :

> "Je prins congié de ce tresdoulz enfant
> Les yeulx mouilliez et la bouche riant." [8]

Alain Chartier made use of the same motif in various ways :

---

[1] Take all these points just the other way about.

[2] Prince, if it is generally everywhere As I know : every virtue abounds ; But many a man hearing me will say : He lies.

[3] Under a bad picture done in bad colours and by the most paltry painter of the world, in an ironical manner by master Jehan Robertet.

[4] The shelved and rejected lover.

[5] I laugh in tears.

[6] Even in laughter the heart is sorrowful ; and the end of that mirth is heaviness.

[7] Lying abed awake and fasting at the board, Laughing in tears and lamenting in song.

[8] I took leave of this most sweet child With tearful eyes and a laughing mouth.

> " Je n'ay bouche qui puisse rire,
> Que les yeulx ne la desmentissent :
> Car le cueur l'en vouldroit desdire
> Par les lermes qui des yeulx issent." [1]

He says of a disconsolate lover :

> " De faire chiere s'efforçoit
> Et menoit une joye fainte,
> Et à chanter son cueur forçoit
> Non pas pour plaisir, mais pour crainte,
> Car tousjours ung relaiz de plainte
> S'enlassoit au ton de sa voix,
> Et revenoit à son attainte
> Comme l'oysel au chant du bois." [2]

Very near akin to the motif of laughter and tears is that of the poet who at the end of his poem denies his own sorrow, as, for example, Alain Chartier :

> " Cest livret voult dicter et faire escripre
> Pour passer temps sans courage villain
> Ung simple clerc que l'en appelle Alain
> Qui parle ainsi d'amours pour oyr dire." [3]

Othe de Granson had already pretended to speak of secret love only " par devinaille." [4] King René treated this motif in a fantastic manner at the end of his *Cuer d'Amours espris*. His valet, with a candle in his hand, tries to find out if the king has really lost his heart, but finds no hole in his side.

> " Sy me dist tout en soubzriant
> Que je dormisse seulement
> Et que n'avoye nullement
> Pour ce mal garde de morir." [5]

---

[1] My mouth cannot laugh, Without my eyes belying it : For the heart would deny it By the tears issuing from the eyes.

[2] He constrained himself to be cheerful And showed a feigned joy, And forced his heart to sing Not for pleasure, but for fear, For ever a remainder of complaint Entwined itself with the tone of his voice, And reverted to its purpose Like the ousel singing in the wood.

[3] This booklet meant to dictate and to describe To pass the time without vulgar mood A simple clerk called Alain Who speaks thus of love by hearsay.

[4] By guessing.

[5] So he told me smiling That I should lie down and sleep And that I should not at all Be afraid to die of this evil.

By losing the impeccable gravity characteristic of them in preceding epochs, the ancient conventional forms of erotic poetry became penetrated by a new meaning. Charles d'Orléans makes use of personifications and of allegories like all his predecessors, but, by some slight surplus of stress, he adds an almost imperceptible flavour of raillery, and this gives them an affecting note, which is lacking in the graceful figures of the *Roman de la Rose*. He sees his own heart as a double of himself.

> " Je suys celluy au cueur vestu de noir. . . ."[1]

Occasionally in his extravagant personifications, the comical element has the upper hand :

> " Un jour à mon cueur devisoye
> Qui en secret à moy parloit,
> Et en parlant lui demandoye
> Se point d'espargne fait avoit
> D'aucuns biens quant Amours servoit :
> Il me dist que très voulentiers
> La verité m'en compteroit,
> Mais qu'eust visité ses papiers.

> " Quand ce m'eut dit, il print sa voye
> Et d'avecques moy se partoit.
> Après entrer je le véoye
> En ung comptouer qu'il avoit :
> Là, de ça et de là quéroit,
> En cherchant plusieurs vieulx caïers
> Car le vray monstrer me vouloit,
> Mais qu'eust visitez ses papiers. . . ."[2]

Not always, however ; in the following lines the comic is not dominant :

[1] I am the wight whose heart is draped in black.

[2] One day I was talking with my heart Which secretly spoke to me, And in talking I asked it If it had saved No goods when serving Love : It said that quite willingly It would tell me the truth about it, As soon as it had consulted its papers.

Having told me this it went away And from me departed. Next I saw it enter In an office it had : There it rummaged here and there In looking for several old writing-books, For it would show me the truth, As soon as it had consulted its papers.

" Ne hurtez plus à l'uis de ma pensée,
Soing et Soucy, sans tant vous travailler ;
Car elle dort et ne veult s'esveiller,
Toute la nuit en peine a despensée.

"En dangier est, s'elle n'est bien pansée ;
Cessez, cessez, laissez la sommeiller ;
Ne hurtez plus à l'uis de ma pensée,
Soing et Soucy, sans tant vous travailler. . . ." [1]

For the spirit of the epoch nothing heightened so much
the acrid flavour of sad and sensitive love as the addition
of an element of profanation. Religious travesty has created
something better than the obscenities of the *Cent Nouvelles
Nouvelles ;* it furnished the form for the tenderest love-poem
which that age produced : *L'Amant rendu Cordelier à l'Observance d'Amours.*

Already the poetical club of Charles d'Orléans had imagined
a literary brotherhood whose members, in analogy to the
reformed Franciscans, called themselves " amourex de l'observance." The author of *L'Amant rendu Cordelier* developed
this motif. Who is this author ? Is it really Martial d'Auvergne ? It is hard to believe it, so much does this poem
rise above the level of his work.

The poor disillusioned lover comes to renounce the world
in the strange convent, where only " the martyrs of love "
are received. He tells the Prior the touching story of his
despised love ; the latter exhorts him to forget it. Under
a medieval guise we seem to perceive already the genre of
Watteau. Only the moonlight is wanting to remind us of
Pierrot. " Was she not in the habit," asks the Prior, " of giving
you a sweet look or saying ' God save you ' in passing ? "
—" I had not got so far in her good graces," replies the lover ;
" but at night I stood about the door of her house, and looked
up at the eaves."

---

[1] Do not knock at the door of my mind any more, Anxiety and Care ; do
not give yourselves so much trouble ; For it sleeps and does not want to wake,
It has passed all the night in solicitude.

It will be in danger, if not well nursed ; Stop, stop, let it sleep ; Do not
knock at the door of my mind any more, Anxiety and Care ; do not give
yourselves so much trouble.

"Et puis, quant je oyoye les verrières
De la maison qui cliquetoient,
Lors me sembloit que mes prières
Exaussées d'elle sy estoient." [1]

"Were you quite sure that she noticed you?" asks the Prior.

"Se m'aist Dieu, j'estoye tant ravis,
Que ne savoye mon sens ne estre,
Car, sans parler, m'estoit advis
Que le vent ventoit sa fenestre
Et que m'avoit bien peu cognoistre,
En disant bas : 'Doint bonne nuyt,'
Et Dieu scet se j'estoye grant maistre
Après cela toute la nuyt." [2]

Then he slept in glory.

"Tellement estoie restauré
Que, sans tourner ne travailler,
Je faisoie un somme doré,
Sans point la nuyt me resveiller,
Et puis, avant que m'abiller,
Pour en rendre à Amours louanges,
Baisoie troys fois mon orillier,
En riant à par moy aux anges." [3]

When he is solemnly received into the order, the lady
who had despised him faints and a little gold heart enamelled
with tears, which he had given her, falls from her dress.

"Les aultres, pour leur mal couvrir
A force leurs cueurs retenoient,
Passans temps a clorre et rouvrir
Les heures qu'en leurs mains tenoient,
Dont souvent les feuillès tournoient
En signe de devocion ;
Mais les deulz et pleurs que menoient
Monstroient bien leur affection." [4]

---

[1] And then, when I heard the window Of the house which clattered, Then
it seemed to me that my prayers Had been heard by her.

[2] So help me God, I was so ravished That I was scarcely conscious, For,
without being told, it seemed to me That the wind moved her window And
she could well have recognized me, Perhaps saying softly : "Good night,
then," and God knows I felt like a prince After this all night.

[3] I felt so refreshed That without turning about or tossing, I enjoyed golden
slumber, Without waking up all night, And then, before dressing To praise
Love for it, I kissed my pillow thrice, While laughing silently at the angels.

[4] The others, to hide their affliction Controlled their hearts by force, Passing
the time in closing and opening again The breviaries they held in their hands,

The Prior enumerates his new duties to him, warning him never to listen to the nightingale's song, never to sleep under "eglantine and mayflower," and, above all, never to look a woman in the eyes. The exhortation ends in a long string of eight-lined stanzas, being variations to the theme "Sweet eyes."

> "Doux yeulx qui tousjours vont et viennent;
> Doux yeulx eschauffans le plisson,
> De ceulx qui amoureux deviennent. . . .
>
> "Doux yeulx a cler esperlissans,
> Qui dient: C'est fait quant tu vouldras,
> A ceulx qu'ils sentent bien puissans. . . ." [1]

Towards the middle of the fifteenth century all the conventional genres of erotic poetry are of a languishing tenor, and bear the stamp of resigned melancholy. Even cynical contempt of woman grows refined. In the *Quinze Joyes de Mariage* the mischievous and gross purpose is tempered by wistful sentimentality. By its sober realism, by the elegance of its form and the subtlety of its psychology, this work is a precursor of the "novel of manners" of modern times.

In all that concerns the expression of love, literature profited by the models and the experience of a long series of past centuries. Masters of such diversity of spirit as Plato and Ovid, the troubadours and the wandering students, Dante and Jean de Meun, had bequeathed to it a perfected instrument. Pictorial art, on the contrary, having neither models nor tradition, was primitive in the strict sense of the word, in respect of erotic expression. Not till the eighteenth century was painting to overtake literature in point of delicate expression of love. The artist of the fifteenth century had not yet learned to be frivolous or sentimental. In the miniatures of that time the posture of lovers embracing remains hieratic and solemn. A portrait of a Dutch gentlewoman, Lysbet of Duvenvoorde, by an unknown master before 1430, shows a figure of such severe dignity that a modern scholar has taken

---

Of which they often turned the leaves As a sign of devotion; But their sorrow and tears Clearly showed their emotion.
[1] Sweet eyes that always come and go; Sweet eyes heating the fur coat Of those who fall in love. . . .
Sweet eyes of pearly clearness, That say: I am ready when you please, To those whom they feel to be powerful.

LYSBET VAN DUVENVOORDE. BY AN UNKNOWN MASTER

the picture for a donor's portrait, omitting to read the words on the scroll she bears in her hand : " Mi verdriet lange te hopen, Wie is hi die syn hert hout open ? " i.e. : " I am weary of hoping so long. Who is he who holds his heart open ? " Pictorial expression knew no middle term between the chaste and the obscene. The rendering of erotic subjects was rare, and what there is of it, is naïve and innocent. Once more, however, we must bear in mind that the greater number of profane works have disappeared. It would be most interesting to be able to compare the nude of Van Eyck in his " Bath of Women," which Fazio saw, with that of his " Adam and Eve." As to the latter picture, it must not be imagined that the erotic element is lacking. Following the rules of the code of feminine beauty of his time, the artist made the breasts small and placed them too high ; the arms are long and thin, the belly prominent. But he did so quite ingenuously and with no intention of giving sensual pleasure. A small picture in the Leipsic Gallery, occasionally designated as belonging to the " school of Jan van Eyck," represents a girl in a room ; she is nude, as magical practices require, and is employing witchcraft to force her lover to show himself. Here the intention is present, and the artist has succeeded in expressing the erotic sentiment : the nude figure has the demure lasciviousness which reappears in those of Cranach.

It is most improbable that the restraint thus displayed in fifteenth-century art, in respect of erotic expression, was due to a sense of modesty, for in general an extreme licence was tolerated. Though pictorial art cultivated it very little as yet, the nude occupied a large place in the tableau vivant. The " personnages " of nude goddesses or nymphs played by real women were rarely wanting at the entries of princes. These exhibitions took place on platforms and occasionally even in the water, like that of the sirens who swam in the Lys " quite naked and dishevelled as they paint them," near the bridge over which Duke Philip had to pass, on his entry into Ghent in 1457. The Judgment of Paris was the favourite subject. These representations should be taken neither as proofs of high æsthetic taste nor gross licentiousness, but rather as naïve and popular sensuousness. Jean de Roye, speaking of sirens that were seen, not very far from a calvary, on the occasion of Louis XI's entry into Paris in 1461, says : " And there were also three very handsome girls, representing quite naked sirens, and one saw their beautiful turgid, separate, round and hard breasts, which was a very pleasant sight, and they recited little motets and bergerettes ; and near them several deep-toned instruments were playing fine melodies." Molinet tells us of the pleasure which the people of Antwerp felt at the entry of Philip le Beau in 1494, when they saw the Judgment of Paris : " But the stand at which the people looked with the greatest pleasure was the history of the three goddesses represented nude by living women."

How far removed from the Greek sense of beauty was the parody of this theme got up for the entry of Charles the Bold at Lille in 1468, where were seen a corpulent Venus, a thin Juno and a hunchbacked Minerva, each wearing a gold crown.

These nude spectacles remained customary during the sixteenth century. Dürer, in the diary of his journey in the Netherlands, described the one he saw at Antwerp at the entry of Charles V in 1521, and as late as 1578 William of Orange, at his entry in Brussels, saw among other items a chained and nude Andromeda, " which one would have taken for a marble statue."

The inferiority of pictorial as compared with literary expression is not confined to the domain of the comic, the sentimental and the erotic. The expressive faculty of the art of this period fails as soon as it is no longer supported by that extraordinary turn for visualizing, which explains the marvels of its pictures. When more is required than the direct and accurate vision of reality, the superiority of pictorial expression at once vanishes, and then is felt the justice of Michelangelo's criticism : that this art aims at achieving several things at the same time, of which a single one would be important enough to demand the devotion of all its powers.

Let us once more consider a picture by Jan van Eyck. In so far as accurate observation suffices, his art is perfect, especially in facial expression, the material of the dresses, and the jewellery. As soon as it becomes necessary to reduce reality in some sort to a scheme, as is the case when buildings and landscapes have to be painted, certain weaknesses appear. In spite of the charming intimacy of his perspectives, there is a certain incoherence, a defective grouping. The more the subject demands free composition and the creation of a new form, the more his powers fall short.

It cannot be denied that in the illuminated breviaries the calendar pages surpass in beauty those representing sacred subjects. To picture a month, it suffices to observe and reproduce accurately. On the other hand, to compose an important scene, full of movement, with many personages, needed the sense of rhythm and of unity which Giotto possessed and which Michelangelo recaptured. Now, multiplicity was a characteristic of fifteenth-century art. It rarely succeeds in finding harmony and unity. The central part of the altar-piece of the Lamb does indeed show this harmony, in the severe rhythm in which the different processions of adorers are advancing towards the Lamb ; but this effect has been obtained, so to say, by a purely arithmetical co-ordination. Van Eyck evaded the difficulties of the composition by grouping his personages in a very simple figure ; the harmony is static, not dynamic.

The great distance separating Van Eyck from Rogier van der Weyden lies in the fact that the latter is aware of a problem of rhythmical composition. He limits himself in the use of detail, in order to find unity ; it is true, without always succeeding.

There was a venerable and severe tradition regulating the representation of the most important sacred subjects. The artist had not to invent the composition of his picture ; for some of these subjects rhythmical composition came, so to speak, of itself. It was impossible to paint a Descent from the Cross, a *pietà*, an Adoration of the Shepherds, without the composition assuming a certain rhythmical structure. It suffices to remember the Descent from the Cross by Rogier van der Weyden in the Escurial, his *pietà* at Madrid, or those of the Avignon school at the Louvre and at Brussels, those by Petrus Cristus, by Geertgen of Sint Jan, the " Belles heures d'Ailly." The very nature of the subject implied a simple and severe composition.

As soon as the scene to be represented required more move-

ment, as in the case of Christ being mocked or bearing the
cross, or in the Adoration of the Magi, the difficulties of the
composition increase and a certain unrest and lack of harmony is the result.   Here, however, inconographic tradition
still supplies a model of a kind, but where it fails him altogether
the artist of the fifteenth century is almost helpless.   W₍
need but notice the feebleness of composition in the scenes
in courts of justice by Dirk Bouts and by Gerard David,
though the solemnity of the subject itself called for an element
of severity.   The composition reaches an irritating pitch of
clumsiness in scenes like the Martyrdom of Saint Erasmus at
Louvain, and that of Saint Hippolytus, torn to pieces by horses,
at Bruges.

And yet here we are still dealing with the representation
of scenes borrowed from reality.   When the whole has to
be created by the unaided imagination, the art of the period
cannot avoid the ridiculous.   Pictures on the grand scale
were saved by the solemnity of their subjects, but the illuminators could not evade the task of giving a shape to all
the mythological and allegorical fancies of which literature
was full.   The illustrations by Jean Miélot for the *Epitre
d'Othéa à Hector*, a mythological fancy of Christine de Pisan's,
may serve as a sample.   It is impossible to imagine anything
more awkward.   The Greek gods have large wings outside
their ermine mantles and " houppelandes " of brocade.   Saturn
devouring his children, Midas awarding the prize, are simply
ridiculous and devoid of all charm.   Yet, whenever the
illuminator sees ·a chance of enlivening the prospect by a
little scene, such as a shepherd with his sheep, he shows the
ability common to the period : within his province his hand
is sure.   The reason is that here we have come to the limit
of the creative faculties of these artists.   Easily masters of
their craft, so long as observation of reality is their guide,
their mastery fails at once when imaginative creation of new
motifs is called for.

Imagination, both literary and artistic, had been led into
a blind alley by allegory.   The mind had grown accustomed
simply to turn into pictorial presentments the allegorical ideas
presenting themselves to the mind.   Allegory linked the
presentment to the thought and the thought to the present-

ment. The desire to describe accurately the allegorical
vision caused all demands of artistic style to be lost sight
of. The cardinal virtue of Temperance has to carry a clock
to represent rule and measure. We see her with this attribute
on a tomb, the work of Michel Colombe, in Nantes Cathedral,
9nd on that of the cardinals of Amboise at Rouen. The
illuminator of the *Epitre d'Othéa*, to conform to this rule,
simply puts on her head a timepiece resembling the one
with which he ornaments the room of Philip the Good.

The allegorical figure can only be justified by a tradition
which has become venerable. Invented all of a piece, it is
rarely satisfactory. The more realistic the mind which creates
it, the more bizarre and factitious its form will be. Chastellain, in his *Exposition sur Vérité mal prise*, sees four ladies
coming to accuse him. They call themselves " Indignation,
Reprobation, Accusation, Vindication." This is how he describes the second. " This dame here appeared to have acrid
conditions and very tart and biting reasons ; she ground her
teeth and bit her lips ; often nodded her head ; and showing
signs of being argumentative, jumped on her feet and turned
to this side and to that ; she proved to be impatient and
inclined to contradict ; the right eye was closed and the other
open ; she had a bag full of books before her, of which she
put some into her girdle, as if they were dear to her, the
others she threw away spitefully ; she tore up papers and
leaves ; she threw writing-books into the fire furiously ; she
smiled on some and kissed them ; she spat on others out of
meanness and trod them underfoot ; she had a pen in her
hand, full of ink, with which she crossed out many important
writings . . . ; also with a sponge she blackened some pictures, she scratched out others with her nails, and others
again she erased wholly and smoothed them as if to have
them forgotten ; and showed herself a hard and fell enemy
to many respectable people, more arbitrarily than reasonably."
Elsewhere he sees Dame Peace spread out her mantle and
break up into four new ladies : Peace of Heart, Peace of Mouth,
Seeming Peace, Peace of True Effect. Or he invents female
figures which he calls " Importance of your lands, Various
conditions and qualities of your several peoples, The envy
and hatred of Frenchmen and of neighbouring nations," as

if politics lent themselves to allegory. It is no living fancy, of course, which prompts him to imagine these quaint figures, but only reflection. All wear their names written on scrolls : he evidently imagines them as figures on tapestry, or in a picture or a show.

There is not a trace of true inspiration here. It is the pastime of an exhausted mind. Though the authors always place their action in the setting of a dream, their phantasmagorias never resemble real dreams, such as we find in Dante and Shakespeare. They do not even keep up the illusion of real vision : Chastellain naïvely calls himself in one of his poems " the inventor or the imaginer of this vision."

Only the note of raillery can still make the arid field of allegory flower again, as in these lines of Deschamps :

> " Phisicien, comment fait Droit ?
> —Sur m'ame, il est en petit point. . . .
> —Que fait Raison ? . . .
> Perdu a son entendement,
> Elle parle mais faiblement,
> Et Justice est toute ydiote. . . ." [1]

The different spheres of literary fancy are mixed up regardless of all homogeneity of style. The author of the *Pastoralet* dresses his political shepherds in a tabard ornamented with fleurs-de-lis and lions rampant ; " shepherds in long cassocks " represent the clergy. Molinet muddles up religious, military, heraldic and amorous terms in a proclamation of the Lord to all true lovers :

> " Nous Dieu d'amours, créateur, roy de gloire
> Salut à tous vrays amans d'humble affaire !
> Comme il soit vrays que depuis la victoire
> De nostre filz sur le mont de Calvaire
> Plusieurs souldars par peu de cognoissance
> De noz armes, font au dyable allyance. . . ." [2]

Therefore the true blazon is described to them : escutcheon *argent*, chief *or* with five wounds—and the Church militant

[1] Physician, what about Law ?—By my soul, he is poorly. . . . How does Reason ? . . . She is out of her mind, She speaks but feebly, And Justice is quite crazy.

[2] We God of love, creator, king of glory All hail to all true lovers of humble mind ! As it is true that since the victory Of our son on Mount Calvary Several soldiers through lack of knowledge Of our arms, make an alliance with the devil. . . .

is given full liberty to take all into her service who want to return to that blazon.

The feats which procured Molinet the reputation of an excellent " rhétoriqueur " and poet appear to us rather as the extreme degeneration of a literary form nearing its end. He takes pleasure in the most insipid puns : " Et ainsi demoura l'Escluse en paix qui lui fut incluse, car la guerre fut d'elle excluse plus solitaire que rencluse." [1] In the introduction to his prose version of the *Roman de la Rose* he plays upon his name, Molinet. " Et affin que je ne perde le froment de ma labeur, et que la farine que en sera molue puisse avoir fleur salutaire, j'ay intencion, se Dieu m'en donne la grace, de tourner et convertir soubz mes rudes meulles le vicieux au vertueux, le corporel en l'espirituel, la mondanité en divinité, et souverainement de la moraliser. Et par ainsi nous tirerons le miel hors de la dure pierre, et la rose vermeille hors de poignans espines, où nous trouverons grain et graine, fruict, fleur et feuille, très souefve odeur, odorant verdure, verdoyant floriture, florissant nourriture, nourrissant fruict et fructifiant pasture." [2]

When they do not play upon words, they play upon ideas. Meschinot makes Prudence and Justice the glasses of his *Lunettes des Princes*, Force the frame and Temperance the nail which keeps the whole together. The poet receives the aforesaid spectacles from Reason with directions how to use them. Sent by Heaven, Reason enters his mind and wants to feast there ; but finds nothing " off which to dine well," for Despair has spoilt all.

Products like these would seem to betray mere decadence and senile decay. Thinking of Italian literature of the same period, the fresh and lovely poetry of the *quattrocento*, we may perhaps wonder how the form and spirit of the Renais-

---

[1] And so Sluys remained in peace that was included with her, for war was excluded from her, lonelier than a recluse.

[2] And lest I lose the wheat of my labour, and that the meal into which¹ it will be ground may have wholesome flour, I intend, if God gives me grace for it, to turn and convert under my rough mill-stones the vicious into the virtuous, the corporal into the spiritual, the worldly into the divine, and, above all, to moralize it. And in this way we shall gather honey from the hard stone and the vermeil rose from sharp thorns, where we shall find grains and seed, fruit, flower and leaf, very sweet odour, odoriferous verdure, verdant florescence, flourishing nurture, nourishing fruit and fruitful pasture.

sance can still seem so remote from the regions on this side of the Alps.

It requires some effort and some reflection to realize that exactly in these artifices of style and wit, we witness the coming of the Renaissance, in the shape it took outside Italy. To contemporaries this far-fetched form meant the renewal of art.

CHAPTER XXIII

THE ADVENT OF THE NEW FORM

The transition from the spirit of the declining Middle Ages to humanism was far less simple than we are inclined to imagine it. Accustomed to oppose humanism to the Middle Ages, we would gladly believe that it was necessary to give up the one in order to embrace the other. We find it difficult to fancy the mind cultivating the ancient forms of medieval thought and expression while aspiring at the same time to antique wisdom and beauty. Yet this is just what we have to picture to ourselves. Classicism did not come as a sudden revelation, it grew up among the luxuriant vegetation of medieval thought. Humanism was a form before it was an inspiration. On the other hand, the characteristic modes of thought of the Middle Ages did not die out till long after the Renaissance.

In Italy the problem of humanism presents itself in a most simple form, because there men's minds had ever been predisposed to the reception of antique culture. The Italian spirit had never lost touch with classic harmony and simplicity. It could expand freely and naturally in the restored forms of classic expression. The *quattrocento* with its serenity makes the impression of a renewed culture, which has shaken off the fetters of medieval thought, until Savonarola reminds us that below the surface the Middle Ages still subsist.

The history of French civilization of the fifteenth century, on the contrary, does not permit us to forget the Middle Ages. France had been the mother-land of all that was strongest and most beautiful in the products of the medieval spirit. All medieval forms—feudalism, the ideas of chivalry and courtesy, scholasticism, Gothic architecture—were rooted here much more firmly than ever they had been in Italy. In the fifteenth century they were dominating still. Instead of the full rich style, the blitheness and the harmony characteristic

297

of Italy and the Renaissance, here it is bizarre pomp, cumbrous forms of expression, a worn-out fancy and an atmosphere of melancholy gravity which prevail. It is not the Middle Ages, it is the new coming culture, which might easily be forgotten.

In literature classical forms could appear without the spirit having changed. An interest in the refinement of Latin style was enough, it seems, to give birth to humanism. The proof of this is furnished by a group of French scholars about the year 1400. It was composed of ecclesiastics and magistrates, Jean de Monstreuil, canon of Lille and secretary to the king, Nicolas de Clemanges, the famous denouncer of abuses in the Church, Pierre et Gontier Col, the Milanese Ambrose de Miliis, also royal secretaries. The elegant and grave epistles they exchange are inferior in no respect—neither in the vagueness of thought, nor in the consequential air, nor in the tortured sentences, nor even in learned trifling— to the epistolary genre of later humanists. Jean de Monstreuil spins long dissertations on the subject of Latin spelling. He defends Cicero and Virgil against the criticism of his friend Ambrose de Miliis, who had accused the former of contradictions and preferred Ovid to the latter. On another occasion he writes to Clemanges : " If you do not come to my aid, dear master and brother, I shall have lost my reputation and be as one sentenced to death. I have just noticed that in my last letter to my lord and father, the bishop of Cambray, I wrote *proximior* instead of the comparative *propior* ; so rash and careless is the pen. Kindly correct this, otherwise our detractors will write libels about it."

There are more charming passages in his correspondence than this : for example, his description of the monastery of Charlieu, near Senlis, where he speaks of the sparrows coming to share the monks' repast, the wren which behaves as if it were the abbot, and lastly, the gardener's donkey, which begs the author not to forget it in his letter. We may hesitate whether to call this medieval naïvety or humanistic elegance.

It suffices to recall that we met Jean de Monstreuil and the brothers Col among the zealots of the *Roman de la Rose* and among the members of the Court of Love of 1401, to be convinced that this primitive French humanism was but a secondary element of their culture, the fruit of scholarly erudition, analogous to the so-called renaissances of classic latinity of earlier ages, notably the ninth and the twelfth century. The circle of Jean de Monstreuil had no immediate successors, and this early French humanism seems to disappear with the men who cultivated it. Still, in its origins it was to some extent connected with the great international movement of literary renovation. Petrarch was, in the eyes of Jean de Monstreuil and his friends, the illustrious initiator, and Coluccio Salutati, the Florentine chancellor who introduced classicism into official style, was not unknown to them either. Their zeal for classic refinement had evidently been roused not a little by Petrarch's taunt that there were no orators nor poets outside Italy. In France Petrarch's work had, so to say, been accepted in a medieval spirit and incorporated into medieval thought. He himself had personally known the leading spirits of the second half of the fourteenth century ; the poet Philippe de Vitri, Nicolas Oresme, philosopher and politician, who had been a preceptor to the dauphin, probably also Philippe de Mézières. These men, in spite of the ideas which make Oresme one of the forerunners of modern science, were not humanists. As to Petrarch himself, we are always inclined to exaggerate the modern element in his mind and work, because we are accustomed to see him exclusively as the first of renovators. It is easy to imagine him emancipated from the ideas of his century. Nothing is further from the truth. He is most emphatically a man of his time. The themes of which he treated were those of the Middle Ages : *De contemptu mundi, De otio religiosorum, De vita solitaria.* It is only the form and the tone of his work which differ and are more highly finished. His glorification of antique virtue in his *De viris illustribus* and his *Rerum memorandarum libri* corresponds more or less with the chivalrous cult of the Nine Worthies. There is nothing surprising in his being found in touch with the founder of the Brethren of the Common Life, or cited as an authority on a dogmatic point by the fanatic Jean de Varennes. Denis the Carthusian borrowed laments from him about the loss of the Holy Sepulchre, a typically medieval subject. What contemporaries outside Italy saw in Petrarch was not at all the poet of the Sonnets or the *Trionfi*, but a moral philosopher, a Christian Cicero.

In a more limited field Boccaccio exercised an influence resembling that of Petrarch. His fame too was that of a moral philosopher, and by no means rested on the *Decamerone*. He was honoured as the "doctor of patience in adversity," as the author of *De casibus virorum illustrium* and of *De claris mulieribus*. Because of these queer writings treating of the inconstancy of human fate "messire Jehan Bocace" had made himself a sort of *impresario* of Fortune. As such he appears to Chastellain, who gave the name of *Le Temple de Bocace* to the bizarre treatise in which he endeavoured to console Queen Margaret, after her flight from England, by relating to her a series of the tragic destinies of his time. In recognizing in Boccaccio the strongly medieval spirit which was their own, these Burgundian spirits of a century later were not at all off the mark.

What distinguishes nascent Humanism in France from that of Italy, is a difference of erudition, skill and taste, rather than of tone or aspiration. To transplant antique form and sentiment into national literature the French had to overcome far more obstacles than the people born under the Tuscan sky or in the shadow of the Coliseum. France too, had her learned clerks, writing in Latin, who were capable at an early date of rising to the height of the epistolary style. But a blending of classicism and medievalism in the vernacular, such as was achieved by Boccaccio, was for a long time impossible in France. The old forms were too strong, and the general culture still lacked the proficiency in mythology and ancient history which was current in Italy. Machaut, although a clerk, pitifully disfigures the names of the seven sages. Chastellain confounds Peleus with Pelias, La Marche Proteus with Pirithous. The author of the *Pastoralet* speaks of the "good king Scipio of Africa." But at the same time his subject inspires him with a description of the god Silvanus and a prayer to Pan, in which the poetical imagination of the Renaissance seems on the point of breaking forth. The chroniclers were already trying their hand at military speeches in Livy's manner, and adorning their narrative of important events by mentioning portents, in close imitation of Livy. Their attempts at classicism did not always succeed. Jean Germain's description of the Arras congress of 1435 is a veritable caricature of

antique prose. The vision of Antiquity was still very bizarre.
At the funeral service of Charles the Bold at Nancy, his con-
queror, the young duke of Lorraine, came to honour the
corpse of his enemy, dressed " in antique style," that is to
say, wearing a long golden beard which reached to his girdle.
Thus got up to represent one of the Nine Worthies, he prayed
for a quarter of an hour.

The word " antique " as conceived in France about 1400
belonged to the same group of ideas as " rhétorique, orateur,
poésie." No one would have thought of applying the word
" poésie " to a ballad or a song in the old French form. This
classical word, which evoked the idea of the admired perfection of the Ancients, meant above all an artificial form.
The poets of this time are perfectly capable of expressing
heartfelt emotions in a simple form, but when they wish to
attain superior beauty, they hunt up mythology, employ
pedantic latinized terms and then consider themselves " rhetoricians." Christine de Pisan expressly singles out a mytho-
logic piece, which she calls " balade pouétique," from her
ordinary work. Eustache Deschamps, wishing to air his
talent, in sending his works to Chaucer, his fellow-poet and
admirer, adds the following lines :

> " O Socrates plains de philosophie,
> Seneque en meurs et Anglux en pratique,
> Ovides grans en ta poeterie,
> Bries en parler, saiges en rethorique
> Aigles tres haulz, qui par ta théorique
> Enlumines le regne d'Eneas,
> L'Isle aux Geans, ceuls de Bruth, et qui as
> Semé les fleurs et planté le rosier,
> Aux ignorans de la langue pandras,
> Grant translateur, noble Geoffroy Chaucier !
>
> . . . .
> A toy pour ce de la fontaine Helye
> Requier avoir un buvraige autentique,
> Dont la doys est du tout en ta baillie,
> Pour rafrener d'elle ma soif ethique,
> Qui en Gaul seray paralitique
> Jusques a ce que tu m'abuveras." [1]

---

[1] O Socrates full of philosophy, Seneca in morals and Englishman in practice,
Great Ovid in your poetry, Brief of speech, well-versed in rhetoric, Exalted
eagle, who by your erudition Have illumined the reign of Eneas, The Island

This is the beginning, modest as yet, of the ridiculous latinism which Villon and Rabelais satirized. This insufferable
manner reappears whenever authors exert themselves to be
exceptionally brilliant, in dedications, discourses, or literary
correspondence. In this vein Chastellain will write " vostre
très humble et obéissante serve et ancelle, la ville de Gand,"
" la viscérale intime douleur et tribulation," [1] La Marche
" nostre francigène locution et langue vernacule," [2] Molinet
" abreuvé de la doulce et melliflue liqueur procédant de la
fontaine caballine," " ce vertueux duc scipionique," " gens
de mulièbre courage." [3]

This far-fetched rhetoric testifies both to an ideal of literary
conversation and to an ideal of style. Like the troubadours
of yore, the rhetoricians and the humanists cultivated literature in the form of an all-round game. Literary correspondence of a rather strange kind springs up. A fervent admirer
of Georges Chastellain, Jean Robertet, secretary to three
dukes of Bourbon and to three kings of France, tried to enter
into correspondence with the poet-historiographer of the Burgundian court, by the good offices of a certain Montferrant who
lived at Bruges. The latter, to soften the old author, who was
at first rather reserved, had recourse to the time-honoured
device of allegory. He evoked the " twelve dames of rhetoric," Science, Eloquence, Gravity of Meaning, Profundity,
etc., who appeared to him in a vision and told him to exert
himself in behalf of the correspondence desired by Robertet.
In the exchange of poetical and rhetorical compliments which
followed, Chastellain's verses are sober, when compared with
the hyperbolic effusions of Robertet.

of the Giants, and that of Brut, and who have Sown flowers and planted
the eglantine, For the ignorant of the language, you will pour yourself forth,
Great translator, noble Geoffroy Chaucer !

From you therefore out of the fountain of Helye I ask to have an
authentic draught, Of which the conduit is wholly in your power To slake
my ethic thirst, I who in Gaul shall be paralysed Till you shall give me to
drink.

[1] Your very humble and obedient slave and servant, the city of Ghent ;
The intestinal inward sorrow and tribulation.

[2] Our French-born locution and vernacular tongue.

[3] Having drunk from the sweet and mellifluous liquor proceeding from
the equine fountain. This virtuous scipionic duke. People of muliebral
courage.

" Frappé en l'oeil d'une clarté terrible
Attaint au cœur d'eloquence incrédible,
A humain sens difficile à produire,
Tout offusquié de lumière incendible
Outre perçant de ray presqu'impossible
Sur obscur corps qui jamais ne peut luire,
Ravi, abstrait me trouve en mon déduire,
En extase corps gisant à la terre,
Foible esperit perplex à voye enquerre
Pour trouver lieu et oportune yssue
Du pas estroit où je suis mis en serre,
Pris à la rets qu'amour vraye a tissue." [1]

In these terms he describes the sensations which the arrival
of a letter by Chastellain caused in him. And, continuing
in prose, he asks his friend Montferrant (whom he calls " friend
of the immortal gods, beloved of men, high Ulyssean breast, full
of mellifluent eloquence "), " N'est-ce resplendeur équale au
curre Phœbus ? " [2] Does he not surpass Orpheus' lyre ? and
" la tube d'Amphion, la Mercuriale flute qui endormit Argus ? "
" Où est l'œil capable de tel objet visible, l'oreille pour ouyr
le haut son argentin et tintinabule d'or ? " [3]
Chastellain showed some scepticism as to this raving enthusiasm. Soon he had enough of it and wanted to bar the
gate which had so long and widely been open to " Dame
Vanity." " Robertet has quite soaked me by his cloud, of
which the drops, congealing like hail, make my garments
brilliant as with pearls ; but what good is it to the dark body
underneath, when my robe deceives the onlookers ? " Therefore let him cease writing in this way, otherwise Chastellain
will throw his letters into the fire without reading them. If
he is willing to speak as beseems among friends, he may rest
assured of George's affection.

---

[1] Struck in the eye by a terrible brightness, Touched in the heart by incredible
eloquence, Difficult for the human mind to produce, Quite obscured by incendiary light Penetrating with almost unbearable rays, To a dark body that can
never shine, Ravished, distraught, I find myself, in my delight, My body in
ecstasy lying on the ground, My feeble spirit is at a loss to go in quest of a
path In order to find a place and opportune exit From the narrow pass where
I am hemmed in Caught in the toils which true love has netted.

[2] Is this not splendour equal to the car of Phœbus ?

[3] The reed of Amphion, the Mercurial flute, which caused Argus to sleep ?
Where is the eye capable of seeing such a visible object, the ear to hear the
high silver sound and golden tintinnabulation ?

Lucubrations of this sort by no means give us the feeling of the measure and harmony of the Renaissance. It all seems to us antiquated in sentiment and style. There is no doubt, however, that these wits considered themselves supremely modern. This Robertet had been in Italy, " a country greedy for renovation . . . on which the meteoric conditions operate to facilitate ornate speech, and towards which all elemental sweetness is drawn, there to resolve into harmony." He evidently believed that the secret of this harmony was in the " ornate speech " and that to rival the Italians it sufficed to bedeck the French style with the ornaments of classicism. Now, in Italy, where language and thought had never been entirely estranged from the pure Latin style, the social environment and the turn of mind were far more congenial to the humanistic tendencies than in France. Italian civilization had naturally developed the type of the humanist. The Italian language was not, like the French, corrupted by an influx of latinism ; it absorbed it without difficulty. In France, on the contrary, the medieval foundations of social life were still solid ; the language, much farther removed from Latin than Italian was, refused to be latinized. If, in English, erudite latinisms were to find an easy access, it was because of the very fact that here the language was not of Latin stock at all, so that no incongruity of expression made itself felt.

In so far as the French humanists of the fifteenth century wrote in Latin, the medieval subsoil of their culture is little in evidence. The more completely the classical style is imitated, the more the true spirit is concealed. The letters and the discourses of Robert Gaguin are not distinguishable from the works of other humanists. But Gaguin is, at the same time, a French poet of altogether medieval inspiration and of altogether national style. Whereas those who did not, and perhaps could not, write in Latin, spoiled their French by latinized forms, he, the accomplished latinist, when writing in French, disdained rhetorical effects. His *Débat du Laboureur, du Prestre et du Gendarme*, medieval in its subject, is also medieval in style. It is simple and vigorous, like Villon's poetry and Deschamps' best work.

Who are the true moderns in the French literature of the fifteenth century ? Those, no doubt, whose works approach nearest to what the following century produced of beauty. Assuredly it is not, whatever their merits may have been, the grave and pompous representatives of the Burgundian style : not Chastellain, La Marche, Molinet. The novelties of form which they affected were too superficial, the foundation of their thought too essentially medieval, their classical whimsies to naive. Should one look for the modern element in the refinement of form ? Sometimes this form, though most artificial, has so much grace that the sweet melody makes us forget the emptiness of meaning.

> "Plusiers bergiers sont en lacz mortelz telz
> Heurtez, boutez, que pou leur déduit duyt.
> Et leurs moutons en maux fortunez nez,
> Venez, vanez, de fers mal parez rez,
> Leurs bledz emblez, ayans sauf conduit vuyd,
> La nuit leur nuit, la mort qui destruit ruit,
> Leur fruit s'en fuit venant aperte perte :
> Mais Pan nous tient en asseurance experte." [1]

This was written by Jean Lemaire de Belges. Much more might be said on this elaboration of a purely formal beauty in poetry. But, taking all in all, it is not here that the future of literature lies. If by moderns we understand those who have most affinity with the later development of French literature, the moderns are Villon, Charles of Orleans and the poet of *L'Amant rendu Cordelier*, just those who kept most aloof from classicism and who did not strain after over-nice forms. The medieval character of their motifs robs them not in the least of their aspect of youth and of promise. It is the spontaneity of their expression which makes them moderns.

Classicism then was not the controlling factor in the advent of the new spirit in literature. Neither was paganism. The frequent use of pagan expressions or tropes has often been considered the chief characteristic of the Renaissance. This practice, however, is far older. As early as the twelfth century mythological terms were employed to express concepts of the

---

[1] Several shepherds are in such mortal snares So much knocked and pushed that it little tends to their delight. And their sheep, born in an evil hour, Are hunted, exhausted, shorn by ill-sharpened shears, Their corn is stolen, having a fruitless safe-conduct, The night is noxious to them ; destructive death rushes in, Their fruit flies, as open ruin comes, But Pan holds us in his expert protection.

Christian faith, and this was not considered at all irreverent or impious. Deschamps speaking of "Jupiter come from paradise," Villon calling the Holy Virgin "high goddess," the humanists referring to God in terms like "princeps superum" and to Mary as "genetrix tonantis," are by no means pagans. Pastorals required some admixture of innocent paganism, by which no reader was duped. The author of the *Pastoralet* who calls the Celestine church at Paris "the temple in the high woods, where people pray to the gods," declares, to dispel all ambiguity, "If, to lend my Muse some strangeness, I speak of the pagan gods, the shepherds and myself are Christians all the same." In the same way Molinet excuses himself for having introduced Mars and Minerva, by quoting "Reason and Understanding," who said to him : "You should do it, not to instil faith in gods and goddesses, but because Our Lord alone inspires people as it pleases Him and frequently by various inspirations."

The purity of Faith was more seriously threatened when, as in the following lines, a certain respect for pagan cults, and notably of sacrifices, is manifested.

> " Des dieux jadis les nations gentiles
> Quirent l'amour par humbles sacrifices,
> Lesquels, posé que ne fussent utiles,
> Furent nientmoins rendables et fertiles,
> De maint grant fruit et de haulx bénéfices,
> Monstrans par fait que d'amour les offices
> Et d'honneur humble, impartis où qu'ils soient
> Pour percer ciel et enfer suffisoient." [1]

This is a stanza of the *Dit de Vérité*, the best poem of Chastellain, which was inspired by his fidelity to the duke of Burgundy, and in which, forgetting his ordinary grandiloquence a little, he gives free rein to his political indignation.

To find paganism, there was no need for the spirit of the waning Middle Ages to revert to classic literature. The pagan spirit displayed itself, as amply as possible, in the *Roman de la*

---

[1] Formerly the gentile nations of the gods Craved love by humble sacrifices, Which, taken for granted that they were useless, Were nevertheless profitable and prolific Of much important fruit and of high benefits, Which shows by facts that offices of love And of humble homage, rendered wherever they were, Were sufficient to pierce heaven and hell.

Rose. Not in the guise of some mythological phrases ; it was not there that the danger lay, but in the whole erotic conception and inspiration of this most popular work of all. From the early Middle Ages onward Venus and Cupid had found a refuge in this domain. But the great pagan who called them to vigorous life and enthroned them was Jean de Meun. By blending with Christian conceptions of eternal bliss the boldest praise of voluptuousness, he had taught numerous generations a very ambiguous attitude towards Faith. He had dared to distort Genesis for his impious purposes by making Nature complain of men because they neglect her commandment of procreation, in the words :

> " Si m'aïst Diex li crucefis,
> Moult me repens dont homme fis." [1]

It is astonishing that the Church, which so rigorously repressed the slightest deviations from dogma of a speculative character, suffered the teaching of this breviary of the aristocracy (for the *Roman de la Rose* was nothing less) to be disseminated with impunity.

But the essence of the great renewal lies even less in paganism than in pure Latinity. Classic expression and imagery, and even sentiments borrowed from heathen Antiquity, might be a potent stimulus or an indispensable support in the process of cultural renovation, they never were its moving power. The soul of Western Christendom itself was outgrowing medieval forms and modes of thought that had become shackles. The Middle Ages had always lived in the shadow of Antiquity, always handled its treasures, or what they had of them, interpreting it according to truly medieval principles : scholastic theology and chivalry, asceticism and courtesy. Now, by an inward ripening, the mind, after having been so long conversant with the forms of Antiquity, began to grasp its spirit. The incomparable simpleness and purity of the ancient culture, its exactitude of conception and of expression, its easy and natural thought and strong interest in men and in life,—all this began to dawn upon men's minds. Europe,

[1] So help me God who was crucified, I much repent that I made man.

after having lived in the shadow of Antiquity, lived in its sunshine once more.

This process of assimilation of the classic spirit, however, was intricate and full of incongruities. The new form and the new spirit do not yet coincide. The classical form may serve to express the old conceptions : more than one humanist chooses the sapphic strophe for a pious poem of purely medieval inspiration. Traditional forms, on the other hand, may contain the spirit of the coming age. Nothing is more erroneous than to identify classicism and modern culture.

The fifteenth century in France and the Netherlands is still medieval at heart. The diapason of life had not yet changed. Scholastic thought, with symbolism and strong formalism, the thoroughly dualistic conception of life and the world still dominated. The two poles of the mind continued to be chivalry and hierarchy. Profound pessimism spread a general gloom over life. The gothic principle prevailed in art. But all these forms and modes were on the wane. A high and strong culture is declining, but at the same time and in the same sphere new things are being born. The tide is turning, the tone of life is about to change.

BIBLIOGRAPHY

Achéry, Luc d' —, *Spicilegium*, nova ed., Paris, 1723, III, p. 730: *Statuts de l'ordre de l'Etoile*.

Acquoy, J. G. R. —, *Het klooster van Windesheim en zijn invloed*, 3 vols., Utrecht, 1875–80.

Acta Sanctorum, see Colette, François de Paule, Pierre de Luxembourg, Pierre Thomas, Vincent Ferrer.

Ailly, Pierre d' —, *De falsis prophetis*, in Gerson, *Opera* I, p. 538, *De Reformatione*, ibid. II, p. 911, *Tractatus I adversus cancellarium Parisiensem*, ibid. I, p. 723.

Alain de la Roche = Alanus de Rupe, Beatus Alanus redivivus, ed. J. A. Coppenstein, Naples, 1642.

Amant rendu cordelier à l'observance d'amours, L' —, poème attribué à Martial d'Auvergne, publié par A. de Montaiglon, Société des anciens textes français, 1881.

Anitchkoff, E., *L'esthétique au moyen âge*, Le Moyen Âge, vol. XX (1918), p. 221.

Baisieux, Jacques de —, *Des trois chevaliers et del chainse*, Scheler, Trouvères belges, vol. I, 1876.

Basin, Thomas —, *De rebus gestis Caroli VII et Ludovici XI historiarum libri XII*, ed. Quicherat, Société de l'histoire de France, 4 vols., 1855–59.

Baude, Les vers de maître Henri —, ed. Quicherat, Trésors des pièces rares ou inédites, 1856.

Beatis, Antonio de —, *Die Reise des Kardinals Luigi d'Aragona*, ed. L. von Pastor, Freiburg, 1905.

Becker, C. H. —, *Ubi sunt qui ante nos in mundo fuere*, Islamstudien I, 1924, p. 501.

Bertoni, G. —, *L'Orlando furioso e la rinascenza a Ferrara*, Modena, 1919.

Blois, Extraict de l'enqueste faite pour la canonization de Charles de —, in André Du Chesne, *Histoire de la maison de Chastillon sur Marne*, Paris, 1621, Preuves, p. 223.

Bonaventura, Saint —, *Opera*, Paris, 1871.

Bonet, Honoré —, *L'arbre des batailles*, Paris, Michel le Noir, 1515.

Boucicaut, Le livre des faicts du mareschal de —, ed. Petitot, Collection de mémoires, VI.

Bourquelot, F. —, *Les Vaudois du quinzième siècle*, Bibliothèque de l'école des chartes, 2nd series, III, p. 109.

Burckhardt, J. —, *Die Kultur der Renaissance in Italien*, 10th edition, Leipzig, 1908.

Burckhardt, J. —, *Weltgeschichtliche Betrachtungen*, Berlin-Stuttgart, 1905.

Byvanck, W. G. C. —, *Spécimen d'un essai critique sur les œuvres de Villon*, Leyde, 1882.

——, *Un poète inconnu de la société de François Villon*, Paris, 1891.

Carnahan, D. H. —, *The " Ad Deum vadit " of Jean Gerson*, University of Illinois studies in language and literature, 1917, III, No. 1.

Caroli ducis Burgundiœ, De laudibus —, *De Morte* —, etc., *Chroniques relatives à l'histoire de la Belgique sous la domination des ducs de Bourgogne*, ed. Kervyn de Lettenhove, vol. III, Brussels, 1873.

Cartellieri, O. —, *Geschichte der Herzöge von Burgund, I Philipp der Kühne*, Leipzig, 1910.

——, *Beiträge zur Geschichte der Herzöge von Burgund*, Sitzungsberichte der Heidelberger Akademie der Wissenschaften, 1911, etc.

Cent ballades, Le livre des —, ed. G. Raynaud, Société des anciens textes français, 1905.

Cent nouvelles nouvelles, Les —, ed. Th. Wright, Bibliothèque elzévirienne, 2 vols., Paris, 1857–58.

Champion, P. —, *Vie de Charles d'Orléans, 1394–1465*, Paris, 1911.

——, *François Villon, sa vie et son temps*, Bibliothèque du XVᵉ siècle, 2 vols., Paris, 1913.

Chansons françaises du quinzième siècle, ed. G. Paris, Société des anciens textes français, 1875.

Charny, Geoffroy de —, see Piaget.

Chartier, Les œuvres de maistre Alain —, ed. A. Du Chesne Tourangeau, Paris, 1617.

Chartier, Jean —, *Histoire de Charles VII*, ed. D. Godefroy, Paris, 1661.

Chastellain, Œuvres de Georges —, ed. Kervyn de Lettenhove, 8 vols., Brussels, 1863–66. Especially Chronique I–V ; Le miroer des nobles hommes en France, Le dit de vérité, Exposition sur vérité mal prise, La mort du roy Charles VII, vol. V ; L'entrée du roy Loys en nouveau règne, Advertissement au duc Charles, Le livre de la paix, Recollection des merveilles, Le temple de Bocace, Les douze Dames de rhétorique, Le lyon rampant, Les hauts faits du duc de Bourgongne, La mort du duc Philippe, vol. VII, etc.

Chesne, André du —, *Histoire de la maison de Chastillon sur Marne*, Paris, 1621.

Chmelarz, E. —, *König René der Gute und die Handschrift seines Romanes " Cuer d'amours espris "* in der K.K. *Hofbibliothek*, Jahrbuch der kunsthist. Sammlungen des allerh. Kaiserhauses, XI, Vienna, 1890.

Chopinel, Jean —, see Roman.

Chronique de Berne, ed. H. Moranvillé, Société de l'histoire de France, 3 vols., 1891–97.

Chronique scandaleuse, see Roye.

Clemanges, Nicolas de —, *Opera*, ed. Lydius, Leyden, 1613.

Clercq, Jacques du —, *Mémoires (1448–1467)*, ed. de Reiffenberg, 4 vols., Brussels, 1823.

Clopinel, Jean —, see Roman.

Colette, Sainte —, *Acta Sanctorum Martii*, vol. I, 532–623.

Commines, Philippe de —, *Mémoires*, ed. B. de Mandrot, Collection de textes pour servir à l'enseignement de l'histoire, 2 vols., 1901–03.

Complainte du povre commun et des povres laboureurs de France, La —, in Monstrelet, *Chronique*, vol. VI, p. 176.

Coopland, G. W. —, *The Tree of Battles and some of its Sources*, Revue d'histoire du droit, V, 173, Haarlem, 1923.

Coquillart, G. —, *Œuvres*, ed. Ch. d'Héricault, Bibliothèque elzévirienne, 2 vols., 1857.

Couderc, C. —, *Les comptes d'un grand couturier parisien au XVᵉ siècle*, Bulletin de la société de l'histoire de Paris, vol. XXXVIII (1911), p. 118.

Coville, A. —, *Les premiers Valois et la guerre de cent ans, 1328–1422*, in Lavisse, *Histoire de France*, vol. IV, 1.

——, *Le véritable texte de la justification du duc de Bourgogne par Jean Petit*, Bibliothèque de l'école des chartes, 1911, p. 57.

Débat des hérauts d'armes de France et d'Angleterre, Le —, ed. L. Pannier et P. Meyer, Société des anciens textes français, 1887.

Denifle, H. —, *La désolation des églises, etc., en France*, 2 vols., Paris, 1897–99.

Denifle, H. —, and Chatelain, Ae. —, *Chartularium universitatis Parisiensis*, 4+2 vols., Paris, 1889–97.

Déprez, E. —, *La bataille de Najera, 3 avril 1367*, Revue historique, vol. CXXXVI (1921), p. 37.

Deschamps, Eustache —, *Œuvres complètes*, ed. De Queux de Saint Hilaire et G. Raynaud, Société des anciens textes français, 11 vols., 1878–1903.

Dionysius Cartusianus (or of Ryckel), *Opera omnia, cura et labore monachorum sacr. ord. Cart.*, 41 vols., Montreuil and Tournay, 1896–1913. Especially Dialogion de fide catholica, vol. 18; De quotidiano baptismate lacrimarum, vol. 29; De munificentia et beneficiis Dei, vol. 34; De laudibus sanctæ et individuæ trinitatis, De passione domini salvatoris dialogus, vol. 35; De mutua cognitione, De modo agendi processiones, Contra vitia superstitionum quibus circa cultum veri Dei erratur, vol. 36; De vita et regimine episcoporum, nobilium, etc., etc., vol. 37 ss; Inter Jesum et puerum dialogus, vol. 38; Directorium vitæ nobilium, vol. 37; De vitiis et virtutibus, vol. 39; De contemplatione, De quatuor hominum novissimis, vol. 41.

Dixmude, Jan van —, *Chronike*, ed. J. J. Lambin, Ypres, 1839.

Douet d'Arcq, *Choix de pièces inédites relatives au règne de Charles VI*, Société de l'histoire de France, 2 vols., 1863.

Doutrepont, G. —, *La littérature française à la cour des ducs de Bourgogne*, Bibliothèque du XVᵉ siècle, Paris, 1909.

Durand Gréville, E. —, *Hubert et Jean Van Eyck*, Bruxelles, 1910.

Durrieu, P. —, *Les très riches heures de Jean de France, duc de Berry*, Paris, 1904.

Durrieu, P. —, *Les belles heures du duc de Berry*, Gazette des beaux arts, 1906, vol. XXXV, p. 283.

——, *La Miniature flamande au temps de la cour de Bourgogne (1415–1530)*, Brussels, 1921.

——, *Un barbier de nom français à Bruges*, Comptes rendus de l'Académie des inscriptions et belles-lettres, 1917, p. 542.

Eckhart, Meister —, *Predigten*, ed. F. Pfeiffer, in *Deutsche Mystiker des XIV Jahrhunderts*, 2 vols., Leipzig, 1857.

Elisabeth, Saint —, *Report of an autopsy of the body of — of Hungary by bishop Konrad of Hildesheim and abbot Hermann of Georgenthal*, Historisches Jahrbuch der Görresgesellschaft, vol. XXVIII, p. 887.

Erasmus, Desiderius —, *Opera omnia*, ed. J. Clericus, 10 vols., Leyden, 1703–06.

——, *Opus epistolarum . . . denuo recognitum et auctum*, P. S. and H. M. Allen, 5 vols., Oxford 1906–24 (–1524).

——, *Ratio seu methodus compendio perveniendi ad veram theologiam*, ed. Basileæ, 1520.

——, *Colloquia*, ed. Elzevier, 1636.

Escouchy, Mathieu d' —, *Chronique*, ed. G. du Fresne de Beaucourt, Société de l'histoire de France, 3 vols., 1863–64.

Estienne, Henri —, *Apologie pour Hérodote*, ed. Ristelhuber, 2 vols., 1879.

Facius, Bartholomæus —, *De Viris illustribus liber*, ed. L. Mehus, Florence, 1745.

Fenin, Pierre de —, *Mémoires*, Petitot, Collection de mémoires, VII.

Ferrer, see Vincent.

Fierens Gevaert, *La renaissance septentrionale et les premiers maîtres des Flandres*, Brussels, 1905.

Fillastre, Guillaume —, *Le premier et Le second volume de la toison d'or*, Paris, Franc. Regnault, 1515–16.

François de Paule, Saint —, *Acta sanctorum Aprilis*, vol. I, pp. 103–234.

Fredericq, P., *Codex documentorum sacratissimarum Indulgentiarum Neerlandicarum*, Rijks geschiedkundige Publicatiën (small series), No. 21, The Hague, 1922.

Fresne de Beaucourt, G. du —, *Histoire de Charles VII*, 6 vols., Paris, 1881–91.

Froissart, Jean —, *Chroniques*, ed. S. Luce et G. Raynaud, Société de l'histoire de France, 11 vols., 1869–99 (–1385).

——, *Chroniques*, ed. Kervyn de Lettenhove, 29 vols., Brussels, 1867–77.

——, *Poésies*, ed. A. Scheler, Académie royale de Belgique, 3 vols., Brussels, 1870–72.

——, *Méliador*, ed. A. Longnon, Société des anciens textes français, 3 vols., 1895–99.

Gaguin, Robert —, *Epistolæ et orationes*, ed. L. Thuasne, Bibliothèque littéraire de la Renaissance, 2 vols., Paris, 1903.

——, *Compendium super Francorum gestis*, Paris, 1500.

Geffroi de Paris, *Chronique*, ed. De Wailly et Delisle, Bouquet, Recueil des historiens, vol. XXII.

Germain, Jean —, *Liber de virtutibus Philippi ducis Burgundiœ*, ed. Kervyn de Lettenhove, *Chron. rel. à l'hist. de la Belgique sous la dom. des ducs de Bourgogne*, vol. II.

Gerson, Jean —, *Opera omnia*, ed. L. Ellies du Pin, ed. II,:Hagæ Comitis, 1728, 5 vols. Especially vol. I, De examinatione doctrinarum, De probatione spirituum, De distinctione verarum visionum a falsis, Epistola super librum Joh. Ruysbroeck, etc., Ep. contra libellum Joh. de Schonhavia, id. contra defensionem Joh. de Schonhavia, Contra vanam curiositatem, De libris caute legendis, De consolatione theologiæ, Contra superstitionem præsertim Innocentum, De erroribus circa artem magicam, Compendium theologiæ, De decem præceptis, De præceptis decalogi, De susceptione humanitatis Christi, De falsis prophetis; vol. II, De nuptiis Christi et ecclesiæ, Expostulatio adv. eos qui publice volunt dogmatizare, etc., Contra impugnantes ordinem Carthusiensium; vol. III, Liber de vita spirituali animæ, Regulæ morales, De passionibus animæ, Centilogium de impulsibus, Contra fœdam tentationem blasphemiæ, De parvulis ad Christum trahendis, Expostulatio adversus corruptionem juventutis per lascivas imagines, Discours de l'excellence de virginité, Oratio ad bonum angelum suum, De monte contemplationis, De via imitativa, Considérations sur Saint Joseph, De triplici theologia, Considérations sur le péché de blasphème, Contra gulam sermo, Sermo contra luxuriem, Sermo de nativitate Domini, Sermo de natalitate b. Mariæ Virginis, Sermones in die S. Ludovici, Sermo de Angelis, Sermones de defunctis, Sermo de S. Nicolao; vol. IV, Meditatio super VII^{mo} psalmo pœnitentiali, Tractatus super Magnificat, Querela nomine Universitatis, Sermo coram rege Franciæ, Oratio ad regem Franciæ, Josephina.

Godefroy, Th. —, *Le cérémonial françois*, 2 vols., Paris, 1649.

Grandes chroniques de France, Les —, ed. Paulin Paris, 6 vols., Paris, 1836–38.

Gratia Dei, Oratio Antonii —, ed. Kervyn de Lettenhove, *Chron. rel. à l'hist. de Belg. sous la dom. des ducs de Bourgogne*, vol. III.

Hanotaux, G. —, *Jeanne d'Arc*, Paris, 1911.

Hefele, K. —, *Der heilige Bernhardin von Siena und die franziskanische Wanderpredigt in Italien*, Freiburg, 1912.

Hintzen, J. D. —, *De kruistochtplannen van Philips den Goede*, Rotterdam, 1918.

Histoire littéraire de la France, XIVe siècle, vol. XXIV, 1862.

Hoepffner, E. —, *Frage- und Antwortspiele in der französischen Literatur des 14. Jahrhunderts*, Zeitschrift für romanische Philologie, vol. XXXIII, 1909.

Hospinianus, R. —, *De templis, hoc est de origine, progressu, usu et abusu templorum, etc.*, 2nd ed., Zürich, 1603.

Houwaert, J. B. —, *Declaratie van die triumphante incompst van den Prince van Oraingnien, etc.*, Antwerp, Plantijn, 1579.

Huet, G.—, *Notes d'histoire littéraire III*, in Le Moyen Âge, vol. XX, 1918.

Huizinga, J. —, *Uit de voorgeschiedenis van ons nationaal besef*, De Gids, 1912, III.

——, *Renaissancestudiën I : Het probleem*, De Gids, 1920, vol. IV.

James, W. —, *The Varieties of Religious Experience*, London, 1903.

Jorga, N. —, *Philippe de Mézières et la croisade au XIVe siècle*, Bibliothèque de l'école des hautes études, Fasc. CX, 1896.

Jouffroy, Jean —, *De Philippo duce oratio*, ed. Kervyn de Lettenhove, *Chron. rel. à l'hist. de Belg. sous la dom. des ducs de Bourgogne*, vol. III.

Journal d'un bourgeois de Paris, 1405–1449, ed. A. Tuetey, Publications de la société de l'histoire de Paris, doc. No. III, 1881.

Jouvencel, Le —, ed. C. Favre et L. Lecestre, Société de l'histoire de France, 2 vols., 1887–92.

Jouvenel des Ursins, Jean —, *Chronique*, ed. Michaud et Poujoulat, Nouvelle collection des mémoires, II.

Kempis, Thomas à —, *Opera omnia*, ed. M. J. Pohl, 7 vols., Freiburg, 1902–10.

Kleinclausz, A. —, *Histoire de Bourgogne*, Paris, 1909.

——, *L'art funéraire de la Bourgogne au moyen âge*, Gazette des beaux arts, vol. XXVII, 1902.

——, *Un atelier de sculpture au XVe siècle*, Gazette des beaux arts, vol. XXIX, 1903.

Krogh-Tonning, K. —, *Der letzte Scholastiker, Eine Apologie*, Freiburg, 1904.

Kurth, Betty —, *Die Blütezeit der Bildwirkerkunst zu Tournay und der burgundische Hof*, Jahrbuch der Kunstsammlungen des Kaiserhauses, XXXIV, 1917.

Laborde, L. de —, *Les ducs de Bourgogne, Etudes sur les lettres, les arts et l'industrie pendant le XVe siècle*, 3 vols., Paris, 1849–53.

La Curne de Sainte Palaye, J. B. —, *Mémoires sur l'ancienne chevalerie*, 1781.

Lalaing, Le livre des faits du bon chevalier messire Jacques de —, ed. Kervyn de Lettenhove, in *Œuvres de Chastellain*, vol. VIII.

La Marche, Olivier de —, *Mémoires*, ed. Beaune et d'Arbaumont, Société de l'histoire de France, 4 vols., 1883–88.

——, *Estat de la maison du duc Charles de Bourgogne*, ibid., vol. IV.

——, *Rationarium aulæ et imperii Caroli Audacis ducis Burgundiæ*, ed. A. Matthæus, Analecta I, pp. 357–494 (Middle Dutch translation of the preceding work).

——, *Le parement et triumphe des dames*, Paris, Michel le Noir, 1520.

Langlois, E. —, *Anciens proverbes français*, Bibliothèque de l'Ecole des chartes, vol. LX (1899), p. 569.

——, *Recueil d'arts de seconde rhétorique*, Documents inédits sur l'histoire de France, Paris, 1902.

Lannoy, Ghillebert de —, *Œuvres*, ed. Ch. Potvin, Louvain, 1878.

La Roche, see Alain.

La Salle, Antoine de la —, *La Salade*, Paris, Michel le Noir, 1521.

——, *Le reconfort de Madame du Fresne*, ed. J. Nève, Paris, 1903.

La Tour Landry, Le livre du chevalier de —, ed. A. de Montaiglon, Bibliothèque elzévirienne, Paris, 1854.

Lefèvre de Saint Remy, Jean —, *Chronique*, ed. F. Morand, Société de l'histoire de France, 2 vols., 1876.

Leroux de Lincy, A. —, *Le livre des proverbes français*, 2nd ed., 2 vols., Paris, 1859.

Liber Karoleidos, ed. Kervyn de Lettenhove, *Chron. rel. à l'hist. de Belg. sous la dom. des ducs de Bourgogne*, vol. III.

Livre des trahisons, Le —, ed. id., ibid., vol. II.

Loër, Theodericus —, *Vita Dionysii Cartusiani*, in Dionysii Opera I, p. xlii.

Lorris, Guillaume de —, see Roman.

Louis XI, Lettres de —, ed. Vaesen, Charavay, De Mandrot, Société de l'histoire de France, 11 vols., 1883–1909.

Luce, S. —, *La France pendant la guerre de cent ans*, Paris, 1890.

Luther, Martin —, *De captivitate babylonica ecclesiæ prœludium*, Werke, Weimar edition, vol. VI.

Luxembourg, see Pierre.

Machaut, Guillaume de —, *Le livre du Voir-dit*, ed. Paulin Paris, Société des bibliophiles françois, 1875.

—— *Œuvres*, ed. E. Hoepffner, Société des anciens textes français, 2 vols., 1908–11.

——, *Poésies lyriques*, ed. V. Chichmaref, Zapiski istoritcheski fil. fakulteta imp. S. Peterb. univers., vol. XCII, 1909.

Magnien, Ch. —, *Caxton à la cour de Charles le Téméraire*, Annuaire de la société d'archéologie de Bruxelles, vol. XXIII, 1912.

Maillard, Olivier —, *Sermones dominicales, etc.*, Paris, Jean Petit, 1515.

Mâle, E. —, *L'art religieux du treizième siècle en France*, Paris, 1902.

——, *L'art religieux à la fin du moyen âge en France*, Paris, 1908.

Mangeart, J. —, *Catalogue des manuscrits de la bibliothèque de Valenciennes*, 1860.

Martial (d'Auvergne), *Les poésies de Martial de Paris dit d'Auvergne*, 2 vols., Paris, 1724. See Amant.

Meschinot, Jean —, *sa vie et ses œuvres*, par A. de la Borderie, Bibliothèque de l'Ecole des chartes, vol. LVI, 1895.

Meyer, P. —, *Les neuf preux*, Bulletin de la société des anciens textes français, 1883, p. 45.

Michault, Pierre —, *La dance aux aveugles et autres poésies du XV* siècle, Lille, 1748.

Michel, André —, *Histoire de l'art*, vols. III and IV, Paris, 1907, etc.

Molinet, Jean, *Chronique*, ed. J. Buchon, Collection de chroniques nationales, 5 vols., 1827–28.

——, *Les faicts et dictz de messire Jehan* —, Paris, Jehan Petit, 1537.

Molinier, A. —, *Les sources de l'histoire de France, des origines aux guerres d'Italie* (1494), 6 vols., Paris, 1901–06.

Moll, W. —, *Kerkgeschiedenis van Nederland vóór de hervorming*, 5 parts, Utrecht, 1864–69.

Moll, W. —, *Johannes Brugman en het godsdienstig leven onzer vaderen in de vijftiende eeuw*, 2 vols., Amsterdam, 1854.

Monstrelet, Enguerrand de —, *Chroniques*, ed. Douet d'Arcq, Société de l'histoire de France, 6 vols., 1857–62.

Monstreuil, Jean de —, *Epistolæ*, ed. Martène et Durand, Amplissima collectio, II col., 1398.

Mougel, D. A. —, *Denys le Chartreux, sa vie, etc.*, Montreuil, 1896.

Nys, E. —, *Le droit de guerre et les précurseurs de Grotius*, Brussels and Leipzig, 1882.

——, *Etudes de droit international et de droit politique*, Brussels and Paris, 1896.

Ordonnances des rois de France, Paris, 1723–77.

Orléans, Charles d' —, *Poésies complètes*, 2 vols., Paris, 1874.

Oulmont, Ch. —, *Le verger, le temple et la cellule, Essai sur la sensualité dans les œuvres de mystique religieuse*, Paris, 1912.

Pannier, L. —, *Les joyaux du duc de Guyenne, recherches sur les goûts artistiques et la vie privée du dauphin Louis*, Revue archéologique, 1873.

Pastoralet, Le —, ed. Kervyn de Lettenhove, *Chron. rel. à l'hist. de Belg. sous la dom. des ducs de Bourgogne*, vol. II.

Pauli, Theodericus —, *De rebus actis sub ducibus Burgundiæ compendium*, ed. id., ibid., vol. III.

Petit Dutaillis, Ch. —, *Charles VII, Louis XI et les premières années de Charles VIII (1422–1492)*, in Lavisse, *Histoire de France*, vol. IV, 2.

——, *Documents nouveaux sur les mœurs populaires et le droit de vengeance dans les Pays-Bas au XVe siècle*, Bibliothèque du XVe siècle, Paris, 1908.

Petit Jehan de Saintré, L'histoire et plaisante cronicque du —, ed. G. Hellény, Paris, 1890.

Petrarca, Francesco —, *Opera*, Basle edition, 1581.

Piaget, A. —, *Oton de Granson et ses poésies*, Romania, vol. XIX, 1890.

——, *La cour amoureuse dite de Charles VI*, Romania, vol. XX, 1891 ; XXI, 1892.

——, *Le livre messire Geoffroy de Charny*, Romania, vol. XXVI, 1897.

——, *Le chapel des fleurs de lis, par Philippe de Vitri*, Romania, vol. XXVII, 1898.

——, *Chronologie des épistres sur le Roman de la rose*, Etudes romanes dédiées à Gaston Paris, 1891, p. 113.

Pierre de Luxembourg, The Blessed —, *Acta sanctorum Julii*, vol. I, pp. 509–628.

Pierre Thomas, Carmelite, Saint —, *Acta sanctorum Januarii*, vol. II (his life by Philippe de Mézières).

Pirenne, H. —, *Histoire de Belgique*, 5 vols., Brussels, 1902–21.

Pisan, Christine de —, *Œuvres poétiques*, ed. M. Roy, Société des anciens textes français, 3 vols., 1886–96.

——, *Epitre d'Othéa à Hector*, Manuscrit 9392, de Jean Miélot, ed. J. van den Gheyn, Brussels, 1913.

Poésies françoises des XVe et XVIe siècles, Recueil de —, ed. A. de Montaiglon, Bibliothèque elzévirienne, Paris, 1856.

Poitiers, Aliénor de —, *Les honneurs de la cour*, ed. La Curne de Sainte Palaye, *Mémoires sur l'ancienne chevalerie*, 1781, II.

Polydorus Vergilius, *Anglicœ historiœ libri XXVI*, Basle, 1546.

Pool, J. C. —, *Frederik van Heilo en zijne schriften*, Amsterdam, 1866.

Quinze joyes de mariage, Les —, Paris, Marpon et Flammarion, without date.

Ramsay, J. H. —, *Lancaster and York, 1399–1485*, 2 vols., Oxford, 1892.

Raynaldus, *Annales ecclesiastici*, vol. III (= Baronius, vol. XXII).

Raynaud, G. —, *Rondeaux, etc., du XVe siècle*, Société des anciens textes français, 1889.

Religieux de Saint Denis, Chronique du —, ed. Bellaguet, Collection des documents inédits, 6 vols., 1839–52.

Renaudet, A. —, *Préréforme et humanisme à Paris, 1494–1517*, Paris, 1916.

René, Œuvres du roi —, ed. De Quatrebarbes, 4 vols., Angers, 1845.

Roman de la Rose, Le —, ed. M. Méon, 4 vols., Paris, 1814.

——, ed. F. Michel, 2 vols., Paris, 1864.

——, ed. E. Langlois, Société des anciens textes français, 1914, I.

Rousselot, P. —, *Pour l'histoire du problème de l'amour*, Beiträge zur Geschichte der Philosophie im Mittelalter, ed. Bäumker and von Hertling, vol. VI, 1908.

Roye, Jean de —, *Journal dite Chronique scandaleuse*, ed. B. de Mandrot, Société de l'histoire de France, 2 vols., 1894–96.

Rozmital, Leo von —, *Reise durch die Abendlände, 1465–1467*, ed. Schmeller, Bibliothek des literarischen Vereins zu Stuttgart, vol. VII, 1844.

Ruelens, Ch. —, *Recueil de chansons, poèmes, etc. relatifs aux Pays-Bas*, 1878.

Ruusbroec, Johannes —, *Werken*, ed. David and Snellaert, Maetschappij der Vlaemsche bibliophilen, 1860–68. Especially II, Die chierheit der gheesteleker brulocht, Spieghel der ewigher salicheit ; IV, Van seven trappen in den graet der gheestelicker minnen, Boec van der hoechster waerheit, Dat boec van seven sloten, Dat boec van den rike der ghelieven.

Ruysbroeck l'Admirable, Œuvres de —, Traduction du flamand par les Bénédictins de Saint Paul de Wisques, vols. I–III, Brussels and Paris, 1917–20.

Salmon, Pierre le Fruictier dit —, *Mémoires*, ed. Buchon, Collection de chroniques nationales, 3e supplément de Froissart, vol. XV.

Schäfer, D. —, *Mittelalterlicher Brauch bei der Ueberführung von Leichen*, Sitzungsberichte der preussischen Akademie der Wissenschaften, 1920, p. 478.

Schmidt, C. —, *Der Prediger Olivier Maillard*, Zeitschrift für historische Theologie, 1856.

Seuse, Heinrich — (Suso), *Deutsche Schriften*, ed. K. Bihlmeyer, Stuttgart, 1907.

Sicard, *Mitrale sive de officiis ecclesiasticis summa*, Migne, Patr. lat., vol. CCXIII.

Stavelot, Jean de —, *Chronique*, ed. Borgnet, Collection des chroniques belges, Brussels, 1861.

Stein, H. —, *Etude sur Olivier de la Marche*, Mémoires couronnés de l'Académie royale de Belgique, vol. XLIX, 1888.

Tauler, Johannes —, *Predigten*, ed. F. Vetter, in *Deutsche Texte des Mittelalters*, vol. XI, Berlin, 1910.

Thomas Aquinas, Saint —, *Historia translationis corporis sanctissimi ecclesiæ doctoris divi Th. de Aq.*, *1368*, auct. fr. Raymundo Hugonis O.P., Acta sanctorum Martii, vol. I, p. 725.

Thomas, see Pierre.

Trahisons, see *Livre des* —.

Uhrig, H. —, *Die vierzehn heiligen Nothelfer* (*XIV Auxiliatores*), Theologische Quartalschrift, vol. LXX, 1888.

Upton, Nicolas —, *De officio militari*, ed. E. Bysshe, London, 1654.

Valois, Noël —, *La France et le grand schisme d'occident*, 4 vols., Paris, 1896–1902.

Varennes, Jean de —, *Responsiones ad capitula accusationum, etc.*, in Gerson, *Opera*, I, pp. 906–943.

Vigneulles, Philippe de —, *Mémoires*, ed. H. Michelant, Bibliothek des lit. Vereins zu Stuttgart, vol. XXIV, 1852.

Villon, François —, *Œuvres*, ed. A. Longnon, Les classiques français du moyen âge, vol. II, Paris, 1914.

Vincent Ferrer, Saint —, *Vita*, auct. Petro Ranzano O.P., 1455, *Acta sanctorum Aprilis*, vol. I, pp. 82–512.

——, *Sermones quadragesimales*, Cologne, 1482.

Vitri, Philippe de —, *Le chapel des fleurs de lis*, ed. A. Piaget, Romania, vol. XXVII, 1898.

Vœux du héron, Les —, ed. Société des bibliophiles de Mons, No. 8, 1839.

Walsingham, Thomas —, *Historia Anglicana*, ed. H. T. Riley, in *Rer. brit. medii œvi scriptores* (Rolls series), 3 vols., London, 1864.

Weale, W. H. J. —, *Hubert and John van Eyck, their Life and Work*, London and New York, 1908.

Wielant, Philippe —, *Antiquités de Flandre*, ed. De Smet, Corpus chronicorum Flandriæ, vol. IV.

Wright, Th. —, *The Anglo-Latin Satirical Poets and Epigrammatists of the Twelfth Century*, in *Rerum britannicarum medii œvi scriptores* (Rolls series), 2 vols., London, 1872.

Zöckler, O. —, *Dionys des Kartäusers Schrift De venustate mundi, Beitrag zur Vorgeschichte der Ästhetik*, Theologische Studien und Kritiken, 1881.

INDEX

Y